THE PIRANHA CLUB
Power and Influence in Formula One

THE PIRANHA CLUB

CLUB

Power and Influence in
Formula One

Timothy Collings

First published in Great Britain in 2001 by
Virgin Books Ltd
Thames Wharf Studios
Rainville Road
London W6 9HA

A catalogue record for the book is available from
the British Library.

ISBN 1 85227 907 9

Typeset by Phoenix Photosetting, Chatham, Kent

Printed and bound in Great Britain by
Mackays of Chatham

Contents

Acknowledgements

This book would not have been possible without the generous cooperation and help of many people and organisations. All of the following, in no particular order, contributed to the research and writing of the Piranha Club, some by sparing time for interviews, some by correcting facts and providing precious insights into people or events and some by having provided valuable information in the public domain: Russell Hotten (and his book *Formula One*), Ted Macauley (*Grand Prix Men*), Steve Small (*The Grand Prix Who's Who*), Ivan Rendall (*The Power Game*), David Hodges, Doug Nye and Nigel Roebuck (*Grand Prix* and, in Nigel's case, many other books, including *Inside Formula One* and *Grand Prix Greats*, and helpful notes), Alan Henry (too many books to mention, but particularly his McLaren and Williams volumes, as well as always generous help and advice), Derek Jewell (*Man and Motor*), Louis T. Stanley (*Behind the Scenes* and *Strictly off the Record*), Bruce Jones (*The Ultimate Encyclopaedia of Formula One*), William Court (*Power and Glory*), Murray Walker (*Formula One Heroes*), Gerry Donaldson (*Grand Prix People*), Jabby Crombac (*Colin Chapman, The Man and his Cars*), Virginia Williams (*A Different Kind of Life*), Brock Yates (*Enzo Ferrari*), Eoin Young (*It Beats Working*, his funny book, and plenty of information and encouragement), Michael Cooper-Evans (*Rob Walker*), Rob and Betty Walker, for their time, anecdotes, wonderful company and delicious lunch down in Somerset, Richard Williams (*Racers*), Eddie Irvine (*Green Races Red*), *Autosport* magazine (always dependable), *Motor Sport*, *F1 Racing*, *F1 News*, *Formula 1 Magazine*, *Eurobusiness*, various websites including GrandPrix.com (formerly InsideF1.com), AtlasF1.com, F1Fanclub.com, Reuters, the Press Association and *Sporting Life*, Maurice Hamilton (always helpful and encouraging), Heiner Buchinger, Eddie Jordan, Ian Phillips, Giselle Davies, Tom Walkinshaw, Jacques Deschenaux (*Grand Prix Guide*), *The Concise Oxford Dictionary*, François-Michel Gregoire (*Who Works*), Flavio Briatore, Bernie Ecclestone, Max Mosley, Ron Dennis, Pino Allievi, David Tremayne, and many other newspapers and magazines, as referred to in the text of the book.

I would also like to thank Frank Williams, Luca di Montezemolo, Jean Todt, Joe Saward, Jock Clear, Craig Pollock, Jackie Stewart, Ken Tyrrell, Peter Sauber, Alain Prost, Paul Stoddart, Bobby Rahal, Jo Ramirez, Jonathan Legard, Stuart Sykes (for long-range eagle-eyed expertise and help and encouragement), Bob Constanduros (great support), Herbie Blash, Alan Baldwin, Tyler Alexander, Bob McMurray, Ann Bradshaw, Ellen Kolby, Mike Doodson, Sid Watkins, Charlie Whiting, Bob McKenzie, Ray Matts, Stan Piecha, Kevin Eason, Derick Allsop, Agnes Kaiser, Pasquale Lattuneddu and Ian Gordon. Special thanks go to Jonathan Taylor, at Virgin Books, for considering the idea and to Martin Noble for turning late and rushed copy into, I hope, a readable book. Special thanks also to the team at Collings Sport, including Marcus Lee, Will Spong, Will Gray, Gary Emmerson, Steven Dove, Richard Hart, Lorraine Varney, Jenny Baskerville, Calvin Rowley and Kevin Hand for their forbearance. Further, and final, very special thanks to my wife Ruth, and children, Josh and Kitty, for putting up with it all. Some will have been forgotten and to you I apologise while acknowledging also the photographers who have recorded so much of the drama, subterfuge and tension down the years.

Timothy Collings
Hitchin
18 July 2001

1 Welcome to the Piranha Club

Money, moncy, money – Part I

No-one outside those who were present knows what happened at the Villa d'Este on the night of 5 September 1991. Few of those who were there have been prepared to reveal the whole truth as the drama surrounding a complex 'transfer deal', which saw Michael Schumacher leave Jordan for Benetton and Roberto Moreno move in the opposite direction, albeit reluctantly, and despite winning a court action against the Anglo-Italian team. But it was there, in the imperial foyer of one of the most spectacular and famous hotels in northern Italy, on the edge of Lake Como, that their clandestine wheeling and dealing earned Formula One's business operations a new and sinister-sounding soubriquet: the Piranha Club.

That night, said many long-standing observers and critics of the sport, something about Formula One changed forever. The once-Corinthian world of Grand Prix racing, a world of pleasure and danger fuelled by adventure and funded by private means, crossed an invisible and barely-perceptible line, shifting irretrievably from sport to business, from competitive rivalry to something more Machiavellian. It was the end of the last vestiges of the golden age, of gladiators in cockpits, of mortality, parties and fun, and the start of a new era of money, politics and intrigue.

Schumacher had driven in just one Grand Prix meeting for the Jordan team after being hired as an emergency replacement for Bertrand Gachot, a temperamental 'pilote', who was sent to jail for assaulting a taxi driver by using a gas canister in London after a traffic altercation. Moreno was a journeyman, but, he had a contract; a source of scant protection, it turned out, once the lawyers and power-brokers set to work on that hot night late in the Italian summer. It was a night that left many unwritten codes trampled in the dust and dew of a magnificent September morning and a night that confirmed that Formula One's future was in the hands of ruthless businessmen and ambitious competitors.

The story of Schumacher's switch from green to blue, from the blarney boys to the knitwear family, stunned the paddock the following day at Monza where Milan's beautiful people, including many models, several racing enthusiasts and soccer stars, had gathered with the regular circus of drivers, owners, engineers, mechanics, reporters, friends, cooks and motor-home staff to prepare for the annual Italian Grand Prix at the Autodromo Nazionale. The late Ayrton Senna, heading towards his third drivers' world championship in four years, was so aggrieved he spoke out with passion at the way in which his friend Moreno, a fellow-Brazilian, was treated – like a pawn in a grandmasters' game of high-octane chess with stakes to match.

But throughout the night before, as persuasive talking and financial offers were filling the hours downstairs, Senna slept above it all in his bedroom. Amid a flow of smoked sandwiches and fine wine, men like Flavio Briatore, Tom Walkinshaw, Eddie Jordan and Bernie Ecclestone, not to mention the Schumacher entourage including lawyers from International Management Group (IMG), argued with other legal representatives and agents, including those working for Moreno, as Schumacher, then just a new tyro from Germany, barely ready to accept his mantle as the 'wunderkind', still growing accustomed to the place settings of his cutlery, and its purpose, at formal dinners, was moved from one team to another, after just one weekend as a Grand Prix driver.

It was cloak and dagger stuff, sparked by his sensational form at the previous meeting at the Spa-Francorchamps circuit, in Belgium, amplified by two applications for court injunctions, one in London and one in Milan, accompanied by many dire threats and wild reports of extraordinary behaviour and completed by a late night agreement, manipulated by many deft hands, that ensured the outcome was that which the sport's controlling interests had sought. The Piranha Club was born and won the day.

Despite every effort they could muster for the fight to retain Schumacher, who had been nothing less than sensational in practice and qualifying at Spa-Francorchamps, Eddie Jordan and his men were unable to hang on to the best young driver of his generation. Their application for an injunction, in London, preventing Schumacher from driving for Benetton, had been heard in the High Court the previous day, but had failed. Yet they fought on, supporting Moreno in his case to retain his seat by taking protective action in court in Milan. Moreno won. He had, it seemed, and thanks to the Italian legal system, kept his seat.

Benetton were thus informed that they had to keep him in their car, alongside his compatriot and friend Nelson Piquet, for the Italian Grand Prix and, furthermore, were warned that they faced possible expulsion from the championship if they failed to do so. Indeed, on Thursday afternoon, Italian bailiffs visited their garage in order that the cars were impounded and law, and with it Moreno's right to a chassis, was upheld. But, by power of attrition, the weight of pressure and the lure of money, Moreno was weakened and overcome and Jordan's scrap for Schumacher was defeated.

> To begin with, when Bernie advised me to see Flavio, we were not moving [said Jordan]. At that stage our position was strengthened by Moreno. He said he was driving and Piquet said he was driving. He had a legitimate case. We were happy to discuss Schumacher driving for us for the rest of the season. But then the whole thing became unreasonable and fell apart. We wouldn't move. We are not a team which is going to be bought. We were not going to prostitute ourselves on an issue we felt so strongly about. In the end, though, we went ...

Benetton, with Briatore, Ecclestone and Walkinshaw working for a mutual interest, negotiated their way into creating the vacancy they needed in order to hire Schumacher. By three in the morning, after a week of legal attrition, days of tension and hours of argument, Jordan's powers were so weakened that he was unable to stop a deal taking place which put Schumacher into a Benetton and ensured that the Italians, with all their multivarious international marketing interests, were able to exploit the young German's burgeoning popularity in his fatherland. The television broadcast rights for coverage of Formula One in central Europe also leapt in value overnight. Jordan was outmanoeuvred; Moreno was forced to leave the job he loved and his contract was dissolved; Schumacher had switched to a richer and better-supported team; Benetton had a driver for the future and an entry into the German market; and Ecclestone had seen his television rights' values soar as another part of his masterplan was executed. And the Schumacher era had begun.

It was a decisive move in the creation of the so-called Piranha Club's reputation, one act in a drama that was part of a far grander play that many felt was a scheme to develop Formula One into a global television spectacular. Significantly, for Jordan, a man of natural intelligence, warmth and sharp instincts, it was also a bitter learning process as he discovered that, in his first season as a team owner, it was wise to move with alacrity and, to borrow a phrase from professional football, get your retaliation in first for the sake of self-protection.

> There was a lot of shouting and roaring. There was a problem between the lawyers representing Moreno, and Benetton. Something silly was said that was interpreted by the lawyer as something quite unethical . . . The meeting went on for hours.

The old days of friendly deals done with a handshake, honoured by gentlemen and confirmed with a happy toast over dinner in the evening were gone. Long gone. This was the night when the lawyers and moneymen took utter control of the sport. The rich men won. The men with helicopters to convey them above the morning mist and dew the following day to Monza were the winners. Those, like Eddie Jordan and his right-hand man Ian Phillips, who stood and watched as the helicopters clattered and rose into the sky, who were to drive down the valley in a hired road car, in their case a Fiat 126, were the losers. It was a lesson they heeded. Like the rest, they knew the Piranha Club would be running the sport from that morning onwards. And they knew, as in the old phrase, if you can't beat 'em, join 'em.

Eddie Jordan is one of the most infectious and likeable characters in Formula One, if not British sport. He has played drums on stage all over the world, he has been featured in the popular British television show *This Is Your Life* and he has dodged, ducked and dived his way through a chequered career from early days as a bank employee in Dublin to becoming one of the richest men in the land. He has done it all with a smile and a joke, never losing his sense of humour or his ability to talk himself in and out of trouble with consummate skill.

As a Formula One team owner, he has stamped his brand on the paddock, the sport and the public imagination. As a survivor, he has demonstrated that anyone can do it – climb, that is to say, from the army of those who live outside the paddock fences, peering in, to become one of the chosen and lucky few whose professional lives carry them from continent to continent as part of the Formula One road show. Jordan rubs shoulders with rock stars, actors, film stars, sportsmen, models and statesmen in his life as a popular public figure, but he has never forgotten what happened to him at the Villa d'Este. Nor has he ever lost touch with his humble beginnings.

Born in Dublin on 30 March 1948, Jordan was expected by his family to become a dentist when, in his late teens, he was enjoying life in his native city. His wit and gift of the gab made him a popular man and the promised comforts of life as a professional fixer of teeth seemed, in some ways, suited to his generous nature. But it was not to be. Jordan wanted something else out of life. So in 1967, instead of sticking to the path towards oral hygiene, he took a different turn and steered instead towards the acquisition of knowledge and wealth. He joined the Bank of Ireland as a clerk. It was a wise decision, an inspired change of direction and it left him well prepared for what lay ahead later in his life as a mogul of the pit-lane and paddock. For three years, he worked happily in the bank, gaining more and more insights into how the world of money operates and how businesses succeed. He was a quick learner, especially where making a deal was concerned. It is, of course, a family trait that he had inherited and one that he has passed on to his own children. Self-confidence, after all, has never been lacking in such talkative Irishmen.

In 1970, however, luck played a part in the life of young Jordan. Due to a strike in the capital, he was posted from Dublin to Jersey, the famous tax-haven island off the French coast. There he came into contact with motor racing for the first time and it left him stunned as he watched racers in karts fighting it out on the Bouley Bay hill-climb. Inspired, Jordan returned to Dublin and bought himself a kart. He taught himself, went on to

5

win the Irish championship and, in 1974, moved into single-seater racing in Formula Ford 1600 cars. That proved satisfactory enough and, with the racing bug biting hard, he decided to uproot from Ireland and move to Britain to compete.

Alas, a major accident at the end of the year left him with two broken legs. He was ruled out of the 1976 season, a blow of almost equal severity to his personal morale, as the fractured legs were to him physically. But he remained determined to race and, in 1977, after much wheeling and dealing, he was in Formula Atlantic racing. The next year, he won the Irish title, a success that prompted him to move on and partner Stefan Johansson in the British Formula Three championship, racing under a banner of Team Ireland. Johansson, of Sweden, was to remain close to Jordan, as, significantly, did most of his early colleagues, drivers and friends. In 1979, Jordan tried racing a Formula Two car, at Donington, and also tested a McLaren Formula One car, recognising, by the time he reached this pinnacle in his personal racing career, that he was unlikely to go much further. At the end of that year, he created Eddie Jordan Racing.

This was the start of the real thing for this ebullient, funny Irishman. His true personality, his business acumen and his sheer enthusiasm for life in general, and racing in particular, came to the fore in a blend of qualities perfectly suited to the world of motor sport. By 1983 he had established himself and he ran Martin Brundle in the British Formula Three championship. Brundle finished second to Ayrton Senna. Competitive and driven by his ambitions, Jordan pressed on. Finally, in 1987, he won the British Formula Three title, with Johnny Herbert driving. Successes followed in the European Formula 3000 series the next year with Herbert and Martin Donnelly paving the way before Jean Alesi lifted the title in 1989 en route to his own long and spectacular Formula One career. The Frenchman's arrival at the top was the final stimulus to Jordan himself and, in 1990, to a chorus of warnings and some disapproval from those who regarded themselves as more prudent, he established Jordan Grand Prix.

The headquarters were a lock-up unit on the industrial estate at Silverstone, within the circuit and close to the track. It was a small beginning. When his first car was built and ready for a public testing, Jordan asked the former British Grand Prix winner John Watson, an Ulsterman, to perform the ceremonies on a cold, damp and foggy day at the old Northamptonshire circuit. A small group of reporters were invited to this inaugural occasion and were served tea, instant coffee in polystyrene cups and sandwiches to mark the day. The car ran in black, unpainted and unsponsored. It was a far cry from the glittering splendour of a hot day by the Mediterranean at the Monaco Grand Prix, but for Jordan it was a first important step towards fulfilling his dream and the relative modesty of his hospitality was in stark contrast to the warmth and sincerity of his welcome as he revealed himself to be an enthusiast fired by a perfectly simple ambition.

In 1991 he entered the FIA Formula One World Championship with Gachot and Andrea de Cesaris as his drivers, one the Luxembourg-born son of a Brussels-based Eurocrat, the other a veteran Italian with a reputation for unpredictability and extraordinary eyes. At the same time, in Formula 3000, he ran Damon Hill, having had Eddie Irvine, Heinz-Harald Frentzen and Emanuele Naspetti the previous year. The names are important because, as time went by, they would recur in the Jordan story, usually to argue the toss after being traded from one team to another, but more often to chew the fat and enjoy his friendship. Jordan, of course, was not only their employer, but for many of them also their personal manager and so, by virtue of controlling their careers, he was able to dictate what they did, for whom they raced and how much of a cut he could take from their contracts. His penchant for management spread far and wide, his flair for making money equally. Like Flavio Briatore, at Benetton, Jordan could see that running a Formula One team was not the only avenue of business open to him through which he could make a decent profit in the early 1990s. Formula One, after all, as he was discovering, was a very, very expensive business and it needed very expansive funding.

But Jordan was no quitter. Nor did he lack personal resources in terms of energy, determination and imagination. As a younger man, as he would frequently recount, he had sold woollen carpets and out-of-date smoked salmon in the Dandelion Market in Dublin. He could sell snow to an Eskimo. When his son, Zac, was at preparatory school, several years ago, Jordan received a telephone call from the headmaster. He was told that boys had been caught smoking. Jordan, a fitness enthusiast, was very upset. But he was less distraught when he heard what the headmaster had to say. 'Mr Jordan,' he told him. 'Zac was not smoking. He was selling Benson and Hedges cigarettes to the boys at £3.50 a packet. Do you have any idea where he may have got them?' As his team was sponsored by Benson and Hedges, at the time, it was not difficult to solve the puzzle. He was delighted. Zac, like his father, was a natural wheeler-dealer, a chip off the old block. And his improvisational business skills were a further inspiration to his father to survive as he began hacking his way through the intensifying financial jungles towards secure membership of the 'Piranha Club'.

In 1991, his first full year as a team owner in the competitive and ruthless world of Formula One, Jordan experienced a wide range of blows and surprises. His car, the nimble, pretty, sleek, green Cosworth-powered and Seven-Up-sponsored Jordan 191 was the envy of many in the pit-lane and frequently out-qualified and out-performed Cosworth's chosen factory-supplied team, Benetton. His drivers also performed with an élan unexpected by many seasoned observers. It seemed they reacted well to Jordan's unique form of man-management, a personal approach that included generous rations of fun and games mixed among the serious preparations. The team often, for example, wore shorts – including Eddie Jordan himself – and treated its sponsors with a refreshing sense of candour and mischief. Jokes and japes, a shortage of cash and a team spirit unmatched by any other team in the championship were the strongest features as Jordan's happy voyage survived one financial knock after another and just about stayed afloat. When they finished fourth and fifth, thus scoring their first points, in the Canadian Grand Prix in June, the team celebrated raucously and Jordan let it slip that, using a financial arrangement he had discovered in Belgium, he had 'bet' against his own success, through a form of insurance, in order to enjoy a payout which would allow him to cover the bonuses for success. The financial house in Brussels was not delighted to read this news. It had agreed a confidentiality clause with Jordan, in advance.

By the time of the late days of the English summer, when Gachot was arrested for assaulting a London taxi driver by using a gas canister as his personal weapon, the bills were piling up and the budget was exhausted. Financially, Jordan knew his team was on its knees. Debts were all around him, including a mounting and worrying amount owed to Cosworth for their engines. If ever he needed to wheel and deal, to duck and to dive, to borrow and beg and find some cash, this was the time. Cosworth were pressing for their money and threatening legal action. Without Cosworth, Jordan could not continue and, even if they managed to struggle through, he needed engines for 1992. It was a grim scenario, made worse by Gachot's idiotic arrest and the attendant bad publicity.

The likelihood of this Irishman, with his hard-working, fun-loving team of men in green, developing an outfit to challenge the likes of McLaren-Honda, for whom Ayrton Senna was on his way to the drivers' title, or Williams-Renault, for whom Nigel Mansell and Riccardo Patrese were heading towards second and third places, seemed remote. But, remarkably, he did. And he survived not only the threats of his creditors and the wiles of the Piranha Club to do so.

> When we arrived at Spa, the cars were sealed away [he explained, referring to the Belgian Grand Prix at Francorchamps in 1991, when Schumacher made his debut]. The local bailiff had taken action. Well, we had just had a torrid two weeks. We had Gachot go to jail. We needed to find another driver and when Michael Schumacher and Ian (Phillips) were trying to get the contract finished, on the Thursday night, we went to the track to find that local Belgian bailiffs had locked up the trucks and the cars. So, we couldn't get them out. They claimed we owed some money . . .

Jordan's memory of the sequence of events, he admitted, was hazy. But, according to Phillips, money was owed to a Belgian driver, Philippe Adams, and his claim resulted in the local courts approving an order to prevent the team from using their cars or trucks for fear that they would be leaving the country without clearing the debt. Action was taken by the bailiffs, said Phillips, on Saturday afternoon after qualifying. 'We found a way of clearing it up, so we could race,' he added.

By this time, both Jordan and Phillips were deeply entangled in a desperate bid to keep the team going, to hang on to the dazzling talent of Schumacher – who qualified seventh at Spa-Francorchamps before destroying his clutch at the start of the race – and to try and find an engine supplier for 1992. It was a juggling act, in terms of energy and resources available, every day for each one of them.

It had started when Schumacher tested for the first time, immediately before the Belgian race, and it continued through the following two weeks to the Italian weekend at Monza. Phillips was busy trying to tie down Schumacher while Jordan was seeking engines and Cosworth, fed up with waiting for their bills to be paid, issued a winding-up order on Jordan Grand Prix. To make matters worse, Schumacher's management team were suspicious of Jordan's plans for the future. They were being fed information, suggesting the team was in a perilous state, which was designed, deliberately, to persuade them to avoid signing any long-term contract.

Schumacher, happy enough to have stayed in a breezy holiday chalet that he shared with his new team chiefs in Belgium, was also reminded that other teams had higher standards of hotel accommodation on offer. Few leading outfits, after all, would have considered asking one of their Grand Prix drivers to share quarters, including the bathroom, with commercial or marketing staff. To his credit, Schumacher was never troubled by this and always said, later, how much he had enjoyed his brief time with the Jordan outfit.

But Schumacher, like Moreno, was a mere pawn in the moves made by the major players at the time. His value was not only in his talent, but also in the fact he was German. Formula One needed a good German driver, but in a successful team with real prospects for the following season, not a team facing a winding-up order from its engine suppliers with little prospect for real sustained success. Furthermore, Benetton, owned by the Italian fashion chain, were looking for ways of using Formula One for marketing their products, their image and the services of the other companies in their group. It was obvious, in hindsight, that Benetton had wanted Schumacher immediately they saw how fast he was at Spa-Francorchamps on the opening day of practice in the valleys of the Ardennes, if not long before.

Walkinshaw, who was then director of engineering at Benetton, where he worked in alliance with Briatore, knew all about Schumacher. Having run Jaguar in the group C world sports-car championship, he had enjoyed close quarters experience of him. He had seen him racing for Mercedes-Benz in the same series and knew he was an exceptional talent. He was, also, in close contact with Jochen Neerpasch, an agent working on behalf of Mercedes-Benz, as their competitions chief, as well as for International Management Group (IMG), and their drivers, particularly Schumacher, who remained under contract to Mercedes-Benz, where he had been developed as a junior driver.

> Neerpasch had been canvassing several teams to see if they were interested in Michael and, of course, I had been impressed with his performances in the Mercedes sportscar and I was keeping an eye on him [he admitted]. I said I was interested in running him [at Benetton], but understood he had a prior commitment to Jordan. I was only interested if the Mercedes lawyers could give me clear legal advice that he was not committed elsewhere. I would want my head examined if I didn't go after a driver of his obvious calibre.

It was the beginning of the end for Jordan's interest in retaining Schumacher long-term. Walkinshaw, a resolute Scot with a reputation for winning at all costs, was not a man who wasted words. He was well-connected within the paddock and throughout the global automotive industry, entirely aware of who was approaching who for drivers and engines for the following year and, together with Briatore, he was building a team to win at Benetton. He had recognised in Schumacher a driver he needed to help achieve his ambitions. Like Jordan, he was a proven entrepreneur, but a man also of widespread success throughout many parts of the motor industry. He had enjoyed success in many automotive programmes ranging from touring cars to sports cars to road cars. But success in Formula One had proved elusive until he caught sight of the potential of Michael Schumacher. With him, in a car packaged to provide the power and the performance he needed, Walkinshaw knew that he could direct Benetton to the world championship.

He saw all he needed of Schumacher, to confirm he could perform in Formula One, in just two days at the Belgian Grand Prix. Walkinshaw was unhappy with Moreno and he wanted to replace him. 'I wanted someone in the second car who would liven things up a bit,' he explained. With that in mind, he contacted Neerpasch, regarded by most of the players in this particular game as the man in control of Schumacher's future, alongside his manager Willi Weber, of course. When he telephoned Neerpasch, he interrupted the German while he was soaking in his bath. Walkinshaw laughed. But they talked.

Jochen agreed to come over to London to discuss the possibility of Michael coming to Benetton for the next race at
Monza. They came over with their lawyers and a contract
and we examined it and satisfied ourselves that indeed,
there was no agreement with Jordan. The only thing was
that there was a block in the contract that if Mercedes Benz
came back into F1 racing, in the following three years,
then they would have the right to take him back. I thought
that it was worth taking that risk and we signed him for
Monza.

Briatore, like Walkinshaw, saw Schumacher as a key figure in
Benetton's future.

The first time I saw Michael was in Spa [said Briatore]. The
first time I spoke to him was in London, a few days afterwards, in my house. He was with me, and Neerpasch, and
we discussed Michael's position with Jordan and it was
confirmed to me that there was no contract. It was only a
one-race deal. I told Michael I was ready to put him in the
car and that we didn't need any money from personal
sponsorship and that was how we did the deal. It was very
important for him to get into the car immediately. For me,
that was no problem. I felt it was important to find someone for the future of the team. We all felt very strongly that
he was our driver for the future.
   My only worry was that he would not have enough laps,
but we did not expect instant miracles. We knew too that
we did not have the best car, but we were working on it.
We wanted a driver for the future. I knew my situation at
the time was not a winning one, but we were looking
ahead and Michael was the first really important step.
Nelson [Piquet] and [Roberto] Moreno were our other drivers at the time. I had already decided what to do and two
weeks before I met with Michael, I had told Moreno what I
wanted to do in the future; that he would not be driving
with us any more and that it was not our intention to
renew his contract.

Briatore and Walkinshaw's matter-of-fact approach to the signing of Schumacher made it seem obvious that Jordan had no
right to believe he had any hold on him. In this age of harsh

legal realities, any notion that Jordan, having been the man to have run him first in a Formula One car, would have a moral first call on his services was treated as an irrelevance. A naïve irrelevance. Walkinshaw said:

> I had no problem with Eddie applying to the court [for an injunction to stop Schumacher signing for Benetton]. He tried on several counts and the judge dismissed every one of them. I think there's been a lot of nonsense on this. The fact is that Schumacher, for whatever reason, had no contract with Jordan. He was a free agent. How anyone can allow a talent like that to be walking around the paddock, I don't know. That's their business. When we were informed of that we went about the proper way of securing him.

To a tough, experienced operator like Walkinshaw, this manoeuvring was all in a day's work. To the struggling new boys at Jordan, fighting on all fronts, every hour was a scrap for survival. Having 'found' Schumacher, thanks to some help here and there, and having survived the legal and financial difficulties of racing at Spa-Francorchamps, they had become engulfed in other problems which distracted them from the more urgent need to sign Schumacher promptly, beyond agreeing a deal with heads of agreement in principle, and prevent him being charmed away in the night. And these distractions, together with the information exchanges that are all part and parcel of the dealers' market that is the paddock in Formula One, undermined them.

'I had a call from Weber on Friday afternoon,' explained Phillips. 'Michael was due to come for a seat fitting on the Monday (eight days after the Belgian race and three before the opening of the Italian Grand Prix). Then, instead of Michael, Neerpasch and Julian Jakobi turned up! We wouldn't let Jakobi near the place. He was working for IMG then.'

As Phillips explained the story, running back through his mind to recall clearly these days now a distant decade away, Jordan interrupted to add his own recollections.

'I refused to let him in. I'd just come back, from Japan, with a deal for Yamaha engines and, at that stage, we were skint. Absolutely skint. And . . . '

'Neerpasch presented a contract to us,' Phillips continued.

'Yes,' interjected Jordan. 'And Flavio [Briatore] was restricting us a little, too, because we were a bit embarrassing to

Flavio's Benettons with our Jordan, with a customer engine, so he made sure that we got stung . . . He made sure we wouldn't get the [Ford Cosworth] engines the following year. But, it was worse than that. Cosworth, at that time, put a winding-up order on Jordan, so I had to run like hell to find an engine!

'I had heard – from Herbie [Blash] and Bernie [Ecclestone] that Walkinshaw, and a few others, were desperate to get this Yamaha engine and that if I didn't move quickly, I would never get it. So, I'm gone to Japan and Ian [Phillips] is looking after things – and all this is flying around the place when I come back on the Monday to find out that Weber had actually had the good manners to ring us and to say "look, please, be careful".

'And, by that stage, Bernie and Flavio and Tom had, I believe, concocted how they were going to get a German into Formula One their way. There had not been one for such a long time.

'It was a very big market that was sports-car orientated and this was their big opportunity. And, it was no secret. Bernie will tell you. He helped to cement the deal between Flavio and Benetton to get Michael Schumacher to join them. At that stage I could, possibly, understand because the chances of Jordan surviving were, in our view, quite good, but in anyone else's view, quite limited.

'He was probably aware that there was a winding-up order about. Flavio would have told him about that and about Cosworth's move, their petition. But we had a Yamaha engine, at that stage, untried and untested . . . '

The significance of the engines was one of the critical issues in the story.

'There was something else,' Phillips explained. 'Neerpasch, on Sunday morning in Spa, came to us and he said we had to run Ford the following year. We were all sworn to secrecy on Yamaha and so we said, "Oh, yeah, we will be . . . "

'But what we didn't know was that Tom Walkinshaw, who was the engineering director at Benetton, was so involved by then. He had run the Jaguar sports-cars against the Mercedes. He was the only other person in the world who knew how good, really, Michael was . . .

'And, at this time, we didn't know of Bernie's involvement in all of this. After Spa, Bernie disappeared to Sardinia, I think, where he was buying some land. He knew we had got the Yamaha deal because he had been instrumental . . . '

Ecclestone has helped Jordan by using old contacts and advising each to help the other to make the deal work.

'We had been lying about Yamaha, because we had to!' Phillips continued. 'So they [Neerpasch and Weber] were using the big Ford angle and when they went to see Bernie and said, "What shall we do?" he told them Jordan had got a deal with Yamaha . . . He squared that away. No problem.'

Jordan joined in again, adding his own personal recollection. 'So, then the fun starts! We said "**** this!" I knew it was happening. I had spies at Benetton. And they must have had spies at Jordan. So everyone seemed to know exactly what was going on. So, it went straight down to court injunctions. They fought it like crazy. We went in London. We knew what was happening. So, we collared Moreno. We paid Moreno to use the same injunction to save his arse, but in the Italian courts. He won. We lost.'

As Jordan and Phillips recalled it, Moreno had the opportunity to stop the entire affair from happening at all. Having won his case, in Monza, to save his seat with Benetton, he was, it was claimed, offered half a million dollars to walk away. The court action in Italy was concluded on Thursday, a day of simmering drama and comings-and-goings in the Monza paddock as the affair unfolded gradually.

'At that stage, they were reconciled to losing him [Schumacher],' said Jordan. 'The financial penalty for losing Piquet was so huge that they would have had to retain him. And they had to give a seat to Moreno. And, then, we were all invited up to the Villa d'Este.'

'No, we were summoned. Summoned,' said Phillips.

'I'd never seen so many lawyers coming in and out like that,' said Jordan.

'And we didn't find our own hotel until Friday night,' said Phillips.

'Ian and I shared a single bed,' Jordan added. 'And Flavio paid for it! He sent sandwiches to the room and they were mouldy old things! And he – Ian, he is not easy to sleep with!' At this point Jordan added descriptive reasons, relating to odours and habits, for this assertion. They are too colourful for publication. 'To do this in a small, single bed in one of the staff out-houses at somewhere like the Villa d'Este is not very pleasant. On top of losing your driver.'

Phillips continued his version of the story. 'We got summoned to the Villa d'Este. When I got to the circuit, I saw Bernie and I told him about the courts and what had been happening. He had got the plans for his house in Sardinia out and he said, "This looks great," and he pretended he knew nothing about it. Then he said, "Leave it to me. I'll sort it out." Then at seven o'clock that night he said, "Get up to the Villa d'Este," and we drove up to Lake Como in our little Fiat 126 rent-a-car ... Bernie was there and we saw Michael.'

Phillips was struck by the change in circumstances since the last race. 'In Spa,' he said, 'we stayed in a holiday camp. Five-pounds-a-night. I shared a bathroom with Michael and Willi. It was a bit like a dormitory! And the next time I see Michael, he is in the Villa D'Este! And they are all sitting there, having dinner, and we were outside ... and Bernie said, "We might as well let you go, there's no money, Moreno's not going to get it and he's not going to get paid," and it went on and on and on.

'Eventually, Bernie came out. I'll never forget it. Eddie, Bernie and I, we went round the side of the staircase and there was this lovely glass cabinet and I turned to Bernie. We had told Moreno, "Don't settle, don't settle," and Bernie told us he had to settle. He said there was no money. I told him that "If nobody sits in that car by the time official qualifying comes on Saturday, at one o'clock, then Benetton will be excluded from the championship. They cannot take force majeure. Moreno is going to sit it out. He isn't going to give in ... " And, half an hour later, he came back and said they had offered Moreno half a million dollars.'

'No,' interjected Jordan. 'They offered it to us first. And we said we wouldn't take it.'

'And we told Moreno not to take it,' said Phillips.

'And, to be fair, the lawyer believed he wouldn't take it,' Jordan continued. 'And Moreno needed to keep his seat, at the time, and we needed money. We weren't prepared to take the money. And we were so strong about not taking the money they then offered it to Moreno, who did take it.'

Phillips said: 'Yeah, at two-thirty in the morning, Moreno took the money ...'

'That is correct,' said Jordan. 'And that is how the Piranha Club was formed. Word just got around the paddock.'

So, it unfolded, Moreno accepted an offer to give up his rightful seat with Benetton for Schumacher. Jordan, without a second driver, then accepted an offer of $125,000 from Moreno to fill the vacancy.

'And we did the deal that night,' Phillips said. 'We had no idea where we were staying. Tom [Walkinshaw] had been wandering around like the wine waiter, spilling it on the carpet! And we still did not know where we were staying. No idea.'

'And,' said Jordan, 'you just couldn't believe how many lawyers there were present there that night. There were waves of them coming in to that place. There were Benetton lawyers, Flav's people and Bernie's people. But they were all so shocked that the family was upset that, in Milan, we had won a case against Benetton!'

'Everyone had been looking for Moreno the whole of Thursday,' Phillips added. 'But he was there, actually, all the time, holed up in our motor home. Nobody, but us, knew where he was. And, of course, the other thing was that we had Marlboro begging us to take [Alessandro] Zanardi. But Walkinshaw had told us, "You can't have Zanardi because I've got him under an option." He had given Zanardi a seat fitting . . . '

'Yes, but at three in the morning, we couldn't afford to take another risk,' said Jordan.

'So, when we left at six-thirty, having had just three hours' sleep in that single bed, we had to go and tell Trevor [Foster, team manager of Jordan] what was happening and to get Moreno fixed up for the car and all the rest of it,' said Phillips. 'Then, we pull up at this set of traffic lights, on the way to Monza, and there's the old Marlboro man there. And he pulled up and said, "Why don't you take Zanardi?"'

'We told him he had an option with Walkinshaw. And he said, "No, he doesn't" and we go on then, the first time we meet Zanardi, he turns up at our motor home at half past eight in tears. "I really want to drive this car," he said. But it was too late then. Walkinshaw had told us what he did to stop us having Zanardi.'

'And then Ron came out with this thing about the Piranha Club, just as we were walking across the paddock at Monza,' recalled Jordan again. 'He said, "Welcome to the Piranha Club." I can remember the moment.'

Phillips went on. 'Everybody was agog. Bernie pretended he knew nothing about it, when he had orchestrated the whole thing. He was able to say we had Yamaha.'

And Ecclestone, it appeared, also had the vision to see how valuable Schumacher was to become to the show as a whole. His talent, in a successful team, would open up a vast new

German market. According to one German source, Schumacher, at the time, was under contract to RTL, the big German broadcaster, whose arrangement with Formula One dictated that if a German driver entered the sport it would double the fee to be paid and if a second entered, it would increase again.

In short, Ecclestone knew that his television business would profit from the arrival of Schumacher and Germany in the Formula One paddock. Of course, the same would apply, in principle, for Jordan as for Benetton, but the latter were considered a more powerful and successful operation with a stronger brand image.

This manoeuvring, furthermore, affected the careers of other men. The Swedish driver, Stefan Johansson, for example, was in Monza during the Italian Grand Prix build-up waiting for a call from Jordan. As a Marlboro-backed driver, he hoped that the fact Jordan were a Marlboro-sponsored team would help assist him in taking the chance to slip into the vacant seat created by Schumacher's departure to Benetton. He never received the call.

Zanardi, the runaway leader of the International F3000 championship, was also waiting for a chance to step into a Formula One car and had pinned his hopes on Jordan. But, on Thursday afternoon, Benetton having decided to dismiss Moreno anyway, they gave Zanardi a seat-fitting. Clearly, Zanardi was being lined up as first reserve if the team failed to land Schumacher cleanly.

Having received £150,000 (pounds sterling) from Mercedes-Benz to give Schumacher a drive in Belgium, knowing that they were prepared to pay £3 million (sterling) the next year to keep him there, Jordan had built up high hopes for the future. In theory, they had secured, he thought, a driver of huge potential and the backing of a dependable supporter. But even before this arrangement had begun to form in his mind, he confronted problems. Prompted by various sources, Neerpasch had started to 'move the goalposts' and make life difficult, as Phillips explained.

When Neerpasch turned up at the factory on the Monday before Monza, he presented a contract and he said, 'These are the conditions for Michael' and he had, basically, taken the space on the whole car! So, we worked all night on doing a version of the contract that we *could* sign. And then, in the morning, we were sitting around waiting for them to turn up when a fax came through from the lawyers with two lines, from Michael. 'Dear Eddie, I am sorry I am unable to take up your offer of a drive. Yours sincerely, Michael.' And, at that very time, Michael was at Benetton, having a seat-fitting. We knew because someone phoned somebody at Benetton.

By the end of Tuesday, on the basis that they could prove he was having a seat fitting at Benetton, after having agreed heads of agreement with Jordan, Jordan had requested his lawyers to apply for an injunction against Schumacher driving for Benetton. The case was heard in London the following day, Wednesday, 24 hours before they were due to arrive in Monza.

We had heads of agreement, which under normal law would have been good enough [said Jordan]. But what happened was that the judge said he could not restrict someone's right to work unless we had signed that other contract, which was unsignable. 'On the basis that that contract is flawed, I cannot give you the injunction to stop him driving for another team until this contract is settled and signed,' the judge said. But they had no intention of signing that contract. So, it was a mistake I will always remember. But, in the heat of the moment, no-one was at fault.

Neerpasch recalled it all, at the time, with some detachment:

Michael Schumcher signed an agreement with Eddie Jordan on the Thursday before Spa. It was an agreement to talk about an agreement. What he signed was a letter of intent. Eddie Jordan offered him the drive, but he needed money. Mercedes-Benz agreed that money and asked for sponsors' space. We talked with Eddie about the rest of the season and also the future, but only on the condition that our money would guarantee a certain space on the car.

I went to see Eddie Jordan on the Monday and we could not agree. A number of teams were interested in Michael and we went to Benetton. They wanted him and it was a straightforward deal. He is paid as a driver. I think the Jordan was a very good car for this year. There was no need to change. Michael wanted to stay with Jordan, but Eddie would not agree with our requirements for sponsor space and he wasn't prepared to discuss our contract. He wanted Michael to sign before Monza. Michael was still a Mercedes-Benz driver, but we released him for F1. At the end of it all, I think it is very important for Germany to have a competitive driver in F1.

Neerpasch also said that Mercedes-Benz wanted to have Schumacher back for their planned re-entry to Formula One in 1993 with Sauber:

It would have been against our strategy to release him. We built up the drivers and we wanted them for our own team. It was sensational, of course, for the F1 people to see Michael at Spa. Everyone was interested in him. We discussed a lot of things. In the end though, Eddie said he was using Yamaha engines and we discussed this and we decided that Yamaha were not going to be reliable or victorious. We wanted Michael to have a season in F1 and we wanted to finance the season for him. We wanted him ready for the following year, for the new Mercedes team for 1993.

At that time, we saw 1992 as a preparation year. We wanted both Michael and Karl [Wendlinger] to get F1 experience. We discussed this with Michael and he decided to stay at Jordan. They were a very nice team and made him feel welcome. He did not want to change. But we discussed it for a long time and, finally, decided to change.

The whole episode, known at the time as the 'Schumacher Affair', threw a shaft of stark light into one of the dark corners of Formula One and contributed towards the creation of the Contract Recognitions Board, an organisation to formalise the legitimacy of drivers' contracts with teams. But that came later, a long time after Moreno was manipulated and paid off amid rumours of threats and retribution among the various lawyers and participants at the Villa d'Este.

Senna, the great and glorious champion of the time, was disgusted at the events. At the hotel, when he learned of what had happened, he told Briatore what he felt of his treatment of his compatriot and friend Moreno. On Saturday afternoon, he claimed pole position. At the subsequent news conference, looking serious and thoughtful, he took the opportunity to give vent to his feelings. He spoke with controlled passion:

> It's difficult to comment in a clean and fair manner, without knowing all the clauses in the contracts, but, as you know, even the best contract in the world, drawn up by the best lawyers, is only worth anything if both sides are really working for it ... What has happened was not correct. It's always the people in the top teams who are written about the most. So, I feel, that unless one of us speaks about it, something like this just goes by and people get away with it.
>
> Moreno is a good driver. He's dedicated. He's a professional. And he had a contract for the whole season. But people just push others who are maybe not in a strong position and they threaten, use their apparently strong position to get a driver to change his mind and to accept things. As a principle, I don't think this was a good move. There were commercial interests involved and future prospects which made certain people do these things ...

Moreno, the fall guy, the man pushed out of Benetton to make way for the new wunderkind's arrival, deserved a word. Upset, threatened, cajoled to take money and give up the seat he had proved was his through legal action, he turned to God for support.

> I think everyone in the paddock was surprised by what happened [he said]. Unluckily, for me, I was alone at the time I was told, as my wife and my daughter were in Brazil. I didn't even tell my wife afterwards because I thought it would hurt her too much. It is very difficult for a person to go through all that alone. Fortunately, I am a religious person. I believe in God. I opened the Bible and I asked God to put me in the right direction and it opened at a good page. That gave me self-confidence and I kept myself together. It was very stressful.
>
> My only problem was that I caught a virus before the race in France, in July. I went to the doctor and took some penicillin. It upset my stomach and I was not recovered for the race. I think it is the only problem I had this year. I

took legal action because I just wanted to defend myself. I had to defend my rights on the contract I had for this year. On the Thursday night, I slept for only two hours and had my seat fitting at seven in the morning. I got in the car, I concentrated and I tried to do my best . . .

2 The First and the Foremost: Enzo Ferrari

When we won, then it was Ferrari who had won, not the driver, because Ferrari was the best car. When we lost, it was always the driver's fault. Enzo was a very emotional person. As a race manager of the old guard, he was of the opinion that a driver should consider himself lucky to be driving for the team.

(Niki Lauda)

My impression was of a man who was not deeply involved in money, but someone who had a great passion for verbal fencing and who had to win . . .

(Gianni Agnelli)

He was a very good negotiator. Very tough. He would argue with me over a dollar for some things. I respected him for that. He was a good businessman. He was a super salesman and he sold himself and he sold his ideas.

(Bernie Ecclestone)

How come we don't get a Ferrari today?

(Pope John Paul II, on climbing from his helicopter during a visit to Maranello in 1988)

I remember Von Karajan telling me, in a letter he sent to me, 'when I hear your 12 cylinders, I hear a burst of harmony that no conductor could ever recreate'.

(Enzo Ferrari)

On a hot late summer's afternoon, at Monza, in 1988, not more than a few weeks after his death, Enzo Ferrari's name was the cause of extraordinary celebration. Already a legend, by virtue of his achievements in life, his reputation was given an even more magical lustre when two of his cars came home in sequence at the end of a dramatic Italian Grand Prix. It was the only race that year when the McLaren-Hondas, driven by Ayrton Senna and Alain Prost, were beaten; the only blot on the Woking team's attempt to deliver a clean sweep of 16 successive race victories.

In the *parc fermée* afterwards, as the cars were scrutinised, Italians stood overwhelmed. Many did not know whether to laugh, or to cry. Gerhard Berger, one of the sport's most popular men, a happy-go-lucky character with a dash of humanity to match his enormous courage, had won, followed home by Michele Alboreto, the last Italian driver signed by 'the old man' in a bid to see one of his own, at the wheel of one of his cars, driving to triumph. The old circuit was soon awash with tifosi, flags and emotion, a sea of black, yellow and red jostling for attention in the sunshine. They all knew what Ferrari meant to Formula One; and to Italy; but this demonstration, and the manner in which it happened, confirmed the status of the name and the team, and with them the man who founded it all, to a much wider audience altogether.

'Ferrari, we followed you in life and now in death' read one of the banners. Nobody, now, it seemed, would forget Ferrari: the name that stood for racing, passion and speed; and the man whose single-minded approach to life and business had enabled him to rule at Modena and Maranello with an almost dictatorial dominance through most of the twentieth century. Ferrari cared more for his cars than his drivers, it was always said. He had a ruthless streak, but some sentimental qualities, too. He could wheel and deal, smile and calculate and then, when the time was right, he could strike like a cobra. If one man originated the characteristics for membership of the 'piranha club' it was Ferrari, a man whose achievements and methods dominated Formula One for so long and whose team continued that tradition many years after his death.

His autobiography was called *Le Mie Gioie Terribili* (My Terrible Joys). Like Rob Walker, he knew that his passion for cars and racing was one that would lead to death for many of his drivers. His son, Dino, died in 1956 when he was only 24 years old and the grief he suffered then stayed with him through the rest of his life. He only rarely played a public role in Formula

One racing, by attending the Friday practice sessions in advance of the Italian Grand Prix, always with dark sunglasses covering his eyes. He used the politics of the sport, the battles between the English *garagistes*, or 'kit car teams' (Lotus, McLaren, Williams, Tyrrell, Brabham and the rest) and the establishment grouped around the old Federation International de Sport Automobile (FISA), later to be integrated into the modernised Federation International de l'Automobile (FIA) by Max Mosley as his chance to learn more and more of his competitors' leanings and inclinations. He was a man who wanted to win, not take sides. He did not play politics; but his methods were as political and cunning as those seen by anyone at any time in the development of Formula One in the second half of the twentieth century.

His was a life that encompassed it all. From a dumbstruck boy, stunned by his first experience of motor racing around the streets of Bologna, to racing driver, to team manager and to team creator and owner, he brandished his enthusiasm with a startling will to win and an air of imperious passion, almost obsessive in its severity, that left many ordinary acquaintances surprised and some shocked. To Ferrari, it was all about winning and virtually any means of doing so were acceptable within the framework of the rules. He admired courage and a heavy right foot. He loved drivers who gave everything to the cause of Ferrari and winning. He cared less for those who calculated and measured their talent and gave less than their all for him and his cars. He could be haughty and hurtful, dismissive and devious, relying on his drivers' sense of awe in giving service to the famous Ferrari team to overcome any need for a decent retainer. The great Juan-Manuel Fangio, winner of five drivers' world titles, drove only one season for Ferrari and left. It is understood he did not appreciate the team owner's attitude towards his drivers.

In his lifetime in motor racing, of course, Ferrari was to be well acquainted with death. He experienced the loss of his son, Dino, and the bloody end of many of his drivers. Yet he continued to race, seeing, beyond the tragedy and the pain and the horror, some kind of reason for it all in the sport to which he gave his every waking hour of thought during the major part of his existence. Like many Italians, he could shrug aside most issues of the day. For him, life was only truly worthwhile when his cars were racing, when he was dominant in his chosen world and when all around him were obedient to his wishes. Like all the best members of the 'piranha club', he was able to mix business and sport, racing, money and pleasure in one dangerous and heady concoction within his team. His life was to be measured, as he may have wanted, in races, pole positions, victories and championships, yet his legacy was a team without a modern structure, emasculated by his lofty arrogance and adhesion to outdated mantras, a team in search of a modern identity to be run for some time under the management of his own illegitimate son, before fresh ideas took over.

Enzo Anselmo Ferrari was born in Modena, Italy, on 18 February 1898, as an icy blizzard swept south down the Po valley from the Appennini. His father, Alfredo, ran a local metal-fabricating business and was keen on sport. The family ran a car. When he was ten, Ferrari and his brother Alfredo were taken by his father to watch a motor race in Bologna, the 1908 Circuit de Bologna, in which Vincenzo Lancia competed with Felice Nazarro. The experience inspired him for life. He had to become a racing driver. After watching several further races, he had made up his mind and, partly as a result, he neglected his education thereafter. This was to be a matter of some regret to him in later life when his use of violet-coloured ink and occasional a pursuit of writing and journalism, two of his other interests, suggested he may have had an artistic side that was separate from his love of cars.

In 1916 his father and brother died in the same year. It was a tragedy that rocked his family to its core and left him wounded psychologically. Never again was he able to form lasting emotional attachments, a factor which may help explain his difficulties in handling relationships with his drivers. In the First World War he was employed to shoe mules, but was discharged in 1918 when he suffered a severe bout of influenza. When he recovered he tried to find work with Fiat in Turin but failed and, after hanging around the city, began working as a handyman for a small car manufacturer called CMN that concentrated on converting surplus war vehicles. As part of this job, he was a test driver, an occupation he enjoyed and which encouraged him to try racing. His first race was a hill-climb at Parma in October 1919. He also entered the 1919 Targa Florio in which he finished ninth.

This experience set him on his career path and, as with most other men who later rose to own and run successful Formula

One motor racing teams, it demonstrated not only a deep love of the sport, and the sheer thrill of racing, but also a determination to follow that course single-mindedly and to succeed. Ferrari's ability to overcome such a difficult early life, his competitive streak and his willingness to take risks, on and off the track, offered a perfect early example of what it takes to reach the top in motor racing.

By 1920 he had found a job with Alfa Romeo, thanks to his friend Ugo Sivocci, who had also helped him find his original work in Turin, and he managed to race one of their modified production cars in the 1920 Targa Florio. In this period of his life, he became close to Giorgio Rimini, one of Nicola Romeo's closest associates, and therefore a more than useful man to know. In 1923 he was racing and winning at the Savio circuit, near Ravenna, where he met the father of the legendary Italian fighter-pilot Francesco Baracca. He was so impressed with Ferrari's courage and self-belief that he presented him with his son's squadron badge, a black prancing horse, which Ferrari placed against the background of the yellow shield of Modena. This emblem was to become, from 1932, the symbol of Ferrari and his cars, a signal of power and strength harnessed in an image of beauty.

In 1924 he won the Coppa Acerbo. It was probably his greatest victory. He recalled it in his book *Piloti che gente* in which he wrote:

I remember with particular satisfaction my victory at Pescara 1924 with an Alfa Romeo R.L. With this car, I had won at Ravenna and at Rovigo, but the Coppa Acerbo I initialled my fame as a driver. In fact, I was able to beat the Mercedes, which was just returning from the success of the Targa Florio. In the Alfa team, there was also Campari with the famous P2, but, unfortunately, he was forced to retire. My mechanic was Eugenio Siena, Campari's cousin. As agreed, since the first lap I should have looked for the shape of Campari's P2 in the driving mirror, if I led the way, and to give way to him with dispatch ... I had a very speedy start and at each lap I repeated my search in the mirror, but in vain. I couldn't see the P2. Worried by his absence, and the chase of Bonmartini and Giulio Masetti's Mercedes, I looked at Siena with a first sign to slow down. But Siena gave a cry where there was not even a shadow of worry about the delay of his cousin. So, I insisted on the first position and I won. Campari explained to me that he had hidden his car in a side street, after having retired due to damage to the gear-change, so that the antagonists would not have realised too soon his surrender.

It was an early introduction to strategy and tactics for Ferrari and one that will be recognised by the latter-day followers of Formula One, recalling the 'team orders' debates of modern times, including Rubens Barrichello's donation of second position to Michael Schumacher in the 2001 Austrian Grand Prix and Schumacher's donation of victory to Eddie Irvine at the 1999 Malaysian Grand Prix. Motor racing was not, and has never been, exclusively the preserve of contests between individual drivers; but it has always contained team tactics, grander schemes and more meaningful and lucrative reasons to compete and perform than merely the sport. Recall here, too, the words of Ferrari's sporting director Jean Todt at the A1-Ring (a name that conjures up images far away from those of the old Oesterreichring, which it replaced, at the same venue), at Spielberg in May 2001.

Do you really think that people in Formula One are only thinking about the sport? You don't think that there are some commercial interests? Major motor manufacturers are involved in order to win, not to work for me, to work for the drivers, for the engineers. We are there to try to deliver wins. Then we are chosen, rightly or wrongly, for the strategy that we are able to build. Sometimes you have to take some decisions. Sometimes you may regret taking those decisions, but I feel very comfortable about the decision that has been taken today.

Todt, one of the modern 'piranha club' members was merely following the tune of his team, his tradition and his business. Yet, of course, there are differing views on what are acceptable tactics, in relation to team orders. And, equally, there have been many differing views on what kind of contractual obligations drivers accept, on whether one team should help another, on what is acceptable in the sport as a whole when massive sums of money are at stake. Ferrari, serious and ambitious, was one of the first men to understand all of this and, ironically,

Todt, obeying the commands of a different kind of hierarchy and a different set of ambitions at Maranello and beyond, may have operated his tactics in a fashion that the old man, and diehard traditionalists, may not have liked.

Plenty of examples abound. One of the most famous came at Monza, in 1956, when Peter Collins handed his car over to Juan-Manuel Fangio to ensure that the Argentinian finished the race and won the drivers' world championship, albeit after taking other drivers' cars on no fewer than three occasions during the season. These acts, also, put the status of Fangio's 1956 title into some perspective, as did Ferrari himself when he said:

> Musso and Collins stepped down for the sake of Fangio, obviously with my consent. Had Collins not handed his own car to Fangio twice, he would with mathematical certainty have become world champion that year, as he well deserved. Instead, Collins and Musso met their deaths without ever being able to win this coveted distinction.

In 1958 Phil Hill, then racing for Ferrari, was asked to drop back to third place behind Mike Hawthorn in the Moroccan Grand Prix at Casablanca to enable the British driver to clinch the drivers' championship. Six years later, at the Mexican Grand Prix, Lorenzo Bandini dropped back behind John Surtees to help the former world motorcycle champion take the drivers' title. Both acts of personal sacrifice obeyed the orders of Ferrari. Both, also, were not at odds with his basic credo, which was that his drivers, when running in a one–two formation, should hold station with the man who originally took the lead not to be challenged by his team-mate.

It was the blatant breaking of this convention, by Didier Pironi, on the last lap of the 1982 San Marino Grand Prix, when he passed Gilles Villeneuve to win the race that moved Ferrari to express his sympathies for the Canadian. Two weeks later, however, Villeneuve died in practice for the Belgian Grand Prix at Zolder when, fuelled by his rage, he lost control of his car at high speed. In 2001, when there was an outcry at Barrichello's predicament, some sharp-eyed observers noted that there was a certain ambiguity about the situation. Joe Saward, writer of the popular 'Globetrotter' column run on the InsideF1 website, observed this and merely questioned if the Brazilian, Barrichello, had the same supplicant number two role as had

Eddie Irvine during the previous four years, when he drove alongside Schumacher at Ferrari.

Of course, if that is a clear-cut reality, then there is absolutely nothing wrong with the situation [said Saward]. Think about Carlos Reutemann's explanation of what happened after he won the 1981 Brazilian Grand Prix against team orders ahead of his Williams team-mate Alan Jones. 'When I signed my contract with Frank there was a "seven seconds" clause in it,' he recalled many years later. 'If I was leading the race by seven seconds, then I could win; if Jones was closer than seven seconds, then I had to let Alan past. We started the race in Brazil, in the rain, and to be honest I never drove particularly hard. Frank just showed me the pit signals to the third place man and, believe me, I never thought Jones was running so close behind. About three or four laps from the lead, Frank put out a sign signalling me that we would reverse the order. I was obviously very upset.'

Reutemann couldn't bring himself to do so. Williams didn't pay him the money due for the win and Reutemann was clever enough never to mention it. As Sheridan Thynne, the team's commercial director at the time, mentioned: 'The fact that Reutemann never queried the absence of payment was an indication of how exceptionally clever he was. Very clever people never fight battles they are going to lose.' Five years later, Williams was again in trouble on the team orders front when Nelson Piquet, who believed that he was team leader, found himself being forced to race team-mate Nigel Mansell with as much ferocity as he was directing at rivals from other teams. 'I didn't join Williams to have my team-mate use the knowledge that I contributed in order to beat me,' he said firmly. Williams added: 'What Nelson thought he was being guaranteed was a repeat of the Reutemann fiasco of 1981, when we controlled, or tried to control, the second driver. Whereas what in fact we discussed was that, in a classic case of one driver leading the championship and needing every bit of support, then we would obviously control his team-mate. But he was not given unconditional priority over the second driver. We took the view that they were both running for the championship and would have to fight it out between them.'

All of which explains just why Ron Dennis and Sir Frank Williams have a subtly different style than Jean Todt and his cohorts at Ferrari. Todt pooh-poohs the notion that everybody in F1 is thinking about the sporting dimension. They are simply there to win. He may be right. But it will be a sad day for F1 if he is proved right in the long term. The sporting aspect of Grand Prix racing has been under assault for too long from too many sides.

This digression, from Ferrari, shows without doubt that strategy, teamwork and the manipulation of racing has always been around and is likely always to stay because motor racing is about the success of the team, its cars and the reputation of the manufacturer. It is about 'win on Sunday, sell on Monday', as many have expressed it; at another level, as the McLaren chief Ron Dennis has often explained, Grand Prix racing is a very big and international business which briefly becomes a sport once every other Sunday afternoon, for two hours, on 16 or 17 days of the year. No wonder, then, that Ferrari smelt his opportunity in motor racing – since it combined his sporting passion with his ruthless business ambitions – and that the sport developed into the modern-day circus that it became, operated at its heart by the club. Even Ferrari, for whom sporting interests were a high priority, may have struggled to recognise it or to love it.

After his success in the Coppa Acerbo, Ferrari gained further victories and was promoted to become a full factory driver. This brought with it an opportunity to drive a car in the French Grand Prix, but such a prospect apparently caused him great anxiety and he suffered a crisis of confidence and did not take part. It was a bruising blow, but he recovered to continue racing in local events, where he was happier, and pursued a new career also in working with Rimini and operating as a general agent of repair and support. On 28 April 1923 he married Laura Garello and soon he had his own distributorship for Alfa Romeo in Modena. In 1929 he started his own racing company, Societa Anonima Scuderia Ferrari, which was supported by the Caniato brothers, Augusto and Alfredo, the heirs to a textile fortune, from Ferrara. By then, Alfa Romeo had withdrawn from racing so he was able to use their cars and technical assistance – he offered them shares in his team in exchange – to provide the vehicles for his drivers. He did similar deals with Bosch, Pirelli and Shell and created a group of keen amateur drivers to which he added Giuseppe Campari and, later, the great coup of recruiting Tazio Nuvolari.

All this suggested great organisational skills allied to an ability to measure risk and a courageous heart. His team had 50 employees of one sort or another when it started and in its first season ran in 22 events, winning eight. It was the biggest team ever assembled by an individual and it was an immediate success. Ferrari had broken a mould by proving he could go it alone, albeit with such support from what the modernists would call 'technical partners'. As so often, Ferrari showed little interest in paying his drivers vast retainers; instead he offered them a cut from the prize money. He supplied a car and all the backing required to perform at the circuit. Alfa Romeo found the arrangement satisfactory and, until 1933, when they were beset by financial problems, they were happy to continue racing with Ferrari.

It was then, barely after shaking off the celebrations of the New Year, that Ferrari faced his first major dilemma when the terrible news of Alfa's plan to withdraw arrived from Milan. He soon resolved it. Benito Mussolini had been moving closer to an aggressive expansion into Africa, with Ethiopia among the prime targets, and this persuaded Alfa Romeo to shift the emphasis of its staff's attention towards war materials. This was not all. The depression was also reducing the market for high performance luxury sports cars and without Alfa Romeo, of course, he lacked a supply of new racing cars. Fortunately, with help from Pirelli who interceded on his behalf, he persuaded Alfa to supply him with six P3s and the services of engineer Luigi Bazzi and test driver Attilio Marinoni. In effect, Ferrari's *scuderia* became Alfa's racing team. By then, too, his life was becoming increasingly busy. His first son Alfredo, known as Dino, was born in 1932 and, with business booming, he had given up racing completely, even in local events. (An interesting feature of the nature of Formula One team chiefs is the number of them who moved from racing themselves into team management and ownership.)

As his team developed, gradually becoming more and more professional, so there were other changes. Alfredo Caniato, who was more content in the carefree days, was bought out by Count Carlo Felice Trossi, a millionaire who loved racing. The *scuderia* looked increasingly purposeful by the week. Then, along came the power of the Germans in the form of Mercedes and Auto Union whose cars set new standards in the 1930s. In 1935 Ferrari recruited Rene Dreyfus who had been with Bugatti. Dreyfus observed that there were real differences between his old team and his new. It was an insight into Ferrari himself.

The difference between being a member of the Bugatti team and Scuderia Ferrari was virtually night and day [he recalled]. I lived with Meo Constantini, the Bugatti team manager. But I visited with Ferrari. With Ferrari, I learned the business of racing, for there was no doubt he was a businessman. Enzo Ferrari was a pleasant person and friendly, but not openly affectionate. There was, for example, none of the sense of belonging to the family that I had with the Maserati brothers, not the sense of spirited fun and intimacy that I had with Meo Constantini. Enzo Ferrari loved racing. Of that there was no question. Still, it was more than an enthusiast's love, but one tempered by the practical realisation that this was a good way to build a nice, profitable empire. I knew he was going to be a big man one day, even then, when the cars he raced carried someone else's name. I felt sure that eventually they would carry his ... Ettore Bugatti was le Patron. Enzo Ferrari was the Boss. Bugatti was imperious. Ferrari was impenetrable.

In this period, Ferrari suffered all the experiences of life. He experienced love (by all accounts, he was a man of vigorous physical passion with many tastes), death, pain, grief and delight through handling many great drivers. Giuseppe Campari, Louis Chiron, Achille Varzi and, of course, Nuvolari, who won a great and unexpected victory for him in the 1935 German Grand Prix at the Nuerburgring (where, after perhaps the greatest single race of all time, having crushed the might of the Germans on home soil, he had to find his own record of the Italian anthem to be played at the victory ceremony, the Germans having been so confident of winning that they had none other than their own available), all did service for the *scuderia*.

By then, however, he had been witness to other events including his first personal experience of seeing one of his cars involved in a bloody accident which killed a driver. This came during the second heat of three at the Monza Grand Prix in 1933, run on the high-speed oval, the Pista de Velocita, inside the park circuit at Monza. Campari was driving a P3 for the Scuderia Ferrari and Baconin Borzacchini a Maserati. After the standing start, they roared away into the moody gloom and never returned. A massive accident on the south curve claimed their lives. According to Brock Yates' account, in his controversial book *Enzo Ferrari, The Man and the Machine*, they had touched wheels at full speed and pinwheeled off the track.

Both men were flung on to the pavement while their cars tumbled crazily through the wire infield fence [he reported]. Borzacchini's Maserati bounced to a stop on its wheels, looking practically undamaged. But its driver was mortally wounded and would pass away a few hours later. Campari, the beloved 'Pepino', was killed instantly. The other two drivers, although their automobiles flipped over, escaped with minor injuries. Standing in the damp gloom of the pits, Enzo Ferrari reeled at the news. Suddenly, the naked brutality of the sport he loved pummelled him and tore at his insides. Here were two men, his old compagnos, now lying torn and lifeless like rag dolls in a muddy ditch. He had steeled himself for such moments. He knew of the flimsy cars and their propensity to buck men off their backs ... He understood the risks, having accepted them himself. But for Campari and Borzacchini to go down together was almost more than he could bear. This would force him to separate the cruel, heartless business of racing from the amiable side of motorsports, the casual talk in bars, the bargaining over the sale of an Alfa to a wealthy client, the workaday routine of the shop. For until that day, he had not dealt with the death of one of his own. Yes, Arcangeli had fallen, and so too had Sivocci and Ascari, among others, but they had not been in scuderia cars. No blood had been spilled on the prancing horse until that evil afternoon and it would mark a turning point for him. From that day onward, Enzo Ferrari would draw a thin, invisible psychic shield between himself and his drivers. On rare occasions, he would let that barrier be penetrated, but for the most part the men who would thereafter drive for Enzo Ferrari operated outside his most intimate emotional boundaries.

Even by the standards of that era, this was a black afternoon, made worse by a further tragedy when Count Czaykowski, a wealthy Polish private entrant who had won the first heat in his massive Bugatti type 53, lost control and crashed in the same place on the south curve. He burned to death in the wreckage. The triple tragedy plunged the world of Italian motorsport into mourning and recriminations. The echo was heard again many times, including May 1994, when in a similarly depressing and black weekend at Imola, both Roland Ratzenberger and Ayrton Senna lost their lives at the San Marino Grand Prix.

Nuvolari, the redoubtable and strong Nuvolari, was deeply affected. He spent the entire night after the races and the deaths in the Monza hospital with the grieving wives of the dead men. When asked how he felt about it all, he said, 'It happens when you least expect it. If we were to drive eternally preoccupied with the dangers that beset us, we would never complete a single lap.' Such thoughts have echoed through Grand Prix motor racing ever since. Ferrari, upset, attended the funerals of Campari and Borzaccchini, hired Louis Chiron, known as the 'wily fox', to replace Campari, and carried on. But a spear had passed through him, hardening him even more deeply against the emotions of his inner and outer lives.

This toughness stayed with him and provided the alternative in his character to the sentimentality that appeared superficially from time to time. It may also help explain why, according to Yates, Ferrari joined the Fascist Party in 1934. He knew that it would help him in business. According to Yates,

> there is no evidence that he was a particularly devoted party member, although the Scuderia's newsletter did assume for the next four years a bellicose tone attuned to party doctrine. Fascist slogans were laced through the text and Ferrari's traditional sniping at his rivals – the Maserati brothers, the German teams and certain drivers and sponsors who had fallen from favour – became more pointed and strident. Ferrari, always the cold-eyed, businessman, was not about to disturb a cosy arrangement with Alfa Romeo because of some silly, essentially irrelevant political doctrine. If Fascism was in fashion and it meant extra racing success for the Scuderia, so be it; Enzo Ferrari would be a good Fascist.

35

The racing continued, but Ferrari rarely made the journey. He spoke French, to a workmanlike standard, but rarely went to France. In 1934, he made one of his final crossings of the Italian borders by going to Monte Carlo, but not to the French Grand Prix. He refused to fly, disliked trains (it was said he was suspicious of them) and did not like the discomfort of long hours behind the wheel of a car on journeys on the poor roads then used in Europe. Apparently, he did not go in lifts either and took a pretty cynical view of many feats of modern engineering.

He was absent, therefore, when the Auto Unions turned out for the French race complete with swastikas on their long and pointed tails while his own driver Chiron, the sophisticate from the south of France, wore blue silk overalls to climb into his shimmering red Scuderia Ferrari Alfa which, eventually, won the race after virtually all else fell by the wayside. It was a signal of further Ferrari battles against the might of Germany, the first of which, sadly, saw the death of the spirited and loved Algerian driver Guy Moll.

This came in the Coppa Acerba at Pescara on 15 August 1934, when Moll, a strange plastic mask protecting his face as he sat upright in his shining red Alfa Romeo, duelled with Luigi Fagioli, in his Mercedes Benz W25, but was killed when, according to Chris Nixon, he crashed at 170 mph after attempting to pass Ernst Henne in a Mercedes-Benz back-up car on a narrow piece of straight road. From the corner of his eye, he noticed Moll's car pitch through a 'gruesome yawning motion that sent it tumbling off the track'. A lap later, the crumpled car was leaning askew against a farmhouse and, according to Yates, 'the broken body of Guy Moll was lying by the roadside ... he died on the 17th lap, which may or may not have had any relationship with Enzo Ferrari's superstition about that number'. Ferrari, later in his life, said Moll was one of his greatest drivers and greatest losses. His death, therefore, further illustrates the rate at which he was hardening his heart through these years.

> I rank him [he said] with Stirling Moss as the only driver worthy of comparison with Nuvolari. In fact, he resembled Nuvolari in certain mental traits, in his aggressive spirit, in the calm assurance with which he drove and in the equanimity with which he was prepared to face death.

In 1937 he suggested to Alfa Romeo that they build a 1.5 litre vetturetta. Instead of accepting his advice, they chose to bring their racing back in-house, purchasing 80 per cent of the Scuderia Ferrari and, at the start of 1938, bringing the operation back to their Portello base. It meant that Ferrari went from being his own man, in charge of the operation, to Direttore Sportivo, working under the direction of Wilfredo Ricart, a despised outsider, a Spaniard. He could not stomach it for long and, in late 1939, decided to depart, agreeing, as part of his severance arrangement, not to compete with Alfa for four years. He is also reported to have been dismissed and the truth may well lie somewhere between the two.

In his own memoirs, he is direct and to the point about his thinking at this time. 'The rift became unbridgeable and led to my dismissal,' he wrote. Clever and devious, he may have planned events to suit him. He also wrote: 'It was during this period, in 1937, to be exact, that I had the idea of having a racing car of my own built at Modena. This was the one later to be known as the Alfa 158.' It was a claim disputed by others, but never settled. Gioachino Colombo, a brilliant engineer with Alfa Romeo, recruited by Ferrari, probably played more than a small part in the idea and creation, by joint effort with Alfa Romeo, of the car to be known as 'the Alfetta'.

It was also at this first meeting between the Alfa engineer, who travelled down the old Via Emilia to Modena, that Ferrari rejected the idea of a mid-engined vehicle with the famous remark that 'it has always been that the ox pulls the cart'. In retrospect, it is easy to laugh at Ferrari; particularly as 20 years later he was to adopt the same intransigent position when the new British teams, led by Cooper, were manifestly proving him wrong. However, it is also an example of his single-mindedness and lack of technical vision, a fact he admitted was a weakness. 'I have never considered myself to be a designer or an inventor, but only one who gets things moving and keeps them running,' he wrote, using 'my innate talent for stirring up men.'

Ferrari was also good, like all the latter-day members of the Piranha Club, at wheeling and dealing, motivating men when he needed to, removing them when their useful days were over. In the building of the Alfetta, he spent his days buying and bartering for such items as steel tubing and sheet aluminium, ignition wiring, fuel, oil pumps, brake components, coolers, radiators, springs, shock absorbers and the rest. He knew nearly every small workshop in the Padana valley and what he needed just as, in later times, many of the British teams were to use the Thames Valley and its hinterland as the region from which they would draw talent and technology. Ferrari also motivated his small team of men brilliantly, commanding loyalty and exacting the maximum. He was obsessed with victory on the race circuit and that obsession transmitted itself to everyone around him. It was all consuming. It consumed most of Italy. It certainly consumed the lives of many of the men who worked almost superhuman hours to please him. According to Yates:

> As the summer heat of Modena bore down on them, transforming the workshops of the Scuderia into a fuming hell of simmering, deafening, maddening motion, he seemed to gain strength. Each night the exhausted team would gather in one of the little trattorias around the neighbourhood to eat and to muse about their progress, finally to fall into bed for a few hours' sleep, before beginning again at dawn.

The project was wracked by intrigues and politics, mostly amidst the Alfa management, where the idea of a Scuderia Italia emerged following the dismissal of Vittorio Jano, Italy's most famous racing car designer in late 1937. Ferrari himself needed to be as opportunistic as ever and when his *scuderia* was taken over, to be absorbed into the new Alfa racing operation known as Alfa Corse, he made sure he benefited well from becoming the sporting director. The 158 finally made its debut at a test at Monza in May 1938, and then raced, in early August, at the Coppa Ciano, where Emilio Villoresi won to the delight of the Ferrari crew. The Alfetta had scored a maiden victory and Ferrari knew how to make a winner.

But success, at this time, could not guarantee happiness. Not for Ferrari, nor for anyone with an eye on the broader international picture. Even so, racing continued; and so did the political chicanery and infighting which was to be a feature of all Ferrari racing teams of the future for the following 50 years. In April 1939 Mussolini moved to annex Albania. As a result, he became King of Italy, Ethiopia and Albania; and he drifted towards an alliance with Hitler while, at the same time, the racing teams of Europe went to Tripoli for Marshal Balbo's annual extravaganza, an event called the Tripoli Grand Prix which mixed elegant parties with a sporting contest that had a reputation for having been manipulated in the past. Maserati were there, and Alfa and Mercedes-Benz with two Type 165s complete with all-new V8 1.5 litre engines. Driven by Rudi Caracciola and Hermann Lang, the Mercedes-Benzs dominated and demonstrated German superiority in all things technical. The Alfa team had to respond and respond fast; within a month, modifications were being tested on the 158s at Monza where, in a high-speed accident 'Mimi' Villoresi was killed. It was a bad episode for Alfa Romeo, for Ferrari and for Italy.

Villoresi's brother, Gigi, who had raced for Maserati, swore, like Nuvolari before him, that he would never take the wheel of an Alfa Romeo again in his life. Both men were true to their word and Gigi was further aggravated and angered by a row with Ferrari himself over insurance. The Villoresi family asked for an insurance settlement, but Ferrari, according to Yates, refused. This is an allegation that is not widely supported. Indeed, many believe the insurance policies were paid for by Alfa Romeo, not Ferrari. It was also suggested that Ferrari claimed 'Mimi' was ill and that this caused him to crash, but this allegation is also contested by others. It turned to a bitter quarrel that was to affect their relationship for the rest of their lives and it was one of his final bad episodes during his long near-20 years experience with Alfa Romeo. His umbilical cord, as he referred to the relationship, was severed. War was all around and the smell of gunpowder in the Alpine air. Yet, before Italy was drawn fully into fighting, he had another idea to activate and it was to be a car known as Tipo 815.

He started a new company, Auto-Avio Costruzioni, producing parts for various clients and using the prancing horse on its note-heads. When the Maserati brothers moved to Modena, backed by Adolfo Orsi, his pride was hurt again. Still stinging from the Alfa Romeo ending, he had returned home to Modena to find his enemies on his doorstep and his reputation under scrutiny. Then, in December 1939, he was approached by two men, Alberto Ascari, only a 22-year-old motor cyclist at the time, and his friend Lotario Rangoni Machiavelli, an enthusiastic amateur racer and wealthy Modena aristocrat. They asked Ferrari to make two small sports cars for the Mille Miglia, reorganised as the Gran Premio di Brescia. It was a heaven-sent opportunity for Ferrari who took the decision to agree to build the cars on Christmas Eve, 1939.

This meeting offered another insight into the commitment and passion for racing which ruled Ferrari's life and dominated his thoughts. Christmas Eve, in Italy, is a very religious and significant day. It is a holy family day. Yet while most families in Modena and Italy were together, eating and praying, he was doing business. In Yates's view, this showed

> not only the singular intensity with which he engaged in business, but also the hypocrisy of his testimonials of devotion to his son and wife. This behaviour was hardly unusual for him and others also found him boring ahead with his work on various Easter Sundays, Christmases or any one of the multitude of holidays and feast days that dot the Italian calendar.

In that cold December meeting, the true team of Ferrari was born and the man himself was reborn. He took control of his own destiny, operating as a hands-on manager and director in a manner remote from that which he adopted in later life when he remained at home in Italy while his team was racing all over the world. His genius for organising his own will to prevail in all kinds of difficult circumstances and to use his own drive and ambition to make things happen was to rise to the fore. The cars were built, they ran and they showed speed and promise, before retiring. Then Italy went to war and Ferrari looked for new opportunities. At 42, he was too old to be called up and to fight. Instead, he devoted his energies to his own war effort, more explicitly, to maximising his own opportunities for profit.

Various accounts of his war work exist, one suggesting that at the prompting of Corrado Gatti, a Turin businessman, who was an associate of Ferrari's friend Enrico Nardi, he should use Auto Avio Costruzione to copy German-made Jung grinding machines under patent. Ferrari found no such patents existed. Instead, he chose to copy the grinders without any permission and found this to be a very successful exercise. Various other accounts suggest he was involved in many others kind of war-related industry, all of which were specialist and profitable, including fabricating gearboxes for the use of Breda engines to be modified for marine use as landing craft for the Italian army. It was also said that he worked for the Brescia firm of Ernesto Breda who manufactured arms for the government.

In 1943, when the Allies began bombing the main industrial centres in the Po valley, to his immense good fortune as seen retrospectively, he was ordered to move his factory to a safer location. Maranello was the place and three adjacent pieces of land and buildings were purchased in the joint names of Enzo and his wife Laura's names, an arrangement that was calculated to offer maximum security to them both. By September 1943, Ferrari's new factory was thriving, his standing was high, the Auto Avio Costruzione business was secure and, the contract that forbade him to use his name in motor racing having run out, the Scuderia Ferrari was out of the shadows again.

During the war, other events of note had made an impact on his life. The most important of these was the arrival of a fair-haired woman called Lina Lardi. Attractive and serene, she came from a nearby medieval village, Castelvetro, and she worked in the Carrozzeria Orlandi, owned by a friend of Ferrari. She became very close to him and was to remain an important figure through the rest of his life and, significantly, bore him a son. But in those times, in Italy, when divorce was well-nigh impossible and such relationships were to be kept away from the public glare, Ferrari's love affair with Lina Lardi was to be a secret one, albeit one that gradually became more and more widely known around Maranello and Modena. Those who knew of it understood it as a sweet and genuine love story, contrary to many later observers who attempted to rewrite the story with a scandalous overtone. It was a real relationship of importance to the man.

As the war ended, the prospects for Ferrari were uncertain. On bad days, they seemed to him to be bleak. In early 1945 Lina Lardi was pregnant, his relationship with his wife Laura was strained and his son Dino, 12, was ill. He was facing the likelihood that he might lose one child and gain another at a time when death and bombs were all around. In April 1945, Benito Mussolini was killed and brutalised on the shores of Lake Como. A few weeks later, on 22 May 1945, Piero Lardi Ferrari was born and taken to live and be brought up in the Lardi home at Castelvetro where Ferrari was to be a regular visitor. It was a time of ending and cleansing in Italy and, for Ferrari, a time of change.

After the Second World War, Ferrari set out to build his own Grand Prix cars and in 1947 he succeeded with a 1.5 litre Tipo

125. This was a car that had been a dream for him and Giaochimo Colombo, who had worked with him in its early creation. When the war ended, Ferrari knew he wanted to build racing cars again, but Vittorio Jano, the designer he wanted most, was unavailable (he was with Lancia). Colombo, however, though working for Alfa Romeo in Milan, was semi-available; having been a member of the now-defunct Fascist party, he was sent on leave of absence while investigations into his activities during the war took place. Various unpleasant deeds, including assassinations, proved these were wild days and to Colombo a move away from Milan to somewhere more peaceful was an attractive proposition.

In July 1945 he drove with Nardi to Modena to the original offices of the *scuderia* to meet Ferrari, weaving through the crater-strewn roads and villages in a pre-war vehicle fuelled by black market petrol. At the meeting, it is said, Colombo was surprised to hear Ferrari suggest that the time was right to build racing cars again, but understood immediately. Ferrari wanted to steal a march, to be a leading competitor and he planned a 1.5-litre vehicle. Colombo proposed that it should be a 12-cylinder car and Ferrari responded by saying 'My dear Colombo, you read my mind.' It is a version of events that suggests that many of the claims made – that Ferrari was the man who had the original idea for a V-12 engine – may not be true. Both men, however, shared a passionate desire to make this audacious and unique idea work, to prove to Alfa Romeo that there was one racing car team in the Padana valley and that that team was Scuderia Ferrari.

Colombo, working while on what later became to be known in Formula One circles as 'gardening leave' – designers like Adrian Newey, leaving Williams for McLaren went through the same kind of process – turned a small room in his Milan apartment into a studio and set to work. Cajoled by Ferrari, he worked at a frenzied pace and asked an old friend, now unemployed, to work on the gearbox. As life returned to normal, Ferrari and his team were toiling and the French, in Paris, were celebrating their freedom by running the Grand Prix de la Liberation in the Bois de Boulogne in September 1945.

The French capital also hosted a meeting of the national automobile clubs of the nations involved (excluding Germany, which was banned from attending) to agree, under the banner of the Fédération Internationale de l'Automobile (FIA), that

Grand Prix racing would resume with a formula that restricted engines to no more than 4.5 litres (unsupercharged) in size or 1.5 litres (supercharged). Ferrari believed a supercharged version of his 1.5 litre power-unit would be competitive and felt reassured that he was on the right lines. The arrival, in Maranello, of a 21-year-old unemployed draftsman called Luciano Fochi also helped; a former apprentice under Colombo at Alfa Romeo, he was job-hunting on a day when Colombo visited the factory with his drawings and he was promptly hired to transform Colombo's sketches into blueprints. This was a critical event as, in November 1945, Colombo was recalled to work by Alfa Romeo, briefed to resuscitate half a dozen old 158s and to triumph while the Auto Unions and Mercedes-Benz hopes lay defenceless.

It was a double blow to Ferrari; the loss of his designer (albeit while working for another company under contract) and the defection of his designer to his most bitter rival (albeit the same company to which he was contracted to work). Dismayed, tired, over-stretched, Ferrari felt helpless himself and, according to Yates,

> was in a bad way, looked haggard beyond his 48 years, his shock of hair, combed back in pompadour style, was peppered with grey, his eyes, always puffy and languid, were red-rimmed with fatigue, his hulking frame slumped behind a desk in the large unheated office

when he was visited by his old friend Luigi Chinetti who had driven from Paris. Chinetti found him easily in the dull two-storey building on the Viale Trento e Trieste, surrounded by the decay of post-war Modena.

Cleverly, Chinetti felt there was something to build on beneath the veneer of Ferrari's self-deprecatory complaints. Ferrari moaned, talked of the difficulties, the rebuilding and the ruin and the challenges ahead. Chinetti, who had heard of the planned 125, by whatever means, talked of his years in America, the massive war machine there that had created methods of mass production and modernity that made Italy look antiquated and laughable. He was direct and factual. He called Ferrari nothing more than Ferrari. Not Commendatore. Not Cavaliere. He told him that if Ferrari produced the cars, he could sell them in America. To Ferrari, it was an illusion, but attractive. His frustrations hurt him. They were made worse, also, by the sound of the Maserati brothers testing their cars on the Abetone road outside his factory when, sometimes, the howl of their engines rattled his office windows.

Ferrari was in anguish, his 125 badly delayed, when Colombo recommended the inexperienced engineer Giuseppe Busso, who was unemployed. He took him on and virtually locked him into the work immediately. Busso settled quickly, but faced a daunting challenge; Ferrari lubricated his way by inviting him to his apartment for dinners with Laura and showing sufficient sentimentality to engage his friendship and loyalty. 'The anguish of seeing him cry many a time when talking about Dino may have contributed to my affection for Ferrari,' he recalled. But the workload was punishing. To speed things, Ferrari hired Aurelio Lampredi as deputy manager of the technical office. It was a move that led to clashes with Busso, but progress.

In December 1946 he held a news conference with the press to confirm that a new line of Ferrari cars was imminent. It was the first such gathering in what was to become a tradition. The visit from Chinetti was still in the back of his mind. But these were dramatic times, the cars were nothing like ready, Ferrari hectored and bullied, Lampredi resigned and then, after pleading from the old man, returned. By 12 March 1947 the first prototype of the 125 was ready for a test drive.

Ferrari himself, by now a bulky man, forced his way into the car as it stood on the cobbled courtyard. Luigi Bazzi, his longtime engineer in charge of the building of the power-unit, was there and nodded as Ferrari fired it up, pulled away and turned right up the Abetone road, heading north from Maranello on the long, straight, tree-lined road. To test his car here, away from the swoops and curves of the Apennines to the south, confirmed that he was, as ever, more interested in power than handling. It was to be the enduring feature of his cars for the next two generations as he used his great powers of self-publicity and persuasion to the full while maintaining his reclusive lifestyle in Modena.

The 125 made its racing debut at Piacenza on 11 May 1947, in a 60-miles race on a street circuit. Franco Cortese did not win for Ferrari, but led by 25 seconds before retiring with three laps remaining with a broken fuel-pump. Maserati won. 'A promising failure,' Ferrari told Bazzi afterwards. The fire was lit. Two weeks later, a Ferrari ran in Rome with Cortese at the wheel around the Baths of Caracalla and won, the first victory by a Ferrari in the company's history, but celebrated rarely due to the poor opposition and its mere academic importance.

The next year, Ferrari registered an official entry for a Grand Prix for the first time at Monaco on 16 May 1948, when Prince Igor Troubetzkoy drove a two-litre Tipo 166. History was made and later the same year, after Raymond Sommer won a sports car race at Valentino Park in Turin, Ferrari was prompted to nostalgic memories of 1918.

It was a very cold one [the winter] and I found myself out on the street again, my clothes feeling as though they were freezing to me. Crossing Valentino Park, I brushed the snow off a bench and sat down. I was alone. My father and my brother were no more. Overcome by loneliness and despair, I wept. Many years later, in 1947, after Sommer had won the first post-war Turin Grand Prix with the 12-cylinder Ferrari, I went and sat on that same bench. The tears I shed that day, though, were of a very different kind.

The absence at this time of the Alfa Romeos was a boon for Ferrari and, in 1949, he made the most of the opportunity. The 125s and their successors, particularly at the hands of Alberto Ascari and Luigi Villoresi, enjoyed themselves, but with the advent of the new world championship in 1950, Alfa Romeo changed policy and re-entered Grand Prix motor racing and outgunned the Ferraris, a decision that resulted in a series of wins. Ferrari's first did not arrive until the 1951 British Grand Prix at Silverstone where the Alfettas were defeated by Jose Froilan Gonzalez, known as the 'pampas bull', driving a 4.5-litre V12 Ferrari 375, a car with an engine recommended by Aurelio Lampredi, who had returned to the *scuderia*. For his historic efforts, Gonzalez's prize was a sports car! Ascari won the next race, the German Grand Prix at the Nurburgring, and with these successes and triumph in the Mille Miglia the legend was under way – although victory was overshadowed by Ascari's crashing into the crowd, killing a local doctor and dragging the team into a long legal dispute. Fangio may have been the world champion, but it was a fortunate win.

Ferrari, adept at spreading his risks and calculating the best approach to business, continued taking a great competitive interest in sports car racing, as was usual at this time, and in 1948 experienced perhaps, some said, his last honest face-to-face meeting with a driver. Nuvolari, his body failing, had been entered for the Mille Miglia (an event Ferrari enjoyed and in which he claimed many famous wins). He was due to drive a Cisitalia, but the car was not ready on time and he took over an open Ferrari 166C, intended for Count Igor Troubetzkoy. He drove like a man possessed, led at Ravenna, lost his engine cover, lost his seat (which was replaced by a sack of oranges) and carried on and on. At one of the last control stops, Ferrari saw him and recognised the poor condition he was in. With tears in his eyes, he begged him to stop. Nuvolari, it was recognised, was the last driver to hold Ferrari's level respect. But he drove on and at Reggio Emilia was forced to retire by a broken spring and he had to be lifted out of the car.

These early adventures in Ferrari's career help explain how racing and his team developed and how his character moulded itself to suit the needs. But he was unable to adapt quickly to new threats to the supremacy he began to establish in the early 1950s (when his Tipo 500, a perfectly prepared competitive four-cylinder in-line vehicle, dominated successive championships while they were run for Formula Two two-litre cars) after Ascari had won the drivers' title in 1952 and 1953. Ascari, a double world champion, won all six of his races in 1952 and five from eight starts in 1953, but he died after moving to Lancia, when he was testing a Ferrari sports car, just weeks after surviving an accident at the Monaco Grand Prix which had sent him into the harbour.

In 1952, in the only race in which Ascari did not compete, Piero Taruffi won, while in 1953, when he missed the French and German Grands Prix, the victories went to the *scuderia*'s newcomer, Mike Hawthorn, who always wore a green jacket and bow-tie, and Farina, respectively. The Ferrari team were also virtually invincible at this time in Formula Two and it was a headline-making shock when they were beaten at Monza in September 1953 by Fangio in a Maserati.

Ferrari's grief at Ascari's death was softened, no doubt, by Fiat's decision to turn over all of the Lancia cars and their designer Vittorio Jano to his team. He continued racing, of course, and began producing Gran Turismo cars, in alliance with Battista 'Pinin' Fafina, that were to enjoy success at Le

Mans and other endurance events. These victories made Ferrari and his cars world famous, but the challenge of competing successfully in two forms of racing, sports cars and Formula One, stretched the team's resources.

A new 2.5 litre formula was introduced for 1954. Ferrari developed the 500's two-litre power-unit into a 2.5-litre power unit for the Tipo 625. But it was no match for the opposition and it was only the withdrawal of Lancia, and the move of Jano to Ferrari, that salvaged their pride. Jano it was who evolved a new V6 initially for Formula Two's 1.5 litre category, but in late 1957 increased it to 2.4 litres for Formula One. In 1958, 1959 and 1960 it powered the Dino 246 and Dino 256 cars, named after his son who died in the summer of 1956 from nephritis, a kidney complaint, four years after contracting muscular dystrophy. Dino's death was a terrible blow to his father.

> I feel alone after a life crowded by so many events, and almost guilty of having survived [he wrote in his memoirs]. And I feel, too, a certain detachment, for in this arid earth that is myself, the plant of hope can thrive only if watered by a son's love.

Following Dino's death, on 30 June 1956, Ferrari's cars entered the French Grand Prix the following day at Reims, the drivers, Fangio, Collins, Castellotti, Portago and Gendebien, each wearing a black armband. Collins, for whom the Old Man had a soft spot, won.

It was in a Dino that Mike Hawthorn drove to the drivers' world championship in 1958, the last season before the full might of the 'kit-car teams' came to the fore. Though great successes were still achieved, notably with Hawthorn, Peter Collins and Fangio, it was obvious that the opposition were growing in cleverness, strength and numbers, particularly the British teams who concentrated on building their own chassis, working on the aerodynamics, but not their own engines. This was their way of concentrating on the traditional weakness of Ferrari who believed power would conquer all.

The Maranello Scuderia was also prone to internal conflict and argument in the years of change that swept through the early 1960s. In the engineering department, for example, when Jano retired, Carlo Chiti, formerly with Alfa Romeo, took over as chief engineer and, with Ferrari prompting cleverly and thinking long-term, was put in charge of designing a new 120-degree V6 power-unit, initially for the 1.5 litre Formula Two season in 1960, but more importantly in readiness for the 1961 Formula One season when the rules changed. At around the same time, the *scuderia* hired Mauro Forghieri, to assist Chiti in the racing programme, thus bringing into place one of the most creative designers and memorable characters in the history of Ferrari. When Chiti left the company, in a great 'palace revolution' at the end of 1961, Forghieri was appointed as his successor and remained head of race engineering for a generation during which he was described as both a 'madman' and a 'genius' by several who worked with him.

The British teams, waiting for their own 1.5 V8s to arrive from BRM and Coventry Climax, were left behind and with the V6 Ferraris out in a class of their own, Phil Hill won the drivers' title at Monza in the most tragic of circumstances, following the death of his team-mate Wolfgang von Trips.

'At Ferrari in those days, you started with a handicap,' said John Surtees, the 1964 drivers' world champion for Ferrari. 'Until Le Mans was over, you couldn't really do the work you wanted to do – and needed to do – in Formula One.' For Ferrari, however, Le Mans remained significant and special until the end of the 1960s as he struggled for consistent success on two racing fronts. To make matters worse for Ferrari, in the 1950s, he suffered a grievous blow when his son Dino died in 1956. He never really recovered and many said it was the defining moment of his life. The grief never really lifted and he rarely attended a Grand Prix again.

In his splendid book *Mon Ami Mate, The Bright Brief Lives of Mike Hawthorn and Peter Collins*, Chris Nixon wrote of the events of 1956 when Peter Collins arrived in Modena and took up residence in the Reale Hotel, a short walk from the Ferrari house at 11 Via Trento Trieste. He recalled that Collins, charming and clever with languages, settled in quickly, ate with the Ferrari staff in the recently opened Ristorante Cavallino, across the road from the factory in Maranello, and enjoyed a close relationship with Enzo and Laura Ferrari. These, too, were the final days of Dino's life and Collins, much the same age as the dying Dino, would visit him often and obey requests to go to the cinema and report back on certain films. When Dino died, Collins was seen as a surrogate son by the Ferraris who offered him the use of a flat above the Cavallino, which had previously been used by Dino. It was also said that Signora Ferrari often made his breakfast and sometimes did his washing. Ferrari, however, disapproved when Collins married and their relationship deteriorated thereafter.

Fangio, unimpressed by his season with Ferrari moved on at the end of 1956 (having won the title, thanks to Collins's handing him his car in the final race). The following year, 1957, brought only more misery. On the Mille Miglia, the Marquis de Portago crashed his Ferrari into the crowd, twelve spectators were killed and Ferrari was charged with manslaughter. In Formula One, with Hawthorn partnering Collins and Luigi Musso, Ferrari failed to win a race as the British teams grew in strength.

The next year, Musso was killed at the French Grand Prix and Collins at the Nurburgring. Hawthorn took the world championship and then retired from the sport just months before being killed in the road accident witnessed by Rob Walker. Ferrari continued, hiring and firing drivers as he felt necessary, men like Tony Brooks, Jean Behra, Phil Hill and Dan Gurney among them. Then came 1961, the shark-nosed 156 and a scrap for the drivers' title between Wolfgang Von Trips and Hill which resulted in the American taking the crown after the German had crashed into the crowd at Monza, killing himself and 14 spectators. Always, it seemed, Ferrari's glories came at a price and, too often, with blood as he stretched his resources to stay in competition.

The V6 carried on racing into 1964 until a new Ferrari V8 arrived to carry Surtees to the title either side of championship wins by Jim Clark in his Lotus Climax. In 1966 a new three-litre formula came into effect. This was meat and drink to Ferrari who had a war-chest of such engines developed from the old days, but a deep reservoir of reserves and a dogmatic approach to the needs of the job were not adequate to guarantee continued success. The V12 was at the end of the road and the less powerful Repco Brabham V8 stole the championships with Jack Brabham at the wheel.

Surtees, disillusioned with the perennial politics of the *scuderia*, resigned and left midway through the season, having won the Belgian Grand Prix at Spa-Francorchamps. Surtees's departure and the failures of the V12 were the start of a period of disappointment for Ferrari. There was only sporadic success. Chris Amon (who recalled that the old man was often more interested in what his drivers did in bed the previous night than in his cars) often appeared set for success, particularly in 1967, but was always cheated by mechanical failure or bad luck.

In 1968 Jacky Ickx won the French Grand Prix in the rain at Rouen, and was still in with a chance for the drivers' title when he crashed in practice in Canada and broke his leg. In 1969 the overweight V12-engined Ferraris were outclassed and looked obsolete as they were drubbed by the mostly Cosworth V8 powered opposition. Worse still, attempts to update the old Ferrari were doomed and when his prototype 'boxer' V12 burst behind him during private testing, Chris Amon decided to abandon Ferrari immediately. He was aghast and he was emotional; and he was wrong because, in the early 1970s, this new flat 12 horizontally opposed power-unit, first developed by Forghieri, came into its own and, fleetingly, won races before a real nadir followed in 1973 when the 312Bs were redesigned to conform to new deformable structure safety regulations and proved utterly uncompetitive.

Ferrari withdrew briefly from Formula One but returned in 1974, with Niki Lauda alongside Clay Regazzoni in the team, as strong as ever. Their pairing was the creation of the team's new manager Luca di Montezemolo, a man whose name was to remain synonymous with Ferrari and Italian sport thereafter. He, Montezemolo, signed Lauda after arranging a secret meeting in London. Lauda flew in from Vienna and Montezemolo from Milan to avoid the inquiring lenses and questions of any prying Italian reporters.

Only bad luck cost Lauda a title that year, but he responded by lifting the drivers' crown the following year with the 312T and again, in 1977, after surviving a horrendous blazing accident at the Nurburgring which cost him the championship (won by James Hunt) in 1976 when he retired from the final race at Mount Fuji on safety grounds in the teeming rain. The 1977 success also confirmed, for Ferrari, a hat-trick of constructors' titles and at a time when the *scuderia* was progressing, with financial involvement from Fiat, into something different from the original team dominated by one man and his ego. Strategic management, originally in the form of Luca di Montezemolo, who joined in 1973 (and left less than three years later, only to return as president of Ferrari in 1991), had arrived and money was an ever-increasing concern to everyone involved in Ferrari and Formula One. But sentiment and honour were still part of the Ferrari mentality.

This was clearly shown at the end of the 1976 season. Hunt had won the title, after Lauda had parked his Ferrari and abandoned the Japanese Grand Prix in the cloudburst at Mount Fuji. The conditions were among the worst ever known in Formula One motor racing, but Lauda, a man with more courage than any other, knew that his retirement would not please or be understood by Ferrari. Lauda telephoned the Old Man from the airport at Tokyo and knew immediately how displeased he was. A week later, Ferrari held one of his chaotic and famous news conferences. Reporters travelled from all over Europe to be there. Yates reported the scene with a comic eye.

At one point [he wrote] a writer addressed him as Commendatore, to which Ferrari growled, 'Look, I'm no Commendatore – I prefer to be called Ferrari. When I go to the barber shop and am called Commendatore I don't object because there are many Commendatori, but if they call me Ferrari that is another matter, understand? Therefore, if you want to call me Enzo, then I shall close my eyes, imagine you are a beautiful girl and I will be even happier.' This was the kind of opaque garble for which such sessions had become famous. Early in the conference, he was asked about the Lauda retirement at Fuji and if he know of anything like it. 'Yes, I know of a driver,' he mused. 'His name was Enzo Ferrari. You don't believe me because you are young men. I was to go to the Lyon Grand Prix, where I was to drive the fourth car. At the time, I suffered a nervous breakdown and I had the guts to say to myself "I have tried the circuit, have come home and have to go back – but I can't make it." As soon as I got over the breakdown, which I suffered in 1924, I went back to racing. Do not forget that I was born in 1898 and that, in 1918, I underwent two chest operations. I have suffered a lot, but God has not abandoned me. Like Lauda, I had to ask myself, when my Dino was born, should I race again? I decided to stop. Lauda decided to go on. I had to keep my word to him even if this should damage Ferrari.' From such jumbles of sentimentalities, distortions and vague inferences, the gathered press were supposed to infer that Ferrari supported Lauda's decision to park the car, but in private . . .

By 1969 the strain, financially, had become acute for Ferrari, no longer the young and vigorous man he was when building up his company, and he had faced up to his financial difficulties by selling a holding to Fiat, who took over his production car business. Ferrari remained in charge of the racing team, with a limited share, but Fiat were the paymasters and a new era had started. It was the start of Ferrari's efforts to stay apace with the rapid developments in the sport brought about by Colin Chapman and Lotus and the response saw Niki Lauda win his two world titles in three years in the mid-1970s when the team was managed by Forghieri and Montezemolo, and then Jody Scheckter triumph in 1979.

After this, despite the power and music of the engines, Ferrari was a team fighting history and struggling to adapt, headed by an ageing old patriarch and autocrat whose ideas and methods were not modern enough to help his team compete. Powerful engines were the heart of the cars, but the chassis were outdated and it was years afterwards that the efforts of Harvey Postlethwaite, who began to introduce carbon-fibre at Maranello following his arrival in the summer of 1981, began to pay off.

Postlethwaite, an engineer with experience at March, Wolf, Fittipaldi and Hesketh, had worked in the design of suspensions, aerodynamics and carbon-fibre; his arrival was designed to permit Forghieri to concentrate on the engines while he developed the new 'Anglo' ideas of aerodynamic efficiency, down-force, road-holding, handling and braking. His arrival was a signal that the Old Man was taking on new ideas. But the old structure, creaking and groaning under the weight of new technology, was not conducive to progress.

> I quickly found that the business was done through the back door [said Postlethwaite]. Through leaks from informants and from the masses of cronies who surrounded the Old Man. There was almost no debate or criticism aired in formal meetings. Ferrari had no interest in, much less control over, the passenger-car side of the business. In fact, he had total disdain for the people who bought the road cars. He called them 'fools', although they were in a sense supporting the entire racing operation. And I was paid by cheque from Fiat. Not Ferrari . . . And there was no interest on Ferrari's part in chassis, aerodynamics or brakes. He

lived in the past, totally distracted by big horsepower, to the exclusion of all else.

This added to the sense of drama and conflict at Maranello as Ferrari requested certain kind of engines be developed despite advice to the contrary from Postlethwaite, who was inevitably thrown into conflict with Forghieri. If this was not bad enough, 1982 was to see a more meaningful, savage and ultimately fatal conflict between Gilles Villeneuve, whose driving and personality were so much admired by Ferrari, and Didier Pironi, his French team mate who had succeeded Scheckter. When Pironi won the San Marino Grand Prix, having broken the unwritten Ferrari agreement that team-mates hold positions by passing Villeneuve on the final lap, at the circuit named after Dino Ferrari, in a race that was boycotted by the FOCA teams, it led to the tragedy at Zolder, in qualifying for the Belgian Grand Prix, where Villeneuve struck the rear of Jochen Mass's March and cart-wheeled off the circuit, dying in a massive and shocking accident.

His replacement, alongside the luckless and seemingly condemned Pironi, was another Frenchman, Patrick Tambay. Despite the protests of the Italian media, who wanted an Italian, it was Tambay who was hired to steer the crimson vehicles of Italian honour to glory. Pironi, much criticised after Villeneuve's death, was almost killed himself at the German Grand Prix at the Hockenheimring when he hit the rear of Alain Prost's Renault in thick mist and cannoned off it and into the air. Unlike Villeneuve, he landed rear first, not nose, and survived with two broken legs. His career in Formula One was over. He later died in a power-boat crash off the Isle of Wight in 1987. The Old Man was reportedly told of the Pironi accident in Germany and replied with just two words 'Adieu, mondiale'. Goodbye, world championship.

More big-name drivers came and went, as did famous and reputable designers, including John Barnard, the originator of McLaren's supremacy, who was watched in 1985 and recruited in 1986. At that time, Piero Lardi Ferrari was constantly at loggerheads with Forghieri, TAG-McLaren were the dominant force on the circuits and Honda were marching over the horizon with a war chest said to have contained more than 300 million American dollars. Barnard's 'arrival', however, was hardly that; as he worked in England in a base known as the GTO

(Guildford Technical Office) and he only travelled rarely, mostly to go the race meetings. He did not work in Italy much at all. Postlethwaite was troubled, Forghieri resigned and joined Lamborghini and Michele Alboreto, then driving for Ferrari, who had at least registered rare victories in Canada and Germany in 1985, compared the hiring of the English engineer to work in England as like having 'a doctor doing brain surgery by telephone'.

The atmosphere was hardly improved by some of Barnard's innovate 'improvements' to the way of life under Ferrari. He banned, for example, the traditional team lunch, which included a generous supply of Lambrusco, at race weekends. He also found the pressure of the media difficult to deal with and admitted that what he termed 'the PR side of this business' was a 'complete pain in the arse, though I recognise the need for it'. At McLaren, he told Neil Lyndon, he spent a lot of his time trying to avoid the media and stay out of trouble.

> I always had the feeling that Ron Dennis [McLaren's team principal] was an unexploded hand-grenade, who could go off at any moment and make a horrible mess of the room. A lot of my time was spent trying to keep the safety pin in.

By the summer of 1987, according to Yates, Ferrari's son Piero was involved in an alleged 'palace coup', along with Postlethwaite. It was no surprise to close Ferrari-watchers. The place was alive with rumour, intrigue and speculation. Barnard knew the political set-up behind the scenes was difficult, but saw it from a slant.

> Harvey has been here for six or seven years and, to some extent, he has become Ferrari-ised [he told Lyndon]. Most of the people in this racing team have been with Ferrari since they left school. They don't know anything else and they don't have anywhere else to go, unless they leave the country. The worst that can happen to them is that, if they screw up, they get moved out of the racing division and into production. If I could have my way entirely, there's a hell of a lot of them who would go; but, to do that, I'd have to get too close myself to the company with the consequence that I might become a victim of the same process.

(Barnard, of course, had been a victim of a similarly ruthless sequence of events himself when, after being approached by Niki Lauda, working on behalf of BMW, he was hired to head a new Formula One team; after approaching two famous drivers and making many plans, he was told the idea was not being supported by the BMW board of directors and made redundant.)

By late 1986 it was clear changes were necessary and Barnard's recruitment was imminent. A further insight into the man and his team came when the British media corps was invited to Maranello to meet the Old Man in mid-September, immediately before the Italian Grand Prix at Monza that year. Alongside him, as always, was Marco Piccinini, interpreter, smoother-of-the-way and Formula One's most velvet-gloved diplomat; and his son Piero Lardi Ferrari, then 41. Asked by Nigel Roebuck if he had any ambitions remaining, Ferrari replied: 'I've been involved in racing since 1919 and, to go on living, a human being must always have new ambitions. At Ferrari, the most beautiful victory is always the next one.' Roebuck also reported that Piero held a 10 per cent shareholding in the *scuderia* at this time. The rest were with Fiat (40 per cent), Enzo Ferrari (49 per cent) and Pininfarina (one per cent).

At the same meeting, Ferrari talked about Senna, whom he admired and had considered signing following his refulgent spell at Lotus. 'Ah, Senna,' he said, when asked. 'We felt it inappropriate to go to Marlboro (who pay our drivers) with the financial expectations which were advanced by the driver. They were, shall we say, *imaginativo*!' In his piece, following this day, Roebuck recalled lunch at the Cavallino across the road and an anecdote of Chris Amon's experiences with the team.

I used to test at Modena all morning and then have lunch with the Old Man [Amon said]. And there was always wine with the pasta. Once, in my early days there, I realised we'd each had a bottle of Lambrusco – you know how easily that stuff goes down – and Ferrari said: 'Good, you'll go faster this afternoon!' I did, too. Believe it or not . . .

And, at the end of the visit, Ferrari waved his arm for quiet and told the assembled British reporters:

I want to tell you that I think Britain a great country and I have done since I went to Brooklands in 1923. You enjoy a fine and old democracy that used to be administered by a great dictator – Churchill. And today you have the good fortune of enjoying a democracy administered by a very strong woman. I hope it carries on. I have no interest in political parties of any kind, only in nations.

By the following year, 1987, McLaren-Honda, with Alain Prost leading, was competing with Williams-Honda, led by Nelson Piquet and Nigel Mansell, for the championship. Jean-Claude Migeot, a French aerodynamicist, was hired. But soon enough the Old Man lost his patience as he saw Barnard, busy with an automatic gearbox, Postlethwaite and Migeot leading his team nowhere. There was a major row. Postlethwaite left and Migeot followed. As the year ended, plans were drawn up in Paris to phase out the turbo-charged engines and bring in a 3.5 litre formula. Some FOCA teams pleaded against this, having invested heavily in turbo development, and a new dispute appeared likely. When a meeting was held in Paris to discuss the issues, Ferrari sent his usual representatives while, on the same day, he hosted a meeting at his Fiorano farmhouse, where Ferrari built a test circuit, with Balestre and Ecclestone. Agreement was reached, said Yates, between them with the support of the man dubbed 'the Pope of the north' and all the words in Paris were to be little more than empty rhetoric of academic value.

It was to be the last meaningful act by Ferrari. The following February, at a grand party organised by the Cavallino restaurant and held in the Maranello factory, he celebrated his 90th birthday. The guest list numbered more than 1,750, the table-clothes were in Modena yellow and after the feast was eaten, 12 cakes decorated with Ferrari's emblem were served. The season that followed was far less colourful. It was dominated by the red-and-white McLarens, by illness and decline, by a disappointment in being too poorly to meet the Pope John Paul II when he toured the valley (though he did, it was said, confess to the Pope afterwards in a telephone conversation). Ferrari, a self-confessed agitator of men, died, aged 90, on 14 August 1988. With him went the last roar of the pioneer and the plutocrat. Two days later, Fiat moved in, announced officially that it would exercise an option to obtain 40 per cent of the remaining shares in Ferrari (leaving the family with 10 per cent) and

Scuderia Ferrari became part of the corporate club, the brand name of a manufacturer in racing with its eye on the bottom line. Some traditions remained within the team, but to gain success Ferrari had to adopt the modern trends, hire international designers and managers and drivers. Team Schumacher was born at Planet Ferrari in the mid-1990s and, in turning the tide, it achieved its rewards even if the means were never quite the same as those of the Old Man and his dreams.

Enzo Ferrari was a remarkable man, involved deeply in racing for more than 50 years, a giant whose shadow remains cast across the sport. His cars have raced on all the roads where races are held. His Ferraris have won in Italy, Britain, Germany, France, Florida, Brazil, Australia and Monte Carlo. They have won in Africa, America and Mexico. They have won long-distance endurance tests, sprints, Grands Prix and sports car races. Ferrari drivers have won drivers' titles and his cars have won constructors' titles. No other racing car manufacturer can match the record or the reputation of Ferrari and the blood-red cars in living, in racing or in death. Argentina in 1953, the Mille Miglia in Italy in 1957, Cuba in 1958, Monza in 1961 . . . all saw spectators slaughtered. Drivers, too, have perished at the wheel of the most famous cars of all.

The man, Enzo Ferrari, may have been seen, by some who did not know him, as a mysterious figure in the end; but those who did enjoyed his company, his humanity and his humour. He was a man who loved racing, but who travelled only rarely to the races. He was a man who many thought did not like to be seen in public, yet he continued enjoying the company of his friends for as long as he could share his favourite Saturday lunches with them. He was a man who appeared to suffer intensely when one of his drivers was killed, but who continued to send men to their death in his machines. He was a man of few friends, seen by many as unapproachable, stern and rough. In a room, no one sat until he had. He was addressed by most people as Commendatore, a rank to which he was promoted by the Italian King before the war, in recognition of his victorious contributions to Italy's reputation. By the mid-1960s he and his cars were icons. In 1962, at his Christmas gathering of news reporters and car correspondents, he announced that every car he produced in 1963 was pre-sold. Then, he was selling about 600 luxury high-speed cars per year and he employed about 300 men. He also produced racing cars, Formula One cars.

No philanthropist, he cared little for losing money. He cared for racing, for the perfection he might one day achieve in his cars, the thrill of the competition and the satisfaction of a victory. Autocratic and often bad-tempered, he had a reputation for not suffering insubordination. Harry Schell said once that he 'was an impossible man to work for'. Few employees lasted more than a year or two. Political infighting was, therefore, part of his life.

In his cars, as in certain parts of his life, he sought power beyond all others. Ferrari was not an engineer, but a man who appreciated engines. He had ideas about engines and made his engineers do things his way. Or go. Similarly, he wanted his own way with his cars. 'My cars must be beautiful,' he always said. 'But, more than that, they must not stop out on the circuit. For then people will say "what a pity, it was so pretty".' It was said that he could lose with honour, though only occasionally, but he could not break down on the circuit with honour. This belief helped drivers consider his cars to be safer than those of most of his rivals.

The American journalist Robert Daley, in his classic study of motor racing, *The Cruel Sport*, wrote that the central fact in Ferrari's life was death.

> But not the death of drivers. It was the death in 1956 of his son Alfredo, called Dino, of leukaemia (in fact, he died from a rare form of muscular dystrophy) at the age of 25. The boy had been bed-ridden part of every year from the age of 16. He kept asking his father why his body was so feeble when his mind was so alert, so eager to live. Ferrari had no answer. He had had much experience in death, but death had never been personal until now.

He had hoped to support Dino's interest in engineering. But his dream died slowly in his son's body. Ferrari found it difficult to come to terms with his death. He kept his memory alive and he visited his tomb every day in Modena. He brooded there and visited again whenever a driver was killed. This sense of grief as motivation is a recurrent theme not only in Ferrari's life, but in those of other members of the Piranha Club. The loss of friends or family is used as a stimulus to work harder, achieve more and succeed.

Ferrari spent long hours, up to 15 hours daily, sometimes including Sundays, at the factory, but it was not all work. He told

Daley: 'A man has no need of entertainment. Entertainment only distracts from his duty. If a man has his duty, that is enough.' He cared little for flamboyant wealth. Unlike some modern members of the Piranha Club, he was not likely to be found on a yacht, launching a power-boat or living it up in London or Monte Carlo or Malaga. He was a local man, an ordinary man of Modena, who worked. In his office, the only decorations were a photograph of Dino on a wall and a black glass prancing horse, a gift from the actor Paul Newman, on his desk.

He was a tough employer. He did not negotiate with drivers. They took his offers or left. At the end of one season, Phil Hill and Dan Gurney asked for a pay rise. Gurney was fired. Hill, whom he wished to keep, was told he was retiring from the sport and would not be racing in his native United States Grand Prix the following month. 'Ferrari decided to give me one last chance,' said Hill. 'And I took it.' He allowed him to race in America, but he did not get a pay rise. As a result, many men who raced for Ferrari did so for the challenge and the thrill, but not for the money. They wanted to prove something to him and to themselves. They were often fast, on a ragged edge, and nervous. Some said they were faintly suicidal. All this appealed to Ferrari.

For nearly 20 years, his secretary was an English woman, Brenda Vernor, from Croydon in south London. She went to Italy on an exchange visit to Perugia, but after a romance with Mike Parkes stayed on with the most famous racing and car organisation on earth. Her recollections paint a vivid picture of life at Modena and Maranello from the 1960s to the end of the twentieth century. Once, she told Jane Nottage of *Formula 1 Magazine*, she had a row with Parkes, in the heat of their relationship and before, following his death, she worked for Ferrari, and she

> took off to Imperia without telling anyone where I was going. Two days after I got there an express letter arrived. It was a handwritten letter (Ferrari always used violet ink) from Mr Ferrari saying 'I don't want my drivers upset, please come back immediately.' So, I did. I haven't got a clue how he found me.

When Parkes was killed in a road accident, driving under a lorry in heavy rain, Ferrari offered Vernor a job.

Mr Ferrari always said that if Mike wasn't around in my life he would employ me as his secretary. When Mike died, he invited me in for an interview. I was terrified of him. I thought, I definitely do not want to work for him, but I had enormous respect for him so I agreed to give it a try.

Vernor found Ferrari's bark was far worse than his bite. She told Nottage:

I think he was a little timid with women. The only woman he would really listen to was his mother, then he'd stand to attention and say 'yes, mother, no, mother'. She was a small woman but with an incredibly strong character. But we used to have a laugh and a joke. He was always commenting on my weight. 'Oh, you've put on weight' or 'Oh, you've lost weight.' He liked to take the mickey. I'm sure that if someone had asked him what I was wearing the previous week he could have told you. He was very observant and he had a wonderful memory. However, he never wanted women in his factory as he said there'd be arguments and problems. So, in the beginning, I was the only woman out of 190 men in the racing department. Fortunately, I have three older brothers, so I was used to being around men. It didn't intimidate me.

She said she found him a precise and exacting employer.

Whenever I took a letter to him, he would change something. It might be a comma or punctuation. But it would always be something. He would never sign a letter in English. He would only sign the letter in Italian and then I'd have to send the English translation with it.

And he was a man of tireless commitment and steady routine.

He was totally committed to the company. He had a very precise routine. Every day, he would go the barber's, then to the cemetery to be with his wife and son, Dino, and then go to his office in Modena. About 11 am he would arrive in Maranello. He always said 'good morning' to everyone. All down the hallways and in the workshops, you could hear everyone saying 'the old man is here'. About 1 pm, or 1.15

pm, he would go to lunch, sometimes taking with him visitors to Fiorano and then he'd be back and work until 8 pm, go home, eat dinner and go to bed.

An austere and serious man, Ferrari expected the same commitment to racing and to his team from everyone. Vernor recalled that he would sometimes call her, at home, at the weekend, when urgent business was pressing.

> I was doing my housework on a Sunday and he would call me and say 'I need to talk to Mr Ecclestone, please call him' and then I'd say 'Alright, I'll call him from home now.' But he would say 'No, come to the office.' So, I'd drop everything, get dressed and go to the office. But nobody minded working hard for Mr Ferrari. It was a pleasure and an honour. In the factory, people would work until 5 am and then go back in again at 8 am. It was all like a family then. We all felt part of one family. If I'd worked over the weekend, I would often come in on the Monday morning and find a little present on my desk with a note. 'Cordiale saluti. Ferrari.' He was autocratic, but fair.

In her privileged position, close to Ferrari and the very heart of the world of Grand Prix motor racing, Vernor learned a lot about the men who ran the early prototypes of the Piranha Club. Of Ferrari, according to Nottage, she said:

> He was always looking after the workers. But people outside his extended family never knew that side of him. However, he did hate people going on holiday. He couldn't understand why they needed to. But apart from that he was very close to the ordinary people. He understood them, as he had come from a poor background. He understood what it was to have nothing and that created an incredibly strong bond between him and the people who worked for him. Maybe that explains the enigma. He made luxury cars for an exclusive few, but he understood and was loved by the people. Now it has all changed. I walk past the factory and I don't see people coming out smiling any more.

Vernor also told Nottage that she believed Ferrari had great respect for Ecclestone and the work he had done in building up

Formula One and fighting for the rights of the teams during the late 1970s and early 1980s, in particular when the teams, represented by FOCA, took on the ruling authority and establishment, represented by the old FISA and the traditional manufacturers, like Renault, Alfa-Romeo and Ferrari.

I admire Bernie [she said]. Like Mr Ferrari, he started off with nothing and he built an empire. They had a lot of contact with each other, but Mr Ferrari was very cunning and clever. He was a great actor and he knew his strength. Without Ferrari, there wouldn't be Formula One. And he used to play that with Bernie. Once, they had an argument and Mr Ferrari said 'Right, I'm coming out of Formula One.' He got Gustav Brunner, who was with us then, to design an Indy car. He knew it wouldn't happen as Bernie would give in and, sure enough, he did and he got what he wanted. Mr Ferrari used to play his part to the full. Today (2001), that car is in the museum.

In an interesting aside, Vernor also mentioned to Nottage that she remained employed by Ferrari. But now, instead of working for the Old Man himself, she was working for his son, Piero Lardi Ferrari, the nominal head of the family which still held 10 per cent of the shares in the *scuderia*. 'Piero is just like his father,' she said. 'He looks like Mr Ferrari and is like him in character. He'll blow up and then it's all over in a few minutes and he gets on with things. He never bears grudges.' Piero Lardi Ferrari was first acknowledged by his father in 1975, when he issued a news release in which he referred to a 'young man intimately related to me'. This was three years before the death of his wife Laura, on 27 January 1978, and probably indicated that the existence of his illegitimate son could no longer be hidden. Following Laura's death, he formally adopted Piero, thus honouring a promise to his mother, and he was absorbed into the family business.

The death of Laura was another profound event in Ferrari's life. They had been married for 55 years, but their union was as much one of expedience and business sense as one of love. For much of that time Ferrari, many have since said and written, behaved with little care for her true feelings while she deteriorated into a condition of mental instability. An enigma, for most of their long marriage, Laura Domenica Garello Ferrari had lived in the shadows of her husband's empire and reputation and died there too. She spent much time away, when possible, particularly at their summer house on the Adriatic. She died, aged 78, just weeks before his 80th birthday, her illness and its causes the subject of persistent rumour, much of it wildly inaccurate and unfair. For Ferrari, Laura had been a woman who changed in life from one person to another as her illness descended and this was a difficulty for him.

Yet through all of this conjecture, rumour, sadness, grief and turmoil, a life of triumphs and tragedies on and off the track, Ferrari remained an extraordinary manipulator of men and events. His power over that maelstrom of political intrigue that passed as his racing department in Maranello had at least prepared him, and his loyal emissary of the time, Marco Piccinini, for the subtleties required as the FISA-FOCA war unfolded in the late 1970s.

Ecclestone, leader of the FOCA teams who were fighting for a fair share of the spoils of the sport and to establish control over its commercial operations, was up against the pompous Frenchman Jean-Marie Balestre, a figure widely lampooned in many European, particularly Italian, publications, one of which published photographs of him in what appeared to be a German uniform. This created uproar and caused a long-running dispute in which Balestre claimed to have been a Resistance spy in the Second World War. In this conflict, between the modern FOCA on the one hand and the establishment FISA on the other, Ferrari knew his value, his best position and his best strategy. He knew, too, that a Grand Prix without a Ferrari in the race would reduce the interest by more than a quarter; indeed, in a survey in the early 1980s, Nigel Roebuck claimed in an article in the British weekly magazine *Autosport* that 30 per cent of any crowd at a Grand Prix race came only to see the Ferraris.

All this gave Ferrari heavyweight value at the box office and heavyweight value, therefore, to both sides in the dispute as they waged battles over adjustable suspension systems, ground effect 'skirts', tunnels, water-cooled brakes and turbo-chargers in a war that was always going to end in a compromise agreement orchestrated by Ecclestone. Piccinini, too, was central to the process as the wrangling continued, always listening to both sides, allowing himself and Ferrari to be seen as part of the establishment, but with a ready ear for the dissidents. Known, by some, as the 'monsignor', Piccinini was as artful as Ferrari. Yates, in his book quoted one close observer of the entire struggle saying 'he was extraordinary . . . Piccinini was everyone's friend at the same time. Everybody was taking sides, but only Piccinini and Ferrari were taking both sides at the same time.' And Ferrari, of course, was able to exploit this situation to the full. He was, after all, a deft politician and a man who, it was said, never really carried a grudge.

That general assessment may not have been true of his feeling towards the group of criminals who, in October 1979, decided to break into the San Cataldo crypt and steal the body of his son, Dino Ferrari. This was an act, said Yates, of a group of 'uniquely depraved individuals'. He was right. It was only when they were caught in the act of attempting to hack their way through the metal casket itself that they were scared off and failed in their mission, leaving behind plastic bags that suggested they wanted to take the remains and hold them for ransom. These criminals were never found or arrested. Ferrari, in reaction, fitted the tomb entrance with elaborate iron gates. Three years later, in his final memoirs, he wrote:

> I never did imagine that the price of notoriety, which I have always paid at every point in my life, would include the destruction of the tomb in which 26 years ago I buried my son Dino. After many events, I feel alone and almost guilty for having survived. At times, I think that the pain is but an exasperating attachment to life when faced with the hallucinating fragility of existence.

At around the time these words were penned, of course, Ferrari was growing old, feeling worn down by life and recovering, also, from another shock: the unsolved disappearance of Carlo Bussi, in the summer of 1978, who vanished while on holiday in Sardinia. At first, it was considered to have been an act of terrorism, a kidnapping, but nothing was heard and the mystery remains unresolved.

The Old Man, however, liked to see a bit of a dog-fight for a seat in his cars. He liked to make his drivers compete for a chance to race and then to push to their limits to impress. Some believed he enjoyed this almost perverse experience. Hill believed there was a sense of a strange tradition for drivers to sacrifice themselves at Ferrari. He won the drivers' title in 1961 after a tough rivalry with his Ferrari team-mate Wolfgang Von Trips who was killed at Monza, in the Italian Grand Prix. The following year, Hill drove within himself. He said:

> They think I should go out there in an inferior car and sacrifice myself to the honour and glory of Ferrari. There have been too many sacrifices already. I won't be another. I won't be one of their sacrifices.

Like nearly all of the ex-Ferrari drivers who served under the Old Man himself, Hill had mixed feelings on his time in the magical *scuderia*. But he would not have changed a day of the experience. Nor would Jody Scheckter, the South African who won the drivers' title in 1979, the last for the team before Schumacher was to triumph in 2000. He joined that year, from the privateer team of Walter Wolf, and arrived with a reputation as a tough, brutally frank, reclusive and professional driver with no time for niceties. According to Yates, Scheckter was approached, as was Lauda before him, by Ferrari 'operatives' who sneaked into Maranello having been met at the same autostrada exit and then been escorted in via a back gate.

'How much do you want?' was Ferrari's opening gambit, small talk having been rejected as useless.

'I am too young to talk about money,' replied Scheckter, to Marco Piccinini, Ferrari's team manager and right-hand man, who acted as interpreter. Caught off-guard momentarily, Ferrari responded and a lengthy spell of haggling ensued. Scheckter's asking price was high and Ferrari's offers were low. Scheckter demanded a six-figure retainer, competitive with other teams, and also wanted 20 per cent of the prize money. Ferrari offered only 10 per cent. In Yates's account,

> the Old Man was fully aware of the wage scales in Formula One and knew that no driver got 20 per cent. He capitulated and accepted 10 per cent. Then Ferrari tried one final ploy. Scheckter demanded payment in dollars. Ferrari agreed, but offered Canadian dollars, which were about 20 per cent less valuable than American. Scheckter balked, Ferrari gave in and the deal was finalised.

In that year, Scheckter worked alongside the legendary Gilles Villeneuve. They were both great racers and therefore had many similarities, but also many differences. Villeneuve, for example, preferred to live in Monte Carlo, not Italy. But Scheckter told Yates:

> I loved the Italians and their way of life. My wife and I had an apartment in Modena and although I didn't speak Italian I felt very much at home. As a champion driver, you are considered part of the family. And, believe me, when an entire crowd of diners rises to applaud you when you enter a restaurant, you appreciate how much they care about their sport.

He said that despite trying to stay out of the factory politics at Maranello, it was impossible.

> Forghieri could be a madman, but he was brilliant and we had numerous arguments. As for the Old Man, you couldn't help but be ill at ease around him. I tried to be very professional. I was there to win races. Nothing else. That was the difference between me and Gilles, I suppose. He was trying to win laps. As for Ferrari, he didn't want to hear about the failing of his cars, especially the engines. I remember one day, I was briefing him on a race and I remarked that the Cosworths had more power than we did on certain parts of the track. Piccinini, who was translating, said 'You can't say that. You can't tell him that the Cosworths have more power.' But Enzo Ferrari was a very special man. You've simply got to respect him for what he did. He was all business with his drivers. I remember, after I won the world championship, he said nothing. No letters. No phone-calls. Nothing. Then, one day, a few weeks later, I saw him at Fiorano. He walked right past me. He gave me a little salute and said 'hey, champion'. But that's the only word I ever heard from him about the title. At the end of the season, they had their annual banquet and a bunch of us – mechanics, test drivers, engineers, the lot – received trophies. Mine was a prancing horse on a little wooden base. One of the legs had broken off and been brazed back on.

Ferrari's prancing horse insignia has now survived him and become synonymous with the marque that has had longer and deeper associations with Formula One than any other. A formidable businessman, a dictator, an autocrat, adept at extracting the maximum from his men and for building up strength in depth, his example remains that which is followed most keenly by aspirant members of the Piranha Club. His cars have been called sensual, emotional and highly strung and he has been criticised for his womanising, his sentimentality and his lack of feeling for families and people, but according to those who knew him, most of this was untrue.

He was, said Pino Allievi of *La Gazzetta dello Sport*, a humorous man, a hard man when necessary, but a man of great curiosity about the world. He remained in contact with his friends, maintained his Saturday lunch sessions for as long as possible with such companions as Scagletti, Benzi, Gozi and sometimes King Gustav of Sweden. He enjoyed teasing his Fiat supporters for a long period by driving a Peugeot. He was also generous and often gave small gifts, a tie or a scarf, to visitors. He read the newspapers prodigiously, watched the television news incessantly and had a mind open for news and ideas. He preferred, said Allievi, to stay at home and look at the world, waiting for visitors to come to him, than to go out and find them. He was tough and demanding, but he was loyal and generous, too.

On one occasion, Allievi recalled, Ferrari telephoned him to complain about a report he had written. 'I am not talking to you any more,' he said, at the end of a long series of objections, before hanging up. Then, an hour later, he rang again to say he had thought again and wanted to smooth things over. He invited Allievi to come to lunch and try a special tortellini made by the wife of a friend. But, he said, there was only enough for two – before adding, with a theatrical pause, that he could bring his wife, but they would have to divide their share of the delicacy to ensure she could eat. The recollection of the call still had the power, years later, to make Allievi smile. Ferrari had powers of persuasion and imagination that were unique.

'He was not a Ron Dennis and he was not a Frank Williams,' said Allievi. 'He was not a team manager at all, but a man who made cars to drive and to race. He was an owner.' Like Allievi, Bernie Ecclestone still enjoys his memories of Enzo Ferrari. Ferrari, he said, was one of the very few team owners in Formula One who had left a strong and indelible impression upon him. 'He was a great man, a very impressive person in every way,' he said. 'A wonderful businessman, a brilliant nego-tiator and a clever leader and motivator.'

Enzo Ferrari was a man who built a racing legend and left a racing legacy.

3 How it Was in the Good Old Days

In his book *Chasing the Title, Memorable Moments from 50 years of Formula One*, Nigel Roebuck dedicated a chapter to one of the sport's last true Corinthian privateers. It was entitled 'Rob Walker – profession: gentleman'. The chapter covers eight pages, a modest offering really on such a wonderful man, but enough to convey the reader to another time, another era. The past, after all, *is* another country – a place where they did things very differently – and Walker, the first private entrant to defeat a factory team in a World Championship Grand Prix race, *did* do things very differently. But, in the 1950s and 1960s, everyone did.

An enthusiast who used his private means (he was fortunate to be born into the Johnnie Walker whisky family) to fund his passion for cars and racing, he was truly a gentleman-racer and team-owner. He was also a success. Between 1958 and 1968, his privately entered team registered nine victories over the factory outfits. He also rose to become a respected and established member of the paddock family and, in the very early days, he was chairman, briefly, of the original forerunner of the modern Formula One Constructors' Association. But his day, his era, was very different from the modern one. And the piranhas were far less of a worry.

It was a time, indeed, when life was treated differently, when opportunities for fun were snatched and enjoyed, while danger was treated as an everyday companion. In Formula One, more than anywhere, it was accepted as a risk of the trade and the price someone had to pay, with terrible regularity, for the pleasure of taking part in the sheer revelry that the sport of Grand Prix motor racing then represented. 'We knew it could happen to anyone, and it happened all the time,' said Walker, whose cars were entered under the label that included his initials, R.R.C. Walker, in full.

In the old days, you'd leave Monaco and everybody would shake hands and say 'goodbye' and then, a week later, you'd all be shaking hands again and saying 'hallo' in Zandvoort, or somewhere like that, and so on. We all knew one another, literally. It was very friendly. It is not like that now, I don't think. There are very few of the original people left . . .

In early 2001, Walker lived with his wife Betty at their family home, Nunney Court, near Frome in Somerset. They were married in May 1940 and had travelled together and lived through more than 50 years' experience of the growth and development of Grand Prix motor racing. To visit them, on an early spring day, was to roll back the years and unpeel memories, layer upon layer, to reveal lives and adventures seen now in monochrome or sepia tints, but which on closer examination provided more purity in hue and shade than any modern Technicolor creation. Rob and Betty lived it. It was not a small industry, nor was it a corporate marketing bonanza. Nor was it a financial opportunity, let alone a chance to become a multi-millionaire. To them, as to most of the teams and people involved, it was a way of life, a tumbling, happy road show that involved risks, made laughs and provided endless fun.

I lived in the circus really all my life and it is a way of life for me [he told Gerry Donaldson for his 1990 book *Grand Prix People*]. As one gets older, I suppose, one's enthusiasm for anything gets a little bit less and the atmosphere is absolutely no comparison to what it used to be. But, of course, we've got all these sponsors now.

The message remained unchanged ten years or more later. By then, however, Walker had given up his shared role – he alternated with Innes Ireland, the former Grand Prix driver – as a Grand Prix reporter for the American magazine *Road & Track* and become a freelance journalist. Aged 83, he still wrote occasional features, as contributions, and, given his venerability and experiences, this was notable in itself. His writing was much enjoyed and praised because it recreated an age and a style that was only rarely reproduced. It also confirmed that Walker existed in an era of motor racing that belonged to the participants themselves and the public who supported them, when serious-minded competitors, like Enzo Ferrari, were in the minority and before manipulators and opportunists came anywhere near the paddock.

Walker, of course, was born with the advantage of an aristocratic background, privilege and wealth when he entered the world on 14 August 1917. As Robert Ramsay Campbell Walker, he had every right to look forwards with confidence and pleasure to a life ahead which was to include a blissful childhood at Scotsbridge House in Rickmansworth and, later, at Sutton Veny, a magnificent Georgian mansion in Wiltshire, school at Sherborne, then university at Cambridge, some exceptional escapades, the purchase of his first Delahaye while still an undergraduate, racing at Le Mans, service in the Fleet Air Arm as a fighter pilot and, then, after the war his long and pleasurable association with motor racing as a private entrant and enthusiast and, later, as a journalist.

As a team chief, he had the joy of running such drivers as Tony Rolt, Reg Parnell, Peter Collins, Tony Brooks, Jack Brabham, Jo Bonnier, Graham Hill, Jochen Rindt, Jo Siffert and Stirling Moss. A tall, confident and somewhat languid man, he simply did things his way and was loved for it. Even at the turn of the new millennium, he still received a permanent annual pass from Bernie Ecclestone to visit any world championship Grand Prix. Perhaps the 'Piranha Club' did not exist, certainly not in full, in Walker's era, but more likely he was able to swim through it with such noble poise that no other fish dared even consider a doubtful thought or act. He is a Boy's Own hero and his story lives up to the myth.

But it was as a team owner and entrant that he earned his place in the club and it was as a team owner and entrant that he achieved great feats in Formula One. These include the first victories in Grand Prix races for the famous marques of Cooper and Lotus. Both were achieved by the RRC Walker Racing Team, humbling the works outfits' efforts. And both were secured with Moss, arguably the greatest driver of all, bar Juan-Manuel Fangio, at the wheel. For Walker, certainly, Moss was someone special and it is in his relationship with the famous English racing driver that much of the character of the age is revealed.

'For me, to have Stirling as my driver, it was marvellous,' he explained, his long almost-drawling voice making each word sound like honey pouring across hot buttered toast.

71

Apart from the fact that he was such a wonderful driver, really in a class of his own, you know, he was also a really good friend. We were great chums and always got along well. In all our years together, we never had any kind of contract at all. At the beginning of every season, we would agree and it was always just a handshake. Of course, the other great thing with Stirling, in those days, was that he was a very popular driver to have. In those days, there was no FOCA to do a financial deal for all the entrants. It was up to each of us to make our own arrangements. There was very little prize money and starting money – appearance money, in effect – was what mattered. And the one driver every race organiser wanted more than any other was Stirling . . .

To Roebuck, Walker was a gentleman from a generation increasingly extinct. He recalled his jokes, his dry-as-Beefeater humour, his stories and his connections everywhere around the world. He reported the occasion when Walker, visiting the Long Beach Grand Prix, booked a room on the *Queen Mary*, then a floating hotel in the Californian harbour. He was greeted warmly 'on board' and was told 'Mr Walker – we're glad to see you, sir. And you'll be pleased to know we've given you your old suite . . . ' Walker recalled being a frequent passenger in the liner's great transatlantic days. 'I was awfully lucky, really. The chairman of Cunard White Star had been a chum of mine at school.'

He rejected many approaches from publishers requesting that he wrote his memoirs. Recalling them, he began: 'Well, Macmillan asked me. . . But, then he died.' And he once explained away missing a French Grand Prix by saying he had other business. 'Oh, I was busy that weekend – we were taking Ginger Rogers to Wimbledon.' All this, as they say, was for real. He enjoyed life, cars and fun. By the time he was a young undergraduate, he had driven many fast and extravagant cars and was in the habit of running up from Cambridge to eat dinner at the Ritz. He raced his own cars for fun and became a well-known amateur. 'I always say motor racing is all I've ever done,' he explained. 'That and the war.'

Before the war, however, he raced at Le Mans in 1939 in his own Delahaye and finished eighth, having done nearly all of the driving himself. Earlier, he had learned, between practice sessions, that he had obtained a degree, much to his surprise. Even this was performed, however, with some style since he began in a pinstripe suit, changed later to a sports jacket for the morning work and, typically, paused for a flute of champagne, as his refreshment, each time he stopped. All for fun in the days when such adventures were within the reach of the rich individual and before the war, the later years of progress and the arrival of the multi-million pound automotive battlegrounds of the late years of the twentieth century swept such innocent times away.

For Walker, then, the war meant service and the return of his pilot's licence. It was taken from him and suspended for life after he enlivened a lunch interval at a Cottenham National Hunt meeting by 'jumping' the fences in a Tiger Moth. 'Unfortunately, a policeman gave my number to the Air Ministry,' he explained with an insouciant drawl of such understated delivery it made nearly every cool remark in the paddock of the new millennium sound wet.

The war had another distinct effect on Walker. It caused him to carry through his promise to Betty to give up racing himself, apart from hill-climbs and speed trials, and to concentrate on running his own cars. It was the culmination of a fascination that started when he was only seven, taken to the Boulogne Grand Prix during a summer holiday in France.

> I found it all fascinating [he recalled]. A taxi driver took us around the circuit in his Citroen and he was highly enthused with the whole thing. My mother was terrified. I was encouraging him as much as possible and he was pointing out the places where people had been killed with great delight, the trees they'd hit and so on. Then, my mother gave me a car when I was still quite young and I drove it up and down a long drive. I used to time myself and then I began to tune the cars. Seeing that I was very keen, my mother gave me the second chauffeur to look after my car and to tune it up and that sort of thing . . . Of course, this was while I was under the age to drive, but I was on my own private property, so it didn't matter.

Once bitten, Walker was hooked. He became virtually obsessed by cars. In 1938, while up at Cambridge, he travelled to Donington Park to see the mighty Mercedes and Auto Unions in action. Later that year, while wandering down Park Lane, he happened to see a perfect 3.5 litre Delahaye Type 135S in a showroom. It had been owned by Prince Bira.

> I absolutely fell for it and, although it was far more money than I had, I was introduced to hire purchase and so I bought the thing – without telling my mother, or anybody. I entered it for a race at Brooklands. That was in 1938. And the next year, I raced at Le Mans, the last one before the war.

If surviving all this unhurt was an achievement, it was nothing to surviving his service with the Fleet Air Arm, a period which included many terrifying escapades and the invasion of Sicily.

> Out of our batch, where there were 260 people, 25 eventually came out alive. So, I had no hesitation in saying 'Yes, I won't drive after the war.' I didn't think I'd ever see another motor race, let alone drive in it!

Still alive, after the war, Walker became an entrant, pouring much of his own money into his effort to wrest the ascendancy from the then-dominant Italian teams of the time.

> I still had the Delahaye, which was the fastest road-going car in Great Britain and I wasn't allowed to race it, so what to do but find somebody to drive it – and that's what started me as a race entrant. I got Tony Rolt. He really was a magnificent driver, who won Le Mans with the Jaguar team, and he drove single-seaters for me. We got a Delage and then we worked up to Connaughts. After Tony Rolt retired, I had Peter Collins, then Tony Brooks and then I had Jack Brabham, who was the first one who drove a full year's Grands Prix for me, and then Stirling Moss came to me and we had this wonderful relationship for five years . . .

It was in the latter days of this wonderful time that Walker first saw hints of the changes that were to come as the teams gradually became more organised. He recalled Bernie Ecclestone's early days among them and the first efforts at organising a group meeting and the preliminary meetings of what was to emerge as FOCA.

The first time I remember seeing Bernie Ecclestone [he said] was on an aeroplane. We all used to all more or less take the aeroplane over ourselves. Or at least we would take a wander about and talk to each other. I think it was one of those aeroplanes in which the rear of it is a sort of big cabin place, where you could drink and things. Anyway, I saw this little man wandering about and I said who's that? And they said 'It's Bernie Ecclestone . . . He used to drive 500s or something.' That's the first time I remember seeing him.

The next time that Walker recalled, vividly, seeing Ecclestone was in 1970 when Jochen Rindt was killed at Monza. 'I remember him walking back through the pits carrying Jochen's helmet under his arm,' he said.

By this time, I was fairly well-known. I'd been the first private entrant to win a Grand Prix, I was the first person to win a Grand Prix for Cooper and for Coventry Climax and I won the first four for Lotus. Actually, I was the first chairman of FOCA, only because they were such a rabble. They had to have somebody. I was called in for a short time until they organised themselves . . .

His laughter was a reminder, a punctuation point, allowing for consideration that this once-disorganised rabble grew to become the modern 'Piranha Club' and as slick and professional an organisation as any in the world. 'I shouldn't have been a member of FOCA anyway,' he said.

I was an invited member. At first, I refused because I thought they were a load of fools and they didn't know what they were doing and, then, I could see advantages in it. As there are now. And, as a member of FOCA I got that. And they said I was the one person, outside the constructors, who they'd like to have. So, I said 'alright I will.' I'd been in motor racing much longer than any of them and I suppose, in a lot of things, I was inclined to take command and to put them more on the line. I didn't say much in these things because I used to laugh so much. They were so funny.

But things were not always so much fun, or so smooth-running for Walker, and there were times in his career as an owner and

75

entrant that he ran into the kind of difficulties and tragedies which have always afflicted motor racing men, particularly those whose cars were crossing regularly from Britain to the European mainland. According to one account in his biography, *Rob Walker* by Michael Cooper-Evans, for example, in 1949, he became drawn into the 'Delahaye case' after his driver Guy Jason-Henry had been arrested at Newhaven for trying to smuggle more than 3,000 watches into the country in a false petrol tank. The false tank, much to Walker's consternation, was fitted to his Delahaye. Worse still, the story – as such stories would in more modern and contemporary times – was reported in bold headlines in all the daily newspapers. Luckily, for Walker, however, he was not implicated in any way and later, when the case was resolved, succeeded after some long and tough negotiations in recovering his car.

But these were truly, by comparison with modern times, gentlemanly days. This became clear when Walker talked of his first drivers.

> Tony [Rolt] was a gentleman driver, and he drove like a gentleman; if someone who was obviously faster wanted to pass him, Tony would move over to let him through. Peter [Collins] was quite different. He was my first professional driver and he really opened my eyes to what the cut and thrust of truly competitive race driving was like. I remember one race at Crystal Palace, which was run in two ten-lap heats. In the first Horace Gould in a Cooper-Bristol got the drop on Peter at the start and then blocked him for the whole ten laps. During the interval, I heard Peter saying to Horace 'if you do that again, Horace, I'll push you off.' Horace did. And Peter pushed him off. And won. Peter had the most incredible will to win.

As Cooper-Evans concluded, it was this will which endeared Collins later to Enzo Ferrari and which, later still, led him to his death at the Nurburgring in August 1958.

Employing professionals, in that amateur era, proved Walker was a competitor with an edge, even if he was also seen as a fun-loving privateer with money to burn. Such competitiveness, of course, is a recurrent feature of all the team owners who have made an impact. That, and opportunism, of the sort exemplified by both drivers and businessmen, seeking the best for their cars and teams. Walker showed these qualities, too, in 1956 when, he said, he made two of the most important decisions of his racing career.

> I was the first person to order a Formula Two Cooper-Climax from John [Cooper] and I lost no time in contacting Alf (Francis, a famous mechanic who fell out with Stirling Moss shortly before) and persuading him to join me.

Both were auspicious moves that contributed to Walker's successes.

One such famous and memorable success came at the Monaco Grand Prix of 1957 when Jack Brabham drove the Cooper-Climax. It was an episode Walker recalled vividly himself and wrote of in early 2001.

> In 1956, John Cooper decided to ask Coventry Climax to enlarge the 1500cc engine as much as they could, as he hoped to use it as a Formula One engine. In fact, the largest they could get it to was 1996cc, and the Formula was then 2.5 litres. Coventry Climax agreed to do this as long as John Cooper paid for all the research into it. At this time, also, the Suez Canal crisis was on and it was thought quite possible that there might be no more racing in 1957 due to lack of fuel. John had not great resources and thought if he paid for this Formula One engine, and there was no racing, it might put his business in jeopardy.
>
> At this juncture, I stepped in and said that I would pay for all the costs as long as I was allowed to have the first engine, and the chassis. This was agreed and they went ahead with building the engine and Coopers built the chassis. It was decided between John and myself that he would have the second car, with Roy Salvadori as his driver, and that Brabham, who had recently come over from Australia, would be my Formula One driver for the year. Actually, I was also his landlord as well, as he was unable to get a mortgage, as he was a racing driver . . .

Brabham's first appearance in Walker's distinctive dark-blue-and-white colours was at Syracuse in March. He was travelling south from Rome to the port of Reggio di Calabria, in the 'toe' of southern Italy, with Harry Schell, when their train broke down in the night in the midst of nowhere. They climbed out of their carriage, on to the track, ran several miles to the next station, hired a taxi and arrived on the quayside just in time to catch the last ferry to Messina. They offered bribes to the ship's captain to make all possible speed, but it was daylight when they reached Sicily where Schell hired a battered Fiat and drove faster than his passenger believed possible only to reach the circuit long after the start of practice. Undaunted, Brabham, who was carrying his helmet and overalls, continued to run towards the pits. After dodging various Caribinieri and track officials, he reached the Walker garage looking hot, sweaty and short of breath, jumped into the waiting Cooper and qualified faster than any other Formula Two car. In the race, he finished sixth and lapped Peter Walker in Walker's Connaught Formula One car. It was an auspicious, if extraordinary, start. Walker, as languid as ever, merely noted that his punctuality showed little sign of improvement as time passed.

The first championship race in Europe was Monaco and we decided to enter the new car, with Jack driving for this race. John Cooper was unable to enter a Formula One car as the second engine was not yet ready and Roy Salvadori was not available. But John entered one of his Formula Two cars with Les Leston to drive it. All that year, Coopers and I entered two separate teams with our own mechanics and I, of course, had the famous Alf Francis as my head mechanic. However, the two teams gave each other co-operation whenever necessary.

In those days, Betty and I used to take a full week over the Grand Prix, leaving England on the Monday, by car, and spending two days driving down, and then leaving Monte Carlo the Tuesday after the race. So it was a time to look forward to, especially as spring was fully on. We always tried to get the nicest possible car so that we could thoroughly enjoy the journey. This particular year we had a 400 Jenson, which was the latest thing. Later on, we improved considerably to have several Gull-Wing Mercedes, and a 300SL drop-head, followed by Facel Vegas and then Ferraris.

We could catch the ferry at Dover at about 10am. Arriving at Calais, we would buy a picnic and then drive on the back roads to a charming old town where there was one of the new Relais hotels, which had to be of the highest standard in food and accommodation. Our second night, we drove beside Alpine meadows to stay in Gap, which is pretty high up and very beautiful and the nightingales sang so much the sound kept us awake. From there, we descended through fields of narcissus and other wild flowers to Nice. We had booked no hotel in Monte Carlo and went first to visit the mechanics and see they arrived safely.

It turned out that Jack, who was on his first tour of Europe, wanted to visit Modena on his journey down, as it was then the home of motor racing. We found the mechanics and team in good shape in a nice little hotel, the San Remo side of Monte Carlo. As we did not know where to stay ourselves, and there was no room in the team's hotel, we enquired around.

We were told of a new hotel, which had just been started at Eze-sur-mer. Before the war it used to be a Russian prince's villa, with a huge private garden, below the corniche. We got a room there and throughout the 27 years we knew it, it grew and grew until it was possibly the most prestigious hotel on the Riviera and owned, always, by the wonderful Squarciafichi family. It had two swimming pools and little cottages carved out of the cliffs besides the main hotel.

We would have a couple of blissful days there before racing. It was all very different in those days. Each team would choose a garage and have it for their overnight work. They would then drive the racing car to the circuit. There were three days' practice, two starting at 6.30am, and the final one, from about 12 noon, on Saturday, which was followed up by a junior race. Sometimes, we used to garage the cars at Eze and Vanwalls were also there and we would hear the cars driving the eight kilometres to the circuit in the early hours, making a shattering noise.

On this particular occasion, we were all at our pits ready to start at 6.30am. The pits were stationed where the pine trees grew alongside the track and you just had a wooden barricade between yourself and the cars, where you kept the spares, and where the wives stood, to do all the timing and lap charts. There were no Armco barriers and when you found the space allotted to you, for your pit, you prayed there would be a pine tree in it that you could hide behind, to protect you from the cars racing past on each side.

When the first practice started, the car was warmed up and everyone was ready except there was no sign of Jack Brabham. We had never tried the car and Jack had never seen Monte Carlo and, of course, only 16 cars qualified out of the 23 entrants. Every moment was vital. When Jack had not turned up half-way through the practice, I got Peter Collins, who had driven for me before and was there as a works Ferrari driver, to do a few laps with the car. He said that he thought it was all right, but obviously he did not want to push it. Jack never did turn up during this practice, but arrived about an hour later. Apparently he was coming from Modena and got lost on the way so we had missed a whole day.

The next morning practice was again at 6.30am and this time Jack was there. He got going straight away and was beginning to do some reasonable times and learn the circuit. He felt the car needed more brakes on the front and was coming in the next lap to have them adjusted. He went up the hill to the Casino and when he came to the bend at the top his brakes locked up and he went straight through the Casino wall. Jack was unhurt, but the chassis was a complete wreck. Fortunately, the engine, being in the back, was unharmed.

In those days, of course, safety features were not as they were to be by the end of the twentieth century and when Brabham locked up and wrote off his car at Casino Square he crashed through the telegraph poles that were there to protect the stone balustrades leading to the side door of the casino itself. It meant, a rarity in those far-off days, an all-night shift for every mechanic around.

John Cooper had brought down a Formula Two chassis for Les Leston to try to qualify [Walker explained]. It so happened that the Formula One engine fitted into the Formula Two chassis, only the fuel tanks were not large enough to run the 105 laps of the race. So it would mean a refuelling stop. We decided to put the Formula One engine in the Formula Two chassis and all my team, and all of Cooper's, worked the whole night to make the conversion, which they managed superbly.

By the next day, the car was ready and qualifying was not until midday on Saturday. We were ready and out straight away, but had no qualifying time at all. So there was a mountain to climb. Jack was learning the circuit well, and getting closer to the last cars qualifying. Then the unspeakable happened and Masten Gregory blew up at St. Devote, spilling oil everywhere.

This made it impossible for anyone to improve times. I resorted to the last hope. It so happened that the marshal on that corner was also the head barman at the Hotel de Paris – and I knew him well. So, I approached him and asked if he would request practice to be stopped while they cleaned up the oil as it was dangerous. This was granted and practice stopped. The corner was beautifully cleaned up. Jack then went for it and not only qualified, but was 15th out of 16.

Race day was fine and nobody considered the little Cooper at the back with its unknown driver. But 105 laps is a long way and cars dropped out and some were passed (an accident at the chicane removed Moss, Hawthorn and Collins). We completed our refuelling and two laps from the finish we were lying third behind Fangio and Brooks.

Then, on the penultimate lap, disaster struck and the Tipo Mona petrol pump broke away from its mounting. The engine died at the old Station hairpin. Jack pushed the car (which was allowed then) half-way round the course, to the cheering of the crowd, and, completely exhausted, he came over the line sixth. Betty Brabham and small son Geoffrey watched from the grandstand at Jack's super-human effort! When we got back to our hotel, I said to my wife Betty: 'Do you realise, darling, we were actually third at one time in a world championship race?' And, she replied: 'But, next year, darling, it will be better.' And so it was. We won it the following year.

Such dry, droll and amusing adventures (and, by the way, the beautiful hotel, mentioned almost only as a throwaway line was the Cap Estel) were not all that occupied the time of a team owner in those days, however. To be part of the racing scene in the late 1950s also involved much hardship, sacrifice and pain.

> We were all very close friends, all of us, in those times [he explained]. But I think the reason for it was the danger. It wasn't unusual to have three people killed in one race. If you went off the road, you had every chance of being killed. Or injured very badly . . .

A glance through the record books proves Walker to be right. Taking world championship Formula One races alone, there were eight fatal accidents in different races between 1953 and 1960. A year without a death was unusual. It continued the same in the 1960s and into the 1970s before, prompted by the leadership of Jackie Stewart, serious action was taken to make the sport safer for drivers, marshals and spectators. But, in Walker's day, for men who had survived the second world war, it was nothing extraordinary to experience danger and death.

> Once [he said]. I think it was in about 1958, and it was at Le Mans I think, the Shell competition manager, who was driving a Cooper, lost a back wheel. It came off and it killed the person six away from us in the pit. We never knew about it at all. It was a bit like a war really.

From the vantage point of experience and age, Walker can look back now and survey the sport and the business with more detached eyes.

> It's all money and greed now, I think [he said]. Whereas in our day it was companionship, joy of the sport, love of the cars and the beauty of the cars and have a jolly good party afterwards.

However, he was there when it began to change. He was one of the originals, yet also part of the fabric of change. He remembered Ecclestone arriving, the first earlier inklings of teams' organisation, the creation of an association among the constructors.

> It's one of those things that grew. It wasn't called FOCA to start with. I think we got Andrew Ferguson from Coopers to arrange the aeroplanes, because everything was done by sea before that. My first Grand Prix win was probably the first time a car was ever flown to a race!

That race, of course, was the Argentine Grand Prix of 1958, won for Walker by Stirling Moss in a Cooper, the first time a privately entered car had beaten the big manufacturers.

> It was at the time of the change from alcohol to petrol and we were to be on petrol in '58 [he said]. A lot of them, including BRM and Vanwall, I think, had a lot of trouble in doing that. I had (Alf) Francis and he had the [Climax] engine going beautifully before the end of the season.
>
> I was in Switzerland at the beginning of the year and I hated it [his mother had brought him up to take to Australia and her family in the winter, but his wife Betty's family were great enthusiasts of skiing]. But I got a telegram from Stirling [Moss] saying could he drive my Cooper because they [Vanwall] hadn't got onto petrol yet. So, I said 'yes', but asked how we were going to get it to Buenos Aires. And he said it was okay because they (the Argentine organisers) had promised to pay for it to get there by air, paying 3,000 dollars. Then, when the little Cooper came out against all these big Ferraris, they were absolutely livid that they'd paid to get this little insignificant beetle-like thing out there. The other teams, including Ferrari, dismissed it out of hand. But at the first practice we rather wiped the smiles off their faces when Stirling was third – and, then, of course, he won the race . . .

Sadly, for Walker, he was absent. Having spent his two weeks of enforced holidays in Rigikulm, Switzerland, playing cricket with his daughter Dauvergne – using a ski pole as a bat and bowling with a snowball – and simply surviving a regimen he described as 'sheer hell', he opted to stay at home as his son Robbie's first half at Eton was due to begin just before the race. He also believed it was more important for the car to have two mechanics available than for him to travel. He was right. And the entire episode had a silver lining as Moss, the following year, when Vanwall pulled out of racing, decided to race full-time for Walker. Their partnership was to produce famous Moss victories at Monaco, in 1960, the first by a Lotus car and achieved 18 months before Colin Chapman's factory team, and later, the following year, at the Nuerburgring. Thus, for Walker, in being absent from Buenos Aires, he missed one of the great triumphs of his own era, but made certain he was around for inklings of the start of another as Enzo Ferrari noted Moss's name and underlined it again and the so-called 'kit car' constructors, dismissed by some European manufacturers as mere 'garagistes', began to organise themselves and the sport for the future.

> I can remember that first meeting in Austria [he recalled later, referring to his first experiences of organised team assemblies]. I remember Colin Chapman being there and Ken Tyrrell. I don't remember Coopers ever being in the constructors. It must have been after they retired. And Bernie, actually, I remember much, much later. They had an organisation. Ferrari, and that manager of theirs, (Marco) Piccinini, always used to come. Well, it was always owners or managers that came. Piccinini was always very sharp on these things. You had to be very careful what you said with him there. But there wasn't a chairman when he started, so it must have been after that!

By then, however, Walker and Formula One had been through one rite of passage and were moving towards another. For Walker, there may have been the freedom of the good old days, but there was also the tragedy of Mike Hawthorn's death, on Thursday, 22 January 1959, in a high-speed road accident on the Guildford by-pass. It was only a month after Hawthorn had retired from racing as world champion for Ferrari. They were good friends and it was all the more tragic that Walker, driving a drop-head Mercedes 300SL, was driving behind him in wet conditions and was first to the scene of the crash. He found Hawthorn stretched across the back seat of his badly damaged green Jaguar saloon with a slight trickle of blood coming from his mouth. It was a reminder, though hardly needed, of the risks involved with cars and speed, but not the only one.

Close friendships were, of course, more the norm then (Walker and Stirling Moss were close friends as well as team owner and driver) than they were to be in later years. By the end of the century, few people involved in Formula One, or in motor racing at the highest levels, had the time to stop for any kind of social informalities. Business was taking over. Yet business was always there in the way in which the sport was developing. It was inevitable. Even Walker, privateer par excellence, as he was, was in need of good business management. By one curious stroke of coincidence, Walker found one good business practice in connection with one of the drivers whose courage and skill were partly responsible for the arrival of Ecclestone in Formula One as a manager and organiser. The driver was Jochen Rindt, but the man involved was a Walker driver, Jo Bonnier, a man who may have been a forerunner of the motor racing business managers that came later. It was an early example of things to come.

In 1964, Bonnier lived in Switzerland. He was a Swede who spoke six languages fluently but he had few close personal friends. Some felt he was cold and arrogant and others said he was aloof. As a driver, he was a good businessman. Walker used him not only to race the cars, but also to act as his agent. He negotiated the starting money, a role hc was well-suited for with his languages and his position of president of the Grand Prix Drivers' Association.

> He was quite shameless about using the clout which this position conferred upon him to obtain good starting money for the team [said Walker]. No doubt, he was encouraged by the fact that under the terms of our agreement, half of it would end up in his pocket.

In Walker's view, Bonnier may have had the kind of talents required to have done what Ecclestone later did for the sport. Another recollection is a good example of his entrepreneurial skills. Walker said:

> Jo had hit upon the very good idea of renting our second car to a local driver in each of the countries in which we raced and making them pay through the nose for it. So, for instance, at the Nuerburgring, while Jo drove our Brabham-BMW, the Cooper-Climax was entered for Edgar Bath, who was the European hill climb champion. I remember that he was dreadfully slow in practice and then blew the engine up on the second lap. So, I don't suppose he really thought he got his money's worth.
>
> There was an even more embarrassing situation at Monza where we had been asked to give a drive to a local Italian hero who raced under the pseudonym of 'Geki'. On the first practice day, we had rather a lot of problems with Jo's car and I'm afraid that apart from fitting into his seat

we paid very little attention to poor Geki. The result was that he didn't qualify in the first session and the next day it rained and, so, of course, he had no hope of qualifying. In view of this, the Italians flatly refused to pay up the agreed starting money for Geki until Jo said 'You chose the driver and if he's not good enough to qualify that's your problem. Not ours.' And they paid up without another word.

It was through this arrangement that Walker was to meet Rindt. At Zeltweg, Bonnier rented the second car to the young Austrian who had been driving brilliantly in Formula Two. It was to be his first Formula One race.

He was absolutely thrilled about it [said Walker]. I remember he had taken the trouble to find out when I was arriving and he met me at the airport. He was such a charming young man, so full of youthful enthusiasm, and so grateful for the drive. He never forgot that I gave him his first Formula One drive and when the Oesterriechring was inaugurated some years later, he said to me 'I want you to be the first person I ever drive round this circuit.' He took me round in a Mercedes 500SEL and it was very touching.

Rindt went on to drive for the Cooper works team and to be managed by Ecclestone.

Thus Walker's long association with motor racing acquainted him with nearly everyone and everywhere. He knew Ferrrai, Moss and Ecclestone, Graham Hill, Chapman and John Surtees. He had stories on them all and experiences to laugh at forever. His special friendship with Moss almost brought him an exceptional deal with Ferrari. In early 1962, when Moss finally relented and accepted an invitation from Ferrari to visit him at Maranello, the driver was asked to name what he wanted, in a car, anything, to accept an offer to race a Ferrari for the man known as 'Il Ingegnere'. Moss said he would only race a factory-prepared Italian Ferrari if it was run in the dark blue and white of Rob Walker's team and if the Walker team took charge of it at the circuits. Astonishingly, Ferrari agreed, but the entire arrangement came to nothing when Moss crashed in a Lotus at Goodwood on Easter Monday that year. He never raced seriously, at the highest level, again.

'I was devastated, of course,' said Walker. 'The team carried on, with Maurice Trintignant, but it wasn't the same. With Stirling, anything had been possible. He was so much better than anyone else.' After that, for Walker, it was a struggle and a gentle downhill slide. He had happy days with Jo Siffert, from 1965 for five years. He called him 'Seppi' and named his victory in the 1968 British Grand Prix at Brands Hatch as the most satisfying of all. It was a home win, but more importantly, a win that was seen as a victory for the team and not only for the driver. 'Betty and I adored Seppi,' he recalled. 'He was a wonderful man, with unbelievable courage and a great sense of humour.'

Siffert's death, in a BRM, during the Victory Race of 1971, was a personal blow. Accidents, fires, misfortunes and other problems followed and eventually saw the Walker team declining as the costs escalated and the pressures became almost unbearable. Final associations with Graham Hill, at the end of his career when sponsorship was arriving, and then John Surtees, into whose team he merged his name after winding up his own operation, came before Walker eased into journalism. He had, literally, spent a fortune on the sport he loved. Thirty years later, with its high-rise pneumatic motor homes and corporate images, he would struggle to recognise it.

4 John Cooper, Colin Chapman and the Rise of the British 'Garagistes'

Rob Walker may have been the last great aristocratic privateer, but he was certainly no snob. He was a man who recognised competitiveness, industry and spirit in others and he had the courage, and the wallet, not to mention the good humour required at times, to back them. His eye for a winner introduced him to many whose development was to play a fundamental part in the development of the 'British revolution' in Grand Prix motor racing; a phenomenon otherwise known as the rise of the kit-car teams, often also referred to in disparaging terms by the European 'grandees' as 'les garagistes'. First and foremost among these were men like John Cooper and Colin Chapman, whose influences on Formula One were different, but equally far-reaching. Their followers, and customers, shaped the sport's history and remained influential a generation later. A glance through the entry lists helps to explain the changes.

In 1955, the main participating teams were Ferrari, Gordini, Lancia, Maserati and Mercedes; a cosmopolitan, if European, bunch. By 1960, the line-up included Aston Martin, BRM, Cooper, Ferrari and Lotus, along with a brief show from Porsche (it had, therefore, taken in a strong British element); and by 1965, it had expanded further to embrace Brabham, BRM, Cooper, Ferrari, Honda, Lotus and, of course, Team Walker (running Brabhams). Here it is worth remembering that Brabham began life with Walker and Cooper.

In 1970, the entry list included Brabham, Yardley-BRM, Ferrari, McLaren, Gold Leaf Lotus, Team Walker (Lotus), March Elf (Team Tyrrell), STP March, Matra Elf, Surtees and De Tomaso. By then, of course, the kit-car teams were growing up, encouraging others to join them and sponsorship had arrived; and another five years on, the entry list was ballooned still greater. It included: Marlboro Texaco McLaren, Elf Tyrrell, JPS Lotus, Martini Brabham, March Beta, Lavazza March, Ferrari, BRM, UOP Shadow, Surtees, Williams, Embassy Lola, Hesketh, Parnelli, First National Citi Bank Penske and Copersucar. This international mixture of brands and bases reflected the early influences of such far-sighted men as Chapman and Bernie Ecclestone.

For the sake of comprehensive neatness, herewith the list for 1980 which paraded: Ferrari, Candy Tyrrell, Brabham Parmalat, Marlboro McLaren, ATS, Essex Lotus, Ensign Unipart, Renault Elf, Skol Fittipaldi, Marlboro Alfa Romeo, Ligier Gitanes, Saudia Leyland Williams, Warsteiner Arrows and Osella. By then, without much doubt, the embryonic Piranha Club was taking shape, money was flowing and, of course, the so-called 'FISA-FOCA war' was on the horizon. For the rest, please consult the usual reference sources, or the 'teams' section at the end of this book. Each will reflect the importance of the Coopers, the Chapmans and the Ecclestones as the old-fashioned funsters of the 1950s and the 1960s evolved into the businessmen of the 1970s and the tycoons of later years.

John Cooper, as those who knew him have always been quick to attest, was a man of jovial spirits and great personal modesty. He had none of the characteristics that one would think of and associate immediately with requirements for membership of the Piranha Club. He earned more laughs than dollars and had more friends than enemies. But like them all, he loved speed and racing. John and his father Charles, who supported him as his business partner, were one of the most unpretentious, yet successful, forces in the history of the sport, achieving great feats with the minimum of fuss from their garages in Surbiton and, later, Byfleet. They had no publicists, no managers and little or no glamour, but they always had a good time. They were the kind of old-fashioned Britons of the first half of the twentieth century who worked as easily with their own hands as with their minds and who could share time and pleasure with anyone. Indeed, some, like Derek Jewell (who edited the splendid book *Man and Motor – The 20th Century Love Affair*) compared John Cooper to old-fashioned film stars of the era. He described him as 'a large, rumpled man, with a square, Jack Hawkins, kind of face ... His hands, which have helped build so many winners, and have poked into their works from Indianapolis to Nurburgring, are rarely in repose.'

The story of John Newton Cooper, of course, is the story of the revival of rear-engine racing cars and of the successes and the popularity of the nimble little vehicles in their dark green and white livery sent out from the old Cooper Car Company's headquarters down in Surrey. He and father Charles, however, had no idea, when they built their first car for the Formula 500 category, with a motor-cycle engine at the rear, that they were making an engineering breakthrough that was to change the history of the sport. It was simply because of basic practicality and cost; it was easier, neater and cheaper than putting it in the front. The old Formula 500 category was a forerunner to the modern Formula Three, a formula for small racing cars powered by motor-cycle engines. It created thrilling racing for the post-war era and attracted many participants who were later to become important men in Formula One, including Ken Tyrrell and Bernie Ecclestone, but it was, essentially, a formula for fun and not one for lavish spenders.

> So, when we came to make our first 500 racer, it was just a hell of a lot more convenient to have the engine at the back, driving a chain [said John Cooper]. We certainly had no feeling that we were creating some kind of scientific breakthrough. Don't forget, our Cooper-Bristol F2 car was front-engine, but we put the engine at the rear in the 500s because it was the practical thing to do ... And, it wasn't until we built the bob-tailed sports-car in the mid-1950's, with its engine at the rear, that we really began to think that we may be on to something. That really was a super little car, light, easy on its tyres, well balanced and cheap. It just seemed so right.

Such modest self-appraisals were typical of John Cooper who regarded the evolution of his engineering philosophy and its later massive successes, including the triumphs over such illustrious names of their day as Ferrari, Maserati and Vanwall, as little more than something good to celebrate.

Their first great victory came in the Argentine Grand Prix of 1958 when Stirling Moss, as we know, won in Rob Walker's Cooper, powered by a 2.2 litre Climax engine. This was the famous day when Moss drove a non-stop race, finishing on tyres worn down to their canvas, assisted by the antics of his veteran mechanic Alf Francis who pretended a pit-stop was imminent in order to lull the opposition into a false sense of security. It never happened and Walker's little blue machine came home first ahead of the grand front-engine Ferrari of Luigi Musso. Before the race, the little Cooper had been ridiculed and almost barred an entry, the promoters showing great reluctance in paying out for a car so small it appeared to be an insult to their event. Afterwards, the result was seen as arguably the most significant in the sport.

John Cooper had helped to create not only a rear-engine car, but with it a prototype of the modern Formula One car; a car that was to become adjustable, to different set-ups; and a car that encouraged a different kind of driving. 'Before that time, motor racing in Britain was more of a rich man's past-time,' explained Cooper, in an interview with David Tremayne published soon after his death on 26 December 2000.

But our cars were so cheap that they introduced a whole new generation of drivers, who took a different approach. Men such as Stirling Moss and Roy Salvadori came into it and were quick to realise that there was money to be made and, as a result, they were much more professional.

Cooper's realisation and his cars' breakthrough made them the dominant force of the late 1950s and a major player in the 1960s when Chapman, with his famous Lotus marque, rose to fame and Cooper employed a young and ambitious mechanic called Ron Dennis, later to become one of the most powerful men in the ever-growing world of modern Grand Prix racing and an influential force at the heart of the Piranha Club. Cooper, who also enjoyed success with the creation of the Mini-Cooper road cars during the period when his Formula One fortunes began to dwindle, retired long before Dennis rose to fame and often marvelled at his successes, but never with envy.

As a member of the 'old school', Cooper always had other things to enjoy in a life crammed with incidents and anecdotes. One prank, which he recalled with glee, summed up the carefree days of Cooper's era when drivers, team owners, managers and the rest all mixed together and shared their work and their fun. It came on 5 July 1958, on the eve of the French Grand Prix at Reims.

It was the night before the race [he explained]. There was this bar where we would all congregate. There were a couple of trees in the courtyard and, after a few drinks, Mike Hawthorn and Stuart Lewis-Evans, had a bet on which of them would be the first to get to the top. Off they went, climbing frantically.

According to Tremayne, whose interview was published on the Inside-F1 website following Cooper's death, another well-known driver, who remained anonymous in this story, came and stood beneath the trees. Within a short time, he sensed something odd.

'He began to notice there was water falling on him,' said Cooper. 'He looked up and there was Mike Hawthorn, peeing on him. "I've always wanted to piss on you from a great height," he shouted.' The chuckle from Cooper added its own touch of authenticity. The following day, Hawthorn won the French Grand Prix, from pole position, clocking fastest lap along the way in his Ferrari. It was also Juan-Manuel Fangio's last race and saw Luigi Musso killed. Lewis-Evans, a close friend of Ecclestone, died later that season, following a crash at the Moroccan Grand Prix in Casablanca, and Hawthorn, on the Guildford by-pass, the following January.

Like Walker, of course, Cooper and his contemporaries lived through the days of death on the tracks. It was a fact of life. It also gave them the sense that life was brief and had to be lived to the full. John Cooper, and Chapman, and to some degree most of the men who followed them, had fully developed senses of humour. Cooper himself was known for being able to turn forward somersaults in public, as a party trick, a little as Walker could tear up telephone directories. Encouraged, of course, Cooper began doing his somersaults on the ashphalt of the pit lane to mark victories by his cars and the triumphs of men like Jack Brabham, Roy Salvadori and Bruce McLaren sent him spinning head-over-heels many times. Brabham, of course, was drivers' world champion twice in succession, in 1959 and 1960, when Cooper were triumphant, winning both the drivers' and the constructors' crowns. The father-and-son partnership, from Surbiton, thus conquered the world, beating the wealthy factory teams.

But Surbiton did nothing much to mark the feats. According to Jewell, the local citizens were less than enamoured with the world-beating efforts of their Cooper family business. He reported the following:

'I suppose Surbiton made a song and dance about it all?'

'They put our rates up.'

'No, honestly?'

'And we had crowds of people at the garage shouting and screaming about our all-night sessions getting cars ready for races.'

'And that's all?'

'Well, our local baker did make us a cake.'

Cooper's enormous and natural laugh blew away any sense of pomp. He cared neither for fame nor disappointment. He was never worried that, after the 1960s arrived and with them the generation of the permissive society, pop music, fashion and youth culture, his Cooper cars were passed by in the psyche of the time by those of his greatest contemporary rival, Colin Chapman. Lotus Cars, like Cooper Cars, were housed in a London suburb. It was Surbiton and Hornsey in those days, but their addresses mattered little once the public learned all about the racing creations of Chapman and the driving genius of Jim Clark. Surbiton, at least, could claim a link with the glamour of Ferrari by a tenuous route after most of the drivers in Formula One at the time took to driving Mini-Coopers.

The Mini-Cooper, like most things in John Cooper's life, came out of a friendship, in this case his friendship with Alec Issigonis, the chief designer and engineer for the British Motor Corporation (BMC).

I'd known Alec for a long time, you see [Cooper told Jewell]. Only the second race I was in, back in 1947, I beat him. We've been friends ever since. He let me have one of the early test Minis. I couldn't believe it. I was so impressed. I took one to Italy and Lampredi, who was chief designer for Ferrari then, saw me with it at Monza. After he'd tried it out, he said 'if that car didn't look so bloody awful, I'd shoot myself'. Soon, all the Grand Prix drivers and their mates had got Minis and were tuning them a bit. I suggested to Issigonis that we should build a good one for the boys. So we converted one, pushed up the engine size from 850 cc to 1000 cc, put on disc brakes and tarted it up generally. Then we and BMC did further development work together and after that we raced them and they rallied them.

By the mid-1960s, production was in excess of 60,000 and the little car with big performance was dominating all the major rallies of the world and the British and European saloon car championships. But this, even though it produced a wonderful cash flow for the little family business, was not enough to excite John Cooper.

> Where racing cars are concerned [said Roy Salvadori, who went from driver to manager in the team], John Cooper is the most excitable man I know. He feels for those cars. In the pits, suddenly, he'll start to fidget with a pencil or something. Then, he'll go walking around the car. Round and round and round. Popping questions. Have you done this? Have you done that? Worrying. He's too experienced ever to tell a driver to go faster. He'll be at the side of the track muttering. 'Now's the time to go slow. Now's the time not to stress the car.' You want to know what he's really like? We were at Silverstone once, practising. John said 'Well everything's wonderful, the sun's shining, the car's handling ok, the brakes are fine and the gearbox is fine . . . There's only one thing wrong. We're two seconds bloody slower than the opposition.'

Such enthusiasm came to John Cooper from his father, Charles. It is not an uncommon feature in the motor racing industry. Fathers often pass their passion down in their genes and through day-to-day life. Other families, like the Brabhams, Chapmans, Hills, Stewarts and Tyrrells have seen a similar phenomenon in different ways. Charles Cooper was the source for the John Cooper passion and the Cooper family success. An apprentice at Napiers, then chief mechanic to Kaye Don, he opened his first garage at Ewell Road, Surbiton in 1933. In the same decade, he built his own miniature Flying Flea plane. It was little surprise that when John Cooper was eight his father gave him his first car, which he drove around the paddock at Brooklands. At 12, he received his second, with a tuned Austin Seven engine, and drove it around Brooklands at 87 mph, continuing until the authorities stopped him.

At 15, John Cooper left Surbiton County Grammar School to become an apprentice at Coopers, carrying with him his dream of becoming a racing driver. Instead, he also went on to work with a toolmaker and then serve in the war, spending four years in secret work on one-man subs and later time in the RAF. After the war, he returned to Surbiton and, with his father, mapped out the future, in chalk, on the floor of their garage. That first rough design, for their first car, set the trend and dictated their future lives. The idea came, too, from odds and ends, but with one purpose: to build a cheap, fast and fun machine that could race in the Formula 500. The constituent parts included a Fiat Topolino chassis, Ford universal joints, a motor cycle clutch and gearbox, parts of a derelict Morrison air-raid shelter (for frame uprights) and a 500 cc dirt-track single-cylinder J.A.P. engine. It went down the back to help save weight and give better traction . . . and it worked.

Five weeks after being chalked across the floor, the car was built and ready to win sprints and hill-climbs. John Cooper raced it and won. He loved it. A second car was built for an old friend, Eric Brandon. He won, too. More orders flooded in and, soon, almost accidentally, the old Cooper works had turned into a car-manufacturing company. A decision was taken to build a dozen and one of the first buyers was Stirling Moss, then a teenager fired by speed. He was to be followed by many others who grew up in these little Coopers, including Peter Collins, Mike Hawthorn, Stuart Lewis-Evans, Harry Schell, Jack Brabham, Roy Salvadori and Les Leston. They were popular because they were fast and they were also durable.

'If I see anybody shunt one of my cars,' said Charles Cooper. 'I like to see them get up and walk away.' For their strength, they were known as 'blacksmith's cars'. It was a compliment. It was also, usually, true. In one example, cited by Jewell, John Cooper crashed into a wall at the Avus circuit in Berlin to avoid hitting two other cars that had collided. He then pushed his car 150 yards to start it again and still won the race, averaging more than 93 mph, which was a record at the time.

Such feats were representative of the Coopers' success. They swamped Formula 500 and moved on via sports cars, through a protracted period in attempting to build a bigger, faster and equally competitive car, towards Formula Two and Formula One. In 1955 they made a breakthrough, with a sports car, when they used a Coventry-Climax 1100 cc engine (derived from a fire-pump power unit) which was bored out again and again and allied it to conventional transmission and also introduced a 'sawn-off back end'. Some called this a Manx tail. Salvadori said:

This car was ahead of its time. So quick, so stable. The perfect streamlining. That sawn-off back created a pressure in the air stream that kept the rear end on the deck. The story got around that John had chopped off the tail because he couldn't get two of the cars in the transporter. Do you believe that? Well, I'm still not sure. He likes to be light-hearted about it. So, it's a mystery.

The commercial success of the Cooper sports car paid for its transformation into a racing car. It won in Formula Two and encouraged further buyers. Success followed, notably the famous triumph in Buenos Aires where the Walker Cooper, worth £3,000, out-performed its rivals, all worth around £30,000 apiece. But the success did nothing to hide or help the company's financial weakness compared to the competition. Cooper drivers were always instructed to keep away from risks and accidents and to nurse their engines sensitively. Car write-offs and blown engines were beyond the reach of their purse.

John had to worry too much about finances [Salvadori told Jewell]. Whenever we got edgy with each other, which was not often, it was because he didn't want to practice as much as I did. He wanted to keep down the chances of a shunt.

The plunge into the deeper waters of Formula One was, by legend, also chalked on the garage floor. Few deny it even if it is more apocryphal than recorded truth. 'Coopers always used to go in for knife and fork methods,' said Les Leston of the story that the 1959 car was drawn out by John Cooper, Jack Brabham and Owen Maddock sitting in the garage. It did not matter. They won everywhere in 1959 and, again, in 1960 when with the opposition catching up and going for rear engine cars, they had a completely new five-speed gearbox. 'That's how we stayed in front that year,' said John Cooper, after watching Brabham win a sequence of races at Zandvoort, Spa, Reims, Silverstone and Oporto.

They did not know it then, but it was the golden age for them all. The Cooper story was not to be sustained; Brabham left to run his own team; Bruce McLaren came to replace him, but without the same stunning and consistent success; the Mini was launched in 1961; Charles Cooper died after a long illness in

1964; John himself survived a big accident in a Mini he was testing at more than 100 mph on the Kingston by-pass; and there was the rise and rise of Chapman and Lotus. In the end, he sold out to commercial interests.

Cooper was frank in his own assessment of the company's decline. In 1965, he said:

> In 1959 and 1960, we had a car that was a year ahead of its time. After that everyone had basically the same kit of parts – with better drivers. Lotus did more development work than we did. In a sense, they had more incentive to develop. They had Jim Clark, who got better and better. And Colin Chapman has added a deal more science to the ideas we introduced ... To win Grands Prix, you need three things – a great chassis, a great engine and a great driver. And they have to go together. If you don't have a great driver, then somehow when your engine goes back to the makers for overhaul, they don't put so much into it. It's a vicious circle, hard to break. And all the time team morale goes down if you're not winning.

In his way, Cooper was admitting that he had reached his and the family's limits. The baton of British engineering enterprise was passed on, from south London to north, from Cooper to Lotus. Stirling Moss saw it happen. He said: 'Racing simply became more scientific. Lotus made the racing car an artistic piece of work, by using science. John's more of a fundamentalist, a terribly talented blacksmith who's done as much as Lotus, maybe more, in a different way.'

> Colin Chapman set the fashion and others followed, but were pale imitations. I regarded Colin as the outstanding racing car engineer and designer of this century. Through his genius, the ordinary cars on the road benefited. His death marked the passing of an era.
>
> (Louis Stanley, in David Benson's obituary of Chapman
> published in the *Daily Express* in 1982)

> I first came to know Colin Chapman during practice for the 1960 Italian Grand Prix. This was at a meeting with John Cooper and Huscke von Hanstein on the day before the 1500 cc Formula came into being. The Press indulged itself

by describing that meeting between Lotus, Ferrari, Cooper and Porsche as the Formula One 'summit'.

(Enzo Ferrari, in his foreword to *Colin Chapman, The Man and His Cars*, by Jabby Crombac)

Colin was a very fair guy. But he would do, and use, whatever he could to gain an advantage, technically. But things have changed now. With me, he was always very up front. I mean, the two guys I respect out of all the people I've met and all the things I've done in motor racing, of all the team people, were Enzo (Ferrari) and Colin (Chapman). Colin was a great guy. A super driver. A super engineer. A good business guy. He was good at using what he had. He used his knowledge, his fame. . . he used everything. He went almost to the limit. He didn't really know where the limit was or what it was. But he was a super guy. A lovely guy.

(Bernie Ecclestone, talking to the author, in Montreal, June 2001)

Anthony Colin Bruce Chapman, the only son of Stanley and Mary Chapman, was born on 19 May 1928, in Richmond, Surrey, where his father owned the Orange Tree public house. Later, they moved and he grew up at the Railway Hotel, in Tottenham Lane, Hornsey, where his father was the manager. Like virtually all the men who became major powers in Formula One, he was obsessed with speed from an early age. He also loved machinery and engineering, was a man happy to take risks and extended that to both his business life and his life in general. He learned to fly at university, believed in what some observers described as a 'minimalist design philosophy' where racing cars were concerned and had a formidable sense of ambition and the commitment and passion to fulfil it. He had a zany sense of humour, boundless energy, a reputation as a very good driver, an excellent pilot, a marksman and good yachtsman. He liked making money, but he could also spend freely and the rise and fall of Lotus, the marque, team and company that was built upon his vision and energy, is a reflection of how much he meant to the business and its success.

In reality, he was Team Lotus and when he died, on 16 December 1982, the spirit of the team, if not its fabric, went with him; that the team continued afterwards for a decade before it went down was a sadness he would have felt deeply if he had remained alive and seen it. Jackie Stewart said Chapman was 'the greatest, most creative, designer of racing cars in the history of motor racing'. Enzo Ferrari, in the fore-word to Jabby Crombac's book *Colin Chapman*, said: 'I have always admired him and remember him as a subtle visionary, a wise interpreter of technical regulations and so talented because of his ability to produce ideas ahead of their time.'

It was Murray Walker, the television commentator, who could claim personal recollections of virtually everyone in Formula One for the second half of the twentieth century, who said of Chapman that he was 'perhaps, too gifted for his own and others' good, but he will forever be remembered for an incredible array of achievements.' Walker also said that Chapman was a flawed hero, but a hero nonetheless.

> There were aspects of the late, very great, Colin Chapman's life that were considerably less than admirable. But the massive impact his tragically short career had on motor sport was such that it transcends his darker side. For a grey man, he certainly was not.

Instead, he said, Chapman was an intense, blinding light that shone bright to show the way to lesser men, and then simply burned itself out.

> Virile, intense, good-looking and charming, Chapman was not only a design genius, but also an inspirational leader, a supreme motivator and an ingenious and gifted business-man who was always prepared to walk closer to the line of acceptable ethics than most of his peers.

This summary helps explain why he, and not John Cooper, is the man more often thought of first as the pioneer who led the way for British racing cars in his era; people remembered Chapman, Clark and Lotus in a way that Cooper was not recalled. There was something else about them, a dangerous and daring dimension; a risk allied to a sense of technical pioneering that offered a certain allure. Lotus suited the age in the 1960s and they became icons of their time while Chapman emerged as a leader and a far-sighted operator with visions for himself, his team, his company and motor racing as a whole.

As a boy, and as a teenager, he lived a normal, but full, life that was alive with dreams. His teenage years, in north London and Wisbech, were dominated by the shadow of the Second World War and he grew up with few privileges, learning quickly, as did his future associates and contemporaries like Bernie Ecclestone, to take advantage of every opportunity. Indeed, he met his future wife, Hazel Patricia Williams, at a Saturday night dance at Hornsey Town Hall in March 1944, thanks as much to the fact that his father helped to organise the event as his own forethought. The Blitz may have ended, but rationing remained tight and the 'doodlebugs' were soon to start falling; hardly auspicious circumstances, but for Chapman it was to be the start of a relationship that spanned the rest of his life.

Even then, however, Chapman the opportunist was a youth of style and ambition, a 16-year-old in a baggy sports jacket and baggy trousers, content to ride home from that first encounter on a bicycle which betrayed his view of the world and his own future: it was painted gold. Earlier in the war, he had been evacuated from London, where he had studied at the Stationers' Company's School, to Wisbech in Cambridgeshire, but in 1944, he was back in the capital, ready for life and hoping to claim a place at London University. The dance at Hornsey Town Hall was an obvious attraction. His father did the catering and organised the event. Chapman could enter without charge. He knew, too, in those days, how to make things happen and get them done.

> I was terribly shy [Hazel told Jabby Crombac]. But so was Colin. What attracted me to him was that he seemed so capable in the way he did just everyday things. Even at that age, he could always get things done and I remember thinking to myself after our first meeting 'Here is someone a bit different. This chap will go places.'

His relationship with Hazel was to be of vital importance to his life in many ways. She gave him an emotional anchor, not least because she played a major part in the start of Lotus Engineering, in 1952, by putting up the initial £25 required to start the company. She also had to experience and survive some of the most testing moments of Chapman's career development. From an early age, he was keen on gadgets and machinery and this, she recalled, was manifested in late 1944 when the Germans were bombing London and Chapman and his father created a device, which could predict where a 'doodlebug' was going to land. 'It was on the roof, and by lining this thing up, on the "doodlebug", they could tell whether it was going to drop anywhere near,' she told Crombac. 'They would then know whether everybody should take shelter or not.'

Her early recollections provide a sharp insight into Chapman the engineer and businessman, as well as the risk-taker.

> When I first met Colin, he had this 'gold' bicycle, but it was not long before he bought a 350cc Panther motor bike which, of course, he always rode with tremendous verve and enthusiasm. My mother hated it because she knew I used to ride pillion. When Colin came to our house to call for me he would leave the bike at the end of the road and walk the last few yards to collect me. We then walked back to the bike so that my mother wouldn't know we were actually going out on it. However, within six months, Colin had an accident on the way to university, crashing through a London taxi with two very surprised old ladies in the back and our biking days were over. In his usual impetuous way, Colin later discharged himself from the casualty department and I came home to find him sitting in his parents' dining room looking somewhat dejected. My mother suggested he buy a three-wheeler to replace the bike, which he in fact did, but only to re-sell it a couple of days later to a friend for a small profit.

Chapman took up his place at University College, London, in October, 1945, to study mechanical engineering. He was not a great academic, but obviously had little difficulty in absorbing all he felt he needed to know from the lectures.

> He used to bomb off to the lectures on his motor cycle [said Hazel], but when he returned, he never spoke about it and you never saw him get his books out. Two or three days before the exams, he might do a little bit of study, go through his notes.

At around this time, together with a fellow-student friend, Colin Dare, Chapman began to buy and trade old cars, after dressing them up. Typically, he borrowed money sometimes from Hazel's father who also provided him with a lock-up garage, at ten shillings a week. 'Which, he never paid,' Hazel told Crombac. She also reported that they went out only rarely to the Saturday dances, which were free, and to the cinema, when they sneaked in through the exit doors.

Cars remained at the heart of his life, however, even after Dare failed his exams, leaving Chapman to carry on alone and to lose all of the £500 profit he had accumulated when the basic petrol ration was withdrawn. This act of government intervention, negative on the surface, had a positive effect. It meant that the value of second-hand cars fell, forcing Chapman to change direction. Chapman was left with, among others, a 1930 Austin Seven saloon. Inspired by a car trial, which he saw, by chance, at Aldershot, Chapman decided to convert the Austin into a trials vehicle, applying not only his engineering knowledge, but also many of the principles of aircraft design and construction that he had also acquired after learning to fly with the University Air Squadron.

With Hazel's support, this rebuilt old Austin Seven was turned into the Lotus Mark I, using alloy-bonded plywood, to improve the rigidity of the old chassis with fully stressed bodywork, but without adding any weight. The explanation for the name was always kept secret, but it was suggested that the exhaustion experienced in building the car was virtually as soporific as the scent of the lotus flower. Chapman never confirmed his reason for calling it a Lotus. He graduated in 1948, did his national service as a pilot in the Royal Air Force in 1949, which maintained his interest in all things mechanical and aeronautical, and, continuing in the same lock-up garage, owned by Hazel's father, used all leave to work on a second car, the Lotus Mark II.

For this he took parts from an Austin Seven and combined them with a Ford 1172 cc engine to produce another trials competitor. This had car headlamps, fitted with a steering device, in the grill. It was another example of Chapman's enterprise, his vision and his eye for detail. While the Coopers might be content to chalk out a design on their garage floor, Chapman wanted everything done as professionally and with as much sophistication as possible. Trials, therefore, were not likely to hold his interest for long and, predictably, they did not. He felt the rules were too loose and the outcome was, too often, a lottery. He turned for something new and found circuit racing; in particular, he found the 750 Motor Club, an organisation that ran a formula designed for cars using the 750cc Austin Seven engines.

The Lotus Mark III, light and competitive, using a softly sprung boxed frame and an independent front axle, was a pioneering vehicle. Inevitably, further success followed and this, with it, brought a demand for his ideas, his parts and his cars. Chapman was on his way and on 1 January 1952, Lotus Engineering was created. The first factory was a stable behind the Railway Hotel and the first full-time employee was his partner Michael Allen, one of two brothers (Nigel was the other) to whom he was introduced by Hazel. Both were aspiring dentists, from Muswell Hill, where their family had a very well equipped garage. This attraction smoothed their mutual co-operation in the building of the Mark III with each brother believing he would soon be able to compete in his own racing car – a dream frustrated by Chapman's need to keep taking parts off the brothers' vehicles to keep his own in order.

Eventually, Nigel Allen decided he would concentrate on dentistry while Michael remained to pursue a future as Chapman's first full-time man. Chapman himself, of course, had to remain a part-timer as he was still working for British Aluminium as a stress engineer, generating funds the business needed, but available only at weekends and in the evenings.

The first product of the Lotus business was the Lotus Mark IV, which was built for Mike Lawson. It was a trials and autocross car that could also be used on the road. Like the earlier models, it used both Austin and Ford components and proved to be a winner. In late 1952, the partnership with Allen ended following a curious sequence of events following an entry with the Consul-engined Mark V1 in the 100-miles sports car event at the International Daily Mail race meeting at Boreham Airfield in Essex on the August Bank Holiday Monday. The driver was Nigel Allen. He spun four times in practice, collecting, said Crombac, several market drums in the process. This resulted in a prompt return to Hornsey for repairs.

The following morning, while returning to the circuit, a milk float came out of a side turning without warning and Allen, in the repaired Lotus, ran straight into it. Allen was unhurt, but his passenger, Pauline Gooch, his future wife, hurt her knees while the car was destroyed. Luckily, it was covered by fully comprehensive insurance and Lotus Engineering survived this blow.

The advertisements, placed by Chapman in the magazine *Motor Sport*, were attracting just enough conversion work and orders for spare parts to keep the company alive until the payout of £800 arrived. It was, however, the last straw for the relationship between Chapman and Michael Allen. They were not enjoying the best understanding as partners and Allen, given the wreck of the Mark V1 as a payoff, left the business. Finally, Chapman was to run the show on his own.

By then, Lotus Engineering was established as Chapman's trade name and in 1953, buoyed by the insurance money, he took the decision to register the Lotus Engineering Company Ltd. Hazel lent him the £25 fee. The directors were A.C.B. Chapman (BSc Eng) and H. P. Williams, according to the new yellow and green stationery which described the company as 'automobile and component manufacturers, racing and competition car design and development ... Manufacturers of the Lotus chassis frame'. The address was 7 Tottenham Lane, Hornsey, London N8. Telephone MOUntview 8353. Business began.

The loan from Hazel was a famous event in the legend of Lotus, but it was swiftly repaid when Chapman discovered she was to move with her family to Cuffley in Hertfordshire. This meant she was no longer within easy reach. So, deciding that action was called for, he chose to repay her £25 loan by buying her an Austin Seven 'Chummy' in which she was able to commute easily to Muswell Hill, where she ran her mother's wool shop. The car gave useful service also to the racing team as the 'tender car' and was later sold to one of the young mechanics at Lotus at the time, Graham Hill. The deal was straightforward – except for one condition; Hazel demanded that Hill allowed her to have the car back once a year to compete in the annual Wrotham Cup car trial. This resulted, of course, in all three of them enjoying the competition together, but with Hazel driving and Hill and Chapman riding as passengers.

This story, too, is typical of the Chapman style. Like Ron Dennis, Ecclestone, Ferrari, Frank Williams and the rest, he was a dealer with a sharp eye, able to identify qualities in people that were often invisible to most others. He was also able to mix charmingly with people from all walks of life. He could make the most of chance encounters and identify anyone with a special talent. Not only drivers, but also ordinary people he met in everyday life. One such everyday encounter led to

Chapman meeting and hiring Fred Bushell, an accountant who was to run his business affairs for the rest of his life and who travelled back from Paris to Norfolk with him on the night he died. Bushell told Crombac:

> I had passed the Tottenham lane workshop many times late at night and seen the lights on in the building. It so happened that there was a gents toilet close by, primarily there for the use of the patrons of the pub next door, where I would sometimes have to make a call. On this particular occasion, Colin was in there, in his cap and overalls, and, as men do, we got talking and he invited me to have a look in the workshop. They were working on a small racing car and he explained to me in his usual enthusiastic way what he and his colleagues were doing. Then he asked me what I did. Upon hearing that I was an accountant, he took me to a tiny cubicle, where there was a trestle table propped up on beer crates, on which were piles of papers. Principally these amounted to a series of open envelopes on which there were columns of figures which he explained was his accounting system and would I like to sort it out for him? We made an appointment to meet a week later . . .

The rest, as they say, was history. 'I reorganised his accounting systems and I turned what appeared to me to be more like a club into a business.' One of Bushell's most significant early moves was to advise Chapman to set up an independent company for racing. In effect, this was the beginning of Team Lotus, launched in 1954. It was done to prevent the racing costs being carried by the commercial part of the Lotus operation, which was going from strength to strength.

The Lotus Mark V, due to have been perhaps the ultimate Austin Seven special, was never built because the Mark VI, built in 1953, launched the company as a genuine small-scale car manufacturer. It used a multi-tubular space-frame and a stressed aluminium floor and side panels. It was so advanced that it caused a stir. It had independent front suspension, was light and rigid and was sold, as a kit, with engines chosen by the buyer. The Mark VII that followed was the first of the 'streamliners' using the designs of aircraft aerodynamicist Frank Costin and the Mark VIII, another beautiful streamlined Lotus, created for the 1954 racing season, was widely regarded as the most potent 1500cc sports car in England. Frank Costin had been introduced to Chapman by his brother Mike Costin. He, previously, had been drawn to Lotus by the interest of his friends and workmates at de Havilland, in Hatfield, where many of Chapman's early 'night-shift' volunteers, including Peter Ross and 'Mac' McIntosh, were employed.

'I saw Colin one evening in the pub' [said Mike Costin]. 'He offered me a part-time association deal to start the following January. The idea was that we would together build the first seven Mark VI cars, which would finance the construction of the eighth – of which we would share the driving!'

The Mark VIII gave Chapman an opportunity to prove he remained a decent driver with competitive ambitions and, on 17 July, in the curtain raiser to the 1954 British Grand Prix, at Silverstone, he beat the works Porsche 550 of Hans Herrmann. It was an example of his talent and determination, in a summer when he competed in Europe by working in his office until Friday evening before driving the car, by road, to the coast, crossing the channel overnight, practising on Saturday, rebuilding the engine on Saturday night, and racing on Sunday. How he managed to find the time to marry Hazel was a mystery, but he did and they wed on 16 October 1954 at Northaw Church near Cuffley, and went to Majorca for their honeymoon.

Mike Costin, a talented practical engineer, joined Chapman, who gave up his job with British Aluminium to go full-time at Lotus, on 1 January 1955. Mike Costin was a glider enthusiast with little interest in cars, but said Chapman 'had that most fantastic ability to motivate people'. They started full-time together on the same day at Tottenham Lane. Frank Costin was retained as a consultant and, with Chapman, went on to help in the creation of the phenomenal Lotus XI, which was accepted as the classic sports car of the late 1950s. It was strikingly beautiful, wonderfully efficient, light and fast; a perfect example of what Chapman had been working towards achieving.

Success in sports car racing was the immediate reward for the Lotus XI, but this was not enough to satisfy ambitions for something greater and grander. As a result, the first single-seat cars were built in 1956, the year when Chapman helped in the redesign of the Vanwalls. According to team manager David Yorke, the Vanwalls of 1955 were derived from a Cooper chassis. But after Tony Vandervell was introduced to Chapman, by

Vanwall truck driver Derek Wooton, they moved from the so-called 'ladder' chassis to the 'space frame' chassis of Chapman.

'Colin came to our racing shop in Acton and he literally scribbled a rough sketch for our engineers and explained to them the principles of space frame,' said Yorke. For good measure, apparently, Chapman then advised them to use Frank Costin to design the streamlined body for the car that helped establish Vanwall in Formula One that year. (Indeed, that summer almost saw Chapman himself race a Vanwall in the French Grand Prix at Reims on 1 July; but a brake problem in practice put paid to that unique dream for him as he collided with the rear of Mike Hawthorn's car. Only one of the two Vanwalls could be repaired in time and, of course, it was Hawthorn's.) The obvious potential for success of the Vanwalls was noticed throughout Formula One and led to Chapman doing similar 'improvement' work on the BRMs for which his payment was a Raymond Mays-converted Ford Zephyr.

The Lotus 12 showed promise in 1957, but was held back by a problematic gearbox. Chapman realised this was a matter of importance and so he hired a young Mk V1 owner, who as an engineering student, had worked at Lotus in his holidays, Keith Duckworth, a man whose future was to have a profound effect not only on Lotus, but Formula One. Duckworth's first full-time job, like many talented men in this business, was in a shed in the Tottenham Lane yard at Hornsey. Later, of course, he was to become very good friends with Mike Costin with whom he went into partnership in 1958, to form Cosworth Engineering, when the pair of them felt disillusioned by the volume of work, and the unreasonable pressure, heaped on them by Chapman. Duckworth left, but Costin stayed on, for a time, after being made an offer, by Chapman, that he could not refuse. It was typical of Chapman; his vibrant imagination, enthusiasm and charm attracted a squad of highly talented men around him, many of whom created long-lasting reputations, but his management techniques were in direct contrast to the sleek modernity of the engineering in which he involved them.

His first experience of the death of one of his own drivers, at the wheel of a works Lotus, also came in 1957, in a Formula Two race at Reims when 'Mac' Frazer, in a 1500cc Lotus X1, crashed and lost his life. Chapman, said Crombac, took this badly on what was a particularly difficult weekend for him. Cliff Allison was jailed after being injured in a road car accident and

Jay Chamberlin was injured in practice, both for the 12-Hours race for Grand Touring sports cars, and Chapman was involved also in a blazing post-race row with the clerk of the course, Toto Roche.

It was the first truly black day for Lotus. Frazer's death was difficult to accept because, just a few weeks previously, he had shared the driving of a special 1100cc Lotus, which delivered a class-winning performance at Le Mans, a triumph that triggered a memorable night's celebrations at the Crazy Horse Saloon in Avenue George V in Paris. Death was to be expected in racing in those times, however, and Chapman, like the rest, had to find the strength to overcome his feelings and continue. That he did this repeatedly, after men like Jim Clark, Jochen Rindt and Ronnie Petersen died following fatal accidents in his cars, spoke of his ambition and passion as a racer, as well as his obsession with moving the technical boundaries whenever possible.

In 1958 Chapman made his move to the top level when he took his Formula Two Lotus 12s to the Monaco Grand Prix with a driver pairing of Graham Hill, promoted from team mechanic, and Cliff Allison. For them all, Allison, Hill, Lotus and Chapman, it was a maiden foray into Grand Prix racing, a mountain climbed, even if the race was won by Maurice Trintignant in Rob Walker's Cooper-Climax. Allison finished sixth, but Hill retired after 70 laps with engine trouble when running sixth. Chapman, whose personal enthusiasm to move into Grand Prix racing was less than that of his drivers and staff, was for once carried along by others.

'I was only interested in Formula Two, sports cars and the Elite at the time and I didn't want to get involved in Formula One,' he told Doug Nye. 'We weren't ready for it. But the drivers were all fired up so away we went.' Later the same year, the Lotus 16 was introduced, at the French Grand Prix, and the Lotus adventure in Formula One was under way, whether the reluctant Chapman wanted it to be or not. By the end of that debut year, Allison had accumulated three points and Hill none. Mike Costin, according to Crombac, spent most of his time checking the cars' chassis and suspensions for cracks caused by the material used being too light.

It was clear [wrote Cromac] that Chapman, who had so far worked only on cars with a relatively low power to weight ratio was having great difficulty in adapting his ideas to single-seat racing cars, especially because of his conviction that saving weight was of paramount importance.

Inevitably, given Coopers' successes, the rear engine Lotus 18 followed for the 1960 season. If the Coopers looked like the solid products of a clever blacksmith, however, the Lotuses were more akin to beautiful, if fragile, prototypes. Like so many Chapman cars, they captured the imagination and they caused a sensation. Innes Ireland, recruited in 1959, to replace Cliff Allison (who had gone to Ferrari), scored the 18's first win, in a Formula Two event at Oulton Park and then, on Easter Monday, beat Stirling Moss, driving a Cooper, in both the Formula Two and the non-championship Formula One race at Goodwood. So impressed was Moss that he asked Rob Walker to buy one for the next world championship Grand Prix, in Monte Carlo. Walker did so and Moss, in his new car, won the 1960 Monaco Grand Prix, beating the much-fancied Ferraris. It was a famous feat, but it could not disguise the fact that, later that year, the Lotus 18's fragility was to be exposed in tragic circumstances at the Belgian Grand Prix at Spa-Francorchamps.

There, in practice, both Moss and Michael Taylor crashed their privately entered cars badly, due to mechanical failure, Moss suffering two fractured legs because of a defective rear hub. Taylor's steering column fractured. He sued Lotus for negligence, obtaining a settlement. Worse still, for Chapman and Lotus, Alan Stacey, a driver who had an artificial right leg below the knee, whose car had a fractured bolt in a steering gear in practice, was killed in the race when a bird flew into his face and he lost control, the second Lotus works driver to die in a Chapman car. Later that year, recovered sufficiently from his injuries to race again, Moss won the United States Grand Prix at Riverside.

But Chapman, the multi-faceted engineer and businessman, was not involved only in Grand Prix racing in this period. By then, alongside his racing feats, Chapman had established new standards again with the Type 14, better known as the 'Elite', an innovative and brilliant sports car built of glass-fibre, the first of its type in the world. Acclaimed and admired for its lightweight, all-round independent suspension and wonderful Coventry Climax engine, it was a great success in competition, but also almost bankrupted the company because Lotus made a loss of about £100 on each vehicle. However, demand for the Seven, the rights for which were sold to Caterham Cars in 1973, and for the Elite led at long last to Lotus moving from the original premises in Hornsey to a purpose-built factory at Delamare Road, Cheshunt in June 1959.

At the same time, the Lotus Group was created, made up of Lotus Cars, for the manufacturing of road cars, and Lotus Components, for the racing cars and customers. The racing team was kept separate, always to be wholly owned, it was intended, by the Chapman family. (Indeed, this remained the structure for the companies even after October 1968, when shares in Lotus were listed on the London Stock Exchange for the first time in a bid to attract the finance needed for further growth. Chapman, at that time, retained 52 per cent and the sale of the other 48 per cent made him, on paper at least, a multi-millionaire.)

The move to Cheshunt was partly the result of the efforts of Chapman's father Stanley. He found a parcel of suitable land for development.

> Stan was very obviously proud of all that Colin was doing and was extremely supportive [Bushell told Crombac]. Colin respected his father immensely for his general worldly business knowledge, but he did find difficulty in communicating with him and they had very different concepts of the speed at which things should be done ... Perhaps, in current terms, this would be called the 'generation gap'.

As the Lotus companies were split into divisions within the group, in 1959, other things changed. Fred Bushell took over as general manager of the cars operation and Chapman and Hazel moved into a new home at Hadley Wood (their second daughter, Sarah, a sister for Jane, had been born the previous winter). Sadly, also, Graham Hill, in acrimonious circumstances, left Team Lotus following the Italian Grand Prix, claiming he was disgusted at the lack of reliability of the cars. He joined BRM, leaving Chapman fuming with rage. Chapman took Hill to court for breach of contract, but lost the case.

Stretched on all fronts, fired by ambition, Chapman charged on. Early in 1960, learning from Mike Costin that Jim Clark, the son of a prosperous farming family from Fife, in Scotland, who had raced against Chapman at Brands Hatch on Boxing Day, 1958, driving a Lotus Elite, was due to test a Formula One Aston Martin at Goodwood, he made sure Lotus were there, too, with the Lotus 18, a formula junior car that had been revealed for the first time at the Boxing Day meeting at Brands Hatch at the end of the previous year. It was equipped with a 997cc Cosworth engine, which was a pioneering leap in technology for power-units at the time, and which Chapman had identified as the right unit for the car after carefully maintaining close contact with Duckworth. Clark was contracted to Aston Martin for Formula One, but free for Formula Two and junior racing. Predictably, Costin approached the Aston Martin team manager Reg Parnell to ask him if he would allow Clark to try the Lotus. It was a sublime opportunity to impress a driver Chapman respected greatly and it led to one of the greatest partnerships in the history of Formula One.

In his own book *At the Wheel*, Clark wrote: 'Oh, my goodness, the Lotus in comparison was absolutely fantastic. I wouldn't have believed any car could hold the road the way this Lotus did . . . the car seemed to be glued to the road.' Soon afterwards, Clark joined Lotus and when Aston Martin withdrew from Formula One, following a poor debut, he was able to race for Chapman in Formula One and Formula Two, showing dominant flair and excellence in the latter to spark a rush of buyers for the Lotus 18. Peter Warr, a long-serving Lotus veteran in two spells, told Crombac:

> They started winning absolutely everything and in no time at all, we had a tremendous order book on the Lotus 18. They replaced the volume of business on racing cars that had been done with the X1. It was a complete switch from sports cars to single seats and that year, 1960, we sold 125 Formula Junior cars. The problem was that, with only about 60 people, we had no more than four months to build them . . .

The following year, Chapman had his first brush with suspicions of political chicanery of Formula One when the formula was reduced from 2.5 litres to 1.5 litres. It was said that the French president of the Commision Sportive Internationale (CSI) Augustin Perouse was involved, along with Enzo Ferrari, in the move for which the European teams appeared to be better prepared than the British. Twenty years later, when the sport's ruling body was trying to dictate the rules as it went along during the FISA–FOCA war, Chapman, Ecclestone and the rest were to be far less accommodating; but in 1961 they did not have the organisation among themselves to be able to fight back.

Then, Chapman was concentrating on cars, not politics, and at the centre of his attention was the creation of the Lotus 21, the famous 'cigar-shaped' car in which, for the first time, the driver was expected to race from a 'lying' position. This was not immediately easy to adapt to for most drivers, but Chapman, though struggling with a massive workload, and who remained pugnacious and determined man at all times, knew it was a challenge that had to be overcome. Hence, during a test at Silverstone, he showed both his skill as a driver, and his acid wit, when he chose to demonstrate to Innes Ireland what real commitment meant. The story, recounted by Crombac, came from Dick Scammell, who said:

> Innes had been complaining about the car and so Colin got into it for a few laps. He just rolled up his sleeves and put on a crash helmet and by the end of his second lap he wasn't far off the time. On his third lap, he was on the time and on the fourth lap he was quicker. When he came in, Innes asked: 'What is it like when you really get on the brakes?' Colin replied: 'I didn't really get on the brakes because I'm not a racing driver, am I?'

In February 1961, Chapman recruited Andrew Ferguson, formerly with Cooper, as his competitions manager. It was an important development because Ferguson, experienced in racing in Europe in Formula Two and Formula One, who knew the circuits and the logistics and the costs well, was to play a prominent, arguably the most significant, part in the creation of the original Formula 1 Constructors' Association (known as F1CA, later to become FOCA), the forerunner to the modern Piranha Club. This happened in 1963, when the French federation planned a series of Formula Two races and wanted an entry agreement with the British teams. Lotus were involved, of course, and this meant Ferguson, backed by Chapman, played a leading role in the creation of an organisation known as the Formula Two Association. It negotiated terms with the French on the distribution of prize money and starting money based on a sliding scale of performances by the teams. In short, it was the junior blueprint for the future arrangements in Formula One and Ferguson was the first representative on behalf of such teams as Brabham, Cooper and Lotus who all saw the potential of applying the same principle of collective bargaining with their senior teams. BRM were invited to join them and the Formula 1 Constructors' Association was formed to negotiate the best deals with race promoters and reduce costs with organised travel arrangements. According to Ivan Rendall, in his book *The Power Game*, Ferguson was paid the princely fee of £15 per annum for his work.

Ferguson, of course, also played a prominent role at Lotus and threw light on the generous side of Chapman's nature when he recalled an incident in 1961 following a non-championship race at Pau in south-west France. Two mechanics, making unauthorised use of Chapman's rental car, had gone out for the night and been involved in a serious accident. Ferguson had to wake Chapman from a heavy sleep (he was taking pills) and escort him to the hospital where one mechanic had been admitted with a fractured skull. Together, they held him down while he was examined, after which Chapman had to find the car to recover his briefcase. Afterwards, back at Cheshunt, he called Ferguson and according to Crombac, the exchange went like this:

Chapman:	'You know what you have to do, don't you?'
Ferguson:	'Yes. I'll fire him.' (Ferguson said that is what he would have done at Coopers.)
Chapman:	'No, no. He's in a terribly bad way. So, make arrangements to fly his mother over to him.'

It was one example of Chapman's generosity of spirit. Equally, typically, he was able to misjudge when to exercise his generosity. At Monza, that year, for example, following the tragic Italian Grand Prix in which Jim Clark's Lotus collided with the Ferrari of Wolfgang von Trips, sending the German off through the fencing at the Parabolica and into the crowd, killing himself and 14 spectators, Chapman showed his affection and care for Clark. The Italian police had seized his car, but he was unhurt, though severely shocked. Chapman, the owner then of a Piper Comanche plane, decided to fly him home immediately, without giving the local police a chance to question him. This aggravated them badly and it was two years before Clark was cleared of any blame.

Another example of Chapman's enigmatic handling of situations and people came after the season-ending 1961 United States Grand Prix at Watkins Glen. Ferrari took no part, following von Trips' death and Phil Hill's championship win at Monza and this allowed Ireland to sweep home and record Team Lotus's first victory. It also confirmed the team's ascendancy over Cooper as the best Climax-powered car. Chapman was delighted and marked the occasion by throwing his cap in the air, a trademark action that was less spectacular than Cooper's somersaults, but just as effective. Afterwards, on the way back to New York in a private plane, Chapman and John Cooper were sitting together as they flew directly over the Empire State Building when the engine unexpectedly cut out. Showing remarkable coolness, Chapman reached down between the front seats to fiddle with a fuel switch and keep the engine running. Clark was on board this flight, but not Ireland. It was symbolic because, soon afterwards, at the London Motor Show in October, he was told that, despite his loyalty and talent, Lotus were not retaining his services for 1962.

To many this brusque dismissal of the man who had worked so hard and delivered his first works victory smacked of an unfeeling and ruthless nature that was often hidden by Chapman's charm. Ireland, who died in October 1993, was devastated.

> I never knew then and I still don't know to this day why I was dropped [he told Crombac]. Obviously, one can make various conjectures. I think one of the factors was that Colin never wanted to pay the full 'works' for two people and I had gone all the way through the business of the first 25 per cent of the starting money, then thirty-three and a third, and by 1961 I was on a full 50 per cent. I had always been faithful to Colin . . .
>
> I had tremendous faith in him and his design ability. I felt that if he was not a genius, then he was bloody close to being one. I never really raced for myself. It was all for Lotus. In those early days, there was not one journalist

writing kind words about Lotus. Chapman was very much the underdog and to me the challenge was 'by God, between Colin and I, we will make Lotus the top dog'. And by 1961, we were just beginning to see the light through the trees. At the end of 1959, I was asked to go with Graham Hill to BRM. But I didn't. Everybody was saying to me 'boy, you want to get out of Lotus – you'll kill yourself'.

You'll remember, I ran out of brakes four times in 1959 and once, at Rouen, I finished up 150 feet down a ravine. But, still, I felt 'if I leave Colin, he is not going to have anybody' and still I had this burning desire that, by God, we had to get it right. As an engineer myself, I knew he had terrific design ability and so my dismissal came as a very great blow to me and undermined many of the things in life which, up to then, I had always believed. You can imagine. It was the deepest upset I ever had – much more traumatic than my two divorces.

Moss, too, like Ireland, experienced the fragility of Lotus cars. (It was in a Lotus 18/21, prepared by British Racing Partnership (BRP) mechanics, as requested by Rob Walker –because his own team were at Pau on the same day to support Maurice Trintignant's victorious entry in the Formula Two race – that Moss crashed at Goodwood on Easter Monday, 23 April 1962. The impact at 105 mph, in front of 75,000 spectators, was shocking. He suffered a badly broken skull, a fractured leg and other injuries and his career was, effectively, ended. The exact cause of the accident was never found and a deal, arranged by Walker, for Moss to run in a Ferrari 156 through that World Championship season, also ended that day). Understandably, Moss said:

> I think Colin Chapman was a brilliant designer. But in my view, he did not give sufficient consideration to the problems that could arise if the car was driven very hard. If you drove a Lotus very hard, as was often necessary, then a wheel would fall off and this happened with me several times. In fact, unbeknown to me, Rob Walker was fitting new drive-shafts for every race because they were simply not strong enough . . .

Chapman found it difficult to dismiss Ireland. He performed the task reluctantly, at the motor show, only when confronted by Ireland. Chapman could only speak to him, said Ireland, while staring at the floor. He could not look him in the eye, but it was a decision he knew he had to take. By then, after all, he knew all about Clark. He believed in him in a quite different way to any other driver he worked with and, of course, the results were to support him.

In the following four years, from 1962 to 1965, of the 39 Grands Prix that took place, Clark, in a Lotus, won 19. He collected two drivers' world titles and only failed to take two more because of mechanical problems while leading in the final race of the season. Clark was the man who made Chapman's Lotus blossom; and he was the driver whose death left him more desperate than at any other time, changing his perspective on racing, accelerating his desire for success by almost any means and casting a shadow over all that followed. Chapman knew how to create a great chassis and where to find a great engine; in Clark he found the great driver that completed the list of three imperatives, cited by John Cooper, to make a perfect winning team. Clark's death took it all away.

From the start, Chapman surrounded himself with men of ambition, dogged determination, quality and vision. His powers of motivation, allied to his imagination and energy, did the rest. These qualities, indeed, pervaded his life and inspired all those around him, leaving his associates, friends and staff with memories of both the energising side of his complex personality and the curt, almost Machiavellian side. 'There was an excitement about him,' said Dan Gurney, who was instrumental in persuading Chapman to race his cars in America where, to his delight he discovered that considerable financial benefits were available for success in the technologically stagnant Indianapolis 500. 'He was a racer to the core and when you were part of his team, you realised that you were working with somebody who was redefining the edge of racing technology. That was a real motivating factor. Believe me.' In the United States, Clark almost won the 1963 Indianapolis 500 at the first attempt, retired while leading in 1964 and then came back to win outright in 1965.

Chapman and Clark were friends, too. This was not usual for Chapman and his business associates. Indeed, Chapman had more affection for Clark than probably anyone else in his racing career. In an interview with Nigel Roebuck, some 10 years after Clark's death, he said:

For me, Jimmy will always be the best driver the world has ever known. In time, probably, someone else will come along and everyone will hail him as the greatest ever, but not me. As far as I am concerned, there will never be another in his class. These days, of course, Grand Prix drivers are just that. They hardly ever race anything else. That's the way the sport has become, perhaps inevitably. But what you have to remember about Jimmy is that he excelled at everything. I think only Dan Gurney was a serious rival in Formula One, but think of Indy, of that sports car race at the Nurburgring with the little Lotus 23, of the saloon car races with the Lotus Cortina, Formula Two . . . Jimmy came close to retiring a couple of times, you know, and I had mixed feelings about that. On the one hand, the idea of going racing without him was almost unthinkable. On the other hand, I loved him as a human being and desperately didn't want him to get hurt. He had more effect on me than anyone else I've ever known. Forget his ability as a racing driver, and his association with Lotus. Forget everything he did for me in that sense. Jimmy was genuinely a good man. Intelligent, totally honest, and in many ways rather humble, it took him a long time to grow up, in the sense of who he was and what he'd done. I wasn't at Hockenheim that day. And, for some time afterwards, I was in a trance really. I've never lost my love of motor racing, but . . . at the same time I can't say I've ever felt quite the same about it since 1968.

This should be no surprise at all. That year was one of heartbreak and triumph for Chapman. His Lotus company produced more than 3,000 cars, made record profits of more than £730,000 and enabled him to go public, sell shares and become a millionaire. His Lotus 49B, pioneering aerodynamic progress in Formula One, was a winner. It carried Graham Hill to the drivers' championship and won for the team the Constructors' title. But it was also the year in which he lost Jim Clark.

Two years earlier, in 1966, when a three-litre formula was introduced for Formula One, Chapman had made a mistake and used BRM engines. He switched during the season to Climax V8s, after losing patience, and the Climax two-litre was given 32 valves. This struggle to find the right power-unit led, however, to another Chapman-inspired innovation that was to have a lasting influence on the sport, the creation of the Cosworth DFV engine for 1967. This was the unit to power the Lotus 49, the first car to use the engine as a part of a mono-coque structure, which won its first race, at Zandvoort, on 4 June, in the Dutch Grand Prix. The DFV engine, a power unit which Chapman had suggested Cosworth Engineering should build with £100,000 sponsorship from Ford, which he secured on their behalf, went on to become the most famous and suc-cessful in Formula One history.

Such innovative thinking was typical of Chapman. It had seen him move from the Lotus 21 and early space frame chassis to the monocoque design of the Lotus 25, in which Jim Clark won three races in 1962 and then the 1963 drivers' and constructors' world championship titles, registering seven victories on the way. The competition stood little chance, such was Chapman's dazzling blend of design flair, enterprising organisation and far-sighted thinking, not to mention the driving of Clark. The Lotus 25, however, owed its inception not to long days of cerebral labour, but to a typically Chapmanesque flash of inspiration. It came over lunch with Mike Costin and others at a restaurant at Waltham Cross, near Cheshunt, late in 1961. Chapman was working on how to resolve a problem with fuel tank layouts when he thought of a design for the first 'mono-coque' racing car and sketched it out on a table napkin.

'Why the devil don't we just take two fuel tanks and bolt the front suspension on to one end and the engine on to the other?' [he said, recalling his thoughts years later]. I remember drawing it on a paper napkin and then I rushed home and started drawing it up that night. Within a week, we had a working scheme out for it and we started building it right away.

Since then, every racing car has been influenced by Chapman's monocoque moment and every designer by his pioneering genius. The Lotus 49, in 1967, introduced the idea of using the engine as a stressed chassis member; the Lotus 72, in 1970, brought the 'wedge' shape; and the Lotus 79, in 1978, brought 'ground effects' aerodynamic systems. For the opposition, it was always a challenge to copy Lotus or fall behind. Chapman led, took risks, tested his fragile cars beyond their endurance and then built winners. Others followed.

Chapman was like a kaleidoscope, a package of many talents, each shining in different colours, at different times and sending out dazzling rays in different directions. He was moody, of course, dedicated to his pursuit of success, and an opportunist, too, in every way. Not only an engineer, he was also a businessman and an entrepreneur of formidable standing. Few could equal him and few could enjoy his level of vision. Thus, when Esso withdrew as a major backer of motor racing at the end of 1967 and the CSI lifted its ban on advertising, on cars, Chapman saw a chance to move swiftly and to profit. Thanks to a stroke of luck involving a former Lotus chief mechanic and one of his ex-girlfriends, Chapman signed Imperial Tobacco as Team Lotus's sponsor for 1968: Gold Leaf Team Lotus was born.

It was a move with far-reaching effects. Tobacco, then a common and popular habit, was to remain the chief source of funds for Formula One for more than 30 years and lead the sport into some of the most extraordinary and memorable controversies of the late twentieth century. Indeed, Formula One's apparent addiction to the weed has often appeared to be as difficult to break as the real thing for smokers hooked on a 20-a-day habit. The later arrival of the famous sleek black and gold livery of the 'John Players Specials' has always been seen, therefore, as spectacular confirmation that this was a seminal moment for Formula One.

Chapman, of course, had no real qualms about trading the patriotic image of his cars, in British racing green, for that of mobile cigarette packets. Tobacco sponsorship was the reward, to him and his team, for many years of hard work, diligent application of imagination and talent, and an unrivalled sense of commitment. It also carried him into the next development phase of the sport: the teams' struggle for organised unity and commercial recognition of their value. This was the time when Bernie Ecclestone came into his own and when Chapman, with so many talents to use, so many directions to follow, so many schemes to complete and commitments to fulfil, was unable to exercise the control, or give the time, that Ecclestone had available to scheme the campaign that led to an ultimate FOCA triumph in the FISA–FOCA war.

His reputation, however, meant that he always attracted massive interest from racing drivers. It was often said that there were many drivers who won, because they sat behind the wheel of a Chapman car; but there were only a few Chapman cars that won because of the man behind the wheel. When this happened, the driver was usually Jim Clark. The two names, Chapman and Clark, have remained almost synonymous in the history of Formula One, but as men they were an unusual couple: a brilliant engineer and charming street-wise salesman, from London; and a reserved, almost shy, Scottish farmer, with a gift for speed. Both loved motor racing and each understood the strengths and weaknesses of the other. When Chapman recruited Clark, he did so to strengthen his own team. The result was clear and the statistics speak for themselves: between the Dutch Grand Prix of 1960 and his death in a Formula Two race at Hockenheim in 1968, at the wheel of a Lotus 48, Clark contested 72 Grands Prix for Lotus, qualified on the front row 48 times, took pole 33 times and won 25 races. He recorded 28 fastest laps and won the drivers' world championship twice (1963 and 1965).

Understandly, Chapman was devastated by Clark's death, caused when the Scot's car went off a wet track at 125mph and hit a tree. The later championship success of Graham Hill was some, but little, consolation. 'The engine and transmission unit, with the rear wheels, finished some 20 yards away,' reported Louis Stanley, the man once described by the Ford chairman, Walter Hayes, as 'the Florence Nightingale of motor racing' for his work, as director general of the International Grand Prix Medical Service and as honorary secretary and treasurer of the Grand Prix Drivers' Association. Stanley flew to Germany with the Clark family lawyer in a Lear jet to investigate the accident. He said:

> The radiator was torn off. The nose section went into another tree. The steering column was broken, steering damper and brake fluid reservoirs were torn away. The tachometer read 7,200 rpm, equivalent to 125 mph on the gearing of the car. The throttle had jammed open due to a combination of maximum throttle cable pull and immense download on the linkage to the fuel unit. There was no evidence of pre-structural failure and Jim Clark was in no way to blame. Such details show how, structurally, today's racing cars have improved. At Hockenheim, Armco barriers would have prevented the Lotus plunging into the forest. Clark might have escaped with minor injuries ... In the sixties, the CSI were

reluctant to enforce elementary safety standards. As a result, our greatest racing driver was killed.

An alternative explanation came from Peter Jowitt, the RAC scrutineer asked by Chapman to investigate the accident. He said he 'found an oddly shaped cut in the tread of the rear right hand tyre. This cut went completely through the tyre, and I could not find any part of the wreckage which could have caused it.' Jowitt, who admitted that his relationship with Chapman at the time was best described as 'armed neutrality' (due to his objections to many of the Lotus cars at race meetings, some of which he had, as a scrutineer, rejected from the event) added:

> There are not too many men of the calibre of Jimmy Clark. I had to revise my view of Colin Chapman. He must have known that he could expect nothing but the unvarnished result of the investigation, but he was absolutely determined to have the truth, no matter how hurtful. He was not the 'Chunky' Chapman that the world normally saw. I felt that he was being tortured (not a word that I would use very frequently) by the thought that he had in some way contributed to the death of a man who was to him very much more than his team leader. I am fairly sure that if there had been some shortcoming, which in any way had caused this accident, he could have simply turned away from racing. Colin's grief was very private. He did not want the results of the investigation published and I think that they never were. The odd bald statement was put out, but that was Colin's way. In later years, I investigated the Jochen Rindt accident for Lotus. It is fair to say that this did not have the same shattering effect, even though it at one time made it appear possible that Colin Chapman could face manslaughter charges in Italy.

This report, by Jowett, was published for the first time in Graham Gauld's book *Jim Clark Remembered*.

To add further drama to the tragedy of Clark's death, there was a curious experience with the plane chartered to fly his body home from Frankfurt. Chapman, who had been skiing at St Moritz with his family at the time of the accident, was on the plane seated alongside the bier. About half an hour after take-off, the pilot's window smashed. According to Stanley, all pressure was lost and the plane had to descend and limp back to Frankfurt. There an emergency plan was put into action, ensuring the Scot, regarded as the greatest driver of his generation, flew home in dignity.

The accidents continued. In 1969, the season which saw the controversial use of full aerofoil wings fixed to the front and rear suspension uprights, there were more, notably those affecting Graham Hill and Jochen Rindt at the Spanish Grand Prix at Montjuich. Rindt suffered head injuries in his accident and went to hospital where he wrote, and released, a statement that expressed his totally negative views on the aerofoils as used by Lotus. Chapman was infuriated. His credo that Formula One was the competitive arena for pioneering technology was under threat. A meeting at the following Monaco Grand Prix, attended by all the executive committee members of the CSI available in Monte Carlo at the time, decided to ban the big wings in a move which was to define the future battlelines being drawn up for the FISA–FOCA war. To no avail, at around this time, Chapman also tried using four-wheel drive in his cars, an experiment he gave up. Graham Hill, back after seven years with BRM, also crashed after suffering a puncture, at Watkins Glen, and broke a leg.

A year later, Chapman experienced further tragedy when Rindt, managed by Ecclestone, was killed during practice at Monza. Rindt had a clear lead in the drivers' championship, which later proved to be enough for him to become the sport's first posthumous champion. He died in the final qualifying session when he braked while approaching the Parabolica. The car weaved and then turned left straight into the barriers, lifting a post with it as it went underneath. This was another shocking experience for Chapman who had been so convinced, by Rindt, that it was better to run the cars without wings, for higher speeds, that he had tried to persuade his team-mate John Miles to do the same, against his will. When the accident was reported to the Lotus pits, Ecclestone ran to the scene, but was unable to do anything for his friend. Rindt was killed instantly although the Italian authorities did not announce his death until his body had been removed and taken to hospital.

The steering wheel itself was prised through the instrument panel and it was this that had torn the front bulkhead out of the car [Peter Warr told Crombac]. Because he refused to wear the crotch straps of his seat harness, Jochen was forced down into the cockpit with his feet tangled up with the pedals and, in the process, his throat was cut by the harness.

Stanley, again, recalled a scene in hospital at Milan where Rindt, a very popular figure, had been declared dead in the operating theatre. He had actually died, as Warr explained, at the circuit when his Lotus 72, running without any rear wing, went out of control.

I left the theatre and walked down the corridor where Colin was waiting with Nina [Rindt] and Bernie Ecclestone. I had to break the news that Jochen was dead. His wife, drained of emotion, was impassive. Colin was in shock. After the Clark tragedy, his attitude to racing had become subdued. Rindt's death underlined the guilt feeling of being involved in a sport that caused meaningless loss of life. The passage of time helps, but it was never quite the same, even Emerson Fittipaldi's championship win in a Lotus lacked the old sparkle. The dilemma was one that we all had to face in those days.

After Rindt's death, Chapman flew his widow Nina back to their Geneva home immediately. All the Lotus cars were withdrawn from the race, including Graham Hill's entry in Rob Walker's new Lotus 72. An inquest started immediately and lasted several years. It was difficult for Chapman, two years after the deaths of Clark and Mike Spence (Clark's replacement who died in testing at Indianapolis), to face up to the whole bloody scenario unemotionally; and the Italians, as always in such circumstances, accused him of homicide. In the end, Chapman was cleared, on a technicality, and decided, of his own volition, to set up another independent investigation, which found that the brake shaft had broken, but this, in itself was not considered to be the cause of the accident. For some, like John Miles, it was merely a signal of the way things were.

They [the Lotus 72s] only came good after I left, following Rindt's accident. It was a pretty rotten period for me, all told, because I didn't feel as though I was in charge of my own destiny when I was a member of Chapman's team. As long as I was driving the Elans, the Type 47 or even the F1 Type 63 four-wheel-drive car, that nobody else had any interest in, I was okay. I felt in control. But once I got into the 72s, I knew I wasn't, partly because of the cars' frailty, partly because of the domineering way Chapman ran the team.

This reference to his domineering style of management was supported by the comments of others who worked for Chapman, particularly in the period after Clark's death. Another driver for Chapman, Jackie Oliver, later to be a team owner at Arrows and a long-time member of the Piranha Club, told Crombac he believed there had been two Chapmans – one before Clark's death and one afterwards.

I think Jimmy's death made Colin a much harder person ... Looking back, I think there was a 'phase one' Chapman, which existed before Jimmy died, followed by a 'phase two' Chapman afterwards, who took a complete change of direction.

Oliver, who drove nine Grands Prix for Lotus in 1967 and 1968, said Chapman was possessive and could be angry for illogical reasons.

Quite rightly, he saw that I was never going to be a true champion like some of his drivers, but on the other hand he clearly thought I was good enough that he did not want to lose me. He didn't want me to go to BRM and yet he could not offer me anything tangible. He was very angry when I left, but that was the style of the man; he had given me an opportunity for four years and then, even though it was he who had set his sights higher and was no longer able to offer me a Formula One drive, he still found it difficult to let me go. Generally, he was always friendly, and also his humour was always laced with the truth. For instance, if I had a crash with the car, he would dig me in the ribs and say 'another one like that and you'll be looking for a job. Ha, ha, ha'! All the time, there were innuendos in his humour ... Ken Tyrrell was, probably, the best team owner, when it came to bringing on new young drivers.

Colin was probably the worst. He would never spend time considering other people's difficulties and problems because he was too impatient. On the other hand, I think he was the only team owner to possess the three most important elements for success. He could find the money. He could design the cars. And he could run the team. Those three qualities in one man are quite exceptional.

Emerson Fittipaldi, driving a 72D, won the title again for Lotus in 1972, when the team also took the constructors' championship, a feat they repeated in 1973, before Mario Andretti, driving a 'ground effects' Lotus 79, complete with the controversial 'skirts', won both titles again in 1978. It was, however, not much to celebrate because the successes were overshadowed again by death, this time that of Ronnie Petersen in a blazing wreck at the start of the Italian Grand Prix, again at Monza, where a multiple collision in a confused start caused the Swede's car to bounce off the barriers. Amid chaotic scenes as the big crowd cheered the sight of the Ferraris leading the field on the opening lap, after a 20-minutes delay, Petersen was taken to hospital with two broken legs, but died that night in the operating theatre following complications. His departure from the race, and his death, handed the title to his team-mate Andretti, the man who, ironically, had quipped the previous year, when he led more laps than any other driver, that his Lotus 78 'felt like it was painted to the road'. Having crashed his Lotus 79 in practice, it was in a Lotus 78 that Petersen perished on that fateful afternoon. For Chapman, heavy with guilt and grief so often, it was another weighty burden and another source of sorrow. He reacted as ever, by burying himself in his work.

Indeed, by 1980, when the long-term sponsorship deal with Imperial Tobacco ended, Chapman had become distracted by the multiplicity of projects in which he was involved (including boat-building) and allowed his concentration, in Formula One, to wane. Essex Petroleum became major sponsors and their controversial chief executive David Thieme, who enjoyed an opulent lifestyle, became an influence on Chapman too. They had met at a sponsors' dinner in Monte Carlo. Chapman, intrigued by the style of an American resident, with connections to the oil business, maintained the contact and the sponsorship deal followed. Essex took over as main sponsors of the team and in February 1980 showed their style when they sponsored a party to introduce the Esprit Turbo at the Royal Albert Hall, in London. The entire place was turned into a dining room, there were clouds of dry ice, racing cars to be run in Formula One and the Indianapolis 500, food prepared by Roger Verge and the staff of the Dorchester Hotel, 1000 guests including, briefly, Prime Minister Margaret Thatcher (a great Chapman heroine) and entertainment from Shirley Bassey. The estimated cost was around one million American dollars. The following year, at the same venue, the singer was Ray Charles.

Thieme threw money around and offered lavish and spectacular hospitality at a time the FISA–FOCA war was on the horizon, following Balestre's election as FISA president, in October 1978, with a manifesto that stated his aim to be the restoration of the ruling body's authority over Ecclestone, the president of FOCA. This 'war' was created by a series of disputes over the regulations that had created instability in the sport, particularly following the introduction of turbocharged engines in the late 1970s. The scene was set with Balestre, supported by the rich 'grandee' manufacturers – Ferrari, Renault, Alfa Romeo – standing against calls from the British FOCA teams to have the turbocharged engines banned while also pushing for a ban on 'skirts', which helped the FOCA teams compensate through their reduced cornering speeds for a lack of turbo power. Chapman, as a great engineer and designer who could invent, was a fundamental force in the war and courted on both sides. Ecclestone regarded him as a very important part of FOCA, but this did not stop Balestre intervening too.

Indeed, but for careful reconsideration following a conspiratorial meeting with Balestre, Chapman might have been pushed into an attempt at taking control of FOCA at the height of hostilities in 1980. The suggestion of a coup d'état was put to Chapman by Balestre, following the rows over the technical regulations, in particular the banning of 'skirts' which exploited the 'ground effects' aerodynamics systems discovered and pioneered by Chapman, culminating in a non-championship FOCA-only 'Spanish Grand Prix' at Jarama, near Madrid, and a threatened boycott, by the FOCA teams, of the French Grand Prix. Balestre had fined 18 drivers for failing to attend his newly introduced and mandatory FISA-run pre-race briefings in Belgium and Monaco and, when the fines were not paid, he suspended their licences to race. In response, Ecclestone, on behalf of the FOCA teams, said they would not take part unless the fines were withdrawn. Balestre refused to moderate his position, the event was cancelled and then the local Federation Español de Automobilismo (FEA) decided to run an event, under FIA rules, with support from the FISA teams. Alfa Romeo, Ferrari and Renault declined and went home.

All this left Balestre angry and frustrated in his pursuit of total power over all motor racing, particularly Formula One. When a compromise was agreed following a meeting in Lausanne, Balestre rejected it and Ecclestone declared that the FOCA teams would break away and run their own series unless he changed his mind. Furious, Balestre began plotting Ecclestone's overthrow as head of the FOCA and, to do this, chose Chapman as his potential 'partner-in-crime'. He approached him at the Le Mans 24-Hours race where Chapman was visiting, as a guest of Thieme, for the first time since 1962, and invited him to talk in the FISA caravan. The Balestre proposal involved Chapman agreeing to a ban on 'slick' qualifying tyres, instead of skirts (which were to be outlawed from 1981), in return for ousting Ecclestone, following a consultative meeting with Enzo Ferrari in Italy. This, said Balestre, would lead the way to peace and the end of the civil war threatening to split the sport.

Chapman, with all the stealth of a master tactician, absorbed the proposal, flew back to England, chose not to oust Ecclestone and, instead, flew to Maranello to see Ferrari along with Max Mosley, FOCA's lawyer and negotiator. The outcome was another in a series of major meetings of the team owners and principals at Heathrow airport where Ecclestone accepted the offer to replace a ban on skirts with a ban on 'slicks' and also agreed to pay the vexed fines to FISA. The French Grand Prix went ahead but, although it was the end of any question of Chapman replacing Ecclestone, it was not the end of the FISA–FOCA war. Apart from anything else, it also reflected the fact that Chapman was a man of enormous importance and influence.

More controversies followed with particular rows about the 'twin-chassis' cars, ongoing disputes about ground-effect 'skirts' and moving aerodynamic devices, bans, fines, angry statements and three seasons in the doldrums (after eight victories in 1978, Lotus went winless until the Austrian Grand Prix of 1982) before Chapman threw his cap high for the last time following Elio de Angelis's triumph, barely inches ahead of the Williams of Keke Rosberg, at Zeltweg in August 1982. In this time, the bluster blew out of Chapman and a sense of disillusionment with the whole business seemed to settle, albeit fleetingly, over his view of Formula One. He still wanted to win and he remained competitive, but some of the ingenuity was knocked out of him by the politics and some of his enthusiasm went too, even if remained a formidable opponent and a far-sighted thinker. Enzo Ferrari, who respected Chapman as a great opponent in every way, recalled:

> We met up at the FOCA meetings which took place here at Modena. In the discussions, he displayed clarity of thought and great determination. Our last meeting was in January, 1981, when we launched the famous Concorde agreement for the regularisation of Formula One.

Yet, it is a tribute to his engineering vision and success, despite his reputation for creating fragile cars and possessing a personality that may have been as much demonic and ruthless as it was charming and generous, when required, that he attracted a series of racing drivers of the highest talents to his team. Clark, Hill, Jochen Rindt, Ronnie Peterson, Mario Andretti, Nigel Mansell and Emerson Fittipaldi were all associated with victories for Chapman. So, too, was Stirling Moss who, driving for Rob Walker, recorded the first victory of a Lotus in the Monaco Grand Prix of 1960, albeit in a privately entered car. Ayrton Senna won, also, for Lotus, after Chapman's death, but during the time when some of the magic remained within the team.

As Chapman's empire had grown, he too had raised his aspirations and expectations in life. In 1966 he had moved Lotus Cars from Cheshunt to Wymondham in Norfolk, and settled his family into a mansion house nearby at East Carleton. Increasingly stretched in all areas, many said he was a workaholic who never knew when to stop. Charming, energetic, visionary, enthusiastic, ambitious, he was driven to the next step, the next deal and the next car all the time, his vaulting sense of his own destiny not allowing him to carry passengers or prisoners nor to miss any opportunity. This above all is what supplied the energy at Team Lotus, where he achieved greatness as a Formula One team owner and as a truly influential member of the 'club' in its years of development, bringing

major team sponsorship into the sport, supporting the entrepreneurial activities of Ecclestone and the organisation of the
business, and which also took him into the DeLorean debacle
which may, to some degree certainly, have contributed to his
death.

The saga which turned scandalous began when John
DeLorean decided he wanted to build a stainless steel 'supercar'
in depressed Belfast and the British Government supplied £54
million (pounds) in funding. The Lotus Group was engaged as a
major consultant. The rest was easy to understand; such huge
funding, argued the cynics and investigators, had to provide an
equally big temptation to all involved as it found its way into,
they suggested, the pockets of such men as DeLorean himself,
Chapman and others including Fred Bushell, of Lotus. Court
proceedings followed in which Bushell was involved, but by the
time the case was uncovering each act and scene of the
'DeLorean Affair', Chapman was dead. A judge, reportedly,
remarked that if Chapman had been alive to face charges, he
would have been sent to jail for 10 years for his part in an 'out-
rageous and massive fraud'.

Many observers believe he worked himself to death. Aged
only 54, he died from a totally unexpected, but massive heart
attack, leaving a chasm behind in his business and in the complex life he had built up around him. He left behind a family
stunned and shattered by their loss, a wonderful, innovative
company making some of the finest cars in the world, an engineering heritage that remained with Lotus, supporting claims to
technical ingenuity long afterwards, and a resounding impact
on Formula One. On the debit side there was financial chaos
and debt, allegations of wrong-doing and wild risk-taking, a
weakness for unrestrained behaviour, bad tempers and over-
bearing management. There were many examples of what
were known as 'Chapman incidents' yet those who worked
around him remained loyal and full of admiration.

In one so-called Chapman incident, at Zandvoort, he became
embroiled in a row with a policeman who barred his way on to
the track before the Dutch Grand Prix. A scuffle followed,
Chapman became embroiled and was pushed over a straw bale.
He recovered, stood up and then threw a solid punch at the
Dutch policeman who fought back. Chapman, realising the use-
lessness of the situation, retreated, but it was too late. Later,
after he had seen his Lotus win the Dutch Grand Prix, he was

approached again by the police and asked to go with them to their station. He said he would not go and another fight followed, during which he tore his shirt. Hazel Chapman, who was there, was hit with a punch. Mechanics moved in and there was a brawl. When Chapman broke free, he ran to the control tower. There, eventually, he was arrested, but refused to spend the night in jail and, finally, he slept overnight in a waiting room before appearing in court in Haarlem. Finally, he was fined £25 after having his fingerprints taken by the police. To many with recollections of that time, it was a typical Chapman incident.

'I think he was an inspirational, intuitive engineer,' said Peter Warr, his right-hand man and manager at Team Lotus, who recruited the Frenchman Gerard Ducarouge as technical director following Chapman's death.

> Nothing was impossible. He would take his immense knowledge and understanding of vehicles, aeroplanes and all things technical and refuse to accept that anything he wanted to do could not be done. He had an almost intellectual arrogance. He would often go against the opinion of respected engineers who held contrary views. His supreme talents were then, first, to make it happen and, second, to motivate the people who had to do the job to believe that it was not only possible, but that it could be done in half the time they reckoned and that it would offer an unbelievable advantage. That's how he got people to perform miracles.

Typically, when news of his untimely death was broadcast, Lotus were testing his latest great technical innovation – active suspension – a feature that was not to be fully developed or totally successful until a decade later when Nigel Mansell, a driver given his first chance in Formula One, was to lift the drivers' title in an 'active' Williams car in 1992.

John Miles, who drove 12 races, some more pleasurable than others, for Lotus in 1969 and 1970, said:

> He combined a very high level of theoretical engineering qualification with a strong instinct about what was right. And, he had an opportunistic streak, enabling him to grasp things which were often accidents – the most notable being ground-effect aerodynamics . . . I didn't have a great

deal to do with him socially, like most of his drivers. We came from such different backgrounds that I found we just couldn't converse on any subject outside cars. I just wish I'd known as much about engineering as I do now, because I could have made a more significant contribution on that front ... When I was sacked, without my knowledge, I have to say that I would have appreciated it if he had done it, rather than hearing about it from Peter Warr. But then, that was the way he worked. He would never do it himself. I suppose he was a bit of a coward ...

Innes Ireland, sacked by Chapman after being the driver to have delivered Team Lotus's maiden Grand Prix victory, was also equivocal in his summary of the man whose massive range of talents provided much of the energy behind the early days of the Piranha Club. He said:

I suppose he was always close to genius in his design ability, but his manufacturing ethics left a great deal to be desired. By that, I mean the machining and so on, the attention to detail in the car's finish. In my view, there was no great engineering skill in the actual execution of the components. I saw this more than most because I served an engineering apprenticeship with Rolls Royce ... I always felt I was racing as much for Lotus, as for myself. Probably even more. So, when he fired me, it came as a double-blow, shaking my basic faith in humanity. After that, Formula One lost a great deal of its meaning for me.

The death of Colin Chapman was not the death of Lotus. The team which had enjoyed two successful decades of innovation and success in the 1960s and the 1970s, which had slid away in the early 1980s and then been revived by the sublime talent of a young Ayrton Senna, struggled on into a painful spiral of financial failures in the 1990s. Senna followed Nigel Mansell and won his first Formula One victory in the rain at Estoril in Portugal in 1985 and recorded the final Lotus victory at Detroit in 1987 in the 'active-ride' 98-T.

In Chapman's wake, Peter Warr became the first of several men to take the reigns as team principal. For them all, it was a thankless and difficult challenge. Warr (1982–89), Tony Rudd (1989–90) and Peter Collins (1991–94), as well as Horst

Schiebel, who worked with Collins in 1991–92, found the task beyond them. The sport was changing rapidly, growing into an industry of global dimensions, in which only the biggest and best-funded teams with corporate partnerships and support could survive. Chapman was a man of such extraordinary, breathtaking talent and vision that, in his era, he could juggle the demands made on his engineering brilliance with those made on his abilities in business.

In both areas, Lotus were unable to find the right successors or the right chemistry. A series of men took control in the role of chief designer or technical director, many of them brilliant. But more than brilliance was needed at Lotus. Chapman had combined brilliance with charm, vision with flair, innovation with entrepreneurial energy and all this with a decent measure of cunning and chicanery. Maurice Phillippe (1970–75), Ralph Bellamy (1974 and 1976–78), Martin Ogilvie (1978–83) and Peter Wright (1980–82) all worked with Chapman as designers before his death. Afterwards, Gerard Ducarouge (1983–88), Mike Coughlan (1989), Frank Dernie (1989–90), Enrique Scalabroni (1991), Frank Coppuck (1991), Peter Wright and Chris Murphy (both 1992–94) followed.

It is no criticism of them to say they were not at Chapman's level; but it is fair, also, to say that the financial chaos that enveloped the team in the 1990s was not of their making, nor the making of any of the team principals who carried the heavy baton. The confusion of the 'DeLorean affair' and the financial controversies left by the associations with Essex made it difficult for Team Lotus to attract the kind of major support from an international partner that was needed. At the very time when the landscape was moving around them, they had no help to stay alert, competitive and mobile themselves and, in an irony that is pregnant with heavy significance, were left immobile, heavy-footed and weighed down by often anachronistic machinery as they slid gently, inexorably and sadly down the grid towards oblivion.

In his book *Strictly Off the Record*, Louis T. Stanley described Chapman as 'a one man legend'. It was apt and accurate.

> From . . . modest beginning [he explained] grew the Lotus Group of companies with ultra-modern factories, test-track facilities, runways for aircraft, boat-building plant and Ketteringham Hall, an impressive country home and

estate. Of the many projects, Colin concentrated on Team Lotus with its separate financial existence alongside the publicly quoted Lotus Group. Colin's obsession was justified with 72 world championship Grand Prix victories, five drivers' world championships, six constructors' world championships and an Indianapolis 500 victory. Enough to satisfy most mortals, but not Colin. Mentally and physically restless, he kept experimenting with innovations. His robust constitution was tested to the limit. Eventually the strain took its toll. After a meeting of the Formula One Commission, in Paris, he flew home to Norwich that evening. In the early hours of the morning, a massive heart attack proved fatal. The responsibility of designing cars, running the Formula One racing team, managing the companies in a competitive market, and the controversial DeLorean deal, proved too much. At 54 years, he was burnt out with overwork. Maybe delegation might have helped, but that was not Colin's way.

And so John Cooper and Colin Chapman, their cars, teams and eras, were different, yet overlapping, equally significant, but in quite differing ways, in the evolution of this group of men who created Formula One. They were a pioneering British element that overlapped a watershed in the sport. One was a mechanic, at heart, and the other was an engineer. One was a pure racer, but with the heart of an ordinary fellow; the other was a complex fellow with manifold business and design and engineering interests, but with the heart of an ordinary racer. One was not in the slightest way political; but the other could not avoid involvement in every scheme afoot. One worked from the south of the Thames, the other from the north; one released control of his business and eased out of the spotlight when the time felt right while the other worked on, carrying an ever-increasing and stressful burden, until it killed him.

Cooper, in April 1965, ensured his company kept racing by merging, for £250,000, with the Chipstead Motor Group, headed by Jonathan Sieff, a scion of the Marks & Spencer store chain. Ironically Sieff had raced at Le Mans for Lotus and had been badly injured in 1960 (driving an Elite, he suffered a monumental crash on the Mulsanne straight because of a puncture caused by a mechanic fitting an ordinary inner tube to a rear tyre, instead of a racing tube, the crash throwing him over a wall and into a neighbouring garden). 'I was getting to the stage when I knew we'd have to give up motor racing because of the cost,' said Cooper. 'Jonathan Sieff saved us really. He had the money. So, the deal was done.'

Cooper stayed on, then, to be managing director and Salvadori stayed to be racing manager. Soon afterwards, the racing department of the business was moved to Byfleet. The Surbition garage remained as a Mini-Cooper servicing station. People, for years, would drive by and, almost absent-mindedly notice it and remark on its ordinariness. Cooper himself would have laughed, but by the mid-1960s, as Chapman and Lotus were rising to their pomp, he was struggling to identify the reasons he had been drawn to motor racing and Formula One in the first place.

> It isn't quite what it was, is it? [he asked Derek Jewell]. Take Fangio. That was driving. Tyre-smoke. Opposite lock on the corners and all that. Driving on the seat of his pants. But now Jim Clark, he lies in the car and he looks like he's going at half-speed, it's so smooth. It's more like driving a plane. You go into a corner at certain revs and you come out at certain revs. Scientific driving. It's brilliant all right, but it doesn't look anything. And racing is suffering because it doesn't. It's a different game on the inside too. In the old days, it was good fun. People did it because they liked it. Now, it's just a business. Just that.

It might have been a remark from any man who was a member of the Piranha Club from any era. It was always a business, striving to be more professional, more rewarding for the teams and the organisers, with better facilities, attracting greater interest and bigger prizes. Cooper and Chapman played their parts in different ways, each calculating their risks in contrasting methods. By 1966, Cooper was still proud to talk of his cars' safety record even if, at the same time, he was attempting to match Chapman by proving he could run a resourceful business with a more scientific approach just as competitively against the slide-rule efficiency of Lotus.

Before that season began, Cooper said: 'Mark you, whatever happens, everyone has go to find himself a driver capable of staying on the road and not killing himself.' At the time, Cooper had never lost a team driver in racing and was comfortable with the record. He knew that of the 16 men who lined up at the start of the 1958 Monaco Grand Prix, won by Maurice Trintignant, seven were dead and three so badly injured they were never to race again . . . but none of them died in a Cooper.

5 Bernie

Some call him the ringmaster. Others refer to him simply as Mr E. He is talked of as the Tsar of Formula One and written about every day. Some talk in awed tones of his power and his achievements. Others simply melt into silence in his presence. He has the humour of a perfect ice-cold dry Martini and a repertoire of wicked one-liners. To some in the paddock, his gleaming grey motor home is described as the 'Kremlin'; to others it is a place of laughter and fun. He is extraordinarily ordinary and amazingly rich. He can talk to anyone in a direct and straight fashion. He is a generous and loyal friend to those he trusts and the enemy nobody wants to have. His career has been surrounded by speculation and intrigue, mostly based on nothing more than rumour and hearsay. But he has achieved astonishing things. He is the master of his world and his world is Formula One. To most people who know him, he is Bernie.

When his mobile phone rings and he takes a call, it could be from anyone; he knows and does business with celebrities, businessmen, industrialists, financiers, politicians, statesmen, prime ministers, presidents and royalty. He treats them all alike. He has made things happen where others saw no life and he has turned dreams into reality for himself and a group of men who, otherwise, may have achieved much less. When Colin Chapman was fighting on several fronts to keep his business empire and racing team afloat, and ahead of the baying pack, Ecclestone was squinting through the whiff of academic and political grapeshot, in the struggle for control, and beyond the technological confusion of the arguments over the rulebooks. He could see a different kind of future. He had a vision that grew to magnificence in the final years of the twentieth century as Formula One spread its influence across the television audiences of the world, captivating millions of viewers, seducing corporate multinational sponsors and drawing the power and wealth of the automotive manufacturers inexorably into its orbit.

Ecclestone's Formula One vision grew not from sole personal ambition or financial greed, but from a deep desire to race, for the exhilaration of it all, and to succeed; and to do these things, he felt he had to have efficiency and proper organisation. He had no grand plans, but moved from one smart deal to the next, accumulating his profits, gathering his wealth, preparing for the challenges and ventures ahead. Driven by an almost insatiable appetite for organisation, information and achievement and a restless energy to build something with his life, he turned his curiosity to his advantage, overcame his lack of physical stature by exercising one of the sharpest minds into an unstoppable force. As others honed their bodies to perfection, he created an empire of businesses interlocked around the spectacle that fascinated him and hundreds of millions around the world.

His brilliant brain, natural salesmanship, clever negotiating skills and innate sense for a deal have set him apart from everyone else to have turned a Swiss franc, a French franc, a dollar or a pound in Formula One. Only Enzo Ferrari and Chapman rose to his highest expectations and levels of respect as men to whom he would doff his cap, if he were in the habit of demonstrating such feelings; but Ecclestone does not work in such formal fashion, though he is old-fashioned in many of his habits and his belief that a deal can be sealed with a handshake. Honour remains a living word in his vocabulary and for that he has many friends. Anonymity, too, is sought whenever possible, but rarely found. He declines to have his name entered in *Who's Who*. His addresses and phone numbers are ex-directory. Calls to his offices are answered by a voice reciting only the final digits of the telephone number. He gives himself no title. Nor does he ask for one.

Many say he is an autocratic dictator, but others talk of him more as a benevolent despot. The truth is somewhere between the two, or it has been. As time passes and the Piranha Club welcomes more and more younger men, rich former racing drivers backed by corporations, or clever executives and entrepreneurs from the world's biggest car companies, his role is slowly diminishing, his grip on the game relaxing. He is no longer the 'micro traffic cop, posted at the crossroads of Formula One' as Thomas O'Keefe described him for Atlas F1 at the turn of the century. He is not surrounded by men in oily overalls any longer, but by men in sharp suits and shiny shoes. Once a racer, he has had to become a controller and a mogul, but he has done so without losing his common touch and his ability to relate to, and understand, the man behind the wheel. Yet, inside him, he knows that in creating the monster that modern Formula One has become he has destroyed the old quasi-Corinthian sport with which he fell in love in the 1950s.

In his long career in Formula One, since buying the Brabham team in 1971, he has seen and achieved more than most and his achievements have helped create the wealth that lubricates the modern business of the highest echelon in international motor racing. Yet his blunt honesty and his expectations cause friction and sometimes pain. In 1993, for example, while talking to reporters at the Portuguese Grand Prix in Estoril, where Alain Prost had announced his decision to retire at the end of that season after winning his fourth drivers' world title, Ecclestone upset the sensitivities of the sporting world when he lambasted the Frenchman for his casual use of Formula One for his own ends and referred also to what he called the natural culling of drivers in the past. He explained afterwards that he was emphasising his point that Formula One would survive, as it had always done, whether great or champion drivers chose to continue or to retire, as Prost had done when he learned, angrily, that his future team-mate at Williams-Renault in 1994 would be Ayrton Senna, not Damon Hill, if he continued. Nigel Mansell had retired the year before, after winning the title with Williams, for exactly the same reason: except that the incoming driver was Prost. This was typical Ecclestone.

> I didn't imagine Prost leaving would make much difference because he had decided to clear off before at the end of 1991 and nobody had remembered him then [he explained]. It's a fact. So then the subject moved on to other drivers leaving and I told another two journalists that in the old days, one or two drivers would get killed each year. But, I said, thank God that doesn't happen any more because we've spent fortunes and done a lot of research to make the cars safe. The point I was making was that, when these drivers were killed, the sport kept going. So, in answer to the original question, it's the same if a driver retires. Formula One will survive. Life is like that. It's

Formula One itself that's most important. It's greater than any individual.

He was reported to have used the expression 'a form of natural culling', but later denied this. 'It's unfair to suggest I don't care about the drivers because it's not true,' he said. 'I would rather see them retire. I don't want to see them killed.'

Little more than six months later, Ecclestone and Formula One experienced their blackest weekend in modern times when on successive days Roland Ratzenberger and Ayrton Senna were killed at the 1994 San Marino Grand Prix at Imola. To those who had felt hurt by his remarks in Portugal, this was a bleak reminder of the truth. Ecclestone's reference to culling, intended, accurate or otherwise, was honest and meaningful and the global shock and grief manifested by this double tragedy was a salutary lesson that confirmed the theme of his message, even if his view that the cars were safer proved to be wrong. It also challenged the sport, through the offices of the Fédération International de l'Automobile (FIA) president, Max Mosley, to shift its moral stance and work even harder on maximising progress on safety, a political swing that reflected the mood of the modern world and one which has been followed diligently by Mosley ever since.

For Ecclestone, however, this was not the first experience of death at the track. Nor the first loss of a good friend. The Brazilian, like many in the Formula One paddock had grown close to the small man (he is five feet and four inches tall) behind the tinted spectacles, the figure in the crisply creased white shirts and dark trousers who controls his empire from the anonymous modern nine-storey office building overlooking Hyde Park (purchased from Adnan Khashoggi for £7 million) or from the steel-grey motor home in the paddock where deals are done with a handshake. They shared many interests in common and enjoyed one another's company. Ecclestone had not wanted to be close friends again with drivers, after earlier experiences, but he was with the charming and fascinating Latin American who won the drivers' world championship three times and established himself as the greatest racing driver of modern times.

In earlier times, he had suffered when he lost his close friend Stuart Lewis-Evans, a modest, slightly built man, born in 1930, who raced in 14 Grands Prix for Connaught and Vanwall in 1957 and 1958 and whose performances promised improving results. Lewis-Evans died, from terrible burns, after a crash in Casablanca during the 1958 Moroccan Grand Prix. Ecclestone had managed Lewis-Evans's business affairs and, after walking away from motor racing, he came back to do the same for Jochen Rindt, the mercurial Austrian, who crashed and died during practice at the 1970 Italian Grand Prix, afterwards becoming Formula One's only posthumous world champion driver. Ecclestone was there and saw how Rindt died, his seat-belt buckle slashing his throat as he slid into the cockpit of his Lotus because he refused to wear crutch straps.

He was also close to Carlos Pace, another Brazilian, who raced for him when he was running Brabham in the 1970s, who died in an air crash in 1976, and Pedro Rodriguez, who died in a sports car race at the Norisring in Germany in July 1971. And he was around to understand the horror of the deaths of men like Roger Williamson, François Cevert, Mark Donohue, Tom Pryce, Ronnie Peterson, Patrick Depailler, Gilles Villeneuve, Ricardo Paletti and Elio de Angelis; not to mention the count-less accidents, including those which left their marks on Clay Regazzoni, Niki Lauda, Didier Pironi, Frank Williams and Martin Donnelly; and the deaths in an aircraft crash of Graham Hill, Tony Brise and five team members at Elstree in 1975.

In short, Ecclestone had lived with death among his closest companions for 40 years before the sport's critics began to pour forth their moral indignation. He had pushed, along with men like Louis Stanley and Jackie Stewart and many others, includ-ing Sid Watkins in latter years, for constantly improved stan-dards of safety. He may also have organised the teams, created a circus that could negotiate en bloc for much higher entry fees and prize money, created a television audience that, after 1994, soared beyond 200 million viewers worldwide for each Grand Prix and turned the ramshackle rich man's pastime of the 1960s, when 'culling' was accepted by many as a grim risk accepted by all participants, into a slick and professional busi-ness that set higher standards in every respect than virtually every other major sport, and along the way become a multi-millionaire, but he had done it by dint of his own vision, bril-liance in business and extraordinary hard work.

If Imola in 1994 saw many viewers appalled by their own macabre fascination in what they were watching, if it drew them into an illogical desire to criticise the sport and its

141

circus-master, it also stimulated a new growth in interest and a new momentum for ever-improved standards of safety. Ecclestone, shrewd and perceptive, took the opportunity to create his own digital television empire at this time, further swelling his own portfolio of businesses, but by taking his own financial risks and offering the teams and the sport a bigger and better return on their own investments. He did not stop to stand and stare, to reel away upset and confused by the gore, as he had in Casablanca and Monza, but, instead, he stood firm through the popular backlash, the hurtful mass of emotional reaction in Sao Paulo when he flew there for Senna's funeral, and helped guide Formula One to new levels of security, safety, organisation and popularity. To Ecclestone, excellence is always the key. He likes to enjoy success. He has a strong interest in winners, champions and leaders. He cares little for the argument that if one team, or one man, is dominant then the show is boring and lacking spectacle.

> When tennis was at its best [he said], you had Borg winning. With boxing, it was Ali winning everything. Everyone wants to see that. They don't care if the favourite wins. But, just in case he gets beaten, they want to be there. People go to see the event and it is the same with Formula One . . .

His views are simple and understandable. He likes a simple life, often preferring a sandwich to a lavish meal (although years of exercising a weakness for smoked salmon and, it is said, Christmas pudding, probably contributed to the need for a heart by-pass in 1999). He is very conservative and traditional in many ways, but capable of a bold and daring decision. He is loyal to his friends, supports his colleagues and associates when they need it and has helped many mechanics and team owners when financial collapses have followed an over-spending campaign in Formula One. In his earlier career in Formula One, when he was president of FOCA, he was often rumoured, always out of his earshot, to have been associated with, or masterminded, the famous Great Train Robbery in England, in 1963. It is a piece of tittle-tattle that is laughable, but which is repeated. Ecclestone sued after a book and a magazine made the allegations.

'I didn't rob the train and I wasn't a part of it,' he said. Asked why the story survives, he explained that one of the gang, Roy 'the weasel' James, a racing driver in his earlier days, wrote to Graham Hill from jail. Hill was driving for Ecclestone at the time. James, he said, had wanted to return to the sport, but Ecclestone told him it was an impossible dream after 12 years in prison. When he discovered that James was a trained silversmith, he commissioned a trophy from him on his release. Like Colin Chapman, Ecclestone was capable of demonstrating that he is as tender as he is tough, depending on the circumstances.

He is also capable of patience and perfect timing. For years, he remained loyal to the BBC who had broadcast Formula One since 1953. But when the time was right, in 1997, he switched to ITV without batting an eyelid. The deal increased the five-year revenue from British television rights from £7 million to £70 million. For Ecclestone, it was a straightforward decision and a straightforward deal. 'It's Bernie Ecclestone and that's it,' said Andrew Chowns, who negotiated on behalf of ITV. 'I haven't known him long, but I find him incredibly decisive.' The BBC was aghast at the speed of the deal and left floundering. When a BBC's senior sports executive phoned to complain that he had not had time even to make a counterbid, Ecclestone told him: 'Sorry. But I knew you wouldn't be able to afford it.' Ecclestone had done his deal and he honoured it. He did not barter.

Such sums of money do not daunt Ecclestone. He lives through them and through the deals. Yet, though he is a rich man, he is not ostentatious. He may have a collection of old racing cars, but he is as likely to be seen doing the family shopping at his local Chelsea supermarket and driving away in an ordinary Audi estate as reclining in a 'supercar'. He enjoys ordinary chores, dries his own dishes, relishes more than anything else the company of his lissom-limbed wife Slavica, a former model for Giorgio Armani from Rijeka, in Croatia, who is six feet and two inches tall, as well as nearly 30 years younger than her husband, and their two daughters, Tamara and Petra.

His courtship of Slavica Malic, according to a report by John Drayton, revealed the softer side of Ecclestone. It began in 1981 when Slavica attended the Italian Grand Prix at Monza, to model leisure clothes. Ecclestone saw her on the pit-wall, looking bewildered, and invited her to his motor home to cool off with a Coca-Cola. She spoke no English. He spoke no Italian.

They communicated through an interpreter, a girlfriend of Slavica's who spoke both languages. She left her number with him, but when he attempted to call her, he could not make the numbers work. According to Drayton, he even rang the Italian police to ask for their help, but without avail.

A few days later, it was said, Slavica mentioned the Englishman she had met at Monza to an Italian photographer and showed him his card. Immediately, he knew who Ecclestone was and they phoned him. Ecclestone invited Slavica to the Las Vegas Grand Prix, she accepted and they met in New York and flew together from J.F. Kennedy airport to Las Vegas. On this flight, Slavica was quoted saying, 'something happened' and they fell in love. Ecclestone then paid for her to enrol for a crash course in English in Milan where she remained based for her modelling work until 1985. Their marriage, following their wedding at Chelsea Registry Office in 1985, has been as happy and successful as any played out in the suffocating pressure-cooker of modern Formula One.

Slavica is one of the few people around Ecclestone who takes decisions for him or tells him what to do. She will sometimes order his food, in foreign restaurants, particularly Italian. Ecclestone told the *Sunday Times* as a joke this was because 'I don't speak Italian, or anything else. I reckon that anyone who doesn't speak English isn't worth speaking to!' Slavica is more than just a wife to Ecclestone. His wealth is tied up in a trust in her name. Effectively, she is worth something in the region of £2 billion or more – she is one of the richest women in England. As Ecclestone said, 'I gave everything I had to Slavica three or four years ago. Lucky woman. She needed a new hat. And I'm not likely to have any more wives now.'

His light explanation covers the truth. He wanted to secure a comfortable, indeed luxurious, future for her and their daughters and to avoid any punitive taxes on his estate if he died. She said that she cared little for business, or money, or Formula One and, like her husband, detested the way in which she had been misrepresented in some areas of the media. 'I will never be a businesswoman,' she explained. 'One day, if I go back to Croatia, I will live on an island and I will catch small fish from my boat and be happy. I would never want to run Formula One.' And, she told the *Sunday Times*, she was angry with her Croatian newspapers. 'The allegations by those papers in my country, that I was a Yugoslav honey spy, that I was told to meet Bernie ... what rubbish.' In common with Ecclestone, she worked hard to make money in her life because her father, a fireman, divorced her mother when she was only seven. Both are as streetwise as any wealthy couple in the world.

'I don't make money, I make deals,' he has said. It sums things up neatly, but hides a multitude of sins like his preferred use of company director as his occupation in his passport. His deals, however, can range from the smallest to the biggest. Once, at the Australian Grand Prix in Albert Park, Melbourne, he arrived on Sunday morning to find that the pit aprons were damp and slippery, causing the teams trouble at pit stops and prompting fear of a serious accident. Taking command of the situation personally, while on a tour with various VIPs, he ordered the purchase of several large rolls of heavy tape. Not, he added, in black, white or grey, but in every colour available to ensure that when the adhesive strips were laid down on the aprons they were visible in team colours – red for Ferrari, blue for Williams and so on. He was even seen, brandishing a large pair of scissors, cutting the tape and positioning it, on his hands and knees, to demonstrate what was required. Such attention to detail typifies him.

After Senna's death, it was Ecclestone who brokered the deal for Nigel Mansell to return to Formula One for a few selected races alongside Damon Hill; when Michael Schumacher burst on the scene, Ecclestone engineered his switch from Jordan to Benetton; he also set up the move which took Jacques Villeneuve from Indycar racing in the United States to Williams, in the summer of 1995 and smoothed many other 'transfers' that enlivened the business, or helped avoid trouble, when the time seemed right. He also considered a £1.5 billion flotation of his Formula One interests, which did not go through, the subsequent share sales that led to German owner-ship of SLEC, the Ecclestone family trust named after his wife (SLavica ECclestone), which owns Formula One Holdings (and so, through this, embraces, it is understood, the entire empire of Ecclestone interests in Formula One), the dialogue, with Max Mosley alongside him, with the European Commission to solve any problems arising from the alleged monopoly position he enjoyed, in the late 1990s, when the relationship between the sport's ruling body, the Fédération Internationale de l'Automobile (FIA), and its long-term commercial rights holder, Ecclestone, through SLEC, was under scrutiny.

It was, of course, also the same Ecclestone and Mosley who went to Downing Street on 16 October 1997 for tea with Tony Blair, accepting a return invitation that had followed the Prime Minister's visit with his family to the British Grand Prix at Silverstone as Mosley's guests in 1996. It also followed the donation by Ecclestone of a £1 million gift to the Labour party made six months after Blair had been entertained in the famous 'Bernie bus' and driven around the Northamptonshire circuit by Damon Hill prior to the race. None of this came to become public knowledge, however, until after the Blair Government announced it was not supporting the pledge of its Health Secretary Frank Dobson, to ban all tobacco advertising and sponsorship, and was instead to give Formula One a special dispensation of eight years in which to withdraw from its seeming dependence on the tobacco industry's largesse (introduced, originally, by Chapman's Gold Leaf Team Lotus in 1968).

The revelations, when made, caused a furore which after an investigation by the parliamentary standards watchdog, Lord Neill, led to the money being returned and Blair apologising on television. Ecclestone received it, but did not bank it for four months. Cool? Yes. Self-consciously cool or pre-meditated? No. In an interview on 18 December 1997 he told me: 'We're very busy at the moment . . . I must speak to the accountants. I don't know when they sent it to me. Maybe we'll put it in the bank after Christmas.' He dismissed the discussions in Downing Street as of little importance, but said he was disappointed with Blair.

> I wasn't asking for anything when I was invited to go and see him. We had a general discussion. I don't remember it because I didn't record the conversation and I don't remember things that are of little, if any, importance to me. I went with Mosley and he did most of the speaking. It was nothing to do with asking for anything from anybody . . .

This is not glib talk. Ecclestone is used to dealing with politicians and government decision-makers. Once, while escorting a party of reporters around his new digital television compound (into which he has invested around £100 million of his own money) at the Circuit de Catalunya, near Barcelona, on the eve of the Spanish Grand Prix, he was interrupted by a call on his mobile phone. Taking the call, briefly, he said: 'Who is it? Okay, okay. Just tell him to hang on for a while. I'll be there in ten minutes or so.' Afterwards, he continued to show the journalists around in his normal witty style. When one asked who had called him, he said, 'Oh, only Carlos . . . King Carlos. He's all right. He can wait. You guys are important. I'll call him back.'

Restless and apparently addicted to work, he rarely takes holidays. In Switzerland, once, when taken there for a skiing holiday by his wife, he is said to have found the experience so dull that he chose to enliven his days in the hotel by buying it and then planning its improvements. His wealth is the subject of much speculation, but it has all been generated by his own work. At various times, he has owned two Lear jets, housed at Biggin Hill, which he owns, and homes in Gstaad, where he bought the picturesque inn mentioned above and Chelsea Square, in London and other places. In 1995, it was reported that he earned more than £50 million in annual salary, an income that made him the world's highest paid executive.

When all that SLEC owns is taken into account, Ecclestone and his wife Slavica have a private fortune which in April 2001 the *Sunday Times* estimated to be worth £3 billion. Yet he often insists that he is broke! That sum clearly helped put them third on the list of the richest people in Britain behind only the Duke of Westminster (£4.4 billion) and Hans Rausig, a food-packaging tycoon (£4.2 billion). He rubs shoulders with Luciano Benetton, Silvio Berlusconi, Eric Clapton, Mark Knopfler, George Harrison and Michael Douglas. Not bad for a boy who went to school through the Blitz, who once told the *Wall Street Journal* that there are two things a man should never talk about – 'money and the night before'. Such quotes, delivered with dead-pan understatement, are all part of the Ecclestone myth, a mask that hides the clever deep-thinker beneath the one-liners.

> He is an extremely competent person [said Stirling Moss, a man of the same generation and interests]. He could take over any part of the [Formula One] operation. Maybe he couldn't actually drive the cars, but he'd be closer to it than you would be. You need a control freak. Generals win battles because they are control freaks and they can organise.

Ecclestone admits he likes things done his own way and he pays special attention to certain details. He is fastidious, as are many of the men at the top of Formula One, about order and organisation.

> If I went into your house and I saw a picture out of place, or crooked, I'd probably straighten it up. I am like that. All I've done I've done honestly. I am just a bloke doing a job. I've never cheated anybody. If I do a deal, I don't need to write it down on a piece of paper. I won't go back. Everyone knows that . . .

Asked in the late 1990s about the phenomenal worldwide interest in Formula One, he was honest in his reply.

> This is a terrible thing to say. But, if you think just a little bit about it, this sudden surge has happened since we lost Ayrton Senna. Suddenly, the world was exposed to Formula One racing. Obviously, it is a tragedy, but that had a lot to do with it. In Japan, Formula One was Senna. It could have been go-karting. But everyone was in love with Senna. And when they lost Senna, they lost all their enthusiasm. Now, we have to find another hero.

Senna's death has been entwined with many current Formula One people's involvement with the sport and the business. For Ecclestone, who has a soft spot for Brazil where he has been honoured by the city of São Paulo, Senna's birthplace, it was a sad blow with a bitter ending. When he flew to São Paulo for the funeral in May 1994 to say farewell to the man who had invited him to his family's seaside home up the coast at Angra dos Reis, he found himself barred from the service. A misunderstanding over an expression he had used at Imola, in the aftermath of Senna's death, had upset Senna's brother. Ecclestone watched the funeral on television from his hotel room while Slavica attended with the mayor of São Paolo. He had been, he said, the 'first guy to have a Formula One contract with him, that we never took up, at Brabham'. In the BBC's television tribute to Senna, Tamara Ecclestone is seen jet-skiing with Senna off the beach in Brazil where he had his holiday villa. To Tamara and Petra, Senna, it was said, was almost an uncle.

According to the most reliable sources, Ecclestone had been eating an apple at Imola when he was told, by radio, that Senna was dead. His family, led by Senna's brother Leonardo, were desperate for news, so Ecclestone took them to his motorhome, away from prying cameras and notebooks, to break the worst to them. As they walked, he threw his apple core over a fence, an action that apparently also upset the Senna family. Inside the motor home, he told Leonardo that Ayrton was dead. Minutes later, however, he discovered that Senna was not dead. The message had been to tell Ecclestone that it was 'his head'. This left Ecclestone to explain the news again, but they were unable to understand him or believe him. And then Senna was declared dead anyway. Criticism, some of it venomous, poured on him from all directions.

> If Senna could know what has been happening since his death, he would be disgusted [Ecclestone told Doodson in 1996]. Thoroughly disgusted with the family, with the way they have operated and disgusted with a lot of the things that have been said. Because he was a gentleman and a realist.

In many ways, so too is Ecclestone.

> Being nice to people to gain something is not in my nature. And, to be a politician, you have to promise them what they want to hear, not what is good for them. I am a deliverer. I like the business to be done fair and square. I am not interested in what other people think of me. If you ask anyone in Formula One who does business with me, you will know that the sport is safe with me. I have enough money not to be corrupt.

Probably his greatest fear is not death, but the possibility that after all his hard work Formula One could end up in the wrong hands. He told the *International Herald Tribune* in 1997 that he

> would hate to see it go down the drain because it was badly managed. If all the teams owned it they would destroy it. They cannot agree on anything. Not even on how to share their money out. They think they can run the business. I know they can't.

The closest the Club came to wondering about the succession, and their immediate future, may have been in the summer of

1999 when Ecclestone, as recommended by his friend, Professor Sid Watkins, who is also Formula One's senior medical officer, had a triple heart by-pass operation. In a statement the FIA maintained Ecclestone's droll approach to such matters. It read:

> FIA vice president Bernie Ecclestone has had a successful coronary artery by-pass graft operation carried out by consultant cardiac surgeon Mr John Wright and his team at the London Chest Hospital. Before discharging Bernie from hospital today, Mr Wright described the operation as 'routine', and said 'Bernie will be back in the fast lane in a couple of weeks'. (Geneva, 16 June 1999)

Bernie was urged to have the operation by his wife Slavica and by FIA medical chief Professor Watkins, who feared he might otherwise have had to carry it out himself in the medical centre at a Formula One race. (Note: Jean-Marie Balestre, honorary president of the FIA and current president of the FIA Senate, had the same operation in 1986.) Later, consigned to a low-fat diet, Ecclestone would often remark that he pined for a meal of fried eggs, butter and lashings of double cream.

Nobody has argued with the claim that Ecclestone has built the modern business. In the Piranha Club, they know who their leader is. They know who made their businesses grow the way they have. They know they have need of a man to run the show, a man who can keep an eye on everything, understand the business, deal with the deals and keep a grip on the club as a whole. He has survived a number of threats to his position from within the club. (At various times, he has left a room, during a meeting, after suggesting that the team principals present decide among themselves who the new leader should be, only to return and find they had spent so long arguing about the air-conditioning levels, or something similar, that no-one had even proposed a replacement leader.) That there is no obvious successor to Ecclestone, the king of the dealers, is a clear testimony to the gap he will leave behind and the scale of his contribution to the business. By hook, crook, leverage and kindness, he has made Formula One the business that it is.

Bernard Charles Ecclestone was born on 28 October 1930, at St Peters in Suffolk. His father was a trawler captain who helped develop his son's interest in engineering. They moved from Suffolk to Bexley Heath, on the Kent fringes of south-east London in 1939. Ecclestone went to school until he was 15 and then left, with the accord of his father, to work for a local gas company as a laboratory assistant. He also studied for a degree in chemical engineering at Woolwich Polytechnic. Smitten by motorcycles and speed, he began racing them before, some have reported, he was old enough to ride them on the public roads. Confirmation of such detail is difficult with Ecclestone because not only does he shun interviews, whenever possible, but he also claims to have an appalling memory for personal details.

While working in the gas company offices, he began trading in second-hand motorcycles and parts, and then second-hand cars while also coming to the conclusion that racing on two wheels, rather than four, was dangerous. He rode Velocette motorcycles at Brands Hatch from the age of 15. 'Incredibly, I woke up several times in hospital, but I never broke anything,' he recalled. After buying out his partner Fred Compton in the Compton and Eccleston firm he built it up and then sold it. He moved to cars, racing in the Cooper 500cc events that were popular immediately after the Second World War. In 1950 he raced alongside Stirling Moss in the 'Formula Three' race for these 500cc cars, that was run to support the inaugural World Championship event, the British Grand Prix at Silverstone. 'He was not a great driver,' recalled Moss, 'but not bad either . . . ' Ecclestone himself confessed: 'I led most of the races I entered. Then, I either fell off, or the car exploded. Or I won.' But he can claim to have been involved in Formula One from the start of the world championship.

As a schoolboy, he had shown his flair for business and an entrepreneurial skill. According to the respected journalist Mike Doodson, a long-time student of Ecclestone's rise to power, he would take the early train to school and buy the entire stock of rolls and confectionaries from his local baker's, all to be sold later, at a decent profit, to his fellow-pupils. Later, he established a weekend business selling watches and pens in the Petticoat Lane market in London before his dealing in motorcycles and cars took all his attention.

'I had a big motorcycle and car business before I was 21,' he said. 'Then I started mucking around in property and things and it all went from there.' The growing volume of this business caused him embarrassment in his job with the gas board and expedited his departure to run his own affairs. He set up his own second-hand motorcycle showroom in east London where, according to early photographs, his now-legendary obsession with neatness was manifested by having the bikes arranged in perfectly straight lines. When he moved on to cars, his stock had to be fitted with new hubcaps and rechromed bumpers to prevent them looking untidy. One of his earliest customers was John Surtees.

Many tales have circulated about Ecclestone's activities at this time as he built up his second-hand car business, some suggesting he knew every trick in the trade, but the overriding theme of the time was his resolve, ambition and sense of direction, and his fastidious attention to detail. That same preoccupation with tidiness is still shown in modern Formula One with the way in which the 26 transporters used for carrying Ecclestone's digital television equipment around Europe are lined up, washed and sparkling clean, in registration plate order, in the car parks at each Grand Prix venue and by the tight control he exercises over the precise size, scale and positioning of the team motor homes in the paddock.

Shrewdly, he made his own decision to concentrate on business, rather than racing, early in his life.

> I realised I didn't want to risk lying in bed for the rest of my life, looking up at the ceiling. I'd been wheeling and dealing since I was 11, buying and selling fountain pens, bicycles, what have you. Then, I went into motorcycles, cars, property and whatever was about. (Interview with Robert Chesshyre, *Daily Telegraph*)

In his twenties, he was proprietor of the second-biggest motorcycle business in Britain. According to John Drayton, his property portfolio included Alembic House, a 1950s block opposite the Tate Gallery where he lived in the penthouse that was later to be occupied by Lord Archer. He also married young and had a daughter from this early first marriage. But he kept this union discreetly out of the glare of his more public life. As a result, the name of his first wife has remained a private affair, despite Ecclestone's success at this time, during the 1950s, as he was building up his car business into Weekend Car Auctions. (Ecclestone has retained a near-legendary status among car dealers of the period as one of the cleverest operators of his generation, a man who never missed a trick.) The business was sold to British Car Auctions in 1971 when, in a flash of typical dry wit, he said he was tired of collecting purchase tax for the British government, which had recently introduced Value Added Tax (VAT). At almost the same time, he bought the Brabham Formula One team.

This foray into Grand Prix racing, with the team built up by Jack Brabham, was not his first experience of Formula One, however. In 1957, when he was wheeling and dealing in the same bustling, trading car-mad London as Cooper and Chapman, while Ken Tyrrell was also falling in love with motor racing, and younger men like Frank Williams were dreaming of the day when they would be able to take part, Ecclestone was demonstrating his acumen and wealth by buying the assets of the Connaught team. He wished to see them competitive again at the top level, racing as his private entry, but this desire was frustrated even after Ecclestone had given it his best shot, including a personal attempt, in one of his two Connaught cars, at qualifying for the 1958 Monaco Grand Prix. This arose, said Doodson, when he saw his nominated drivers fail to qualify and, in frustration, jumped into one himself. The result was no better. A similar failure to qualify was experienced at Silverstone later in the year.

His Connaught adventure saw him also send two cars, to be driven by his friend Stuart Lewis-Evans and Roy Salvadori, to New Zealand to race in the Tasman series with an instruction to enjoy the sport with the cars, but to return without them. Ecclestone, in fact, asked the drivers to sell them, a task they approached with some trepidation. In Ecclestone's recollection, a deal was performed by Lewis-Evans, though other sources claimed it was made by Salvadori, to trade the cars for the princely exchange of a stamp album. According to the New Zealand journalist Eoin Young, it was Salvadori who told him about the trip and the unusual proposed deal while they were together. Young told Salvadori that he felt it would be wise for him to telephone home to England and speak to Ecclestone to confirm the deal was approved before completion.

When he came off the 'phone [said Young] all the colour had drained out of his face. I could see that he had taken a bit of a verbal battering! Can you imagine it? Selling

153

Bernie's cars for a load of old stamps! Of course, the deal was off.

Sadly Lewis-Evans died from serious burns on 25 October 1958, six days after he had crashed while racing in the Moroccan Grand Prix at Casablanca. It was a very hard and personal blow to Ecclestone. He had been close to Lewis-Evans as a friend and as his business manager and had caught the Formula One bug from him. Afterwards, he returned for a period to the more ordinary world of running his various other business interests, which flourished under his guidance to include properties.

By the mid-1960s he was involved in Formula One again, this time after meeting Jochen Rindt, to whom he was introduced by Salvadori (by then manager of the Cooper team). He agreed to manage Rindt's business affairs while his career was soaring with Chapman's Lotus after spells with Cooper and Brabham. This spell gave him a clear opportunity to study Formula One at close quarters and to see the potential he was to exploit later after he entered the sport himself as a team owner. When Rindt was killed at Monza, in the 1970 Italian Grand Prix, having won enough points that year already to secure the drivers' title, Ecclestone was badly hit again, but this time he did not turn his back on the sport. Instead, he bought Motor Racing Developments (MRD), which owned the Brabham team name, when the team slumped following Jack Brabham's retirement and was being run by another Australian Ron Tauranac. Ecclestone offered Tauranac a reported £200,000 for the entire business in November 1971 and then set about the transformation of the team.

As owner of Brabham, he was a revelation and a success. He brought in Ralph Bellamy from McLaren and then, when Bellamy left for Lotus, put Gordon Murray, a tall, trendy and hairy South African ('I found him standing in a corner under a dust sheet,' quipped Ecclestone) in charge of the design and engineering. He delivered a series of beautiful winners. Under his leadership, Nelson Piquet delivered two drivers' world championships to the team in a pioneering era when the philosophy of most of the British 'kit car' outfits was to find whatever means possible, within the loopholes provided by the regulations, to win. Lap times ruled, but unlike most of his contemporaries, Ecclestone was always looking around at other aspects of the sport at the same time. His purchase of Brabham had brought with it a membership of the Formula One Constructors' Association (FOCA), the organisation he was to transform from something akin to a rural parish council to one of the most powerful organisations in world sport: the Piranha Club itself!

Indeed 1970 was something of a watershed year. The major teams entered for the world championship at the start included that of Rob Walker, who had provided a Lotus for Graham Hill; Brabham, for which Jack himself was still driving; Surtees, for which John Surtees himself was driving; and McLaren, for which Bruce McLaren was to compete. By the following year, 1971, when Ecclestone was in charge at Brabham, Hill had moved and joined him, alongside Tim Schenken, Jack Brabham had retired and McLaren had been killed, during a private test at Goodwood. Surtees was to struggle on, but the Walker team had gone and, rising on the crest of a new British wave, was replaced by the all-conquering Tyrrells (in their second season), March (also in their second year) and sporadic appearances by early forerunners of what was to become the magnificent Williams team. It was a changing of the guard; the Ecclestone generation were on the block.

In England, at the time, much else was changing. The 'Swinging Sixties' were giving way to the more liberal and licentious Seventies, a more permissive society was settling into British life, hair was any length, authority was there to be challenged and the establishment only existed to be ridiculed. Rock music, free love and the hippy generation arrived and Formula One was ready to embrace it all. The days of good men in cravats, blazers and flannels were gone, swept aside by a tidal wave of popular cultural changes that made it easy to see that, with global television on the horizon, this was the time to unite the teams and create a commercial circus, fuelled by noise, colour and speed, that would conquer the new media world. Ecclestone could sense it all, even if, at that time, he could not know where his desire for change and progress would take him.

By 1972 Ecclestone was installed as the man running FOCA, even if he was nominated only as its secretary or administrator (he always eschews titles, even today). Six years later in 1978, he became president, having succeeded in developing the association from a loose negotiating agency, which represented the teams' interests in talks with race organisers, to a body that would soon take total control of the commercial rights and television revenues generated by the circus all over the world. He achieved this through rigorous discipline, sticking to high standards and expectations and by unifying the teams to guarantee their presence at every race. His dislike of untidiness remained at the core of his work as he sought, in his own view, to improve everything for everybody – for the teams, the organisers, the fans and the ruling body. Once, he said, his refusal to take odd offers of sponsorship for his Brabhams, because the strange stickers looked too untidy (he preferred to run the cars in plain white), resulted in a shortage of funds and parts. 'It was in Belgium,' he recalled. 'We had five cars, but only four engines and 12 tyres. I still don't know how we managed . . . '

Working long hours, paying enormous attention to detail and relishing the challenge of running both Brabham, as a championship-challenging team, and FOCA, who were locked in a lengthy struggle for power with the FISA and its president Jean-Marie Balestre, placed great strain on Ecclestone in the 1970s and early 1980s but, while Chapman (who had probably an even greater workload and agenda of responsibilities) floundered, he appeared to thrive on it. Piquet won the world championship for him in 1981 and 1983 and his team continued to deliver respectable performances, as the competitive standards rose inexorably along with the costs before, in 1988, he decided to sell and concentrate solely on his job of 'running the business'. From then on, he was the man in charge of the Piranha Club boys.

As team owner at Brabham, Ecclestone was an undoubted success. Resourceful, demanding and ambitious, he expected things done his way. Or else. His promotion of Gordon Murray was a moment of sublime inspiration. His creations, allied to Ecclestone's Chapmanesque grasp of how to find a way to take advantage of any loopholes, or gaps, in the rulebook, helped carry Nelson Piquet to two drivers' titles, but the team never had a strong enough line-up to land the constructors' title. Instead, Motor Racing Developments (MRD), based at Weybridge, became a team of character and legend.

Stories of Ecclestone's allegedly extraordinary behaviour helped pass many a long night in the paddock; some true, some false. One popular tale claimed that, soon after buying Brabham in the winter of 1969–70, he witnessed one of his mechanics (unbeknown to the hapless mechanic) losing his temper with himself and hitting his workbench with a spanner. Ecclestone, showing remarkable calmness, took a hammer and threatened to hit the mechanic's car. 'You smash up my property and I'll smash up yours,' was his explanation, according to Formula One folklore. In another similar incident, it was said that Ecclestone found the Brabham workshop in a very untidy condition and, in his rage, pulled a telephone out of its wall socket. Then, he told his assembled workforce, according to the popular lore, that if he ever found the place in such a mess again he would close it down.

Piquet's departure, at the end of 1985, had signalled that Ecclestone's real glory days at Brabham were past and the tragic death of Elio de Angelis, killed while testing a Brabham at Le Castellet in 1986, confirmed the feeling. Murray, the designer of the BT44, with split-nose radiators, the BT45, the BT46B, a one-race sensation that was banned after winning because it was a fan car, and the BT52, which Piquet drove to triumph, left. Ecclestone then withdrew Brabham from competition. He sold MRD to Alfa Romeo hoping it would lead to the creation of his long-awaited 'silhouette' racing series using high-performance saloon cars. This was a venture that almost happened, but never did.

Then in 1988 Fiat, owners of Alfa Romeo, sold the Brabham name and team to a Swiss financier, Joachim Luthi, but this deal also foundered because although they resumed racing, using Judd engines, the new owner ended up in prison for tax evasion. After this, Brabham was owned by the Japanese Middlebridge Group, who sought to revive the team's fortunes, but met only disappointment. In 1992, in a final desperate bid to succeed, an Italian woman Giovanna Amati was given a chance, but she was replaced by Damon Hill who had the distinction of qualifying the dreadful BT60B at Silverstone and Budapest. The Hungarian race was the last to witness a Brabham on a Grand Prix starting grid. After Ecclestone, Brabham had quite simply faded away.

The finest thing that happened in motor sport was the creation of FOCA [he said in 1992]. In the old days, it was FOCA's role to kick the lazy amateur organisers the 1970s, then the 1980s and the 1990s. We kicked them into becoming professional and running their races efficiently, to make money so they could pay. The reason I imposed high prize funds was not because we needed the money. That had nothing to do with it because the amount of money that a team gets from a race is a very small percentage of its budget. What it did to was to make the organisers work harder and become more efficient.

Among the changes that Ecclestone affected were improvements to all the paddock facilities. A visitor from a distant Grand Prix, in the 1960s say, would probably not recognise the high level of the infrastructure today. A state-of-the-art purpose-built circuit like Sepang, at Kuala Lumpur, where the Malaysian Grand Prix takes place, is light years away from the old circuits. But when Ecclestone was making modernisations and changes, he faced resistance and complaints, particularly from the public, who were no longer able to enjoy free ease of access to the drivers and the teams.

If you go to a football match, you cannot walk on to the field. I cannot go to watch tennis at Wimbledon and expect to walk on the court. If I could get in, the worst thing that might happen to me is that a tennis ball might hit me. In racing, it could be a lot worse. They, the public, should not be allowed in the paddock. This is a working area. You don't go walking into a car factory without some security card. The paddock is our factory . . .

His reference to security cards was deemed a little futuristic in 1992, but it was soon to become reality. His business acumen, of course, was astonishing; according to *Autosport* magazine, he ran, in 1993, the most profitable company in Britain, making a profit of £15 million from a turnover of just £18 million. By the end of the 1990s, electronic turnstiles were installed and operating at every race in the world, ensuring that each and every person who entered the paddock was registered in and out. All the teams, their members, the drivers, their managers and additional staff, not to mention the media, were issued with plastic passes the size of credit cards, with an electronic swipe facility. It gave Ecclestone a chance to show who was in charge and also to exercise his sense of humour. One seasoned journalist, who chose not to attend the Brazilian Grand Prix, found at the next race he attended that his seasonal pass was not working. Instead of the usual message informing him that his pass was valid, the electronic readout indicated that he was being rejected for non-attendance at the full calendar of races.

Only after raging at various officials did he discover the episode was a deliberate practical joke concocted by Ecclestone (who has also celebrated some team owners' birthdays with funny messages via the same means).

> Self-discipline is very important for me [he said, as if by way of explanation]. I am a perfectionist. I think that sometimes this lets me down. I do also have a temper. I get upset with stupid people and I will explode. But then I will apologise and, after five minutes, I'll have forgotten ... I operate in a field where things are not discussed too much. If I have to sort something out, and make it work, I will just do it; I certainly won't go and discuss it with the press first. There is no room for failure or waiting around in Formula One. It is just the quick and the dead here.

Arguably the biggest battle, almost certainly the most significant, in Bernie Ecclestone's Formula One career came with the advent of the so-called 'FISA–FOCA' war in 1979–81. It may now seem like a distant memory, but to those involved it was all-consuming. It was about the future of the sport, who would control it, how it would be controlled and by what administration. It was a struggle between the continental European 'grandees' and traditionalists, who sided with the proud and strident Frenchman Jean-Marie Balestre, elected president of the Fédération Internationale du Sport Automobile (FISA) in 1979, in a group that included Alfa-Romeo, Ferrari and Renault, manufacturers who in simplistic terms favoured the use of high-powered engines, in particular turbo-engines, over aerodynamic experiments, against the British constructors, like Colin Chapman's Lotus, McLaren, Tyrrell, Williams and Ecclestone's Brabham, the 'garagistes', whose innovative cars were too often capable of beating the more cumbersome and powerful cars of their opponents. Also on the British side was the new March team, one of whose owners was the clever and resourceful Max Mosley, son of the controversial British politician of the 1930s Sir Oswald Mosley and Diana Mitford, sister of the writer Nancy Mitford. This Oxford-educated physics graduate and barrister was an unlikely ally for the former south London second-hand car dealer, but together they formed one

159

of the most formidable double acts not only in the history of motor racing, but any walk of life in the second half of the twentieth century.

Like Ecclestone, Mosley was a racer. He had driven in Formula Two (indeed, he was on the grid at Hockenheim in 1968 when Jim Clark was killed) and he understood the physics and engineering in racing cars. He had helped create March, together with his friends Robin Herd, Alan Rees and Graham Croaker in 1970 and shared the widespread sense of frustration, articulated by men like Colin Chapman and Ecclestone, at the way in which the old Commision Sportive Internationale (CSI) was running the sport. The original Formula I Constructors' Association (FICA) was started by Andrew Ferguson, the Team Lotus manager, in 1964, to represent the interests of the constructors – and particularly the early British 'kit car' teams of the time – with the ruling body, the CSI, FICA (or FOCA, as it became) was also concerned, as Rob Walker revealed, with the details of making improved travel arrangements, improved hotel bookings and the negotiation of improved deals with promoters.

But it was all done in a haphazard way until Ecclestone took control in the 1970s, delivering the kind of deals that had previously been talked of only as dreams. 'Yes, Bernie, that's a good idea ... why don't you just get on with it,' was the gist of the established teams' reactions to his ideas. By 1978, he was not only supporting the moves for vastly improved medical facilities (the 'prof' became Formula One's 'FOCA surgeon' in 1979) at all circuits, but also standing up alongside Chapman in the technical battle which raged over the banning of aerodynamic 'skirts'. By 1979, when the CSI was reformed as the Fédération Internationale du sport Automobile (FISA) to control and adminster the world championship events of the Fédération Internationale de l'Automobile (FIA), when Jean-Marie Balestre was appointed as the president of FISA, Ecclestone had become president of FOCA with Mosley as his close legal adviser and strategic ally.

The high point, or the nadir, depending on your viewpoint, of the war came in 1980 when the championship was wrecked by a series of rows over technical rules and many races were cancelled, or only run as either FISA or FOCA events. In these, only the teams affiliated to that organisation took part. Goodyear, the tyre suppliers, were so concerned at the situation that they

Above Alain Prost and Eddie Jordan discuss a matter of balance in the business, a fine point of political action or the likely pay-outs from the club... The Frenchman, who won four championships as a driver, has not found life as comfortable or rewarding on the pit wall as in the cockpit. The Irishman, who abandoned dreams of a successful racing career to concentrate on the business of ownership and management, has proved that it is possible to enter Formula One, join the club and succeed. Two contrasting tales from two brilliant and passionate men.

Left Tom Walkinshaw has a reputation for being one of the most competitive of a highly-competitive group of men in the Formula One paddock. A successful self-made multi-millionaire, he has won as a driver and as a team chief and has played a significant role in the club and with such teams as Benetton, Ligier and Arrows.

Above Patrick Head and Frank
Williams have shared more pain and
pleasure than any other current duo
of team chiefs since they began
running the Williams operation
together in the 1970s. Both are
recognised as pure racers with sharp
minds and a boundless enthusiasm for
competition, a combination that has
helped their team become one of the
greatest in the sport. But it has been
at a cost: Williams was badly injured
in a road accident in 1986 and the
team has suffered the loss of men
much loved as drivers and friends.

Right Peter Sauber is the quiet Swiss
member of the club, a man content
to stay in the shadows and leave
others in the limelight. His team have
moved steadily through the rankings,
remained steadfast and secure, but
rarely threatened to steal away the
glory and the honours. Curiously, his
team is based in Switzerland, a
country that has banned international
motor racing events.

Above Luca di Montezemolo is the uncrowned prince of Italian commerce and was once the organiser of the 1990 World Cup soccer finals held in Italy before becoming president of Ferrari. He is a smooth operator, at home in English words and rural castles as well as the pit lanes and the paddocks of the world. He has guided Ferrari into the modern corporate era and out of the grip of a past that weighed on the company's shoulders.

Left Flavio Briatore brought colour and spectacle to Formula One and the club when he was given the task of guiding Benetton to success in the 1990s. Though he knew nothing of Formula One at the time, he quickly demonstrated that a resourceful, clever and hard-working approach would pay off as he moulded the team into a youthful and successful organisation that lifted the drivers and constructors championship double in 1995. Here he is pictured with his girlfriend Naomi Campbell, the supermodel.

Above Jackie Stewart, here shown
enjoying a champagne shower after his
team's maiden victory at the
Nurburgring in 1999, in the European
Grand Prix, is a survivor of dangers as a
driver and as a team owner. Together
with his son Paul, he created Stewart
Grand Prix, persuaded Ford to support
him, and, eventually, sold out to them
in a move that set an example to others
and left him with some memorable
moments from club membership to
ponder.

Right Ron Dennis has built McLaren
International into one of the great
teams in the sport's history almost
through his own sense of
determination, vision and sheer hard
work. Formerly a mechanic, he has
accumulated as much experience at
every level of the sport as anyone in
Formula One history and he has
become a powerful and influential
member at the heart of the club.

Above All smiles on the pit wall as Bernie Ecclestone enjoys a moment of horseplay with the top drivers. David Coulthard, Michael Schumacher, Mika Hakkinen and Rubens Barrichello enjoy a joke with the man known by many as 'the bolt' or, more simply, as Mr E. Ecclestone enjoys such moments of levity as he can escape from the constant pressures of running the global show that he has built from almost nothing into one of the biggest sports businesses on earth.

Left Max Mosley, the arch-politician and silver-tongued orator, has played a subtle yet influential role in the development of Formula One throughout the Ecclestone era. A former racer who grew up in the sport, he has brought his education and experience to bear where necessary on the art of solving problems and guiding the leading administrators towards a secure future. Once a team owner, he is now the president of the sport's ruling body, the Federation International de l'Automobile (FIA).

Right Enzo Ferrari, the first and the foremost, was the archetypal Piranha Club man of the early years. He enjoyed describing himself as a manipulator of men, but he was also a passionate racer devoted to the growth of his business and his team during a long and famous lifetime's association with the sport.

Below Bernie Ecclestone has created the modern Formula One by spending 30 years of his life in the business from team owner to ring master, organising, negotiating, planning and delivering on his promises. Respected by all, he has enjoyed a fabulously successful career that has seen him rise from selling motor cycle parts from his mother's kitchen table to running all the commercial affairs of the biggest regularly-televised global sport.

Left John Cooper, pictured with Jack Brabham, was the man who created Cooper cars, moved the engine to the rear and, in effect, pioneered the modern era of Grand Prix cars as we know them today. But Cooper was an honest and simple man without a devious nature and his 'clever blacksmith' approach to the sport came at the end of the innocent era.

Below Jack Brabham, driver and team owner, won the world championship in both roles. His team, sold to Bernie Ecclestone, was among the famous names for many years, but failed to survive into the modern era as Formula One evolved from a club for rich playboys into a global hi-tech business.

Above Rob Walker inspects the detailed preparation on one of his privately-entered cars in the days when Formula One remained open to gentlemen of sufficient private means to enjoy the racing and have time for some fun afterwards. Walker ran Cooper and Lotus cars to spectacular and famous victories, gave Stirling Moss a seat and became one of the great characters in the sport during his long career in the business.

Right Colin Chapman, pictured with Jim Clark, formed one of the most successful team owner and driver combinations in the history of Formula One when he and the brilliant Scot were establishing Lotus in the 1960s. Clark's death in 1968 devastated Chapman, but he continued to make Lotus one of the greatest names of all before his own sudden death in 1982. Chapman was one of the most innovative and bold men to have worked within the club and played a major part in the growth of Formula One.

threatened to withdraw. The future of Formula One looked bleak, confused and messy; indeed, it was to remain so until the end of the wholly unhappy and bitterly remembered 1982 season. Ecclestone and Mosley were probably the only two people who knew exactly what they were fighting for and precisely why. Chapman and the rest appeared to be heavily preoccupied with their own affairs, even though the Lotus owner remained involved in the politics and, at one stage, seemed close to accepting a proposal, put to him by Balestre, to lead a coup d'état to depose Ecclestone at the head of FOCA and settle the affair.

After sleeping on it, he pulled out and Ecclestone stayed in charge to call the Frenchman's bluff and then, in January 1981, announce the creation of the World Federation of Motor Sport and a new championship. This carefully timed and calculated move forced Balestre to come to the negotiating table where Ecclestone and Mosley reached the compromise deal, known as the Concorde Agreement (after the address of the FISA offices in Paris, where most of the negotiating took place) that still exists as the binding document, revised on a regular basis, between the teams and the ruling body, which lays down the foundations for the administration of the sport. It has, to some degree, remained a vexed subject ever since.

It was not straightforward of course. The negotiations, which took place on 19 January 1981, lasted for a reported 13 hours and ended not with an announcement in the capital of France, but a news conference chaired by Enzo Ferrari, who was flanked by Ecclestone and Balestre, at the Ferrari headquarters at Maranello in Italy. To the 'grandees' it seemed a great victory had been won as Balestre claimed that the FISA would continue to act as the sport's governing body and control the rules; but Ecclestone knew he had lost only a battle in the real war; he and FOCA had emerged with the right to control the commercial side of Formula One, including all the television rights, and to handle the distribution of all the revenue. It was the key move in his career and in the development of the business. Yet, the truth, revealed many years later, is that the deal was done not in Maranello or the Place de La Concorde, but in a nightclub, several days earlier. According to Ecclestone, it was 'a shady nightclub . . . where we met the head of Philip Morris, Jean-Marie and myself. Jean-Marie was enjoying the publicity so much that we agreed to do the deal and then keep it quiet for a while. No one knew.'

A little more than a month later, following weeks of heavy negotiations involving teams of lawyers at the Place de la Concorde, the first agreement was signed and sealed. Its contents were declared secret and confidential, never to be revealed by any of the parties involved and most team owners, who are party to it through their membership of FOCA, give a withering look at anyone with the temerity to make leading enquiries on any of the details. In general, however, it is understood that the revenue distribution has been the most vexed subject (the prize money aspect, also a jealously guarded secret is far less significant than widely believed and is only a very small proportion of the overall revenue).

A year later and another controversy erupted when the drivers went on strike at Kyalami in South Africa on the eve of the season-opening South African Grand Prix. Led by Niki Lauda, their natural leader, and Didier Pironi, the Frenchman who was Gilles Villeneuve's team-mate at Ferrari and president of the Grand Prix Drivers' Association (GPDA), the man whose actions in 'unfairly' winning the San Marino Grand Prix that year were to lead to Villeneuve's death, the drivers departed the circuit in a bus after deciding that they would not accept certain contractual restrictions which bound them to their teams. Ecclestone led the teams' discussions and the final negotiations with Pironi, which resolved the issue. The race eventually took place. Ecclestone, through his ability to negotiate swiftly and take control, had emerged as the man to lead Formula One into the future. But the passage was not smooth and many storms lay ahead.

Ecclestone's achievements punctuate the modern growth of Formula One. His decision to embrace television, to organise the teams for regular races and broadcasts, his calculated decisions on deals and promoters and partners have brought untold success. Yet he remains as enigmatic and intriguing after more than 50 years in motor sport, and more than half of them in Formula One, as ever. His habits, his human weaknesses, his idiosyncratic behaviour still prompt as much affection as admiration or awe. And his complete lack of sentiment in all business decisions still causes resentment and anger. When, for example, he agreed to switch the Australian Grand Prix from Adelaide, where it had been one of the most successful and popular events on the calendar, to Melbourne in 1996, he received hate mail and reported death threats from both the South Australians who felt their event was being hijacked by the Victorians and the local Albert Park protest groups who wanted to preserve their trees. Indeed, when he was first shown plans for the new circuit by the proud local promoters, the Major Events Corporation of Melbourne, he surprised them by revealing in the most obvious way his poor eyesight.

According to one report, he literally lowered himself on to the map, his nose and thick-rimmed spectacles only inches away from the plans and, using a finger, followed the proposed track's route around the park. The swish executives were stunned. This was no cool demonstration of superhuman powers, but a display of everyday weakness. But, it was typical of Ecclestone who went on to give unstinting support for the planned race in Melbourne and particularly its creator Ron Walker, and inaugural chief executive Judith Griggs, a lawyer (originally from Adelaide) who had also worked for Ecclestone in London, that he should be prepared to show himself in this way. He never backed off in helping to support Griggs during the worst protests and threats by the 'yellow ribbon protesters' who wanted to save Albert Park and in his direct style articulated his belief in the bulldozers that were moving trees and earth to make a high-quality racing circuit. When the works were finished, and when the park had been transformed into a park containing arguably the world's prettiest track, Ecclestone showed his gratitude to Griggs' fortitude in his own way by sending her a special gift. It was a solid silver cement mixer, nearly the size of a small football, with an inscription that read: 'To Judy, earth mover of the year'.

Such a gesture of loyalty and humour was typical of Ecclestone. No-one is quicker with a riposte. Asked about his successor, as the man in charge of the club, he told Brad Spurgeon on the *International Herald Tribune*:

> Formula One is like a big stage for a pop concert. Teams come and go over the years, like stars come and go. Elvis died. Things still went on. When I go, the same thing will happen. Formula One will continue.

And asked about his own future, his retirement or death, he is just as pungent. He told me, in London, in December 1997:

Well, do you know what my wife Slavica said to me? She said they will bury me in the bus. They will have to dig a big hole do it all in one go and bury me and the bus in an F1 paddock somewhere. So, I said to Slavica, that if I am not dead in 20 years, I shall retire. I am 67 now. So, add that up. It means I will be 87 before I start to stay at home at weekends . . .

6 Never Look a Gift Horse in the Mouth

I think that what the participants should be doing is exactly what was agreed to do when we invented the Concorde Agreement. That was that the teams would, in fact, be the people that would really write the technical regulations, along with the people from FISA. It would be the FISA that would police the regulations that we agreed . . . And this is basically what happens. So, it's not a case of anybody having that much power. There's nobody knows better than the teams what's going to happen in the future. The trouble is that not being . . . well . . . It's not a case of not being straightforward. But it's difficult for somebody, who has got something in mind that they want to do next year, to tell everyone else now. Obviously . . . What's happened is quite refreshing. I'm sure you'll agree with Max now. When he became president of the FISA, he was in a position to look through things that had perhaps been hidden in a cupboard for years. It's like somebody entering a company and realising that things were wrong and we shouldn't be running the business like this. He had a good look through all the sporting and technical regulations and he realised that some of the technical regulations had been breached for some time and it just needed somebody to do something about it.

So, said Bernie Ecclestone, speaking at a news conference at Hockeheim, Germany, in July, 1993, following a meeting with the club. To the next question – Do you think all the regulations need to be rewritten now? – Ecclestone said: 'These technical regulations were really written to propel aeroplanes and now we've got jets . . . so they need to be brought up in line with today.'

As always, Ecclestone's mixture of fractured grammar, precise illumination and hilarity left his listeners more entertained than educated. His opinions showed that the successful
campaign in 1991 which led to the election of Max Mosley as
president of the FISA was considered to be a benefit to the
sport in general and the teams in particular. But it was also
clear that he was ready to lead the way towards the banning of
the then controversial so-called 'electronic driver aids' such as
active suspension, traction control and braking systems.
Mosley, the educated, sophisticated and urbane lawyer whose
family history carried a reputation, had swiftly made his mark
in his early days with the ruling body of motor sport from La
Place de la Concorde following his election as FISA president
on October 1991. His popular victory was hailed, by many in
the sport, as a triumph for common sense over buffoonery. It
also ensured that the old double act of the two greatest 'poachers', Mosley and Ecclestone, would take up senior residential
positions among the 'gamekeepers'.

By 1991, of course, Ecclestone was the major commercial
power broker in Formula One and the sport was no longer a
sport, but a serious business, and it was on the way to becoming
the global showcase for the car industry that it grew into by the
end of the twentieth century. In 1970 BRM and Ferrari were
considered to be the two truly big teams in the pit lane. By the
late 1990s BMW, Mercedes-Benz, Ford, Honda, Fiat, Peugeot,
Renault and Toyota were either involved, or had been, or
intended to be; the one-time chaos club, run by the funsters and
blazer-blades of the 1950s and 1960s, had grown up and grown
out of all recognition. Ecclestone had created a sports-business
that was capable of claiming the world's third-largest television
sports audience behind the soccer World Cup and the Olympic
Games. This progress saw a series of 'characters' in the sport,
too. Some survived. Some failed.

Some even went to prison. Akira Akagi, who took over the
March team once partly owned by Max Mosley, was jailed for
fraud. Joachim Luhti, who purchased Brabham, went the same
way. Fred Bushell, Colin Chapman's right-hand man for so long,
was sent to prison, too, for his part in the De Lorean scandal.
Ted Ball, whose company Landhurst Leasing was linked to various financial affairs including those of the former England football coach Terry Venables, while he was at Tottenham Hotspur,
and vain salvation bids with Brabham and Lotus, was also sen-

tenced to three years in prison for corruption in connection with the receipt of improper payments. He had reportedly been supplying money to keep the teams afloat, but when Landhurst Leasing went into receivership with debts of more than £44 million it was the end of the road for the teams and him. The early 1990s were a particularly tough and demanding time for the teams as the costs of competing escalated and money became more and more difficult to find.

In 1992, during the Belgian Grand Prix at Spa-Francorchamps, Andrea Sassetti, the owner of the Andrea Moda team, was arrested and jailed for forgery. Another team owner, the self-declared anarchist Jean-Pierre van Rossem, a Belgian who refused to bathe, clean his teeth or trim his hair, who had purchased the Onyx team, was arrested for writing false cheques, but evaded conviction by going into politics. Some of these men were likeable, but many were either loathsome or intimidating.

> We've been too democratic really [said Ecclestone]. We never really bothered to vet people in those days and we just said 'let them have a go at it' and that was it. Some of them, if you looked at them, you might say were like hooligans. But they weren't.

The evolution of the business and the elevations of Ecclestone and Mosley to positions of authority within the establishment of the sport soon ensured that the most questionable characters were flushed out. But the process, from the aftermath of the FISA–FOCA war, when the teams took control, to the corporate clean-up of the mid-1990s, was not rapid and saw many colourful adventures along the way. Like the television pictures, it may have looked pretty on the surface, but if you wiped away the make-up, it was not so pretty underneath. 'He was a strange one,' laughed Ecclestone, when Luhti and others were mentioned.

> I knew him because it was Brabham and I was still running it and I knew him like I know anyone now. I don't think he was a villain. I think he had ideas about what he was going to do with the currency market and it all went wrong. Van Rossem? I heard he was somebody who was going to take over and sort me out and do whatever ... I remember

walking up and saying 'Who is this guy?' He was sitting down on the grandstand and I said, 'I'm Bernie Ecclestone. You don't know me, but it appears you want to sort me out and do something and you've got your opportunity now'. . . 'Agh, no, who said that? I never said that! I don't mean this.' In the end, he was as good as gold. He was alright. No problem. And Ted Ball? Another guy like that. They just get involved and get bold and start believing they can do things. I don't believe any of these people set out to be villains. A villain in my opinion is someone who sets his stall out to be a villain. You know what I mean. Somebody sets out to be a burglar. They must want to be a burglar. They break into the house. In these cases, I think people have got ideas and can't carry them through. And then they get carried away and do things they shouldn't do, thinking they're going to get out of trouble, like a gambler starts stealing, thinking he's going to win in the morning. They didn't set out to steal.

To understand this period in the development of the Piranha Club, it is necessary to revisit the late 1970s, to recall the rise of Colin Chapman and his Lotus cars, to note the ambitions of Ecclestone and others, like Frank Williams, Ron Dennis and Ken Tyrrell, whose enterprise and vision provided the foundations of energy and commitment on which the sport was built. All, then, were entrepreneurs who shaped history with their invention, ability to improvise and their competitive spirits. But there was another factor, too; the opposition they faced in the shape of the new FISA president Jean-Mare Balestre and his alliance with the old 'grandees'.

It was a classic struggle through 1979, 1980, 1981 and 1982 that resulted, in the end, in the formation of a close-knit and formidably clever group of people whose common goal, the success of their teams, their companies and their sport, ensured the growth that has sustained Formula One ever since. Since then, they may have poached each other's drivers, staff, ideas and sponsors, but, in essence, they have fought together against most outside threatening foes in a way that would have pleased Chapman, if he had lived to see it. In 1981, after his 'twin chassis' Lotus 88 was banned from taking part in the Brazilian Grand Prix in Rio de Janeiro, he issued a statement which reflected not only the civil unrest among the teams at the time, but also deep concerns for the future.

We have witnessed the changes that have taken place in Grand Prix racing and, unfortunately, see what was fair competition between sportsmen degenerate into power struggles and political manoeuvrings between manipulators attempting to make more money out of the sport than they put in. If one does not clean up this formula, it will end in a quagmire of plagiarism, chicanery and petty rule interpretation forced by the lobbies manipulated by people for whom sport has no meaning.

It was the task of the teams in the wake of Chapman's death, when Ecclestone was building the commercial foundations of the business, to clean up the sport in tandem with the ambitions of Balestre. In this period, the men whose teams have become some of the strongest surviving brand names of all came to the fore. This was the time when the club worked out its rules, put down roots and became firmly established. And it was in this period that Mosley's deft touch established himself as a subtle influence and he could be seen as the sport's politician and diplomat for the long-term future. The manner of his rise and the style of his campaign, successful as it was, to take the presidency of FISA from Balestre, and then take control of the FIA and reform the entire organisation, reveals much about the man and the modern structure of Formula One. As a result, Mosley has been seen by many team principals as a poacher turned gamekeeper, a former FOCA man who changed sides and assisted in the 'loss' of the teams' commercial rights as Ecclestone took control.

A curious, loud, contradictory character, lampooned by many for a long time, Jean-Marie Balestre was born on 9 April 1921. During the Second World War he was involved in youth movements, allegedly served in the French SS, claimed he worked for the French Resistance and was arrested in 1944 by the Germans. It is also said he spent two years in a French jail. His wartime activities were controversial and have been the subject of much debate and conjecture. He founded the magazine Auto Journal, built a publishing company and in 1952 was a founder member of the Fédération Française du Sport Automobile (FFSA). His career in motor sport administration carried him, by 1978, to the presidency of the CSI, which he transformed into the FISA. As its head he fought against the teams' and their association, thus lining up against Ecclestone and Mosley in the FISA–FOCA war. In 1986 he became the president of the FIA, a post he used for a five-year spell of bombastic announcements before Mosley stood against him in 1991.

It was clear, as he sat before the media at the Circuit de Catalunya, a modern creation built in the north-eastern hinter-land of Barcelona, on the eve of the 1991 Spanish Grand Prix, that Jean-Marie Balestre was an angry man. He was also dumb-founded and found it difficult to hide his feelings in his manner and his words. Only once previously during his unbroken run of 13 years in power had the Frenchman who ruled the FISA and the FIA like a personal empire faced any opposition to con-tinuing supremacy. At 70, with major heart surgery only five years behind him, the strain of an election campaign was the last thing he needed. He knew that his opponent, the astute, educated and tough Max Mosley, was extremely well prepared for the task. He knew too that Mosley was perfectly qualified for the post, having been a racing driver, a team owner, a team manager and an administrator.

Balestre wanted to make his usual impression and he was at his most colourful and flamboyant. As he entered the room, there were cheers, many of them ironic, and from the back rows of the assembly calls of 'Vive la France'. The self-styled Charles de Gaulle of motor sport responded by pulling flowers from a display on the platform and throwing them into the crowd of assembled reporters. It was theatrical, blatant and ridiculous, electioneering and what followed was almost absurd. Balestre argued with a sound system engineer and then had a row with his interpreter. Local Spanish technicians adjusted the sound system. The inter-preter was replaced; but Catalan pride in hosting their first Grand Prix at this new circuit was hurt. Balestre then talked at length.

Afterwards, during a period of questions and answers, he was asked about his monopoly of power in Paris. He replied that he was 'the boss' and that 'you all know what is a boss . . . A boss is the boss.' He compared his duties running three major motor-ing organisations to a game of croquet and had most of the room in stitches of laughter. It was Balestre the buffoon at his best. Few objective and impartial observers of this scene were sur-prised to learn, some months later, that it was this very claim to being the 'boss' of three key areas in motor sport that was to be the target of Mosley's campaign to oust him. The only previous attempt to unseat Balestre had come from another Briton, Basil Tye, but this one from Mosley was to be more carefully planned and more successful. At the plenary conference of the FISA in September, Mosley circulated his unofficial manifesto in which he highlighted Balestre's monopoly of power and questioned it.

The second son of the British politician Sir Oswald Mosley and Diana Mitford, Mosley was born on 13 April 1940. His childhood and upbringing had seen him educated in England, Ireland, France and Germany. He had his father's political skills and much of his mother's charm and sense of adventure. She was one of the six famous Mitford sisters who took the European social scene by storm in the 1920s – and Diana and her sister Unity were later associated with close friendship with Adolf Hitler. Mosley spoke several languages with a fluency that would not leave him disadvantaged by Balestre's position in France. He was a contrast to the Frenchman and an appealing alternative for anyone seeking a break with the past and a step into a less-confrontational period for the sport. Mosley had won a place at Christ Church College, Oxford, and earned a degree in physics. He had been secretary of the Oxford Union, read law at Grays Inn, in London, qualified as a barrister and practised law from 1964–69, when he was a specialist in patents. He was interested in politics, but his father's involvement in the British Union of Fascists in the 1930s, for which he was interned (Mosley's earliest recollections of his father are of visiting him in prison) made such ambitions impractical. Instead, curiously, following a trip to Silverstone in the early 1960s, he was drawn into motor racing.

He entered club events and graduated to Formula Two. He founded the London Racing Team with Chris Lambert and, after Lambert was killed in an accident involving Clay Regazzoni at Zandvoort, in August 1968, he joined Frank Williams's Formula Two team as a team-mate to Piers Courage. In this period Mosley participated in the race at Hockenheim in April 1968, when Jim Clark was killed and also raced regularly with such famous rivals as Graham Hill, Jackie Stewart and Jochen Rindt. (Balestre, in his campaigning, claimed frequently that Mosley was born with a golden spoon in his mouth and had all the privileges and advantages that he, a self-made man, had earned for himself.) At this time, Mosley was a risk-taker who sought fun and adventure and experienced several close scrapes. In 1962 he was arrested after a fracas with anti-Mosley demonstrators and was later cleared of threatening behaviour at Old Street Magistrates Court. His defence was that he was protecting his father. Mosley was also a member of the

Territorial Army and trained as a parachutist. In some ways, he was a latter day Rob Walker. But he lived in a different era.

By 1969 Mosley knew he was not a potential champion driver. He retired from competitive action and instead became the M in March Engineering, together with Alan Rees, Graham Coaker and Robin Herd. Herd, a brilliant young engineer and designer, was much in demand and, by another twist of fate, could have joined Rees in another team with Bernie Ecclestone, who was anxious to start one of his own, and Jochen Rindt as the driver. It was Herd's Oxford friendship with Mosley that sealed the future, but it is strange to consider that Ecclestone and Mosley's paths crossed so long ago when each had similar, but conflicting ambitions. Despite establishing itself as one of the most successful racing car production companies and winning many championships, March struggled in Formula One. Jackie Stewart won the 1970 Spanish Grand Prix in a March, run by Ken Tyrrell, but only two 'factory-entered' victories followed and, frustrated by the lack of progress, Mosley, who was increasingly drawn into the work of Ecclestone's FOCA activities, left in 1977. He became the FOCA legal adviser, a leading player in the FISA–FOCA war and, after taking three years out of the sport, was appointed the inaugural president in 1986 of the Manufacturers' Commission, a role that also gave him a chance to sit on the World Motor Sports Council. Swiftly, he became an important part of the machinery of administration within international motor sport while at the same time being involved in the establishment of Simtek Research, in 1989, with Nick Wirth, then a 23-year-old engineer at March. He sold his shares in Simtek to Wirth when he became FISA president.

All this meant that Mosley knew just what he had to offer when he challenged Balestre for the presidency of FISA in 1991. In his manifesto, circulated that year, he attacked the Frenchman's monopoly of three key jobs. He wrote:

Each one of them requires the full-time attention of an active and competent person. It is simply not possible for one man, however able or vigorous, to manage all of them simultaneously. The attempt to do so has led to significant problems: indecision, mistakes, proposals which are countermanded, unnecessary controversy, unavailability of the president, confusion, lack of consultation and so on. Moreover, the three posts are in conflict . . .

He also suggested that to have one man enjoying such power and, with it, an uninterrupted run of 17 years in power, was 'rather too long'. Of his own experiences, he reported:

> I was involved in the promotional organisation of world championship Formula One races in many different countries over a five-year period and in the negotiations which led to the signing of the Concorde Agreement. And, as president of the FISA Manufacturers' Commission, I have represented the world's motor industry on the World Council for the past five years and have thus become very aware of the needs of rallying and touring car racing.

He was clear and articulate in his argument and the evidence for his election seemed overwhelming. He added:

> Typical of what I am trying to say is that the reason no-one has stood against Balestre until now, since the days of Basil Tye, is not that everyone agrees with him, but that there has been no-one who thought they could do the job better. It's because they fear, rightly or wrongly, that the consequences could be adverse. That's completely wrong. If I am elected, if people stand against me and lose, I will still want to work with them and, equally, if they won, I would expect to continue working with them. As in any proper and civilised club, it should be an open thing. The idea that the FISA is the property of one man, and trying to take the presidency from him is like trying to take his house or his car, is alien to any properly run club. A tremendous re-organisation is needed.

Balestre responded with a six-page letter to the delegates, signing himself as president and friend, making a variety of claims and counter-claims, suggesting some 'obvious and dishonest manipulation' had taken place. He also complained that Mosley's lawyers had 'unscrupulously attacked my age and the state of my health' and, for good measure, suggested that Mosley had been attempting to 'brainwash his readers with an accumulation of false truths'. The posturing and the pomp were amazing. When asked if he had anyone in mind to succeed him, Balestre replied:

I see many people, but I would say without modesty that I am happy to hear important people saying that I am the best. I don't know if I am the best. But I am happy that I am one of the rare Frenchmen to have won the confidence of the English. That is very difficult for a Frenchman ... But I am respected. I am a president who has authority and I want to stay in office as long as possible. If I am no longer the president, I shall die immediately! If I am no longer the president, I shall lose all my oxygen.

Thanks to his carefully planned and managed campaign, during which he spent much time on the telephone while on a family holiday in Italy, Mosley was successful.

I thought I'd get one of the clubs around the world somewhere to put me up for election against him [he explained]. I did a lot of canvassing, but there weren't too many ready and brave enough to take me on because they knew failure would be certain death for them! It is one thing to vote in a secret ballot and have no focus fall on you and quite another to put your head over the parapet and reveal you are supporting a complete outsider like me against a well-established and much-feared man like Balestre. In the end, it was New Zealand who decided to back me. They were fed up with the way the federation was being run.

Mosley won the election by 43 votes to 29.

Almost immediately, following his own declarations, he gave one year's notice of his resignation in order that another election would enable his efforts to be judged after a year. In 1992, he won a four-year term of office during which he engineered the merger of the FISA into the FIA. In October 1993 he became president of the FIA for a four-year period, won re-election in 1997 and, following a close collaboration of the International Touring Association (AIT) with the FIA, created a powerful pressure group over which he has presided with aplomb. It has given him a high political profile and earned him much respect even if he has not shaken off the idea that he and Ecclestone operate together, as if in tandem, in making the commercial, political and sporting decisions which dictate the running of world motor sport.

People always think of the two of us together [he said]. I like to think of Bernie as a close friend. That, of course, is a completely different thing from being under his influence. The thing about Bernie and me is that, in 1971, we were elected by the Formula One teams to represent their interests. In one way, or another, we were always the elected representatives of FOCA. So, of course, we have worked together very closely. But since 1983, although we see each other and have discussions, we have not worked anything like as closely as we did before. And we haven't always agreed about everything by any means.

Mosley's promise was to effect a silent revolution. When he took office, however, he found more needed to be done than he expected.

Tremendous reorganisation of the commissions is needed. One or two new commissions are needed and it is essential to have a strategic planning commission immediately to look at fundamental reforms. Overall, the only area that works properly is Formula One and, at the moment, that is the area where most time is spent. I think that is a great mistake.

He also said that he saw no need for the president of FISA to become involved in anything like a sporting referee. This was a clear reference to the controversial manner in which Jean-Marie Balestre had interfered following the collision between Alain Prost and Ayrton Senna in the 1989 Japanese Grand Prix at Suzuka.

In his own way, Mosley has quietly revolutionised everything within the FIA since he took office. But there have been plenty of instances where he has stepped into the limelight to make a forceful point or maintain his own influence. In 1995 at the San Marino Grand Prix, for example, at an event held under sombre circumstances just 12 months after the deaths at Imola of Roland Ratzenberger and Ayrton Senna, he used the anniversary as a platform to appeal for probity and professionalism after a year of excessive controversy, death and intrigue had encouraged the world to watch Formula One as if it were a sporting adjunct to a late-night horror movie. The 1994 season had seen two drivers killed, a spate of other

serious accidents, a series of sporting controversies including
the removal of a fuel filter by Benetton-Renault, the suspension of Michael Schumacher because he ignored a black flag
at Silverstone during the British Grand Prix (after he had
passed Damon Hill on the formation lap) and, ultimately, a
tumultuous finish in Adelaide where Schumacher won his
first drivers' title after a collision which removed both his and
Damon Hill's car from the contest. The 1995 season had
started with a controversy in Brazil where Benetton and
Williams were found to be using irregular fuel. They lost their
points scored in the race.

> I suggest that an honest and adult attitude is required [he
> said]. Everyone involved – the teams, the sponsors, the
> technical experts – must bear in mind that fundamentally
> this is a sport. It may involve a great deal of money. It may
> have huge commercial interests at stake, but the moment
> anyone at the top of Formula One is more interested in the
> money than the result, the whole thing will collapse.

Mosley, of course, has survived many attempts to dislodge him
from power. One came, just a month after the tragedies of
Imola, at the 1994 Spanish Grand Prix at Barcelona where certain team owners and principals held a meeting. The teams
were upset at the way in which Mosley had handled the post-
Imola fallout, calling for more and greater safety measures
which would add to their costs. A grumble among them grew
collective and then revolutionary, amid calls for a strike if their
own demands on how things should be were not met. When the
Benetton principals Flavio Briatore and Tom Walkinshaw
returned to their motor home, they announced: 'Mosley is finished. He is gone. From now on, the teams will run the sport.'
The strike never happened, the coup d'état never happened
and Mosley remained in charge. Another revolution bubbled
below the surface in 2000, when Ron Dennis and Frank
Williams, two of the long-serving members of the club,
expressed their dissatisfaction with the FIA's appeals procedure. They sought guidance from the European Commission,
with whom the FIA had only recently settled a long-running
dispute over television rights. Eddie Jordan was also unhappy
and sided with the McLaren and Williams owners. But Mosley
was ready. When a meeting took place on 6 September at the

Hilton Hotel at Heathrow Terminal 4, he was armed heavily and had fired the first shot.

In a letter addressed to Williams that was sent the previous day and circulated among all the teams, Mosley had virtually torn his opponents to shreds. In this, he wrote:

If you were truly concerned about the FIA Court of Appeal, I would have expected you to make a formal approach to the FIA. The first step would probably have been a written memorandum setting out your misgivings together with your proposals for reform. That would have been followed by at least one meeting. There is a whole process, which any reasonable person would go through before seeking to involve an outside agency. The fact is that you did none of these things. You have occasionally said something, but never made any serious attempt to get things changed.

He reminded Williams also that he had accepted the system when he, belatedly (for reasons relating to another internal dispute within the club) had signed the latest Concorde Agreement. The letter continued:

As you and Ron [Dennis] know well, it is open to anyone to start their own motor sport series. The organiser of such a series would obviously have all the commercial rights, as well as full sporting control, subject only to normal safety precautions and the basic requirements of the International Sporting Code. As I explained to you last night, it is what Ron should do if he wants to manage an international motor sport series himself. I wrote to him the other day telling him this. Ron has no role in the FIA Formula One World Championship apart from that granted him, in common with other teams, by the Concorde Agreement. Unfortunately, he finds all this rather difficult to understand.

The cutting irony and deft reasoning, made public, undermined the 'rebels' position at the meeting at Heathrow and another brief barrage of Mosley completed his triumph. The attempted coup on the palace was all over before anyone had known it had started. The team principals and owners apparently swept the event under the carpet although, as one later revealed, it was more a case of many of them lacking the courage to follow through their promised actions when faced by Mosley's counter-attack. Mosley, later, said:

> Ron seems to think he has some sort of mission personally to manage Formula One. He does not seem to understand that the FIA Formula One World Championship belongs to the 120-odd FIA member countries which founded it in 1950 and have run it ever since.

It was an episode that provided a classic example of how the political structure which supports the Formula One business has evolved. The teams, once so powerful as a unit led by Ecclestone and Mosley, have become important companies, joined forces with major manufacturers and corporations. They need a pristine image and a well-run publicly open and accountable operation as much as the sport at large. Mosley, in his own way, has guided the business and the teams in that direction albeit, as Dennis pointed out, that he believed Mosley would arbitrarily change the rules to suit himself. 'You know,' he explained. 'It's always been the case that whenever I have been told what I should be doing, I have been inclined to do precisely the opposite.'

Given their long shared experiences together in motor racing, and particularly in Formula One, it is little wonder that Max Mosley, Bernie Ecclestone, Ron Dennis, Frank Williams and the rest, including Ken Tyrrell, in particular, before his retirement in 1999, developed a close bond. It would be an exaggeration to say they were like a secret society, but there are enough examples of secrecy and their closeness to suggest it. Mosley raced for Williams' Formula Two team before either of them earned fame or, in Williams' case, a fortune (Mosley has enjoyed considerable independent wealth all his life and his position with the FIA, as president, is nominally an unpaid post).

Dennis was a mechanic for the early Cooper team, worked for Jochen Rindt and went with him to Brabham. Rindt was managed by Ecclestone. Tyrrell ran the Cooper Formula Two team. All these connections are normal, just part of the maze of life, especially a motor racing group of people such as these. It is no surprise, therefore, that these men, the veterans of the club, have stuck together and maintained close relationships, alliances sometimes, as the years have gone by. Even though various political, technical or sporting situations have arisen which moved them to different sides of the arguments, they have retained each other's respect. They are the inner circle and it easy to understand why. At meetings, when they are all present, it is their voices, more often than not, that are heard the most and which lead the way. If Mosley is absent, Ecclestone often takes charge.

Note-taking, or official minutes, had not been encouraged much down the years and often the meetings of the Formula One Constructors' Association have been described as extraordinary, disorganised or even ridiculous. (In one famous paddock anecdote, that may well be apocryphal, it is said that the former Lotus team manager Peter Warr was asked to act as a minutes secretary in order to comply with a request for records to be kept. His record of the meeting covered two lines and showed that the meeting opened and closed.) But that is a third-hand generalisation, not a fact, and anyone with personal experience of any discussions with any of these men as individuals could not mistake their ability, in virtually any subject. Hard-headed businessmen they may be, entrepreneurs, racers, risk-takers, control-freaks, fastidious and ambitious and fuelled by power, but they are not frivolous or blessed with time to waste.

Within the club, too, there are other clubs, like senior committees. These are the serious policy-making groups. The bigger groups, which include far-flung team principals with less experience to attend and learn, are not as effective in real terms. In 2001, the teams and their owners or principal representatives included Ferrari (owned by Fiat, normally represented by Jean Todt, the sporting director, rather than the company president Luca di Montezemolo), McLaren (part-owned and represented by Ron Dennis), Williams (owned and represented by Frank Williams), Benetton (owned by Renault, represented by Flavio Briatore), British American Racing (owned by British American Tobacco, Adrian Reynard and Craig Pollock and represented by Pollock), Jordan (owned and represented by Eddie Jordan), Arrows (owned and represented by Tom Walkinshaw), Sauber (owned and represented by Peter Sauber), Jaguar (owned by Ford and represented by Bobby Rahal), Minardi (owned and represented by Paul Stoddart) and Prost (owned and represented by Alain Prost). Of these 11 men, only two (Pollock and Rahal) were university graduates, a fact of minor importance, but one that demonstrates how heavily 'streetwise' and battle-hardened by either life itself or life in motor racing the majority of them have been. Of the total, only Prost could claim to be a successful ex-Grand Prix driver, though Jordan, Rahal, Walkinshaw and Williams, in varying degrees, had considerable experience in other formulae, Rahal having been highly successful in Indycar racing in the United States and having competed briefly in two Grands Prix.

The heart of the club has been formed by the inner circle of British teams, those men whose teams had been part of the formative years of FOCA. In particular, this meant Williams and Dennis, but in modern times, it is believed, included Pollock, Jordan, Walkinshaw, Rahal and Briatore. In 2001, when the future of the sport was threatened by the actions of the major manufacturers who were members of the European Car Manufacturers' Association (ACEA) and threatened to create a breakaway series, this group of British teams held regular monthly meetings of their own at a famous hotel-restaurant, Le Manoir aux Quatre Saisons, at Great Milton, in Oxfordshire. At these meetings, the team principals discussed the latest moves and negotiations in relation to the ACEA with Dennis, understandably, often leading the way thanks to his close relationship with Mercedes-Benz and Daimler-Chrysler. In their own way, these secret discussions reflected the original divisions between the British teams and the European mainland manufacturers and the suspicions that remained between them. Prost, Sauber and Todt would be included in meetings held at race meetings or, if convenient, at additional meetings held at Heathrow airport in advance of the meetings of the Formula One Commission. These were usually focused, of course, on preparing for points on the agenda, but they were rarely as dedicated to forming policy for the club and its members as the lunches at Le Manoir.

Ron Dennis was born in Woking on 1 June 1947. He lived and grew up in the town, leaving school at 16 to become an apprentice mechanic at the Thompson and Taylor garage, close to the old Brooklands racing circuit at Byfleet. For a spell, he did a part-time vehicle technology course at Guildford Technical College. When Thompson and Taylor was taken over by the Chipstead Motor Group, which had also swallowed up Coopers, the tender-aged Dennis was transferred to the Cooper production line and helped build Formula Two and Formula Three Cooper racing cars. At 18, keen and proficient, he moved again and became a mechanic with the Cooper Formula One team for the 1966 season. He had achieved a goal. He had found his way into motor racing which, in his own words, was a difficult business to break into in the 1960s.

> People just don't understand what F1 was like then [he said].
> No sponsors, no brand names on the cars except,
> occasionally, a fuel company. If you wanted to get into
> racing, there were three ways: as a driver, as a team owner
> or manager, or as a mechanic. I had a passion for the job
> and it was the only avenue available to me. I wouldn't for
> one minute demean the role of the guys who work on the
> cars today, but it was completely different in the 1960s.
> When I started with Cooper, it was hard for people to accept
> my age. My first Grand Prix was the Mexican in 1966. I was
> 19 and the next mechanic in the pit lane was 20 years older.
> It was a mature person's job, so it was not easy to achieve
> acceptance. Even then, it was expensive to send someone
> around the world and maturity was the important
> ingredient for a mechanic. I didn't have the maturity or the
> experience, but I certainly had a lot of commitment.

His first driver was Jochen Rindt, the proud Austrian, who was managed by Bernie Ecclestone and who later became the sport's only posthumous world champion, and his first car the Cooper-Maserati of that summer when England won the World Cup and Harold Wilson was Prime Minister. When Rindt left Cooper for Brabham in 1968, Dennis went with him. This may suggest that Dennis liked the arrogant Rindt, but he did not. 'He was arrogant and really didn't treat people properly,' Dennis told Alan Henry, for his book McLaren: The Epic Years.

> Especially, the mechanics. I recall at the 1967 German
> Grand Prix, Roy Salvadori (the team manager at Coopers)
> telling him that he'd better hurry up and get ready,
> because it was almost time for the start. Rindt just replied
> 'They won't dare start the German Grand Prix without me.'
> So, one of the other mechanics looked up and muttered
> rather acidly 'Why don't you pop down the road with your
> helmet and fill it with ten pounds of potatoes?' I left
> Cooper at the end of 1967 and it was several months to the
> first Grand Prix of the next year. I only went to Brabham

on the express condition that I didn't work in the production shop and was therefore involved in building the prototype Formula One car for the 1968 season. I just developed a good relationship with Jack and, before the season actually started, he asked me to work on his car. So, I said 'Ok, but you break the news to Rindt.'

Dennis was therefore, at 21, working as chief mechanic for the great Jack Brabham. The three years he spent at Brabham taught him much not only about working as a mechanic and racing, but also about the business of Formula One. When Brabham retired, at the end of 1970, Dennis, who had effectively been in charge of the team for the final two North American races of the season, took the decision to set up on his own. Teaming up with a fellow Brabham mechanic, Neil Trundle, they formed Rondel Racing, which opened for business in February 1971, in Woking. For Dennis, his friendship with Trundle was one of the most important of his career. They had met for the first time when Trundle, new to the team, was cleaning out the gearbox bell-housing on Rindt's Brabham BT26 in the paddock at Zandvoort. Dennis made a playful remark about doing certain jobs 'the Brabham way' and provoked Trundle. Despite the inauspicious beginning, it was the start of a long-lasting friendship. Their first ambition was to compete in the European Formula Two series with one car, to be driven by the promising Australian Tim Schenken, but thanks to the arrival of the ambitious young Frenchman Bob Wollek, who had done well in Formula Three, supported by plentiful backing from the oil company Motul, this plan was enlarged to embrace a bigger team.

> Ron Tauranac loaned us three Formula Two chassis, we sold them at the end of the year and paid him the difference [Dennis told Henry]. So, he effectively created a cash flow, but it was also good for him because we were the only ones running his cars really competently. We bought the engines from Bernie Ecclestone, which had come back from the South American Formula Two Temporada series as deck cargo. They were covered in corrosion, but we tidied them up a bit and then went on to use them.

Rondel Racing used a pale blue transporter that year. It looked smart, but it was, in fact, a revamped and refurbished vehicle that the team rescued from premises in Maidenhead. It was stripped down, cleaned up and repainted by Dennis, Trundle and a group of friends from their local pub. Such benevolence (the drinkers were repaid for their efforts with liquid refreshments) was typical of the times as was the generosity of Graham Hill, then a Formula One driver for Brabham. Seeing Dennis and his helpers building up the BT36 for Wollek, he wandered in for a chat. When Dennis asked him if he would take part in some early-season races for him, Hill said 'yes'. He finished second in the season-opener at Hockenehim and won at Thruxton on Easter Monday.

More good luck came Dennis's way when, in an effort to raise funds by finding sponsorship, he and Trundle produced a brochure on Rondel Racing, which explained their ambitions and objectives. This was another typical piece of Dennis forethought and attention to detail, alongside his fastidiousness about order and cleanliness within the team. According to Henry, the father of Dennis's former fiancée, who was an antiques dealer, had a regular customer who was a Ferrari owner. He passed on this piece of information and Dennis promptly sent a brochure out. The man turned out to be Tony Vlassopulos, a successful shipping broker in the City of London who was a great racing enthusiast. He agreed to help the fledgling Rondel Racing team in their maiden season and took over as company chairman. Dennis, as so often, had demonstrated a knack for finding the money as well as keeping the team in order and the reward was in seeing Schenken finish fourth in the European Trophy series that season.

The following year, 1972, was progressive for Rondel Racing, with the team using Brabham BT38s and consolidating their early efforts, but it was a turbulent and near-tragic one for Dennis. In the early part of the summer, he was involved in a serious road accident, which left him badly injured and in hospital for two months. He suffered head injuries and, some said, the blow left him changed forever. While in hospital, he did a lot of reflecting on his life and, afterwards, moved into management.

> In fact, it was probably the most positive thing that ever happened to me [he said]. During that period, I managed the company as opposed to participating in the engineering side. I suppose the accident allowed me to break free of that for the rest of my life.

Associates who knew him before and after the accident later joked that it may have given him the chance to break into management, but it cost him his once prevalent laid-back approach to life, altered his sense of humour and changed him as a person. Indeed, some said, it was as a result of this accident that 'Ronspeak', the serious heavily woven language adopted later by Dennis in formal surroundings, was invented. True or not, the accident certainly changed him and his life and soon afterwards, he was planning his own cars.

Dennis commissioned Ray Jessop to design a Formula Two car for the 1973 season with sponsorship from Motul Oil. Success followed, but it was Formula One that was in Dennis's mind and in the course of the season Jessop was commissioned to design a Rondel F1 car. Unfortunately, it never ran because the 1973 Oil Crisis intervened, forcing Motul to reduce its lavish spending on motor racing. Rondel Racing was also brought to a standstill, but the team's reputation had been made in the previous two years by their immaculate presentation and orderliness. This was noted by various sponsors, including Marlboro, before Dennis left. The Formula One car project was then taken over by Vlassopulos and his friend Ken Grob. For reasons as obvious as the creation of the name Rondel, it was called the Token and was driven in 1974, when Rondel Racing ceased trading, by Tom Pryce, David Purley and Ian Ashley.

Dennis started again in 1975 when he established a new team called Project Three. Manufacturers and sponsors, in particular John Hogan of Philip Morris (which owned the Marlboro brand), who had earlier worked for Coca-Cola and helped Rondel find money, had been impressed by his earlier efforts and asked him to run teams on their behalf. He was involved in the BMW Junior Team, for Formula Two, and, later, the ICI March team, before he launched Project Four, which enjoyed considerable success in Formula Two and Formula Three racing.

In this period, his drivers included many future stars including Eddie Cheever and Stefan Johanssson. The team won the British Formula Three title in 1979 and 1980, with Chico Serra and Johansson, who was by then sponsored by Marlboro. At this time, the astute Dennis benefited from an unexpected development that arose from the appearance and order of this team. In 1979, BMW had introduced their M1 'supercar' and Dennis was commissioned to prepare a number of them for the one-make 'Procar' series that was run in support of several European Grands Prix that summer. Better still, for Project Four, they entered their own Marlboro-supported M1 with Niki Lauda, in that 1979 series, and won the championship. Swiftly, therefore, in one successful move, he had taken his team forward into a Grand Prix environment, won a title and demonstrated efficiency, order and speed to the top sponsors of the day.

Formula One, naturally, was always on his mind and, he knew, that to succeed in building his team to that level he would need an experienced and top-class designer working for him at his base in Pool Road, Woking. Dennis made approaches to Gordon Murray, then making his name at Brabham, and Patrick Head, at Williams. Both were settled and declined to move. Then he spoke to John Barnard, a man of independent mind, who at first appeared to show little interest in the idea. Dennis persevered, pointing out to Barnard that he would have a completely free hand in the design, engineering and technical side of the operation, and their discussions were more fruitful. When Dennis showed Barnard a carbon-fibre composite rear wing from one of the BMW M1 cars, it jogged him into considering using such highly advanced material to build a complete Formula One chassis. He could see the benefits and the two joined forces with Dennis attempting to find the £350,000 they estimated would be enough to support the idea and Barnard, just returned from working in America for the Chaparral team which won the Indianapolis 500 in 1980, concentrating on making Formula One history.

By then, Barnard was already a seasoned design engineer. Born in Wembley in 1946, he had studied at Brunel and Watford technical colleges, worked for Lola, alongside Head, for McLaren, alongside Gordon Coppuck, and for the Parnelli Indycar team in California, before moving to Chaparral in Texas. He and Dennis were a formidable partnership; strong-minded, perfectionist, outspoken and prone to loud arguments, but capable of achieving the heights. The Marlboro men knew this, thanks to Hogan's watchful eye, and knowing also that McLaren, since the death of the team's founder Bruce McLaren in testing at Goodwood on 2 June 1970, had struggled to maintain the same level of momentum and purpose, they hatched a scheme to merge Dennis's Project Four with the McLaren team. Teddy Mayer, the senior executive of the original four-man team that began McLaren, had offered Barnard a job back at McLaren when he returned from America; but he had wanted him to work alongside Coppuck. Barnard said no; he wanted Coppuck out if he was to join.

Marlboro, the sponsors of McLaren, had suggested a merger with Project Four in 1979. They did the same in 1980, with a sharper tone of warning and, as a result, in September 1980, Dennis and Barnard and Project Four became part of McLaren International, the new company which was to grow rapidly and become a force in Formula One for the following two decades. Dennis and Mayer were appointed the joint managing directors and Coppuck left, leaving Barnard with a free hand and none of the distractions he had perceived to exist under the previous and more informal regime.

Dennis, in the role of dealmaker, was out of the Ecclestone mould. Always ready for the next step, never satisfied, restless and fussy and competitive, he was also a bad loser. All these qualities began to come through as he and Barnard transformed McLaren. The more carefree days of the team's origins were left behind as they carried McLaren International forward as a strong, innovative organisation, characterised by attention to detail, excellent preparation and total commitment. Barnard finalised his design for the new carbon-fibre composite car and they forged a deal, thanks to a little help from Steve Nichols, an old friend of Barnard's, with Hercules Aerospace, of Salt Lake City, a company deeply into carbon-fibre technology, to supply the necessary materials for the MP4 design. When it was launched in early 1981, it was heralded as a breakthrough and much was made of the fact it was stiffer, lighter and more impact-resistant than the normal aluminium honeycomb monocoques. Furthermore, Barnard said the number of components used was reduced from around 50 sections of aluminium to just five main panels. The MP4 car put McLaren, and Ron Dennis and John Barnard, firmly on the Formula One map.

Although Dennis was a shy man in many ways, he was also extrovert in others. Indeed, he was a bag of contradictions. He could be ultra-cautious on certain issues and highly adventurous with others. However, early in 1981, with the launch of the MP4, a standard-setting car in terms of concept and appearance (it was beautifully finished and made a major impression when it made its first appearance at Long Beach, where it was on show only and did not race, but succeeded in making the M29 look suddenly out of date), Dennis knew he was involved in something special. He told Henry: 'I have told Marlboro that we will win at least one grand prix this year.' That season, 1981, also saw the banning of the so-called 'sliding skirts', an action taken by Jean-Marie Balestre to clamp down on cornering speeds and halt the momentum of the 'ground-effect' British kit car teams. To beat the regulations (as all the teams did in those days), Dennis's McLaren team fitted a progressive 'double-spring' system which was designed to compress down hard on the suspension at speed and then ride up to conform with the ground clearance rules when the car slowed down and came into the pits.

Dennis's prediction came true at the British Grand Prix, at Silverstone, on 18 July 1981, when John Watson drove splendidly to take advantage of the retirements of the turbo-powered Renaults and claim an historic triumph. It was Ulsterman Watson's second career victory and hugely popular with the British fans. It also followed his strong third place finish at the Spanish Grand Prix, at Jarama, and then second in the French Grand Prix at Dijon. It may have owed something to good fortune, but it was a merited success. It was a breakthrough for Dennis. He was now a victorious Grand Prix team owner and Barnard was a victorious designer and technical director.

The following year, Dennis was ready with more deals. He lured Niki Lauda out of retirement and he persuaded TAG (Techniques d'Avant Garde, a Luxembourg based holding company established in 1977 by Akram Ojjeh, a Franco-Lebanese entrepreneur, who had sponsored Williams since 1980, which specialised in high technology work) to invest in the development of a very special 1.5 litre turbocharged engine from Porsche. These two deals gave him leverage and power and he was able to approach the German manufacturer as a customer and order the power-unit he wanted made to his own specifications, or more specifically, to Barnard's detailed specifications. The shy engineer, with a dry sense of humour, always knew exactly what he wanted. This engine was ready for 1984, leaving Lauda to partner Watson through two interim seasons as the 'package' and the team was developed. The decision to approach Lauda, who had famously walked out of Formula One while midway through practice with Bernie Ecclestone's Brabham team at the 1979 Canadian Grand Prix, claiming he was 'bored driving round and round in circles', was an inspired move by Dennis.

By 1981 Lauda, as he had suspected, was bored with setting up and running his own airline. He brought massive publicity to the McLaren team and prepared the way for the period of dominance that finally arrived when Dennis's meticulous planning and preparations, coupled with another stroke of sublime opportunism, paid off. When he took joint control of the team in 1980, before establishing himself in sole charge within a year, Dennis found his resident drivers were Watson and Alain Prost. Watson stayed, under new ownership, but Prost was lured away by Renault, unconvinced by Dennis and Barnard's persuasive visions of the future. That he was wrong was proved when Prost was dismissed by Renault at the end of 1983 and left without a drive. As an admirer of his ability, Dennis could hardly believe his luck and swiftly signed him for a retainer that was regarded as a coup.

> I had nothing else then and Ron knew it [said Prost]. It embarrasses me now that I signed for so little money, but, at the time, I didn't care. I was away from Renault and that was all that mattered.

Prost's arrival, of course, meant that the well-liked and dependable Watson was out. The man who had been a teenage mechanic to Rindt had grown into a decision-making opportunist with an impassioned ambition to realise; and he knew that a combination of Lauda and Prost would take him there. The McLaren-TAG combination became one of the most formidable forces in Formula One history, winning world titles with Lauda in 1984 and Prost in 1985 and 1986. Even the breakdown of Dennis's close relationship with Barnard and his departure to Ferrari could not stem the tide, though Dennis needed to step back and make adjustments, periodically, to maintain his team's phenomenal development and rate of success.

When, for example, it was clear that Williams' partnership with Honda was producing a triumphant package in the late 1980s, Dennis's reaction was to compete fiercely, to obtain the Honda engines, if necessary to deprive Williams of them and, at the same time, to create a virtual 'dream team' by partnering Prost with the superbly talented, if temperamental, Ayrton Senna for 1988. Together, they won 15 of the 16 races on the calendar and Senna, emerging on top in what became one of the most bitterly contested driver pairings in the sport's history, won his first drivers' championship.

It was in that season that Dennis remarked, as a joke to journalists who ribbed him for being a few minutes late at a news conference, that 'we are here to make history, you are only here to report it'. This was a comment that did little to reduce a growing impression that his and McLaren's massive roll of success had loosened his links with the ordinary man in the street, the kind of man who enjoyed a joke and a pint in the pub and who would laugh at such memories as the day when Jack Brabham failed to win a race only allegedly because his chief mechanic, Ron Dennis, had not given his car enough fuel to go the distance. It seemed, then, he had gone a long way from the days when he asked for help from friends in the pub to prepare a car. Such public comments, however, betrayed something else. The official face of Dennis, the owner, director, manager and strategist, was more and more in demand and becoming more and more verbose and stereotypical; but the private man, once known as a great practical joker, a generous spirit and a risk-taker, was disappearing from view. And the truth of the 'Brabham race', when Dennis merely followed orders by enriching the mixture and taking the blame, seemed less and less important as people swallowed the apocryphal story.

Prost, famously and infamously, had his revenge on Senna in 1989 after the pair collided at the chicane at Suzuka, in the decisive and season-ending Japanese Grand Prix. Senna, despite recovering, driving across the chicane, and finishing first, was disqualified in a move loudly supported by the bombastic Jean-Marie Balestre. Prost departed afterwards for Ferrari, but Dennis's McLaren steamroller continued to win championships with Senna in 1990 and 1991 before Williams, fully recovered after being dropped by Honda because they refused to take a Japanese driver (he went to the declining Lotus team with a supply of engines), became the dominant force again with Renault. Dennis, far-sighted and astute in business beyond racing, had persuaded TAG to join forces with McLaren, when the Porsche engine project came to an end, in the creation of the Tag McLaren Group, with a series of ambitious programmes in mind, including the creation of a 'supercar' called the McLaren F1.

TAG took a 60 per cent holding in McLaren in 1984, Mansour Ojjeh, the motor racing-obsessed son of TAG's founder Akram

Ojjeh, showing enormous enthusiasm for the move. It meant that the company, TAG, which had taken over and transformed the fortunes of the once-ailing Swiss watch-makers Heuer, was a majority player in the team and Dennis had found a long-term partner, albeit one that had been introduced to Formula One by Frank Williams. The McLaren F1 was one result, a dazzling achievement, but the timing of the F1's arrival was unlucky; recession worldwide meant that it appeared at the very time when the supercar market was shrinking. In racing, however, the F1 showed its pedigree by dominating the Le Mans 24 Hours race. The McLaren Group, with TAG support, developed rapidly under Dennis and his partners and added car manufacturing, electronic systems and marketing services to the racing team operation.

When Honda withdrew from Formula One following a late decision at the end of 1992, however, Dennis was caught virtually unprepared. He had no engine supply organised and, despite trying various options, ended up being a Ford-Cosworth customer. This meant that Senna, unarguably the greatest driver of the day, was saddled with an under-powered car. At the end of 1993, during which he delivered the finest performance of his career to win the European Grand Prix in torrential rain at Donington Park and recorded four more victories, he left for Williams, where Prost, in a Renault-powered car, had won his fourth title that year, succeeding the 1992 champion Nigel Mansell who had stormed off to race in America when he learned that Prost had been signed to join Williams. Without competitive engines, and without Senna, Dennis and McLaren endured three lean years before their next key partnership, with Mercedes-Benz, which started in 1995, began to bear fruit. The omens were not good at the beginning when Nigel Mansell was recruited and found the MP4/10 not only 'not to his liking', but also not to the measurements of his lower abdominal girth.

By 1997 they began winning again and in 1998 and 1999 Mika Hakkinen won the drivers' world title, defeating a powerful challenge from Michael Schumacher and Ferrari each time. The fruits were harvested off the circuit, too, as Dennis, the man who began his motor racing career as a mechanic, became a multimillionaire not only through his success with the team, but also by selling some of his shares as the world's car-makers began amalgamating and Formula One embraced a new corporate era. In 1999, he sold a quarter of his 40 per cent stake in McLaren to

Daimler-Chrysler, Mercedes' parent company, in a deal that secured his family's long-term future and also ensured stability for his team. Not bad, at all, for a boy who had left school at 16 to be an apprentice mechanic. *The Sunday Times* rich list in 2001 said he was worth £160 million. He was probably worth far more.

His money has been his passport to a life that may have been beyond his wildest dreams in his early years in Woking. His American wife Lisa, however, is a woman with her feet firmly on the ground and this ensures that Dennis retains his own contact with normality. If he has appeared, at times, to have been aloof or distant, it may have been his natural shyness and concentration on his work, rather than any real arrogance in him and, certainly, as he has matured he has mellowed though few of his team employees, past or present, believe he has slackened off in his drive to win everything, everywhere, all the time. Indeed, some have suggested that his energy is as powerful now as ever, and his tempers, when thwarted, as spectacular as at any time in the last 20 years. His single-minded outlook was demonstrated in September 1992 during a news conference at Monza, when Dennis confirmed he had signed Michael Andretti for 1993, and admitted that he expected Honda to withdraw from being McLaren's engine suppliers.

> I probably understand Ayrton Senna better than anyone else and I have absolutely no problem with his desire to put himself, at every opportunity, in a position to win. There are all sorts of words that you can use, maybe even with a violin . . . You can talk about loyalty, you can talk about good times shared, you can talk about all sorts of emotional things. But this is a business about winning races and Ayrton lives for winning. So, I accept completely that if there is a better opportunity for him to win a race, then, no problem.

At the time, Dennis refused to tell Senna, his friend as well as his best driver, what plans he had for engines in 1993 and beyond. In the end, Senna, unhappy, frustrated and loyal to Dennis, stayed on for a year of satisfying racing, but without a driver's title to show for it. In 1994 he moved to Williams only to be killed in the San Marino Grand Prix at Imola. It was a tragedy that deeply affected Dennis who had harboured a real belief that Senna would return to McLaren. In January 1994 he told Eoin Young:

Our relationship last season was extremely good. I don't see Ayrton driving for Williams for a couple of years at the end of our relationship because I think he's driven by an intense desire to win Grands Prix and world championships and he will put himself in the best possible position to do that after two years at Williams. His first objective is to win. The second is to achieve the best commercial package.

In the same interview, Dennis confirmed to Young that he had told his team not to show 'undue emotion' after winning a Grand Prix in the 1988 season because that was what they were there for. 'We all became a little uncomfortable with our successes because of rubbing salt, and during that period we were deliberately low key.' In 1988 McLaren won 15 of the 16 races.

Through all his success, however, Dennis had not won any love or popularity from the media or the public, although he had earned respect from everyone. When his team went through a difficult period, usually between technical partners capable of supplying a winning engine, he found it difficult to cope with the attitude of some critics who seemed to revel in McLaren's problems as they sought to recover and rise again. Sometimes, it seemed Dennis wanted to prove he was different to everyone else, above it all, a member of a higher breed of racing team and that his membership of this club was little more than a convenience to enable him to prove his team's overall superiority when time called for it.

I have a belief that everything is important in life and everything is important when you are trying to achieve high levels of success in any business; certainly in Formula One. I believe that at all times you should have the best, or at least try to have the best. This is not simply about money. It is mainly about commitment. We try to inspire it into the very fibre of everyone's approach to their work for the team. Winning is not just about winning on the circuit. It is about winning off the circuit, too. Consequently, when people pass less than favourable remarks about things that we do, most of the time those remarks broadly reflect the fact that they recognise that we have higher standards than they have achieved.

It had never been Dennis's style or object to be liked for his professionalism and his sense of purpose. His will to win, his competitive streak, was as steely as that in any driver and often prevailed over them. His negotiations with Senna were often protracted and intense; once, when they were a million pounds apart, they settled their difference by agreeing to toss a coin: Senna lost. On another occasion, Dennis won a bet with Senna by eating a prescribed amount of hot peppers and surviving. This determination made him a winner in the restaurant and has helped make him a winner on the track with his team. But it is allied to a willingness to be pragmatic, plan long-term and think big.

> If you are in Formula One, you strive for perfection and you look everywhere for improvements [he explained]. Not just in the chassis or the engines, but everywhere. There is that common desire to be better ... What you really need is the ability to second-guess what is going to happen; not at the next Grand Prix, sometimes not even next year, but what is going to happen in the longer term. You need to be constantly gearing up with that in mind, and that is where I think I need to apply my time.

As a thinker, a planner and an organiser, Dennis has naturally played a strong and influential role in the 'club' for many years, always making his opinions known, fighting for the constructors' rights and defending the image of Formula One itself. Many inside the Piranha Club believe Dennis is the most obvious natural successor to Ecclestone as the ringmaster.

In 1991 the magazine Management Week ran a cover story that asked of Dennis: Is this the best manager in Britain? He had clearly made a big impression. After Colin Chapman, whose death coincided with his own arrival and rise, Dennis was seen as an innovator with courage and judgement. He has built up his own team, taken his own risks, introduced the carbon-fibre monocoque, built a wind tunnel, developed his own turbo engine, created in alliance with TAG a successful electronics business within the group to work for more than 60 high-tech customers, including rival teams, done deals, found partners, raised money and fought on issues of conscience. The expansion of McLaren, the rapid progress in Dennis's own career; both are evidence of a man on a mission.

When there is conflict between his goals and the ruling body, or any other authority, his frustration and irritation is plain to see, as it was when, as one involved in the British Racing Drivers' Club's efforts to resolve the long-term future of the British Grand Prix at Silverstone, he was reportedly close to losing his self-control during moments of near-rage as the owners of Brands Hatch, who had secured a contract to run the race, stood firm. He was also very upset, it was said, when plans to develop a circuit at Lydden, near Dover, were stalled by the intervention of other parties connected with the Brands Hatch owners. His temper tantrums at such times are loud, explosive and demonstrative. The same deep sense of desire to succeed, or fear of failure, affects both his business life and his motor racing.

> The pain I feel of failure is such an incentive to succeed that you don't need anyone barbing you or motivating you. I am just a terrible loser [he admitted]. When I say that, I don't mean in a sporting sense. I may be able to go and have a drink and feel relaxed, but the pain is there all the time. It's the eyes opening on Monday morning when the first thing that comes into your brain is 'was there a Grand Prix, the day before, and the second thing is where did we finish?' And if it is anywhere other than first, the next thing is . . . hell.

His views spread far and wide across motor racing and reflect a great ambition. In 1993, when he was under pressure to resolve engine suppliers for McLaren and to retain Senna as a driver, he was also deeply concerned at the way in which Max Mosley was controlling the sport. In particular, at that time, he was worried about the way in which the technical regulations were due to be revised with the banning of electronic systems like traction control, anti-lock braking and active suspension.

> Our opposition, which is a strong opposition, is to the introduction of change in a manner that is inconsistent with the regulations, because then we would not have the ability to exploit our investment [he said]. I think that you have to try to bring to bear common sense and logic. But you have got to bring it to bear where people's egos don't get damaged . . . because this is a very ego-driven subject

at the moment. Public debate is the problem. It is not constructive to finding solutions.

These were strongly felt opinions. Dennis believes he and his associates among the best-funded and best-run teams in Formula One, the men who sit at the heart of the club after years of service and success, are most qualified and responsible for shaping its future. It is a position that has often left him in conflict with other parties, often particularly the ruling body and Mosley. He had built his team, almost literally, with his own hands and survived the Darwinian tests thrown at him. It was this system that had his support. Let the rich grow rich, if they know how; let the poor perish, unless they find the means to survive, compete, succeed and join the rich. In the Piranha Club, you eat, or are eaten; as Bernie Ecclestone said, it is a place for the quick and the dead.

> You must not be under any illusions [said Dennis]. The issues that are on the table at the moment [the banning of electronic driver-aids in 1993] are not about money. Money is the camouflage on a fundamental desire to remove from the 'haves' the technical advantages that the 'have-not' teams do not have. There can be no stability until the teams come together and form a balancing power base opposite to that of the governing body. This is completely normal in all sports. There must be a balance. The problem is that the teams are divided. They are divided because the uncompetitive teams are trying to drag back the competitive teams, in terms of technology ... There are different forms of survival. If your objective is to survive by reducing the cost of Grand Prix racing, that objective is not achievable. Grand Prix racing is the pinnacle of motor sport. It has the money that is reflective of 500 million people watching it every other week. That level of media exposure justifies a certain level of investment. And that level of investment is going to be used by the teams who have the biggest share of the voice, to maintain their positions. That value is reflected in income – and our team will use that income to maintain its position. Those are the fundamental economics of Grand Prix racing. The smaller teams must get their acts together. Not from a financial point of view, but from a technical point of view. They

195

have got to kick out the dead wood and they must employ people who can effect change. There are no miracles in motor racing. Nobody can wave some magic wand over the back eight cars on the grid and suddenly have them at the front. It is just not possible. If they are not capable, they will die.

This was a critical period for Formula One when the balance between governing body, teams and commercial rights was under examination and when, also, the technical regulations were revised to improve the racing, reduce the costs and ensure that the poorly-funded teams could compete. It was difficult, however, for Dennis. Just at the very time when Mosley was coming to terms with the shape of Formula One and its image, an overhaul which was accelerated after Ratzenberger and Senna were killed at Imola in 1994, McLaren were struggling, but investing in the future. Furthermore, there were new influences at work. Men like Flavio Briatore, representing a group of external commercial interests not connected directly with motor racing, had arrived. Briatore was to run the Formula One team owned by Benetton, a knitwear, clothing and fashion business, in a style that challenged the old methods and the establishment. Dennis and the veterans of the survival game were not keen to make room at their club table for him. Ken Tyrrell, in one unguarded moment, called him 'a t-shirt salesman'. It was a remark that motivated Briatore and Benetton and, in the 1990s, his mere presence in the sport, his alliance with Renault, his style of management, carried Formula One into a new media-conscious, high-profile, corporate age. Ecclestone's brand was at the show business end of sport and the worldwide car industry was ready to move in.

Dennis was not ready for this in the late-1990s when the power slipped inexorably away from the club and into the hands of Mosley, at the FIA, and Ecclestone, whose long-term commercial rights deals with his own companies left the FOCA teams out in the cold, subservient to the show dancing girls at the Palladium, no longer holding any equity in the brand or the business and facing a series of difficult decisions. For some, it was the right time to sell – as Tyrrell did in selling his team to British American Tobacco – or to grow, rebuild for the future and, armed with a strong plan and good funding, establish a team brand that would retain long-term value. This was the Dennis and McLaren route. But he still found it difficult to accept that the sport was changing so much and that control of the purse strings was slipping out of the teams' control in a manner that was entirely contrary to the original outcome of the FISA–FOCA war. By the early-1990s, however, Mosley was in charge of the FIA, the old FISA had been disbanded and replaced by the World Motor Sports Council, broken down into specialist commissions, and Ecclestone, in his roles as a vice-president of the FIA, president of FOCA, and commercial rights-holder, was running everything else. The teams, like fat cats lazing in the sun and fed too well for too long, had been too concentrated on themselves. The show went on, but they did not own it; they were the chorus lines and some were the lead singers now. When they realised what had happened, they cried 'wolf' and 'thief' because the show they had built up was snatched out of their control.

For men like Dennis, Williams, Tyrrell and the rest, it was and always had been about racing. Certainly, there had been others for whom the money was more attractive, in varying degrees, than the sport. These were the men who were comfortable to lose, to fill the middle and the rear of the grid, to operate on tight budgets and draw well from the funding. There were new arrivals, too, men who worked with one eye on their next material possession, their bank balance and their personal wealth. Where team owners were once content to fund their own shows, the new breed expected to work hard, take some risks and make millions if they could and treat the racing as the means to this end. Winning, or success if it came, was a bonus. This was anathema to Dennis. It was about winning or losing.

> The thing that gets you out of bed in the morning and into the factory is the desire to produce a car that is better than anyone else's [he said]. If the desire is to get out of bed and make money, then your philosophy works. The best way to make money in Grand Prix racing is to fulfil your main objective and that is to win races and the money follows.

To these men, the true racers, it did not matter if there was a big crowd, or if there was worldwide television coverage or none at all.

The point is we're here to win races and not to increase the television. We don't come to increase the gate. Hopefully, the show that takes place with that objective is good enough to attract the media exposure. But you can't let the media run motor racing because then you'll have a show and a show is not motor racing.

The racing man in Dennis is obsessive. So, too, is the private man and the businessman. He rarely shows emotion.

I am knowingly devoid of emotion during a Grand Prix weekend, but that is for two reasons. First of all, I try to be focused. And my level of focus, I think, is pretty high. Secondly, I see emotion as a weakness and not as a strength. If you can control your emotions by being cool, calm and collected, and it is not by accident that cool, calm and collected are all together, you will shape your own destiny from the basis of a firm mindset.

Dennis's approach to life is obsessive and meticulous in all areas including the politics of the sport and the business. His standards are high and he expects the same around him at all times. At his holiday home, a villa near Cannes in the south of France, he keeps to the same levels of maintenance and expectation. He does not let things slip. This relentlessness can be tiring for people around him. It can also lead to raised eyebrows among visitors unused to such personal fads as bans on shoes or food upstairs. Like Ecclestone, he probably could not resist noticing and wanting to straighten a picture on a wall in a friend's house. Like them all, however, he has little time for socialising and holidays. Perhaps, not enough time for friends. In the mid-1990s, he admitted:

We [McLaren] will always change anything, at any time, if we think it is for the better. There is nothing that escapes that philosophy. Including myself. I think I really shocked my people the other day when I said that in a post-race debriefing. I asked myself, 'Is there anyone to do a better job than me?' I concluded that there wasn't so I eliminated that option. That comment was made in a period when I was explaining that there were no Holy Cows in the company. There just aren't any. Even if we are winning every single race, if I could see something that could be improved upon, whether it was an individual, a component, a part of a mechanism, or a system, it would be changed. That is why we're able to stay at the top for so long . . . We evaluate everybody on the outside and on the inside. You have to, if you are serious. It applies to all levels of the company. I saw a young chap working in another team and he was in a specific junior position, but his motivation, his attention to detail and his commitment shone like a light. I phoned him personally. He couldn't actually comprehend that it was me phoning. Now, he works for us and the job he is doing is better than anyone in the pitlane. I watch everybody and everything all through my life. I drive myself crazy with trivial things, things that people don't even look at. I just want things to be as perfect as they can be. In my home, I am just an absolute perfectionist. I don't know how my wife puts up with me sometimes.

Ron Dennis remembered the day he walked across the paddock at Monza and welcomed Eddie Jordan to the Piranha Club. He remembered why he used that expression, too.

If you are in Formula One and you are not a competitive individual, and I mean anywhere in F1, you are going to struggle and have a tough time. It is a cut-and-thrust business where the rewards for success are massive and the penalties for failure and punitive. When you go into a Grand Prix environment, you are constantly trying to outmanoeuvre and out-think your opposition and I don't mean only in how you are going to run the car in such a way that you win. I am talking about every single aspect of Grand Prix racing: the politics, the sponsorships, the way you portray yourself, how you race, how you look, how you attract investment and how you optimise or shape your performance. You can conceptualise that it is like being in a tank of piranhas. Let's say one of these piranhas snaps at a tail by accident and suddenly one fish weakens. The rest of them have got to decide whether they eat it up or hold back. If I were swimming around in a tank with Frank Williams and Ken Tyrrell, I would feel a lot more secure than I would be with other Formula One colleagues who shall remain nameless.

The respect and affection that Ron Dennis holds for Frank Williams is genuine. Luckily, it is reciprocated. Williams admires the unemotional, tough, hard-headed businessman and racer that Dennis has proved himself to be, successfully, over and again. Williams, perhaps more than most of Dennis's competitors, knows also that Dennis will perform like a Piranha when the need, or the opportunity, arises. He is fully capable of taking advantage of any situation that will give McLaren an edge and damage a rival. Dennis and McLaren have approached and taken sponsors, engines, engineers and designers from Williams throughout the years of their rivalry. Williams has responded in kind. Between them exists a relationship of mutual understanding and trust, a code developed by the old rules of the 'club' in the original FOCA days. They have grown up together in Formula One. Williams, reduced to life in a wheelchair following a terrible road accident in 1996, knows that Dennis will not shed tears for him and understands this. He shed no tears himself. But the two have a strong professional relationship borne out of years of competition.

When Dennis was asked if he believed that Williams's road accident had helped Williams achieve greater things as a team chief, he was typically honest in his reply.

There are ups and downs to that. The down is that because of reduced mobility everything takes much longer and I won't have a second thought as to where he would prefer to be; jogging down the M4 or in a wheelchair. However, it's not all negative and one of the most positive aspects is that he has to be totally and utterly focused on every single decision because he's got to think things through. He's got to train his mind to retain a lot of data because he can't flick through pages easily and I think probably he's put body and soul into that because he is so determined. The whole physical thing, the discomfort, of going to every Grand Prix works, too, because he has taken that now as part of the process. We don't talk a lot, both of us, because of our characters. We tend to talk to each other when there is a common problem. I wouldn't phone Frank up for a chat. But, then again, I wouldn't phone anyone up for a chat. Talking comes from necessity.

If there are similarities in Dennis and Williams, there are also many differences, just as there are plenty of similarities and differences between their two teams. At McLaren, Dennis has created a group of businesses under TAG McLaren Holdings and his main partner is Mansour Ojjeh, who represents the TAG investment, while Daimler-Chrysler own the other sizeable shareholding. His racing team, McLaren International, is owned by the group in which TAG, a company created to provide a business link between Saudi Arabia and the rest of the world via investments in property and farming in the United States and Latin America, as well as Europe, have invested heavily. Dennis, who took a stake in TAG Heuer, did well from its flotation in 1996 and this success enabled him to become a very rich man. This activity and this partnership showed how Dennis has worked as a businessman. By contrast, Williams has restricted himself to racing and to a long and loyal partnership with his friend Patrick Head, the technical director of the Williams team. Williams, who was knighted in 1999, owns 70 per cent of Williams Grand Prix Engineering and Head the rest. Together, they have built their empire, rarely venturing beyond Formula One racing, retaining a focus on their core business as a single venture and always keeping a close eye on costs.

There is nothing swish or glamorous about the way Williams go about their work. While Dennis has moved from one ambitious pre-set plan to the next, and at the turn of the century was finalising McLaren's move to a state-of-the-art campus headquarters, named Paragon, by Dennis, to include all of the fragmented parts of the operation, including a proposed university for engineers, Williams were always investing in the team. While Dennis and his men were always likely to be seen in perfectly pressed and fashionable suits, Williams were as likely to make do with comfortable tweed jackets. In a way, McLaren, as reflected by their image and presentation, are the designer cup of perfect cappuccino while Williams remains as synonymous with England as a cup of tea. To some, Dennis has become the epitome of the modern breed of cosmopolitan Formula One entrepreneur while Williams has remained, above all, a quintessentially English racer.

The Williams team's success comes from stability, from everyone knowing his own job and doing it 100 per cent, while trusting a fellow team-member to do his job 100 per

cent and not look over his shoulder. They've got utter belief
in each other and their performance shows it,

said one of racing's most astute observers, Tom Walkinshaw,
owner of the Arrows team. It is a statement that has remained
true from the day the team started winning. Williams's unadul-
terated enthusiasm and Head's engineering excellence and
integrity have been the keys to a series of successes. Their
racing has risen above everything and enabled them to survive
emphatically and successfully despite massive blows and setbacks. Indeed, Williams himself has overcome an accident and
personal injury that would have ended lesser men as well as
other setbacks, including the deaths of drivers and friends, loss
of sponsorship and business mistakes. He has succeeded in
spite of everything, his team straddling 30 years of Formula
One, from one era to another, as winners and champions and
his life can be divided into two lives, the one before his accident
in 1986, and another in the years afterwards when, as a quadri-
plegic, he was confined to a wheelchair with constant nursing.
Yet, while Dennis was said to have amassed a fortune of £160
million by the end of 2000, Williams had accumulated, according to the Sunday Times, £95 million. Not bad, for a self-made
man who once ran his breadline business from a call box.

To understand Williams, think of fighter pilots, long-
distance runners and matadors. He has the same sense of
courage and sheer guts, massive determination and powers of
endurance, a recognition of bravery and elegance in action
and the kind of boundless love of his life, his work and his
team that can inspire feats otherwise thought of as impossible. One passage, from the moving book A Different Kind of
Life written by his wife Virginia Williams in the years after
Frank's accident, demonstrates his extraordinary courage and
nobility. It came, soon after the accident in the south of
France when he broke his neck and she flew to visit him at
the Timone hospital in Marseille. After a brief meeting with
Nigel Mansell, Peter Windsor, then working for Williams and
the man who was in Frank's car when it careered off the
road, and Professor Sid Watkins, the neurosurgeon brought
into Formula One by Bernie Ecclestone, she met Professor
Vincintelli. Patrick Head had travelled with her and was
there, too. There in a medical room, Vincintelli explained, in
French, that her husband, whom she had known to be a man

of enormous vigour and life, had broken his neck. Virginia Williams wrote:

> There was no escaping the question I had to ask. I took a deep breath. 'Is he paralysed?' Professor Vincintelli nodded slowly. I wanted to cry loudly and violently, but the presence of those five men in the room prevented me. A couple of tears did escape and ran down my face . . .

She then explained how, numbly, she was taken to visit Frank, her hair was tucked into a plastic hat, she was dressed in a gown and her feet were put in rubber boots. After walking through the stifling heat in the corridors and through two doors, she reached her husband's room.

> Frank lay motionless on the bed, covered from the waist down by a thin white sheet, a human being in a forest of machinery [she wrote]. Behind him monitor screens bleeped and flashed, recording every conceivable bodily function . . . His hair was matted with dried blood, the inside of his ears and nostrils encrusted with it. Even his fingernails were black with blood. Overriding all my other reactions, I felt an irrelevant sense of outrage that no-one had even bothered to wash him.

Her description continued. Suffice to say, her husband was in a desperately poor condition, having recovered from a massive accident in which he had been very seriously injured. He was covered in bruises, cuts and stitches. He was breathing with great difficulty. Virginia stood almost transfixed. Then, she said, she became aware of something. She wrote:

> I became aware of a slight pressure against my stomach and when I glanced up I saw that Frank was looking at me, his eyes bloodshot and unfamiliar, but the gaze as piercing as ever. Somehow, he had forced his arm towards me. He was trying to say something, but his voice was little more than a whisper and I bent over to catch his words.
> 'Did my arm move?' he asked slowly.
> I nodded, speechless.
> 'What have they told you, Ginny?'

203

I was unable to answer him. Patiently, he rephrased the question, struggling to articulate each word.

'Have they told you that I'm paralysed from the neck down?'

Haltingly, I told him that I thought they had said it was a possibility. There was a long silence. Hot tears streamed down my face.

Frank watched me dry-eyed. He was so much braver than I was. As I fought to control my sobs, he spoke to me again very clearly.

'Ginny, as I see it, I have had forty fantastic years of one sort of life.' He paused and stared at me unblinking. Then he said very slowly and deliberately, 'Now I shall have another forty years of a different kind of life . . . '

The son of a Royal Air Force officer, Frank Owen Garbett Williams was born at South Shields, in north-east England, on 16 April 1942. His mother was a schoolteacher, separated from her husband, a pilot, during the Second World War. She then brought him up alone at nearby Jarrow where, despite circumstances, he managed to fall in love with all things mechanical and maintain an interest in the doings of Newcastle United. He went to Catholic boarding schools in Liverpool and at Dumfries, in Scotland, where he developed his passion for motor racing and began to hitchhike around Britain to attend race meetings. It was in this early life that he developed his extraordinary personal resolve, his determination and his ability to endure all setbacks. When he left school, he joined the Rootes Group in Nottingham as a management trainee, but he remained fired by the idea of motor racing.

In 1961 he saved up and bought his first car, an Austin A35, from Graham Hill's company Speedwell Conversions. He entered it for his first race at Oulton Park. Once bitten, he was addicted and he went on racing, funding his activities through work, among other things, as a grocery salesman. When he damaged the A35, he replaced it with an A40. On the racing circuit, he met people and made friends, including other aspiring young racing drivers like Piers Courage and Jonathan Williams. Both had more money available for their racing than Frank, but this was an obstacle, as always, that he was able to surmount using his mixture of charm and wit. Above all, he had fun. He was a man of restless dynamism and people loved to be around him.

'It was all done on a shoestring in those days,' he recalled. 'We did not take it too seriously. We were rebuilding second-hand cars, bartering for components and so on.' By 1963 Williams had moved to London where he shared a flat, in Pinner Road, Harrow, with Courage, Jonathan Williams and Charlie Crichton-Stuart. It was a centre for all of his friends interested in motor racing and Sheridan Thynne, later to become commercial director for Williams Grand Prix Engineering, was another who was part of the scene at the time. In this period, Frank operated a spares parts business, using his flat as a base and a public telephone box on the street as his lifeline to his customers.

Finding it difficult to fund his own racing career, he became Jonathan Williams's mechanic and travelled to Formula Junior races all over Europe, developing his natural talent for languages, a gift which, in turn, helped his business as he took orders for the spare parts, manufactured in Britain, to keep his business alive. He tried to continue his own racing career in Formula Three, but realised by the end of 1966 that it was not going to happen. As a roving mechanic, with a gift of the gab, he had worked also for Crichton-Stuart and, in 1964, Anthony Horsley. While working for Horsley, he was given a chance to race in a single-seater Brabham, in return for looking after the team, but he enjoyed little success.

The following year, he set himself up in a business selling racing cars and Frank Williams Racing Cars, established in rented premises in Slough, became an official Brabham agent. This business gave him a chance to race a Cooper Formula Three car in which he finished fifth in one race, at Skarpnack, in Sweden. Afterwards, having been given the starting money, he sold his Cooper to a Swedish driver for a profit that was useful to keep him funded at a time when he had spares stocked in lock-up garages all around Harrow. By October 1967, this trade had grown up, too, and he was embarking on another new career — as a team owner. Frank Williams (Motor Racing) Ltd ran Courage, in a Brabham in a Formula Three race at Brands Hatch. Courage, a member of a rich brewery family, but a man obsessed, like Frank Williams, with the thrill of motor racing, won the contest. The two were very good friends and their joy was shared.

In 1968 he ran Courage in Formula Two in a Brabham-Cosworth BT23C, while running a Formula Three car for

Richard Burton and he later ran Tetsu Ikuzawa and Tony Trimmer in Formula Three with some success. This was not enough, however, to match his real ambitions and in 1969 Williams took the plunge into deeper financial risks and managed to buy an ex-factory Brabham BT24 car and entered it in the Tasman Series with Courage driving as they operated on a truly tiny budget with some support from the British tyre company Dunlop. He fitted it with a Cosworth DFW 2.5 litre engine and Piers did well in Australia and New Zealand, inspiring grander dreams.

These were realised in the acquisition of two BT26-Cosworths in which Williams went Grand Prix racing. The team, led by the two 27-year-olds, Williams and Courage, scored two second places, at Monaco and Watkins Glen, that year while also running cars in Formula Two and Formula Three. Frank also showed his early knack of finding sponsors at this time, too, when he persuaded Ted Williams, the owner of a company making machine tools, TW Ward, to pay for a sticker on the Brabham. It was the team's first real non-industry sponsor.

At the 1969 Italian Grand Prix, at Monza, Williams, who spoke fluent Italian and French, met Alessandro de Tomaso, the Argentine head of the Italian sports car firm. Impressed by Courage's performance in finishing second behind Graham Hill at Monte Carlo, he offered Williams a deal in which De Tomaso would build a Cosworth-powered car and Williams would run Courage in it in the 1970 world championship. The chassis was designed by Giampaolo Dallara with Tim Schenken entered as the second driver for the team. Unfortunately, what started as a year of great promise turned into a season of tragedy for Williams as Courage was killed at Zandvoort on the 21st lap of the Dutch Grand Prix. He was lying seventh in his Williams de Tomaso-Cosworth at the time when the car hit a bump, or suffered a puncture, and flew off into an earth bank. The car burst into flames and Courage was killed immediately. 'I saw the news on television and I was devastated for Frank,' said Virginia Williams. 'I had only once met Piers, but I knew their relationship had been much more than driver and employer.'

Indeed, it had. Courage and Williams had a special bond. On one occasion, Courage and Jonathan Williams had persuaded Frank to strip off and run down the railway line at the end of their garden, for a bet. When he was safely outside, they locked the door and left him trapped stark naked outside as a tube train of startled commuters went by. Together they had shared their ups and downs in motor racing, eating 'five shillings suppers in a café on the Pimlico Road'. Virginia Williams recalled the Frank of those days vividly.

> He worked seven days a week, every week, which I found astonishing. He was also a perfectionist. Whether he was dealing with cars, driver or nuts and bolts, he was reluctant to settle for second best. The cost of his choice and his ability to pay for it were minor considerations. Since there was a strong perfectionist streak in my own personality, I could identify with that. But what I loved most about Frank was his wicked sense of humour. It wasn't the sort of humour I'd been a party to before. In my circle of friends, the men tended to be rather conventional and serious. In contrast, Frank had a schoolboy naughtiness about him, which came from an utter lack of respect for authority. He was always teasing people and winking at unsuitable moments; he didn't take the same things seriously that most people did. He was anti-establishment, anti-respectability, anti-responsibility. I found this outlook on life slightly scandalous and at the same time very exciting.

With Courage's death, a part of Frank Williams life ended on 21 June 1970.

Desolated by Courage's death, he nevertheless kept the team going, but his relationship with de Tomaso finished at the end of the year. 'As a businessman, as well as on an emotional level, it was total despair when Piers died,' he told Tom Rubython, of Eurobusiness magazine, in October 2000. 'He was the darling of society and he generated a lot of interest from sponsors. It was just beginning to grow. Afterwards, I found myself seriously insolvent, peanuts figures today, but very important at the time.'

In 1971, after a winter of charming birds out of trees for sponsorship, he had raised enough funding to run a customer March Formula One chassis for Henri Pescarolo, who was backed by Motul Oil, in the world championship and to maintain and run three Formula Two cars. Pescarolo's contribution was around £38,000, which was supported by £10,000 from Ted Williams's tool company. A third deal, worth another £10,000, came with the Italian company Politoys. It was an ambitious move as he employed only ten people at the time and, predictably enough, in what was then seen as typical Williams style, he often had to be in several places at once as he was also running a three-car Formula Two team. In one instance of his over-worked and pressurised life, described by Virginia Williams, Frank flew home from Colombia, where he had entered a Formula Two series, when the chassis on both cars split open. The next race was seven days away, but rather than withdraw, Williams removed the chassis from each and then made the return trip to the March base at Bicester for repairs and reinforcement, having carried the two chassis as hand baggage, returning to Bogota in time for practice for the next race. This, in anyone's language, is certainly the kind of commitment Ron Dennis talked of and admired and it was to serve Williams throughout his development of his team.

In 1972, buoyed by a further £10,000 in personal sponsorship from the Brazilian Carlos Pace, Williams ran a second car. It was a bonus, but not enough to lift the team out of its trough of endless debts and worries (alleviated slightly by a loan of £4,000 from Virginia, who sold her maisonette to raise funds and help him out). When Courage was killed, Williams was left with a lorry, two engines and some components at the end of the season. 'But the heaviest thing we had was loads of debt,' he often quipped. The debt stayed with him, but thanks to the arrival of Bernie Ecclestone in the Formula One paddock, he was able to survive and compete because of the gradual vitalisation of FICA and the introduction of subsidised, organised travel. By 1973, somehow or other, Williams was able to build his own cars (the first had appeared in 1972, the Len Bailey-designed Politoys FX3, but it was destroyed, in spectacular style, by Pescarolo on its first outing in the opening laps of the British Grand Prix at Brands Hatch). Such setbacks were mere challenges to overcome again to Williams and his career is chequered with examples of his ability to beat the odds.

From 1973 to 1976, he soldiered on. Helped by sponsorship from Marlboro, who switched from BRM, and the Italian sports car company Iso Rivolta, the 1973 season was completed, but then Marlboro moved to McLaren, leaving Williams to struggle. By 1975, the costs were rising so steeply that it was clear Williams needed more than a few generous sponsors; he needed a partner and Walter Wolf, a burly Austro-Canadian, who had made a fortune selling oil equipment, took over 60 per cent of the team in 1976. Wolf also purchased the cars and assets of the Hesketh team in a £450,000 package that included hiring Harvey Postlethwaite as designer, a move that meant Williams's newly arrived appointment Patrick Head was ousted. None of this did the team any dramatic good, however, and in frustration Wolf chose to bring in Peter Warr, from Lotus, as team manager. It was a signal, to Williams, that his days as the inspirational dynamo in that team were over and they ended when, in January 1977, Wolf took the team to Argentina, but left Frank behind. He had become a fund-raiser and little more. He left and Head went with him. But Williams, though disappointed, was not bitter. Indeed, he looked back on those days as an invaluable lesson.

> The previous part of my business life was very inept, always trading on the brink of insolvency and learning a lot of lessons the hard way. Then I sold control of Frank Williams Racing Cars to Walter Wolf and I learnt more from him in a year than in my previous 10 years.

This left him to start again, without a FICA membership, and, in 1977, he set up Williams Grand Prix Engineering with Head as his senior engineer and technical officer. They began trading and racing from an old carpet warehouse in Didcot, Oxfordshire, where they kept a March 761 chassis, purchased from Max Mosley for £14,000 and four second-hand Cosworth DFVs, all taken for a knockdown price. In the formation of the company, Williams held 99 per cent of the equity and Virginia, who he had married in August 1975, one per cent. Head, astonishingly talented and loyal, was not offered his holding of 30 per cent, transferred from Virginia's one per cent and 29 per cent from Frank, until a decade later. Williams, however, knew his value.

> He is a truly gifted natural engineer – his engineering kingdom is world renowned. He has made the material difference to the way we have designed and produced racing cars since 1970. And he has outstanding presentation and integrity.

Head promptly proved himself as one of the finest designers with the FW06 and FW07, the latter his first ground-effects car, as Williams did everything possible to raise money and keep his team going. Enterprisingly, he decided to seek support from outside the usual British companies and, thanks to some help from Crichton-Stuart, Williams won backing from Saudia Arabia in 1978 when the name of the Saudia airline appeared on the FW06 driven by Alan Jones in the British Grand Prix at Silverstone. It was in this year, too, of course, that the FICA changed its name to FOCA, that Ecclestone took over as its president and chief executive from Peter Mackintosh and that Jean-Marie Balestre was elected president of the CSI. To say, therefore, that Williams was in at the start of it all, in terms of the prelude to the FISA–FOCA war and the rise of Ecclestone, the club and the enrichment of the sport, would be something of an understatement.

> Securing finance was very difficult, but we had a good story to sell, so we got some reasonable funds [recalled Williams]. It wasn't a lot at first, but the money eventually slopped into the team, which meant we were able to pay our bills. It was sufficient to give us a good start. Not just a fresh start, but a good start.

The 1970s were years of change. They saw remarkable alterations to British life and the remarkable rise of Frank Williams and his team. He went from being an enthusiastic former amateur driver and racing car dealer, relying on cars carrying various obsolete parts bought second-hand from wealthier teams and drivers prepared to pay for the privilege of risking themselves in Formula One, to world champions in 1980. His team went from being the scruffiest of chorus girls in the theatre of motor racing, the back of the grid extras, to the pace-setting stars in the limelight. 'You cannot say Frank started with nothing,' said one of his friends. 'He started with much less than nothing!'

In the first full year as a constructor, the Williams outfit made a profit of £593 on a turnover of nearly £487,000. Twenty years later, the profit was more than £8 million on a turnover of more than £53 million. For that, Williams thanks the Saudi deal as the one that put him on the map. 'So much of what we achieved can be traced back to that sponsorship from Saudi Arabia,' he said. 'It set in train so much. It was a catalyst.' In the first year, Saudi Airways paid £30,000 and in the second £100,000. The money was welcome and significant. It opened the world up for Formula One. When Williams and Head unveiled the FW06, at Didcot, in December, 1977, the presentation was attended by Saudia's director general Sheikh Kemel Sindhi, later to become Saudi Arabia's deputy minister of aviation.

It was a seal of approval for Williams and his team, at long last, and he made the most of it. In 1978, he flew to Riyadh to meet the Saudi royal family and other Saudi companies followed the airline's example. At that year's Monaco Grand Prix, the motor racing-loving Prince Sultan bin Salman introduced Williams to his friend Mansour Ojjeh and this led to the arrival in the sport of TAG, but initially as Williams's backers for the 1978 world championship and investors in research work for the team's new car. It paid off spectacularly at the 1979 British Grand Prix when Alan Jones took pole position and Clay Regazzoni won the race in the ground-breaking FW07. In 1980, Jones won the drivers' world championship and the team took the constructors' title. The dream was turning to reality. The change in his fortunes was almost a shock to Williams at the time. Referring to 1978, Williams told Doug Nye:

> I was almost speechless. It was a completely new world to me. I had difficulty coping with the sudden enormity of it. Alan [Jones] was among the quick boys. It was like one of Piers' drives. It was as if I had been in prison for 10 or 20 years of a 30-year sentence and somebody had suddenly come up with the key and set me free. My initial reaction was 'Bloody hell, I'm not sure I can cope with this. Help. Please, let me inside.'

In addition to his enthusiasm and energy, and an ability to enjoy life and relax despite mounting worries and problems (he ran long distances as a hobby virtually every evening for many years before his accident and was close friends with Sebastian Coe), Williams was shrewd and had foresight. He anticipated, more easily and successfully with wisdom, future events and had spread his interest in sponsors beyond the Gulf before the oil crisis of the early 1980s arrived. Names like Leyland, Mobil, ICI, Canon, Labatts and Camel all found their way to the Williams cars as the budgets grew, costs rose and standards reached new levels. 'Being in Formula One in the 1980s was no easier than in the 1960s or the 1970s,' said Williams.

In 1981, Jones and his team-mate Carlos Reutemann dis-agreed over team orders and both left. Keke Rosberg arrived and promptly won the drivers' title in 1982 and in 1983 Williams formed a new partnership with Honda as engine sup-pliers. It was a far-sighted move, but by the time it bore fruit with Nelson Piquet winning the 1987 title, ahead of his team-mate Nigel Mansell, the man who made the team had been paralysed and confined to a wheelchair. It was only after the accident, on 8 March 1986, that Honda began talking of moving on and transferring their supply of race-winning engines to McLaren. Ron Dennis, the opportunist, the piranha, saw his chance. The Japanese company found it difficult to understand how to do business with a man in a wheelchair and so, with 18 months of their agreement remaining, breached their contract. Their supply went to McLaren, Senna and Prost, for 1988, when they also continued with Lotus who partnered Piquet, of Brazil, with Satoru Nakayima, of Japan.

> I was caught short with Honda [admitted Williams]. The Honda guys said they could go with McLaren or with us, but that we must take a Japanese driver. Patrick and I are cocky bastards and we didn't want to be dictated to. We told Honda that we decided our own drivers. That was a mistake ... I don't think it helped when the Honda guys saw me looking a bit rough in hospital at a time when McLaren had Prost and Senna, as well as a lot of money from Marlboro. Honda worked for five years with Ron Dennis, but then left him too ...

Again, as with the episode when the TAG group switched its Formula One allegiance from Williams to McLaren, there is no bitterness with Williams who has revealed that his relationship with Mansour Ojjeh ended only when Williams declined his approaches to buy a stake in the team. 'We declined a deal with Mansour,' he said. 'Well, we didn't decline a deal. Mansour wanted to buy into us and we did not make the ground sufficiently fertile for such a deal to happen ... ' As to the Honda engine supply deal, it has been reported that Dennis visited Williams in hospital after his 1986 accident to assess the situation and concluded that he had an opportunity to move for it. Dennis recalled, significantly, that it was his invitation to Mansour, to sponsor a 'TAG' turbo engine, which had been very influential.

It meant, for Williams, another recovery and a new start with Renault who, literally, came to Estoril for the Portuguese Grand Prix of 1987 and knocked on the team's motor home door in the paddock. A series of titles followed, with Mansell, Alain Prost, Damon Hill and Jacques Villeneuve in a spell when every race saw a Williams at the front of the field. It ran until 1997 after which it was BMW's turn to put their name forward as technical partners to the sharpest racing team of modern times.

> We've done a clever deal [with BMW]. What BMW has bought is the naming of the team [the team is called BMW Williams] and the right to choose the colours. But it has zero marketing rights. We do all our own deals. It's our business. We run the team.

Success, in the end, made Frank Williams a wealthy man, but he has also been recognised for his achievements. In 1987 he was awarded a CBE for his services to motor racing and, in January 1999, he was knighted. He is also a holder of the rare foreign award of France's Légion d'Honneur for his efforts in cooperation with Renault. Yet these honours have scant effect on the way Williams conducts his business or his life. He has eschewed the use of titles and concentrates on his office, his racing and his bank account just as he always did.

> I am responsible for the amount of money going out and I worry that the money will turn up every day, worry and worry and worry. I wouldn't say that I was mean. But Williams does not throw money around, although where money is necessary, whatever it takes, we spend it.

The death of Ayrton Senna at Imola in 1994 was a colossal loss to Williams and the sport and left Frank and others facing culpable homicide charges for many years before he and his team were cleared of blame. If it did anything, it reminded everyone involved of the fatal dangers in the sport and the sacrifices many people have made to participate and succeed. It also revealed the extraordinary sensitivity and generosity of many of the team chiefs in Formula One, their natural big-heartedness and genuine concern for others at a time when they are also obsessed with their own racing lives. This was clear from the way in which men like Bernie Ecclestone, in particular, and

Ron Dennis, offered any help possible to Virginia Williams, following Frank's accident. There are too many examples to list, but just one from that time shows how it was then. Not only did Ecclestone, like Dennis, supply planes, helicopters and air-ambulances for Williams at the time of the accident itself, he also made certain he had full and proper nursing support afterwards; and later that year, apart from providing his own personal support to the family and the team, he showed the kind of understanding, wit and practical assistance that is synonymous not only with him, but with Formula One as a whole.

On Friday, 11 July 1986, Ecclestone sent his helicopter to Boxford House, where the Williams family lived, and collected them for the flight to Brands Hatch and opening practice day for the British Grand Prix. At the circuit, an advertising hoarding three feet high was covered with the message 'Welcome Back Frank'. Williams spent that day, and the next, amid his team for the first time in months. Like most people with serious spinal injuries, he was supposed to spend a year in hospital, not four months followed by a will to return to work as soon as possible. But on Sunday, when he was tired and stayed at home to watch the race on television, the same helicopter arrived to take Virginia to the race with their son Jonathan.

Nigel Mansell won and, prompted by Patrick Head, Virginia stood on the podium to accept the cup for the winning constructor. She could hardly speak. She knew Frank was at home watching.

Even in the midst of triumph [she wrote later], I grieved that things could not have been different. I knew that I would never again be able to watch Frank's familiar figure sitting on the pit wall, listening patiently to his headset, his face set in its customary impassive expression. Never again see him stand up with a huge happy grin as the chequered flag dropped. Never again see him striding about minutes later formulating a strategy for winning the next race. From now on, he would have to watch all his races from the sidelines, or worse, like today, on television.

She was right but amazingly, in 1987, Williams travelled with his team to every Grand Prix on the calendar and he has done the same, with only a few races missed, ever since. And, along the way, they collected a few more championships.

'Television has become a place for people who want to expose their values with their brands,' said Williams in 2000 when the viewing figures for each race were reported to be upward of 340 million.

> So, they use Formula One. We are part of the gang exploiting that. You take the deals as they come, while they are available. It is very difficult, especially as people are not exactly queuing up, but our marketing guys have done an outstanding job for this company.

Not least, Williams himself. Admired in the paddock for his character and personality, his shrewdness and economy, he has emerged as a living motif for his company and his team. When he described his feelings about his handicaps and his life, in Eurobusiness in October 2000, he was as precise and direct as ever.

> I'm aware of my own inabilities, deficiencies and handicaps, that's all you need to know. I can't write. I can't stay late. But I can work weekends and I'm not inefficient. I can guide people, suggest deals, watch the money, all that sort of stuff. I would describe myself as a day to day manager.

Some daily, some manager, some man.

7 Corporate Ferrari Raises the Stakes

In 1957 Esso paid Rob Walker a lump sum of £5,000 to support his racing and run his garage. His uncle was the chairman of Dunlop and they added a further £3,000. Further help came to his privately run racing team from the spark plugs companies, Lodge or Champion. Luckily, having been born into a wealthy family, he had inherited £1 million, when he was 28. It helped. So, too, did Stirling Moss and Formula Two. He could race in Formula Two and generate funds to help him race in Formula One. In 1957, it cost around £30,000 to run a two-car Formula One team for a season.

> It was better to enter the non-championship races because they knew, in the championship, that you had to go, so they [the race organisers] weren't so willing to shell out [explained Walker]. But, in Formula Two, if they got one big name, like Stirling, then they gave you almost all they had. It helped tremendously and Stirling was marvellous, of course. But for me, it was not really a business. It was a hobby. I had a racing account and, when it went broke, I just put some more money in. I sold a house, or something. That's how it worked. If it had been a real business, I wouldn't have lasted five minutes.

Walker also witnessed the zany early meetings of FICA, during 1968, when commercial sponsors were permitted for the first time and travel and other costs rose dramatically. As the 'care-taker' chairman of the meetings, he was present when they sought to reach accord on how to negotiate a sensible passage to a new era by reaching agreements with the race organisers and the BBC, then broadcasting Formula One on a limited highlight basis.

I saw they were only concerned with their own interests and you would get Ken Tyrrell, Colin Chapman and Teddy Mayer all arguing and getting nowhere. They were always arguing with each other. I remember one day in Austria when there was a wonderful row. Andrew Ferguson was the secretary at the time and he was saying what a hell of a job it was to find an aircraft to carry all the cars there and how much it was costing. Then, Ken Tyrrell said, 'I reckon I could do the whole thing before breakfast,' and Andrew said, 'Well, if bloody Superman can do the whole thing before breakfast he can have the effing job.' It was like that all the time.

In the end, together with Chapman, Walker helped guide Formula One from his era, of the golden age, into the commercial age from which it has ballooned into a modern global industry.

In 2001 Shell paid Ferrari around £17.5 million to supply fuel and lubricants and appear as a high-profile part of the marketing package in which Michael Schumacher propelled himself in the defence of his drivers' world championship crown. Bridgestone supplied the tyres for the team and paid a further fee of more than £1 million. Marlboro, the cigarette brand, owned by Philip Morris, which had once seemed to be the preserve of McLaren, paid Ferrari around £40 million. A list of other companies' names enlarged the Fiat-owned team's budget for the year towards £200 million. The team founded and run, for so long, by Enzo Ferrari, had no need to race in Formula Two. It was a success, a major business making a major profit, under the guidance of Luca di Montezemolo. Installed as chairman (by 90 per cent shareholding parent company Fiat, and its owner Gianni Agnelli, his friend and mentor), in 1991, Montezemolo had driven Ferrari, the team and the company, back to triumph from the edge of disaster.

By 2001 he had also reorganised Ferrari's management structure in a way that echoed, in Formula One, the balance of power of the past and the political manoeuvrings that were characteristic of the Enzo Ferrari years. His sporting director and team principal, at Ferrari, was Jean Todt, a diminutive Frenchman, installed in 1993 to take over the daily administrative strain of the factory and the team and to act as the team representative at FOCA meetings. Todt, the man given the job of protecting Ferrari's interests, was never to be an inner member of the club, but, because of the reputation and importance of the Italian team's name, a voice that was listened to with care. At race meetings, where the paddock wags referred to him as the 'Napoleon of the pit lane', he was a prominent figure on the pit wall, in Ferrari team meetings and around the offices of the circuit.

Together with the deft touch of Montezemolo, he built the Ferrari team that included Schumacher, Ross Brawn as technical director and Rory Byrne as designer and aerodynamicist, the latter two men defecting from Benetton where they had guided the German driver to the world championship in 1994 and 1995. Their transfer took some of the controversy and suspicion, associated with the Schumacher triumphs, with them from Enstone to Maranello. It added an additional layer of intrigue to a team that already reeked of drama, history and tradition; it also gave the team a cutting edge on the track, in the pit-lane and in the stewards' towers of the world as the modern corporate Ferrari, stripped down to become a lean fighting machine but funded by the biggest budget of all, did everything possible to end two decades of failure and recover the glories of its past.

Montezemolo's record was reflected in Ferrari's growth. Turnover of the company went from £250 million in 1995 to £400 million in 1999 and profits soared from only £1.2 million to £18 million in the same period. The Formula One team, without a drivers' title since Jody Scheckter in 1979, ended its long drought in 2000 when Schumacher led Ferrari to a magnificent double of drivers' and constructors' championships in the same season. Yet, still, old habits persist. Enzo Ferrari's illegitimate second son, Piero, retains 10 per cent of a team whose principal, Montezemolo rarely travels to races and who holds even rarer meetings with other team chiefs only when they visit Italy. This maintenance of tradition, of course, has kept alive the allure and mystery of Ferrari's image, ensured the brand retains a singular popularity around the world and set an example, in commercial exploitation of that brand, to all the other Formula One teams. In short, the new corporate Ferrari, under Fiat and Montezemolo, post-Enzo and post-endless-years-of-failure, has blazed the trail that others, some of them newcomers, have followed.

Even if he is not a regular diner at Le Manoir, or present at the Heathrow hotels when summits are called, Montezemolo plays his part in the way the club works because he is the man who represents modern Ferrari in the boardrooms of the world and because, as they all know, Formula One without Ferrari would be unthinkable. Furthermore, Montezemolo knows the business and has done for many years since he was the team manager in the successful years with Niki Lauda 20 years earlier.

> When I came back to Ferrari in 1992 [said Montezemolo] I asked myself why there had been no real success since the 1970s and it was difficult to give a precise answer. Back then, I was lucky enough to be there with Lauda. The basic elements were mechanical – engine, gearbox, suspension and so on. We needed to have strong knowhow and, then, there was a strong competition between Ferrari and Ford. In the 1980s, the British developed a very sophisticated understanding of aerodynamics and composite materials, wind tunnel testing, electronic suspension and it was not in Ferrari's mentality. It was not in the natural knowledge of Italians. We have always been weak in aeronautics. But we tried to do our best and now, at last, I think we are catching up with help from some very special people.

Montezemolo bridges the generations, like Ecclestone, Mosley and Williams. He remembers the old days of the 'garagistes' and the original FOCA meetings. When Jaguar's name entered Formula One at the end of the 1990s, he was prompted to nostalgia.

> I like their green [he remarked]. It puts me in mind of the green of the Lotus of Jim Clark. And I remember the fantastic people of those times. Men like Colin Chapman, Ken Tyrrell and Teddy Mayer from my first constructors' meeting at an hotel near Heathrow. I remember those things romantically now. For me, in those days, the engines were music, not noise.

Born in Bologna, a law graduate from Rome university and a veteran of top jobs with Fiat, Cinzano and being in charge of both the 1990 World Cup finals in Italy and Italy's America's Cup challenge, Montezemolo is an arch-politician and, to some degree like Enzo Ferrari himself, a manipulator of men. He is a strategist and a decision-maker and a man with an appreciation of many good things in life, including individual excellence.

> This is a most unusual company [he said, in 1992 after rejoining Ferrari]. Enzo Ferrari was most unusual and he ran the scuderia along unorthodox, but brilliant, lines. He never studied marketing, but he knew just how to make customers fight and drool over the few cars we sold every year. I, too, am not a conventional style manager, and that is why I am here. Of course, I worked with Enzo Ferrari, I understand the loyalty and fanaticism there is in this team. He knew everyone by name, and they would do anything for him. We have lost some of that, and it is my job to bring it back.

Montezemolo wanted other changes, which included alterations to the club and the running of the sport in the 1990s.

> We are very close to the second era of the modern Formula One. That is my feeling, and for two reasons. First of all, the world is changing. We cannot go in a different direction from the rest of the world. I have a very clear picture in my mind of the next 10 years, from an economic point of view and 'attitude' point of view. We have to follow this, or we are out of the world. Secondly, in Formula One, the limits between the different authorities are not clear. Sometimes, Bernie [Ecclestone] represents the regulations and sometimes he represents the money of the teams and vice versa. I want to see a clear structure with clear definitions and with one president at the top so that everyone can agree.

As a lawyer, and an organiser, Montezemolo has developed his own way of managing Ferrari and their Formula One renaissance. He has pushed hard, recruited the best available in any area at any time, including Schumacher, rebuilt from the bottom up and fought for every point at every corner, in every race and, when necessary, in every appeals and court procedure. This has, at times, seen the team enveloped in uproar and controversy. Two clear examples were in the fallout after the European Grand Prix at Jerez in 1997, when Schumacher drove into Jacques Villeneuve's Williams Renault, damaged his own car and reputation, lost the race and the championship and ended up having his runners-up place in the championship stripped from him and in the aftermath of the Malaysian Grand Prix of 1999, when Ferrari successfully appealed against their disqualification from winning in Kuala Lumpur at a hearing in Paris surrounded by massive media hype. In both events, not only Ferrari's reputation, but the image of the sport itself went on trial.

The cynics, some would say they were realists, conceded that by the mid-1990s money, not sporting ethics, ruled the tracks. Similarly, they said, the club was in danger of becoming overrun by piranhas. Other men were now in the sport, in the midst of the business and using a different set of rules. Men like Flavio Briatore, who was running the Benetton team that won the world championship of 1994 and 1995 with Michael Schumacher, his engineering director in that team, Tom Walkinshaw, the owner of a vast empire of automotive industry businesses including Tom Walkinshaw Racing (TWR) and other British firms, were described frequently as among those who were prepared to win at almost any price. Todt, at Ferrari, was a pragmatist and an employee. He would scheme and work for Ferrari to win, at almost any cost. Eddie Jordan, a flamboyant figure, dedicated racer and sharp operator, may have belonged to the older school; but not newcomers like Craig Pollock, representing his interests and those of British American Tobacco, or Bobby Rahal, for Ford and Jaguar. The face, the style, the very essence of the club was changing and developing as each race passed and, in general, the sport was moving into an era of greater transparency.

Todt was head of Peugeot's world rally team when he took a call from Bernie Ecclestone in July 1992. He was asked to contact Montezemolo, who wanted to talk to him. It took Montezemolo a year, after meetings at his home near Bologna and at Todt's in Paris, before he succeeded in luring Todt to Ferrari. Like so many club men, Todt is a meticulous perfectionist who works extraordinary hours, shows extraordinary loyalty, sacrifices most of his own private life and personal time to the team. He loves mental arithmetic and mind games and finds it very difficult to switch off when he is away from Maranello or a race circuit.

I never switch off, either personally, or my mobile phone [he said]. It is on 24 hours a day so my people can always contact me. I need to know what is going on and I need to know that everyone is happy. I have an anxious character so it is very difficult for me to relax.

This may account for a report that suggested that when Todt first met Ross Brawn, to discuss the post of Ferrari technical director with him (having, it was said, been rebuffed by his first target Adrian Newey, then with Williams, because his wife Marigold did not like the town of Maranello), the big Englisman arrived at the little Frenchman's hotel room in Monte Carlo to find him wearing nothing more than his underpants. 'It was the first time I'd been interviewed by someone wearing only their underwear,' joked Brawn. According to a report by Jane Nottage for *Formula 1* magazine in May 2001, Todt is close to Ecclestone and Briatore. Nottage quoted Todt saying:

Flavio and I are very different. He is surprised by my way of doing things and I am surprised by his way of doing things, but it is complementary. I don't have a lot of free time and he is fun to be with. With Bernie, it is different. He was the catalyst for my meeting with Luca di Montezemolo, so we had a good relationship before I joined Formula One. I have great respect for what he has achieved. I like Peter Sauber very much. He is very sincere. I also have good contact with Gerhard Berger, Alain Prost and Jean Alesi, but there are a lot of people I don't see . . .

The absence of such names as Dennis, Jordan and Williams suggested the old Anglo-Continental divide remained tangible in Todt's view of the politics of the club even twenty years on from the FISA–FOCA war.

High in the neon-lit half-darkness and loud ear-bashing atmosphere that filled a single vast room in a high-rise tower block that looked down across Ropongi, a slim, young man in jeans and black leather sat sipping a soft drink in the VIP enclosure of one of Tokyo's biggest and best-known discotheques. He was famous, German, happy and successful; and he was fighting to recover from the biggest hangover of his life. Three days earlier, Michael Schumacher had won the 1995 drivers' world championship for Benetton-Renault and embarked on a drinking spree and party at the circuit hotel in Aida, where he had triumphed in the Pacific Grand Prix. The celebrations included a notorious wet t-shirt contest, judged by the applause of the men in the room, contested by every female within reach and the damages caused by spillage of champagne, beer, food and wine resulted in a bill of around £20,000. Schumacher enjoyed it all. He mixed his drinks and smoked cigars and laughed. He had a good time.

Next to Schumacher, surrounded by a group of friends, team members, celebrities associated with Fuji TV and various hangers on, sat his Benetton team chief Flavio Briatore. Grinning, tanned, rich and satisfied, he was enjoying himself, too. Briatore did not care that his successes in turning the perennial mid-grid nobodies of Benetton into a championship-winning team had been tainted by suspicions that his cars were not always in conformity with the rules. He, too, was celebrating, but, in the back of his mind, he was worried. He knew that Schumacher was leaving Benetton to join Ferrari and that he had to mould a new team around his new signings, Gerhard Berger and Jean Alesi, who were moving from Ferrari to replace him. Briatore was confident because he is always confident and he believed his ability to raise sponsorship would ensure he could fund continued successes for the team. He had, after all, always found ways of bringing in money and then using that money to buy the talent he needed to make a winning team. It had been the method he had used to create the triumphant 'Schumacher team' and the method that had inspired the first use of the epithet 'Piranha Club' to describe Formula One.

Born on 12 April 1950 at Cuneo in northern Italy, Briatore had transformed Benetton and made a big impact on Formula One. His insistence on media-friendliness, dazzling communications skills, high-profile marketing techniques and plenty of glitz and glamour at all times around the team's garage and motor home had turned Benetton into the 'happening' young team of the mid-1990s. Schumacher was encouraged to be a beaming and victorious leaping athlete on the podium, model girls were invited for photographic shoots, television cameras and rock music were welcome in the pits and, all the time, Briatore talked about the show and the party and the lifestyle. His chequered history, rarely discussed and even less frequently revealed through interviews, suggested a past that he wished to forget and explained why the here-and-now and the future mattered to him so much more. He brought an air of mystery, intrigue, glamour and dark purpose with him to his team and the paddock and a flash of light to the sport.

Briatore grew up in northern Italy in the mountains. His parents were teachers. He left school at 18. He worked as a ski instructor and in the restaurant business before, after various adventures including, allegedly, a spell with the French Foreign Legion (an unproven story), he worked on the Italian stock exchange in Milan. There, in the 1970s, he met Luciano Benetton whose chain of fashion clothing shops was just starting to take off and to succeed. By 1982, after spending most of the previous decade in various undisclosed roles in Italy and around Europe, Briatore became the Benetton Group's principal representative in the United States. The gaps in his curriculum vitae, innocent or otherwise, have certainly added a touch of the unknown to his reputation. In 1979 Benetton had only half a dozen shops in America. In less than ten years, this had grown to 800 or more and Briatore was rich and growing richer. He began to fly regularly between New York and the Virgin Islands, became a partner in the famous Regine's nightclub and enjoyed a flamboyant lifestyle in the circles of Italian-Americans.

When the retail boom, that saw Benetton stores spreading rapidly across most of the United States, came to an end, Briatore was taken to Australia, as a guest of Luciano, to see the 1988 Australian Grand Prix in Adelaide. Despite being unimpressed by the event, he was taken by the commercial opportunities and was soon appointed by Benetton to become the team's marketing director. Soon afterwards, by mid 1999, he ousted the old management team and took control in circumstances that left many of the original team very bitter. As managing director, he took over as team principal and set off to fulfil an ambitious plan by adopting methods which were far more aggressive than those used by his predecessors and most of his rivals. Ruthless decisions were taken, the victims of which have declined to speak of their experiences in any detail. Briatore had ambitious plans and believed in them. 'Formula One is the only sport that is worldwide, covered by television and runs every two weeks,' he said. 'You have millions of people watching it. The message is very clear. Very quick.'

John Barnard was hired, at great expense, to revamp the technical structure of Benetton and then, when he left, Briatore formed a liaison with Tom Walkinshaw. Luigi Montanini, the Ferrari chef and pasta expert, was lured to Benetton. On Walkinshaw's guidance, he recruited Michael Schumacher and built a new team around him, winning the 1994 drivers' world championship in controversial circumstances at the end of a tragic year in which he also purchased the Ligier team, to gain their supply of Renault engines for Benetton in 1995. In this he succeeded and Schumacher led Benetton to the drivers' and constructors' double, but at a cost. Walkinshaw moved to take over Ligier, who took a supply of Mugen-Honda engines, Schumacher left for Ferrari and was followed by both Ross Brawn and Rory Byrne in 1997. These events, of course, lay ahead of Briatore that night in the Japanese discotheque, but when they unfolded they added further to his brief, colourful and complex career in Formula One.

He often made it clear that he saw Formula One not as a technical exercise, but as a sporting adjunct to show business. One night in London, early in 1994, he invited selected groups of reporters to his apartment in Chelsea for a private dinner. He was using his charm and persuading the media that he was a man of character and substance, as managing director of Benetton, and that those who accused him of being little more than a gauche arriviste, a t-shirt salesman, were underestimating him.

I am a businessman [he said that night]. I am not interested in devoting myself to Formula One for 20 years, but I think the potential is very strong and that only 20 per cent of that potential is being used. All the team owners are orientated towards the technical side, rather than the entertainment side, and this is a big fault. Every meeting that I go to, people are talking about pistons and suspensions. Nobody goes to a race to see that kind of thing. Nobody's interested in active or passive systems. Nobody comes up to me after a race and says 'Flavio, your active system is so bloody beautiful.' People come to see Schumacher and Senna racing each other.

In 1996 he purchased a substantial stake in the Minardi team, but sold it back to Gian Carlo Minardi and his partner Gabriele

Rumi when a deal to sell to British American Tobacco was not supported by them. Instead, BAT purchased Tyrrell. In 1997 disillusioned by the lack of success at Benetton and his own disappointment with Minardi, he was replaced at Benetton by David Richards. After taking a break, Briatore moved on to set up a trading business, Supertec, which marketed the former supply of Renault engines prepared by Mecachrome for customers in Formula One. This kept him occupied and well-funded from 1998 to 2000 when he rejoined Benetton, after Renault had bought the team, with a brief to prepare for a full assault on the world championship in French colours in 2002.

In this period, when he launched various other business ventures, including the Billionaire Club in Porto Cervo, Sardinia, he began a relationship with the British model Naomi Campbell that ensured he kept a high profile in the European magazines and newspapers and made certain that he was regarded, still, as the most provocative and colourful team principal in the paddock. He also maintained a close relationship with Bernie Ecclestone, which ensured the rumour mill was always busy with conspiracy theories and that Briatore was as well-informed as possible, a factor he shared in common with every man in the Piranha Club and the pit lane.

> Flavio is good company [said Ecclestone]. I've had dinner with him. You're right. He has a different approach. He's not a racer, by any means, by any shape or form. I think he'd like to be. He'd like to think he was. But he isn't. He is, shall we say, quite different and he's done – which I am happy about for him – very well out of being involved. When he first came over, Mr Benetton said to me, 'Would I look after him?' Nobody knew him. Benetton was going to stop. I said, 'Don't stop,' and he said, 'Well, I don't know who's going to run it, but I've got a guy in New York ... I've bought him over. Would you look after him?' And that is how it happened.

Tom Walkinshaw, the son of a Lanarkshire farmer and market gardener, was born on 14 August 1947. Like Briatore, he was always a restless entrepreneur, but unlike the Italian, he loved motor sport and turned what was once his great hobby into a fabulously successful business empire, employing more than 1,000 people turning over more than £135 million in 30 companies by the mid-1990s, and all built around motor racing. Shrewd, tough and dedicated, he was a resourceful organiser and tactician capable of improvising to win races when required. His career began when he took an interest in a local garage owner, in Scotland, who raced Minis after first discovering speed on one of his father's tractors. He then began racing his own MG Midget in 1968 at Ingliston circuit near Edinburgh, finishing his first race intact.

> It was an ordinary private car [he recalled]. I drove it to Ingliston myself and drove it home again at the finish. I even managed to finish third in my first race. It's a big incentive to keep it together when you're actually depending on the car to get you back and forth.

He graduated to race a Lotus Formula Ford 1600 and then attempted to run in the British Formula Three championship, but a sponsorship problem ended that and, after excursions in Formula Two, Formula Three and Formula 5000, he was diverted into touring cars by Ford in 1974. In a Ford Capri, he won his class in the British championship and two years later set up Tom Walkinshaw Racing. His racing and business careers took off and in 1984 he won the European Touring Car Championship, having also shown he was as adept at running teams for others as for himself.

As Britain's most successful saloon car driver, he knew what it took and, in 1982, he ran Jaguars in the European championship and Rovers in the British series in 1982. This was to result in success and controversy as the TWR Rovers were stripped of the British title at the Shawcross Tribunal of Inquiry in 1983 when it was ruled that they ran with illegal rockers and bodywork. Rover switched to the European series to race against Jaguar, with whom Walkinshaw continued and he won the European title that year in a Jaguar XJS, winning the Spa 24-Hours race along the way. This success led to a close relationship between Jaguar and TWR and the creation of a sportscar programme which ran successfully for six years, the highlight being Jaguar's sixth win in the classic Le Mans 24-Hours with the TWR-designed XJR-9 in 1988.

By the late 1980s, the two became synonymous with success. Jaguar won the world sportscar championship and the Le Mans and Daytona classics while Walkinshaw also began building cars for the IMSA series in America and for Holden in Australia. His expansion and success led him to be elected chairman of the British Racing Drivers' Club (BRDC), but he was ousted from that position following a controversial plan to establish the Silverstone Motor Group, in which the BRDC purchased half of Walkinshaw's garage businesses for a reported £5 million. Later, he bought the shares back for less than half the price. If this was a signal of his alert business mind and eye for an opportunity, his move to join Briatore at Benetton as Engineering Director in the early 1990s showed an equally keen ambition to succeed in Formula One at a time when he was also producing Jaguar XK220s as road-going cars for sale and then running Volvo's team in the British Touring Car Championship.

The move to Benetton came about after a series of meetings with Briatore, which had originated with a lunch appointment to discuss the joint development of a semi-automatic gearbox. After four lunches – 'Italians always make their deals over a bowl of spaghetti, don't they?' said Walkinshaw – they reached agreement in June 1991.

> We'd planned to go into Formula One with a TWR team in 1992 or 1993, but the economic climate was getting difficult and it made sporting and business sense to buy into an existing team. Benetton's aspirations were the same as mine.

His liaison with Briatore was always seen as likely to be a bruising relationship on both sides, particularly as Walkinshaw bought a 35 per cent equity in the team which was scheduled to rise to 50 per cent, and it was no surprise when, after moving to Ligier, Walkinshaw made attempts to buy that team, much to the dismay of the French who hoped to see the team return to French ownership. Finally, Walkinshaw lost patience with the Ligier–Briatore situation and instead, in late 1996, took control of Arrows from Jackie Oliver, not long after celebrating another success at Le Mans with a TWR-designed Porsche and a new deal to build road cars for Volvo. Arrows were renowned as the team that had never won a race in nearly 20 years, since their formation in 1978, but the challenge of turning also-rans into victors was one that Walkinshaw could not turn down and he made Oliver an offer that was too good to be refused. 'Tom and I have both got the same objectives,' said Oliver, when the deal was first announced.

Maybe the style will be different, but the intention will be the same so I cannot see any reason why there should be a disagreement ... I think people should look at it positively. It is not unusual for a number of key people to go from team to team in this business. If you look at Benetton, for example, it is made up – apart from Flavio Briatore – of a group of people who were senior members of other teams prior to Benetton. So why is it so strange to think that the same principles cannot apply with Walkinshaw taking over Arrows?

Showing his usual courage and determination, Walkinshaw promptly surprised most of Formula One by recruiting world champion Damon Hill to race for Arrows in 1997 and switching from Brian Hart power to a supply of factory Yamaha engines and Bridgestone tyres. It did not work out, Hill's best result was second, after leading, in Hungary and, after financial problems set in the following year, Arrows struggled despite running a John Barnard-designed A19.

In 1999, the team was refinanced by a consortium involving Morgan Grenfell Private Equity taking a 70 per cent stake and the introduction of Nigerian Prince Malik Ado Ibrahim as commercial director. Prince was unable to deliver on his promises and it was not until a sponsorship deal with Orange in 2000 that his Arrows team revived their fortunes. For Walkinshaw, it was just another frustration in his Formula One efforts with Arrows, but he was involved in so many interests and projects outside the sport that it was little wonder. While Williams remained focused on only one objective, he was maintaining his enthusiasms across a wide range of business and sport, including rugby, a sport he loved but had to abandon, as a player, because he both broke ankles in a racing accident. In 1997 he bought Gloucester Rugby Club and in 1998 he became chairman of English First Division Rugby, but also continued to find time to ski and shoot.

In 2000 he also ventured into new activities when he signed a deal with the Moscow City Government to create and develop an international motor racing circuit on Nagatino Island. This was another famously entrepreneurial and controversial project, which was dogged by drama including an attempted assassination of the city's deputy mayor, Iosif Ordzhonikidze, in a gun attack on his car. He required a four-hour operation to save his life, but his driver died, as their car was raked by 30 bullets. This incident suggested, as Ecclestone had opined frequently in the past that Moscow has an image as a city run by organised crime. Yet, after a promotional trip to the Russian capital in May 2001, he said:

> We have eight venues seeking Formula One rights at the moment, but I believe that this is where the next event should be. It is about time we had a round of the world championship in Russia. As soon as the circuit is ready we will be here.

Walkinshaw, unruffled by the violence and the mafia, said:

> People have been shot in London as well. As far as I am concerned it was not connected. It had nothing to do with Formula One . . . We signed a contract with the mayor of Moscow, not the official who was attacked.

While Walkinshaw was looking for his best way into Formula One, Ken Tyrrell was waiting to find the best way out. Eventually, struggling against rising costs and mounting odds, not to mention his inclination to accept that, at his venerable age, he should consider retirement, he sold to the Craig Pollock-headed British American Tobacco funded organisation, built around Reynard's manufacturing base, that became the British American Racing (BAR) team with Jacques Villeneuve as the main driver. 'Uncle Ken' had seen it all.

As the founder, inspiration, leader and later chairman of the Tyrrell Racing Organisation, he was involved in Formula One for more than 30 years. He had seen the rise of Bernie Ecclestone, the mercurial achievements of Colin Chapman, the power of Enzo Ferrari, the tenacity of Frank Williams and the resolute ambition of Ron Dennis. He had won drivers' titles with Jackie Stewart, mixed with celebrity and royalty, travelled the world, stayed in the best hotels and resorts and enjoyed the company of stars from every walk of life. Despite registering his last victory as a team owner at the United States (East) Grand Prix in Detroit, in 1983, he maintained a phenomenal level of enthusiasm through the final 15 years of his membership of the club.

In Monte Carlo in 1996, on the eve of the Monaco Grand Prix, he explained why, aged 72, he had remained at the epicentre of the sport for so long. 'Firstly,' he said. 'I still like doing it and, secondly, for the past 29 years, it has been my sole source of income. It is my only business.' At the time, his son Bob was the managing director (commercial) and Harvey Postlethwaite was the managing director (technical). 'I just keep an eye on things now,' he said. 'I like to go in and keep busy and make sure they don't spend too much money and that sort of thing.'

Robert Kenneth Tyrrell was born on 3 May 1924 in West Horsley, Sussex. He joined the RAF in 1941, met his wife Norah in 1942, married her in 1943 and had two sons, Robert and Kenneth. He trained as an airframe fitter, left the RAF in 1946, after qualifying as a flight engineer gaining experience flying in Halifax and Lancaster bombers. After the Second World War, he formed Tyrrell Brothers, a timber business, with his brother Bert, in Ockham, and in 1951 he went to Silverstone, in a coach party organised by his local village football team, to see the BRM race.

> We could have gone anywhere [he explained]. Brighton or any other resort. But, instead, we loaded some crates of beer into this charabanc and off we went. I sat in the grandstand at Stowe corner and I was particularly interested in the supporting race, which was for 500 cc Formula Three cars. One of them was driven by Alan Brown, who lived near me. A few days later, I knocked on his door and asked to see his car. I had never seen one before. At the end of the season, I bought it off him and went racing myself.
>
> I went down to Brands Hatch and I thought 'this is the life'. I drove from 1952 to 1958 before I realised I was not an outstanding driver. I won one international race (in Sweden) and a few national ones, and then it dawned on me that I was not going to be a star. So, instead, I went and started running a Formula Two team for Cooper.

Within a year, the entrepreneur in Tyrrell had persuaded him to run his own team and he formed the Ken Tyrrell Racing Team, to run two works Formula Junior Coopers. Later, in 1963, he changed the name to the Tyrrell Racing Organisation, but continued operating from the same wooden planked office in the timber yard in Surrey. His drivers included, in the early days, Jack Brabham, Bruce McLaren and Masten Gregory; he also gave John Surtees his first race on four wheels.

When John Cooper was badly injured in a road accident in his Mini-Cooper, 'Chopper Tyrrell' took over the running of his Formula One team. Early in 1964, when his driver Timmy Mayer, brother of Teddy Mayer, was killed in a crash in Tasmania, Tyrrell was left without a driver for his budding Formula Three team and, heeding a piece of advice from the Goodwood track manager Robin McKay, decided to test out a young Scot called Jackie Stewart. He had equalled the lap record in an old Ecurie Ecósse Cooper Monaco. McLaren was there to set target times, in a new Formula Three Cooper, and Stewart equalled them in three laps. Tyrrell signed him on the spot.

So began the adventure that was to carry them both, with support from Matra, Elf and Ford, to the drivers' and constructors' titles in 1969. Tyrrell recalled that when he first suggested the idea of running a Matra chassis, Stewart scoffed. But he tested it at Goodwood and finished the day convinced the car was one of the best-handling vehicles he had ever driven. The Tyrrell-Fords produced later carried Stewart to further glory in 1971 and 1973.

> We worked hard and we enjoyed ourselves. The sport has changed a great deal. It has become more and more professional. We had to go out and get sponsorship for the team, as always, but in the later years it became very hi-tech and very expensive.

In addition to his successes, Tyrrell also suffered tragedy and none more so than the death of the promising French driver Francois Cevert in 1973. He also operated without a sponsor in 1981 and enjoyed enough triumphs in the late 1960s for his cars to be talked of in the same breath as Ferrari or Lotus. As a member of the club, he was known for his towering tempers, his manner of talking loudly from a great height and his ferocious defence of his own principles. It was Tyrrell who stood alongside Ron Dennis and Frank Williams in a refusal to sign the latest Concorde Agreement of the mid-1990's because he believed, as they did, that Bernie Ecclestone was taking too big a slice of the growing television cake.

But Tyrrell was always one of the old school, a man who saw the world as it was and who took as much interest in other sports as in his own. He was a keen Tottenham Hotspur supporter who could always be relied upon, after qualifying late on a Saturday afternoon, to remember all the football scores from England, having listened to them on his transistor radio. And he loved cricket. In 1968, at the German Grand Prix at the Nurburgring, following practice on the daunting 14-mile leviathan, he strolled over to Stewart, still sitting in his car. The famous Scottish driver flipped up his visor and complained about his car's handling, wheel-spin and discomforts, the water on the circuit and the danger and futility of it all. When Stewart finished speaking, Tyrrell leaned into the cockpit and said: 'You think you've got problems? England are 86 for six!'

In 1988 he admitted that his first year's sponsorship brought £80,000 to the team. But, he added:

Today, that would buy just two Ford-Cosworth engines, in kit form. We will need 15 engines this year. In 1968, an engine cost £7,500, so I suppose prices have risen in line with inflation. We pay £40,000 per engine now and it takes another £3,500 to have it built.

Twenty-two years later, another team, Benetton, once sponsors of Tyrrell, once run by Briatore and Walkinshaw, now sold to Renault, was paying £15 million for a supply of engines, for the 2000 season. They were coming from Supertec, Briatore's marketing firm and Benetton were ruing the day they parted company with the flamboyant Italian, along with a payoff worth around £2.5 million . . . No wonder so many people refer to him as the man with the golden handshake. In Formula One in the 1990s, he had the knack of being in the right place with the right deal at the right time. But while Briatore prospered, Tyrrell struggled to survive as he had always after the Stewart era. In 2001, after selling his team, he was fighting to recover from cancer. The author chose to leave him in peace and wish him well, which accounts for this briefer than deserved entry on his part as a member of the club.

The decade of the 1990s saw rapid change in the financial and political conditions prevailing in Formula One, as a whole, and for the Piranha Club, in particular. This came as a result of the evolution of the Concorde Agreements between the teams, through FOCA, and the sport's ruling body, the FIA, and the part played in the creation of these agreements by Bernie Ecclestone, as the man controlling the commercial rights of the sport. Ecclestone's position as the commercial rights holder, in a separate and independent role from his position as head of the FOCA made it a vexed passage for all concerned. The teams, particularly the long-established core members of FOCA who had fought in the FISA–FOCA war, were loath to see what they saw as the hard-earned fruits of their years of labour being taken from them by one man and one organisation, albeit that Ecclestone and his companies were reliant on Formula One and the teams and that he was seen as, to some extent, one of them.

To some, in their most vehement and angry states of mind, it was tantamount to a commercial hi-jacking of their work. It was this feeling which led to prolonged disagreements over the 1997 Concorde Agreement and the position taken by Ron Dennis, Ken Tyrrell and Frank Williams, representing their teams, McLaren, Tyrrell and Williams, in refusing to sign or support it during the summer of 1996. The 1997 Concorde Agreement followed the agreements of 1981–86, 1987–91 and 1992–96 and was intended to run until the end of 2001. The evolution of the balance of power and wealth couched within these deals revolved around several issues, but one in particular irked the trio of principals from the three well-established and 'rebel' teams. Teams, indeed, that won 18 of the constructors' world championship titles from 1970 to 2000 and 20 of the drivers' titles. This was the transfer of the commercial rights licence from FOCA, which had previously sub-contracted its execution to Ecclestone and his own Formula One companies, to Ecclestone and his company Formula One Promotions and Administration (FOPA) directly.

In 1992, FOPA was reported to be Britain's most profitable company, making a profit of more than £15 million on a turnover of little more than £18 million, that suggested the ratio of profit was 80 per cent. In 1993 Ecclestone was Britain's highest-paid employee with wages of £45 million, an income he matched again in 1994. This surge in earnings suggested that income and profits had surged at FOPA in the early to mid 1990s as a result of the massive rises in television revenues. In Britain ITV were understood to have paid ten times the sum that the BBC paid previously for the analogue rights to broadcast Formula One and this increase, allied to the understanding that Britain is one of only 120 countries with a deal to broadcast the world championship, indicated that the income from television had risen dramatically.

These increases were no secret. The teams knew about them. They knew, too, therefore that their value as part of the show had increased. But they were no longer, strictly speaking and in equity terms, a part of the show. They were only performers. They had no stake any more in the theatre itself. Ecclestone, however, was prepared, in the new agreement, to increase the teams' share of the commercial and television revenue generated through Ecclestone's activities within the Concorde Agreement to grant the teams a share of the income increased to 47 per cent. The FIA was to continue to take 30 per cent and the Ecclestone companies 23 per cent. All this added up to massive income for everyone with the teams taking a percentage for appearance money and a further cut based on performance and stories of team flotations and share sales becoming fashionable.

Trouble, associated with the new 1997 Concorde Agreement, broke into public view late in 1996, however, when in the build-up to the Belgian Grand Prix the FIA chose to release certain details about the proposals and the issues at stake. These included propositions for two-day Grands Prix, 17 races a year and a new financial package. Tyrrell and McLaren refused to sign; Williams signed and then, at a meeting in Hockenheim, in July 1996, when Mosley outlined his views and the options available to the teams, he withdrew. The three rebel teams believed they were not due to receive a fair share of the escalating profits from television that were due to flow in and that the proposals did not reflect their rights as part of the Formula One show. They argued that Ecclestone was making too much money from the rising television income, granting licences to promoters, holding races, trackside advertising and hospitality; they wanted more; they provided the show. The FIA, in the driving seat, decided that the new agreement could be introduced and enforced without the three rebel teams' signatures, but that they could take part in the series but without, of course, as much political power or income as previously. This was explained to the eight remaining signatory teams by Mosley at a meeting in London in early August 1996. They could be readmitted to the agreement if 80 per cent of the signatory teams agreed . . .

The background to the split, between old and new, triggered by the obvious realisation that the two men who led the teams into the FISA–FOCA war, Ecclestone and Mosley, had jumped ship and joined the blazered establishment, or at least (in Ecclestone's case) taken up a new position closer to their sphere of influence, emerged in the early to mid-1990s. It came out when Ecclestone revealed in 1995 that he was investing enormous sums of money in a digital television project, designed to ensure that Formula One could offer its viewers the best broadcasting images and sound. In 1996, at the German Grand Prix at Hockenheim, the service began with the DF1 satellite channel broadcasting into Germany, Austria and Switzerland. The owners of DF1 were understood to be German media mogul Leo Kirch and his partner, owning 49 per cent, Rupert Murdoch, of BSkyB. Deals followed with Canal Plus of France, who sold their service into European and South American countries, and Telepiu of Italy. The digital compound set up by Ecclestone to supply the service cost him more than £35 million initially and additional improvements, transport and upkeep charges. It was a huge investment and a huge gamble.

Mosley defended Ecclestone's claim to sole sovereignty over television rights for Formula One. He said:

Two or three years ago, Mr Ecclestone made an enormous investment in digital television at a time when almost everyone was saying that he would lose every penny. It is now looking as though digital television is going to be a great success. That's good for him because he took an enormous risk and may now be profiting from it and it is even better for the teams because although they took no risk at all, they don't have to meet any of the cost involved.

Not everyone agreed with that view. Some felt Ecclestone was milking the opportunity given him by the teams and not giving enough back. Mosley did not take that view and on 20 August 1996, he took his opportunity to force the issue when, at a meeting of the FIA's World Council called to discuss a fine imposed on the world rally champion Colin McRae, he introduced the subject of the new Concorde Agreement, without any prior consultation with the Formula One Commission (on which both Dennis and Williams sat as members), and it was formally voted through. The Piranha Club had been outmanoeuvred by two of its own kind, two men who had left for higher offices and richer opportunities.

Among the significant changes it carried with it, the new agreement allowed for changes to be made to the sporting and technical regulations of Formula One with agreement from 80 per cent of the signatory teams and for the votes on the Formula One Commission, regarded as the single most important political voice in the sport, to go to the top five signatory teams in the previous year's world championship together with the team that has appeared in the most world championships overall (Ferrari). In effect, it meant the three non-signatory teams, McLaren, Tyrrell and Williams, had been left on the sidelines. The old bonds of the FOCA teams were broken.

The jealously guarded secret structure of the distribution of prize money was also discarded, it was said, and replaced by a proposal for television income to be split up with the teams receiving 50 per cent and that income itself to be divided equally between the signatory teams as entries and all of the competing teams, with a weighting for previous results. It meant that the three rebel teams, the outfits with the greatest traditions, records and reputations in the sport, other than Ferrari, were punished for standing on a matter of principle. Dennis, clearly aghast and angry at the way things unfolded, remained tight-lipped.

> It is inappropriate for me to share my knowledge of the subject with you. I hope that the whole issue will remain within the teams, within the FIA and Bernie, within the group, because I don't think it serves any function for the parties to air their views. It is far more constructive to find solutions to the areas of disagreement.

He knew the sums of money involved, but, as ever, they remained untold. However, it is understood that by the late 1980s, Ecclestone was charging promoters and race organisers up to £10 million to stage a Formula One World Championship event and that his income from this source alone was in the region of £120 million annually; none of which flowed back to the teams. On top of this, it was known that race organisers were also, as part of their agreement to stage a race, handing over all rights to their trackside advertising and hospitality to the Geneva-based Allsport Management, run by Paddy McNally. This organisation developed the popular and successful Paddock Club, which helped contribute towards another source of income worth around £50 million per season. None of this went to the teams either, but they were aware of the likely arrival of the new concept of 'virtual advertising' (a system of permitting electronic images to be superimposed on different logos on trackside advertising hoardings to suit different markets in relation to their legislation on tobacco advertising and sponsorship) and they were keen to have some say on how this worked and who took the revenue.

Understandably there were prolonged discussions, disagreements and rows. On the Thursday before the 1996 Italian Grand Prix at Monza, the team principals met again at the Ferrari headquarters at Maranello, a meeting, which echoed the old days of Enzo Ferrari holding court to sort out the running of the business. Curiously, of course, the three teams that had most history other than Ferrari were absent, but Ecclestone, having held a meeting with Williams to discuss a compromise, spoke on behalf of all. The rebel teams' proposals for that compromise were considered at the Maranello meeting, approved and later announced by Mosley at the Monza race. It amounted to a probable peace settlement, but there were few details revealed. 'All three teams will be part of the Concorde Agreement,' said Dennis. 'It might happen quickly or it may take a period of time, but it will be before the start of next season.' He was right. It was not quick.

One of the alterations that eased into existence during this period of talking and arguing was the role of Ecclestone within the FIA. He had been made a vice-president of the old FISA, with special responsibility for promotional affairs, by Jean-Marie Balestre in 1987, a role that was transferred into the FIA following Mosley's reformation, but one that ensured he has visibility and responsibility in both the teams' organisation as the long-time head of FOCA and that of the ruling body. It was this position of his, with 'vested interests', that played a part also in attracting the interest of the European Commission in the late 1990s and led to the sport becoming more transparent and understandable. The Maranello meeting had seen an overhaul of the Formula One Commission proposed too. It was to be increased from 13 members to 14, with the addition of Ecclestone as the commercial rights holder, to

a group comprising Mosley, as the FIA president, four promoters, two sponsors and six team representatives, including
Ferrari. At the same time, significantly, it was proposed that
Ecclestone as the rights holder should become a signatory to
the Concorde Agreement itself – a move that meant, if confirmed, that finally, 15 years after the 'war', the poachers had
taken over and the club was in control, one way or another.

None of this led to a swift settlement of the dispute over the
Concorde Agreement and, in March 1997, the squabbling continued; the rebels had not agreed with anything and the signatories were not prepared to give them the same rights they had
supported. At this time, the sport was therefore run under an
agreement to which three top teams and two new teams,
Stewart and Lola, were not signatories. Furthermore, Williams
and McLaren, aware they were losing substantial television
income, threatened to take legal action. The signatory teams
were not impressed. They were adamant that the three rebel
teams should not re-enter the club with the same terms, conditions and privileges that the others had agreed to; nor should
they suffer a reduction in their income to allow the others back.

The crux of it was that if the television income had to be
divided between 10 teams, instead of seven, it would mean less
for each team. Furthermore, a return to the fold by McLaren
and Williams would virtually certainly see them rejoin the
Formula One Commission as one of the top five performing
teams and see Arrows and Sauber replaced. In political terms,
beyond the commission, the re-entry of the rebels would be significant, too; under the new 1997 agreement, proposals for
change needed to have only 80 per cent support and this was
achievable if such renowned conservatives as Dennis and
Williams were not voting at team principal meetings.

The dispute and the arguments simmered on throughout
1997 until the rebels decided to take their case to the European
Commission by lodging a formal complaint, citing the Concorde
Agreement as being in violation of the Treaty of Rome. The
letter of complaint was akin to a flame flickering beneath the
blue touch paper of an explosive keg. At the same time, a new
Concorde Agreement to run from 1998 to 2008 was being discussed, an accord that, it was planned, would replace the trou-
blesome 1997 one. By mid-1997, it had become a critical issue
not only for the rebel teams, but for Ecclestone because he was
preparing for a flotation of his Formula One Holdings empire, a

project that had been delayed endlessly for various reasons since it was revealed earlier that year. Indeed, it was reported that during a meeting of the team principals held at Silverstone in July 1997, there were 15 issues in the new accord that required further scrutiny; but when they met again at the Nurburgring in September, these had increased to a list of 126 points of disagreement raised by the rebel teams. Ecclestone and Mosley, who attended the Nurburgring meeting, were not impressed.

All of this left the club in a bit of a state at this time with seven signatory teams operating under the vexed 1997–2001 agreement, and enjoying a cut of about £8 million per annum each from the television money as well as political clout and recognition, while the rebels pursued a form of equality and some justice through the European Commission. This situation persisted throughout 1997 and was not resolved, finally, until early 1998 when, finally, a new long-term Concorde Agreement was drawn up and signed on Friday, 22 May 1998, at the Automobile Club de Monaco, in the presence of His Serene Highness Prince Albert of Monaco. After approximately 35 drafts had been sent back for revision, the final one supplied an accord that could guarantee the security of the sport and the business for 10 years, certainly until the end of 2007, according to the majority of the teams.

It is this Concorde Agreement under which Formula One has been run ever since; and it was this deal that was used to gain clearance from the European Commission for Ecclestone to go ahead with his proposals for a flotation of Formula One Holdings. The signatories to the new deal on that Friday evening were: Ron Dennis (McLaren), Frank Williams (Williams), Eddie Jordan (Jordan), Tom Walkinshaw (Arrows), Jackie Stewart (Stewart), Alain Prost (Prost), David Richards (Benetton), Craig Pollock (Tyrrell-BAR), Gabriele Rumi (Minardi) and Ecclestone. On Saturday morning, Max Mosley and Luca di Montezemolo (Ferrari) added their signatures, leaving only one team unrepresented: Sauber. The reasons for this were unclear. It was suggested that they ranged from a problem with the paperwork to jealousy that Ferrari were due to receive a substantial payment for agreeing, like the other original signatories to the 2007 Concorde Agreement, to cancel their support for that one. The most likely, however, was that because Sauber are based in Switzerland, and therefore outside the

European Union, and that their commercial director Fritz Kaiser had an interest in the team and some of its major deals, he wished to exploit his position, and his team's, by using some leverage by delaying team owner Peter Sauber's signature. Whatever the details of this delay, it was soon resolved.

Thus the deal under which the club operated at the turn of the twenty-first century was, finally, settled. According to good sources, the distribution of the income from promoters, television, commercial sales and merchandising remained highly secret, but retained much of the complex system that had been in place for the previous 15 years or more. This had always meant that payments were made calculated on the positions of cars and teams at various times during a Grand Prix weekend. Payments were made for the top 20 qualifiers, for positions at quarter, half and three-quarters distance in the race, as well as at the finish, and that only the top ten teams in the championship received payments for their performance overall in the previous half-season. This system had been in place for years and, though it clearly punished the weak and under-funded teams who failed to enjoy success, it was accepted. The rich got richer. It was Darwinian, but it was the way things were in Formula One – and the way, essentially, they have remained.

It was understood that the new Concorde Agreement retained some of these strange arrangements, but cleaned them up. As always, it was difficult to find reliable confirmation of any information given other than that the total revenue generated goes into one general 'pot' before being distributed. The gross is then 'split' three ways between the teams, the commercial rights holder and the FIA, with the teams receiving around 49 per cent of the total. That revenue, due to the teams, is then paid according to a complex formula that, it is understood, ensures twice-yearly payments (made in June and December) for entry and participation and further payments based on various other factors including performance (in the previous year) and history (over three years). Teams that do well are paid better than those that fail. The team that fails to finish in the top 10 suffers for its failure.

Ferrari, successful and popular and an imperative part of the show, has the strongest bargaining position and in 2000 received approximately £16 million for its presence, from the television income stream, compared to BAR, which received only £4 million. BAR failed to score any points in the 1999 championship and suffered as Prost did in 2001, having failed to score a point in 2000. In the vernacular of the paddock, if a team finishes 11th, it misses out on the travel budget completely; it is not just a saying, it is true. Yet for most Formula One teams, the old FOCA entry and prize money distribution, now enhanced to include television and commercial rights income, represent little more than 20 per cent of their gross budgets as the costs have soared and the level of sponsorship income has soared with them.

Bernie Ecclestone retained a straightforward view on life throughout the 1990s, indeed through all of his 30 years' involvement in Formula One. Speaking, in Montreal, during the 2001 Canadian Grand Prix weekend, he said:

The way I look at it is that we were like boutiques, or were like a shopkeeper that goes to market in the morning, buys the fruit and vegetables, puts it in the bag, brings it home, puts it out on the stall, sells it, takes the cash, in the morning goes to the bank, banks the cash, goes to the market . . . you know? And that's how we operate. We buy the best fruit because we're there in the morning at six o'clock and we know what's good and bad. And we get the best prices. And the teams are becoming supermarkets now.

So, you're losing that guy that goes to the market. Maybe that guy doesn't go any more, he sends someone else and maybe that guy doesn't quite know what fruit to buy and what's the best price. But, because the supermarket is so big and the turnover is so great, it's no longer so important that you can buy the fruit at the best price. So, it's changed. When we were at Brabham, I think we had about 60 people who were manufacturing the cars and racing them, doing the whole lot. Now these teams bring 60 or 70 people to a race and they've got 300 people at the factory. So, it's changed . . .

A question to Ecclestone, from the author: *There are a lot of different people in the top jobs now, with different outlooks, some of them coming in only because they want to take money out . . . is that true?*

Yeah, you're right. With the old days with Teddy Mayer at McLaren and me, it was different. I bought Brabham because I retired. I was 40 years old and I wanted to retire and enjoy my life and travel the world with a race team. So, I thought I could afford to run it. And that's what I did. We were all a bit like that. We were all racers at heart then. Now, it's all a bit different. People come in and they can see the commercial benefits of being in Formula One.

What would have happened to you, do you think, if you had not won the FISA-FOCA war?

If we hadn't won?

Yes.

I don't know. No idea. I didn't think about two things. I didn't think about losing, for a start. And I didn't think about if we did, what we would do . . .

Why did you win?

Why? Because we were right. We were absolutely right. What we wanted to do was honest and it was the correct thing to do.

Do the small teams get a fair share of the income, compared to the big teams?

The big teams all get all that is necessary to make more money . . .

What about changing the distribution?

I can't remember the last time it was discussed. This distribution (system) has been going on this way for 25 years. The amount of money that is paid is based on the previous year's results. It's a fixed amount. And there are payments made after each race. It's fair, but it's unfair, too, if you follow my meaning. Maybe, as you quite rightly say, it's too loaded in favour of the rich teams. But the amount of money the teams actually get, the big teams anyway, is such a small percentage of their overall budget that it's not really making a difference. Maybe in the case of Ferrari, it makes 10 per cent of their budget, or less. And in the case of a small team, maybe 30 per cent.

And you?

I like to think that what I'm doing is good for everyone, including myself. Good for everyone else, too. I like to do deals . . .

8   Tempestuous Times

Part I: 1994

Like a beautiful field of golden wheat, enveloped by the darkest of storm clouds, the 1994 season was overshadowed by the tragic events at Imola during the weekend of the San Marino Grand Prix. But it was a year of controversy and intrigue in many other respects. Accusations of cheating and chicanery flew in all directions and many seasoned observers remain convinced that Ayrton Senna's death at the Autodromo Enzo e Dino Ferrari during the race on Sunday, 1 May, only 24 hours after the death of Roland Ratzenberger, was due in part to his simmering fury caused by believing that a rival team was breaking the rules. Senna had left McLaren, after winning the previous season-ending Australian Grand Prix in Adelaide, to join Williams, the seemingly invincible Renault-powered team of the moment; his old nemesis, Alain Prost, the 1993 champion, had retired when he learned of the Brazilian's imminent arrival, leaving the way open for him to partner Damon Hill. Senna's move coincided with other changes, including the banning of all electronic driver aids, including active suspension, anti-lock and power braking, traction control, fly-by-wire throttle control and continuously variable transmission. Some believed everyone would obey the new rules. Others just hoped.

In Brazil, on home soil in Sao Paulo, Senna took pole in his Williams-Renault. He was under pressure. He was in a new team, a champion team, but he was also starting the season under a three-race suspended suspension, for punching Eddie Irvine at Suzuka the previous year, and facing a strong challenge from the Benetton-Ford tyro, Michael Schumacher. In the race, Senna led to the first pit stops. Then Schumacher came out in front and stayed there. Senna, in hot pursuit, finally spun off and stalled after the second stops. Schumacher eased off to win comfortably. Senna's former team, McLaren, using Peugeot engines for the first time, also had a day to forget. They were without a champion, without a recognised race-winning engine supplier and back at square one. But Benetton, re-invented by the image building of Flavio Briatore and the shrewd team management of Tom Walkinshaw, were winning. Neither Senna, nor many at his old and new teams, liked it.

When Senna took pole in Aida, in Japan, at the Pacific Grand Prix, and then spun off on the first lap, allowing Schumacher another straightforward victory for Benetton, he was more upset still. Senna felt, and told some close friends, that the Benetton was a car with some extra, that it used a form of traction control. His feelings were never proven. There were suspicions, too, that Ferrari were using similar unauthorised devices to improve their cars' performances amid fears, fairly widespread in the paddock, that the ruling authority, the FIA, did not have the technical expertise to police its regulations reliably or consistently. In Aida, the FIA technical delegate, a 'poacher turned gamekeeper' named Charlie Whiting, who once worked for Bernie Ecclestone as a mechanic and member of the Brabham team, listened carefully to the fluttering sound of Nicola Larini's Ferrari engine. He investigated and he found it was fitted with a rev-limiter. Some suggested it could be interpreted as a traction control device. Sensibly, avoiding a headlong confrontation and major controversy at the second race of the year, he suggested to Ferrari that they disconnect the device while its legality was investigated. Many members of other teams felt that Ferrari had been cheating, but had been treated gently. It was a mood that set the tone for the rest of the year; one controversy was to follow another.

At the next race, the San Marino Grand Prix, Rubens Barrichello survived a massive accident in practice, Ratzenberger was killed in qualifying, Senna was killed in the race, debris from Pedro Lamy's Lotus car flew into the crowd, where several spectators were hurt, after it collided with JJ Lehto's Benetton, a wheel bounced off Michele Alboreto's Minardi, after a pit stop, hitting four mechanics, who were all taken to hospital, and the weekend ended in death, shock and police activity as the Williams team had its cars impounded and the blame was thrown in all directions. Senna's funeral, in Sao Paulo, attracted worldwide attention; Ratzenberger's only European. Team staff, the paddock people, the media and the administration of the sport were joined in one in stunned and sad bereavement. But what seemed like a nightmare weekend almost seemed to continue to lay a trail through the season as it unfolded.

Despite the best efforts of the ruling body, the FIA, and its president Max Mosley, who announced a series of measures to slow the cars, more accidents followed and a major one at the Monaco Grand Prix where Karl Wendlinger, like Ratzenberger, an Austrian, was left in a coma after a collision with the barriers in his Sauber-Mercedes, hit the recovering circus hard. Wendlinger remained in a coma for 19 days, but the race went on after a minute's silence in memory of the two dead men whose places on the grid were remembered by the clearly symbolic absence of any cars on the front row. It was a heart-wrenching, tearful, stomach-churning and exhausting month, the May of 1994, but it ended with hopeful signs as it was reported that Wendlinger's condition was improving and in the way that Damon Hill, like his father Graham, in 1968, when Jim Clark was killed, rose to meet the expectation of his team and emerge as a leader in the vacuum left by the Brazilian's death. Hill did what was best for him and the team by winning the Spanish Grand Prix at Barcelona, ahead of Schumacher's Benetton, on 29 May.

But Schumacher, irresistibly, surged back. He won in Canada, ahead of Hill, in his Williams-Renault, and again in France, where Hill had taken pole position just ahead of his latest team-mate, the recalled-from-America 1992 world champion Nigel Mansell. Mansell's return, at Ecclestone's behest, came at the expense of a youthful David Coulthard, the Williams team test driver. The start at Magny-Cours, where Schumacher surged between the two Williams men, to lead and then to win left many close watchers of the race suspecting something special worked very well for the Benetton car and its German driver. Hill, however, even if he shared some of the suspicions that were never proven, chose not to complain or cause trouble; he simply wanted to beat Schumacher, especially on a level field in England.

At Silverstone, he took pole, by just three-thousandths of a second, from Schumacher. But on the formation lap, the German caused uproar by overtaking Hill. He was given a five seconds stop-go for penalty, transmitted to Benetton by a message from the race officials. Briatore and Walkinshaw argued with the stewards while Schumacher stayed out, racing.

Eventually, he was black flagged to come in, but refused to obey. Eventually, he did. Then, he rejoined second and finished, but was later excluded from the result for his antics. The stewards then fined Benetton £25,000, but reinstated Schumacher. Finally, a special meeting of the World Motor Sport Council was held, Schumacher was banned for two races, removed from the result of the British Grand Prix and Benetton's fine was increased to $500,000.

At the same time, the FIA issued an enigmatic announcement in which it said that Benetton was one of three teams using computer systems capable of breaching the technical regulations. A furore followed. McLaren and Benetton were fined $100,000 each for refusing to release their cars' systems' software. From tragedy, Formula One had moved to travesty and controversy. Yet there was worse to come as Schumacher appealed against his punishment following Silverstone, German fans threatened to set fire to the forests surrounding the Hockenheimring, if Schumacher was banned from racing in the German Grand Prix, and Hill required a police escort in and out of the circuit after receiving death threats.

This chaotic series of events was followed in Germany by a fire, which engulfed Jos Verstappen's Benetton at a refuelling pit stop. The blaze overshadowed Gerhard Berger's victory for Ferrari, the Italian team's first success in four years, and was followed by more controversy when it was found that Benetton had removed a compulsory filter from their refuelling rig, a move that increased the speed of their pit stops. Racing under appeal, Schumacher won in Hungary and Belgium, but his victory at Spa-Francorchamps was annulled when he was disqualified after the race because of irregular wear to a skid-block fitted to the underside of his car.

The team argued, but the disqualification stood and, the following day, Schumacher, in the midst of a summer of controversy, appeared in Paris for his appeal hearing against his two-race ban following the Silverstone black flag fiasco. He lost and so missed the Italian and Portuguese Grands Prix while Benetton managed to evade serious punishment on their removal of the fuel filter by hiring the famous and very expensive British advocate George Carman to represent them in Paris. On his return to the track, Schumacher suggested on the eve of the European Grand Prix at Jerez in Spain that Hill, who won both in Italy and Portugal to revive his title challenge, was not a truly world-class driver. More controversial headlines followed, as they did when they reached Adelaide to settle the championship outcome and Schumacher took the title only after colliding with Hill in the most suspicious circumstances.

It was Schumacher's first championship triumph, the first by a German and it was won by only one point following a deliberate move to create a collision. To add a touch of pantomime to the sad, bad, sometimes mad year, Mansell, back for the last three races with Williams, won the season-ender in Australia, but his original Formula One team, Lotus, collapsed under the weight of debt. The administrators, Robson Rhodes, revealed that Lotus owed £7 million to Landhurst Leasing, which was also in receivership. It was a signal of the times, but in all of this, while drivers died and the teams fought over technical rules and regulations, the television viewing figures showed a steady increase. 'I suppose there is nothing that is bad publicity, is there?' reflected Bernie Ecclestone from the distance of seven years when he looked back, during the 2001 Canadian Grand Prix, on the events of 1994.

> It happened, 1994 just happened. I mean, people told me after Ayrton got killed that that was the end of Formula One. Bye-bye. Bye-bye. At that time, much as I was close with his family and he used to call us from Brazil to talk to the children, I said Formula One is bigger than any one person. I hope it is. It proved it, truly, really, that it is.

Part II: 1997

At 1327 GMT on 11 November 1997, the Press Association in Britain reported: 'Formula One teams Williams and McLaren were today cleared of attempting to fix the result of last month's European Grand Prix in Jerez, Spain.' It was the end of another *cause célèbre* in the litany of controversies that chequered the sport in the 1990s and concluded a long weekend of wild claims and counterclaims that had blazed across the front pages of the world's print media. It was a big story, nearly big enough to overshadow two others on the same day, but not quite: Michael Schumacher had escaped with a 'let-off' for his 'road rage' ramming attack on Jacques Villeneuve at the European Grand Prix and Bernie Ecclestone, it was revealed, had donated £1 million to the British Labour party at a time when Formula One was seeking an exemption from anti-tobacco legislation concerning advertising and sponsorship in sport. Nothing could stop Formula One claiming space on the front and the back of most national newspapers at the same time.

Schumacher, the tarnished champion of 1994, had gone to face the extraordinary meeting of the World Motor Sport Council of the FIA, held at the British RAC Motor Sports' Association headquarters, at Colnbrook, near Slough, with a grimace and without much grace. He had refused to apologise to Villeneuve, the new champion, for steering his Ferrari into the Canadian's Williams Renault during their Spanish showdown on 26 October and he had denied it was deliberate. Instinctive, yes, he said; deliberate, no. Yet nobody at the hearing and few of the 350 million worldwide television viewers who had watched the showdown in Spain believed him.

The Schumacher story, however, was but a part of a greater piece of Piranha Club chicanery as Ferrari, in turmoil and embarrassment, made a bid to create a wild smokescreen around their star driver. By delivering a transcript of a recording made of conversations that took place between the Williams team and Villeneuve during the European Grand Prix to *The Times* newspaper for publication on Saturday, 8 November, the agents acting on Ferrari's behalf merely dragged themselves, the Italian team and the sport into disrepute. The ploy created uproar, but also helped Schumacher escape with only seven days' enforced work for the FIA in promoting a European road safety campaign in 1998 and the loss of his runners-up position in the 1997 drivers' world championship when the decisions of the hearing were announced.

Instead of triggering sympathy for the Ferrari team and their desperation to end 18 years without success, the revelation of the so-called 'Jerezgate' tapes did the opposite. It also confirmed that some teams in Formula One, and some of the people who run them, were capable of stooping to virtually any measures to improve their own hopes of success. In this case, to tap into a radio frequency for spying purposes, then to record conversations, the measures taken were understood to be not only unsporting and unethical, but also illegal. The suggestion that Schumacher's instinctive action in ramming into Villeneuve's car came only as a result of knowing that other teams were conspiring against him was as laughable as it was deplorable. His lunge came only after he learned that his car had a water leak and was therefore unlikely to go the distance anyway. It was not McLaren and Williams who were involved in desperate and deplorable tactics, stooping to a form of sporting espionage to rescue their hopes. It was Ferrari, the once crimson beauties of the pit lane, but now daubed in sponsors' logos like the rest, and ready to try anything for success.

To most close observers, Ferrari had attempted to use a smear campaign to justify Schumacher's actions. *The Times*, given the transcripts, published them without adding balancing comment from either the McLaren or Williams camps. Understandably, both Ron Dennis and Frank Williams were livid that a newspaper of such standing and reputation could behave in such a way. They were angered, too, by Ferrari's behaviour in circulating the transcripts of the tapes among leading Formula One staff and selected media, a fact that became apparent when Bernie Ecclestone received a copy of the transcript and used it to taunt the teams during a meeting in London prior to the Colnbrook meeting. The transcripts, Ferrari attempted to suggest, proved that McLaren and Williams colluded to fix the result of the Jerez race. The McLaren drivers, Mika Hakkinen and David Coulthard, it was suggested, were asked to protect Villeneuve from attack by Ferrari's Eddie Irvine in exchange for being allowed to pass and finish the race first and second. This they did with Villeneuve, nursing a damaged car home following his collision with Schumacher, claiming third place and, with it, the drivers' world championship.

'I am extremely disappointed that such a prestigious newspaper should print a story not supported by the facts,' said Dennis, reacting to *The Times* story printed on Saturday, 8 November. 'We can't see any logic in perpetuating what appears to be a deliberate attempt, by a rival team, to tarnish the very successful images of McLaren and Williams.' Dennis vehemently denied his team would ever consider using scanning or other devices, as Ferrari had, to listen to rival teams' communications during a race. 'We have never done it and we never would,' he stated. He added that McLaren used a system of encrypted signals to prevent rival teams listening to their communications (though this did not prevent their conversations being recorded, decoded and transcribed for the FIA hearing). Frank Williams was equally disappointed and angry. 'I'm very disappointed to discover that Ferrari are listening to other teams during the races,' he said. 'But not really surprised.' He dismissed all suggestions of collusion as nonsense.

> Our only concern was that Jacques was not held up unnec-
> essarily and we talked to a number of teams about that.
> The Jerez circuit was not an ideal place to hold the final
> round of the championship because of the difficulty in
> overtaking. In fact, the only time Jacques had a problem
> was when Fontana's Sauber let Michael Schumacher
> through without any problem and then cost Jacques 2.5
> seconds in five corners.

Williams left it unsaid that Fontana's Sauber was powered by a Ferrari engine, a fact that pointed to inter-team agreements to support Schumacher.

Dennis also made it clear he did not believe that there could be any realistic connection between the 'Jerezgate' tapes scandal and the long dispute over the non-signing, by McLaren, Tyrrell and Williams, of the 1997 Concorde Agreement. He believed this even though many commentators suggested such connections may exist and be linked, also, to a wish to pressurise the 'rebel' teams into agreeing with the accord, and signing it, at a time when Ecclestone was proposing a £2 billion flotation of his Formula One empire and wanted to present the sport in an excellent light. A further controversy over Schumacher's driving was also regarded as undesirable.

> Above all else, we are a sport [said Dennis]. And the gov-
> erning body has a difficult task when it comes to effecting
> judgement on many of the issues that come out of the com-
> petitive world of Grand Prix racing. The environment of
> Formula One is even more charged at the moment
> because of the commercial and regulatory conflicts, which
> have continued for two years, but these issues are very
> close to being resolved ... I don't believe that the FIA or
> Bernie Ecclestone would jeopardise their hard work and
> commitment to resolving these very important issues by
> involving themselves in the stories published by *The
> Times*.

The feud had started long before in the history of the relationship between the British garagistes and their European continental opponents. Much mutual distrust had engendered a strained relationship made worse by Ferrari's desperation to break their barren run. The nature of the Japanese Grand Prix, run at Suzuka on 12 October 1997, was also a factor. Villeneuve had gone there with a lead of nine points over Schumacher, with two races remaining. He needed only to score two points to win the title. Nothing, it seemed, could be more straightforward, or so simple; but Ferrari, knowing this, needing to lift themselves for one last fight, had a plan to wreck the party. They worked night and day to make it work and, with a shade more luck and better judgement, it may have done. But, instead, it ended in a cloud of dust and criticism at Jerez.

Eddie Irvine always liked to return to Tokyo. So, too, did Jacques Villeneuve. They had grown up there. They knew the city, the night spots and the shops and restaurants. It was a place where they felt anonymous and relaxed. They both went to Tokyo to unwind in the build up to the Japanese Grand Prix in 1997. To win the drivers' title for Williams, Villeneuve needed two points. To help Michael Schumacher do the same for Ferrari, Irvine had to obey team orders, let his team-mate win, if possible, and keep Villeneuve as far away from the front as possible. Both knew their jobs. Both were ready for the task ahead and both relished the prospects as they travelled down to Suzuka in readiness for the race.

A huge crowd filled the circuit every day. They played in the sprawling amusement park, ate western food like candy floss and hamburgers, spent money on Formula One merchandising and mobbed anyone seen in a racing team jacket. Drivers were unable to stroll through the park to the circuit. Some went by helicopter. Others went by mini-bus. The brave ones risked a scooter through the packed masses of people. At the top of the hill, inside the paddock, amid the half-opened packing crates and technical cases, the tension was palpable. This race was all about Williams and Ferrari, Villeneuve and Schumacher, Frentzen and Irvine. All four, ironically, had spent some previous time in their careers racing in Japan and had big fan clubs.

Villeneuve was reading a biography of the Doors singer Jim Morrison. He said he was not interested in any kind of unsporting activity, no subterfuge, no tactics. He just wanted to go out and race to show what he could do and he wanted to win the championship. Jock Clear, his race engineer, said. 'He has identified Michael as just another human being. He believes he can beat him in a straight fight. He knows the car is capable of doing the job and psychologically, he is quite strong.' In qualifying, Villeneuve lived up to his billing as the champion elect. He was fast, very fast and unbeatable for speed and he took pole position. Then, however, came the news that he had ignored yellow flags during Saturday morning practice, not for the first time in the season. Almost unbelievably, the stewards decided that he was excluded from the race. He could not take part and that meant Schumacher, second fastest in qualifying, would have a clear run. Williams were in uproar. They appealed and, pending the outcome of that appeal, it was decided that he could take part in the race, but that points scored would not count unless the appeal was a success.

The race was a vicious dogfight, tactical, pragmatic and ugly. Villeneuve, his concentration rattled by the appeal and the furore beforehand, was never fully competitive and he finished fifth. The key man in the race, however, was his old Tokyo friend, Irvine. Starting on the second row, just behind Villeneuve and Schumacher, he knew he had to make a good start, but did not. Then he recovered and drove an inspired almost sublime race to take the lead.

> I couldn't believe I had lost just one place at the start, to Hakkinen's McLaren [he said]. There had been no game plan before the race, but Michael and I had talked about places where we could overtake. I said it was possible on the outside of turn six and he didn't reckon it was, so he was only half-surprised when I came past. I was quite prepared to take Hakkinen, but I must admit it was very satisfying to pass Michael as well. It wasn't a problem for Michael because he knew I could afford to take more risks when trying to overtake Villeneuve, who led from the start.

When he came upon Villeneuve in the fast left-hander called 130R, Irvine swerved to the outside to avoid his blocking move and swept into the lead. It was a personal dream realised for him, to be in front, leading his favourite race, but after only 20 laps he was ordered, by Ferrari, to slow down and allow Schumacher to make up the 12-seconds deficit and let him through, but at the same time to ensure that Villeneuve, by then third, stayed there.

It was amusing being part of such teamwork, but predictably perhaps, I was on the losing end of it [said Irvine].
The responsibility of racing for someone else's world
champion prospects kills some of the immediate enjoy-
ment. But, at the end of the day, I was there to do a job.
That might not have been so bad had I not lost time with
my second pit stop. When Frentzen pulled out of the pits
after his stop, he came straight across and onto the racing
line at the point where I was doing 180 mph. It was totally
out of order, more dangerous than going flat out past a
yellow flag, the offence for which Villeneuve had received
a one-race ban.

Frentzen finished second, Irvine third, Mika Hakkinen fourth
and Villeneuve fifth, subject to appeal. On paper, Schumacher
had regained the whip hand with thanks due to Irvine and the
Ferrari plan.

Within a week, Williams withdrew their appeal and
Villeneuve, instead of being one point ahead of Schumacher
with one race to go, was one point behind. To those who
retained clear memories of Adelaide in 1994, the parallels were
eerie. 'The man who goes into Jerez in the lead is in a position
where, as we've seen a number of times previously, he can be
very aggressive with the person behind and if both cars don't
finish . . . ' said Patrick Head, Williams technical director,
musing on the possible outcomes and recalling not only
Adelaide, but the 1990 Japanese Grand Prix at Suzuka where
Ayrton Senna, in a McLaren, deliberately collided with Alain
Prost, in a Ferrari, at the first corner to end their races, clinch
the drivers' title and exact revenge. For Villeneuve, understandably, it was a major disappointment.

He was not the only driver to have passed yellow flags while
the marshals were attempting to move Jos Verstappen's Tyrrell
Ford from the straight before the 130R corner. Five others,
including Schumacher and Frentzen, did the same, but they all
received suspended one-race bans. Villeneuve's punishment
was an immediate ban, but he was not told until long after dark-
ness on Saturday night, hours after he had claimed pole position.

This has been the most difficult weekend of my career [he
said later]. It would be easier to accept this kind of thing at
the beginning of the season, but when the stakes are so

high, at the end of the season, it is hard to accept its being played like that. But there are rules and I am not the one who is making them.

When the appeal was withdrawn, he was pragmatic about it, understanding that it was more important to be certain of racing in Spain, in the final race, than to risk everything for two points, as Max Mosley had warned if he proceeded with his appeal.

In Spain, the tension continued. Schumacher was 20 minutes late for the Thursday afternoon news briefing, behaved in a languid fashion and tried to appear relaxed and haughty. The questions centred on deliberate collisions, yellow flags and possible controversial outcomes. Villeneuve said he could not live with himself if he won a championship after forcing a deliberate collision. Schumacher momentarily blanched. In free practice, Irvine blocked Villeneuve who jumped out of his car in the pits and gave the Ulsterman a piece of his mind. Qualifying was equally tense and was settled in bizarre fashion by the sequence of the fastest laps, not their times. Villeneuve took pole with a time of one minute and 21.072 seconds. Schumacher was second with the same time, exactly, and then Frentzen was third, again with exactly the same time. No-one could believe the time-screens. 'The whole thing seemed unreal,' said Irvine, who qualified a distant seventh, out of the fray this time.

When the race started, it was all about the men at the front. Schumacher started superbly, so did Frentzen. Villeneuve caught up and Frentzen let him through for second on lap eight. He stayed second, apart from the pit stops, until lap 48 when, chasing hard, he saw an opening on the inside of Schumacher's Ferrari as they approached the Dry Sack long right-hander at the end of the back straight. Villeneuve went for it, drew level and eased his front left wheel ahead of the Ferrari before Schumacher, responding in the most calculated fashion, pulled across to the right. His front right wheel rammed the sidepod of Villeneuve's Williams. Both cars were damaged, but it was the Ferrari that bounced off the circuit and into a gravel trap, leaving Villeneuve to drive on, nurse his damaged vehicle to the finish, allow the two McLarens to pass him and take the title in third position.

Hakkinen claimed victory, the first of his career ahead of David Coulthard, but amid various recriminations and some amazement at the end of an extraordinary weekend. The stewards, very surprisingly, failed to see or understand the collision in which Schumacher made his 'road rage' attack on Villeneuve and, describing it as 'a racing accident' took no action against him. But Mosley did. Barely 24 hours after the race, he had been called to appear before an extraordinary meeting of the World Motor Sport Council in Paris on 11 November. (The venue was changed on 6 November, the day after Mosley, Ecclestone and Ferrari sporting director Jean Todt dined at San Lorenzo in London.) It ensured several days of keen anticipation and provided Ferrari with the time to try and suggest the trial ahead was a case of collusion, not collision. They failed and the reputations of two very successful teams remained untarnished, but many people close to the events remained bitter and resented the suggestion that teams like McLaren and Williams would agree to fix a result . . .

In Montreal, in 2001, on the eve of the Canadian Grand Prix, Frank Williams recalled:

> I know what you're referring to . . . Jacques slowing up, when he was in the lead, and conceding places. We, subsequent to the accident, were very lucky to remain on the road and running. It was clear that his left or right front wheel alignment was out, because the tyre was looking more and more sorry for itself, as the remaining laps unfolded. We were trying to slow him down, which we did and which made Ron's (Dennis) task a bit easier because he was desperate for his Mercedes partners to win a race. We were desperate to conclude the championship and it subsequently turned out that we were very lucky to slow Jacques down simply because the battery was suspended and only held in place by two wires in bends where he was still pulling 4G. Oh, yes, he shouldn't have finished the race. He should have stopped immediately. The other point to remember is that the quickest man that day was Frentzen. He followed team orders by dropping back and holding up everybody. But not, obviously, the McLarens. He did his job very nicely. He was blindingly quick that day and it was his race, but it's another point to remember

that he went to the wrong point. He went to the McLaren pit and as he drove out he took all the McLaren guns and gave us a lot of free equipment when he came to our pit!

Asked about the alleged 'collusion' with McLaren, Williams was as adamant as he had been in 1997 that Ferrari had been bending the rules.

We don't talk to McLaren during the race. We just talk to our own drivers, backwards and forwards as all the teams. The only significant conversation was to get Jacques to slow down and fall back and bring the car in. Ferrari decided to make a little side bet as Michael had thrown it away. In a number of European countries, it is a criminal offence to eavesdrop on other people's radios. Not telephones, but radio conversations. A criminal offence! Which is, of course, of no consequence to Ferrari. Whatever was said on the radio, although it was totally innocent, it was unmissable. And the law, most specifically, applies in Spain as well as in Britain. With all our radios, you have to apply to the ministry and the relevant authorities to use their frequencies. There are heavy fines if you wander off yours because the whole world has radio frequencies, which are very carefully maintained and controlled. There are some very tough laws about it, too. Telephone tapping in the States is a serious criminal offence as it is in Spain, and certain other European countries. Eavesdropping on radio frequencies is a criminal offence, but I don't mind saying that's of no consequence to Ferrari, who operate to their own laws, always have done, always will do.

Jock Clear had moved with Jacques Villeneuve to join British American Racing when the 1997 champion left Williams at the end of 1998. He retained his close relationship with him as his race engineer and as a close friend. He remembered the late summer tension of 1997. He had not forgotten the intrigue and subterfuge of the final two races. In Germany, at the Nurburgring, on the eve of the 2001 European Grand Prix, he recalled the events with objectivity and insight when he met the author and was asked to remember the atmosphere in the build-up to the final race.

The championship had been, I suppose, in my mind, manipulated at some point to make a good showing in the last race [said Clear]. But, obviously, I am a bit biased about that. In Suzuka, we got disqualified. Having been on pole position, we got disqualified and basically we were allowed to race under appeal in a deal which was later retracted, but certainly I felt that that disqualification, on that weekend, was harsh and although [it was correct] to the letter of the law, there was nothing [seriously wrong]. Basically he was not slowing down under a yellow flag. Jacques had transgressed a couple of times already that season and there was consternation. At the end of the day, it was his own silly fault and you would have thought under the circumstances that he could have been a little more cautious. We weren't cautious enough and didn't really show that we were slowing down. The yellow flag was on a straight and Jacques' opinion was you don't slow down, if you slow down on a straight then someone goes into the back of you. He had his opinion, but anyway, the upshot of that was that we, having been nine points ahead going into the Suzuka Grand Prix, when all we needed was two points from Suzuka and we would have won the championship . . . Well, we were basically out of the race. We raced under appeal and then made every attempt to help the rest of the field overtake Michael by driving particularly slowly for the first five laps, but the only person brave enough to make any attempt to overtake was Irvine, who was, of course, Michael's team-mate.

Jacques realised what was going on and he realised that the best thing he could do, under the circumstances, was, effectively, to make the action from the front. So, that's what he did and he did it very well. After that, once we had got into the race and once things had panned out, we were powerless to stop Michael winning the race. We could simply have driven off into the distance and won the race, but of course we would have been disqualified afterwards and Michael would have been given it if he had finished second, which he probably would have done. There was little we could do. But it did mean that it went to the last race and that left a little bit of a feeling of frustration because you thought it would have been nice to finish it off in Suzuka. We were quick and we were on pole and we could have won

the race. It was frustrating, but was probably our own stu-
pid fault, given that we knew we were under the eye and
we also knew that there would be every pressure from every
television company in the world to make a race of it in Jerez
and not to have the championship decided with one race to
go.

Any opportunity to fall over we knew we were going to
be given – and we tied our own laces together! Having said
that, we went to Jerez one point behind Michael, which
changed completely the flavour of Jerez. That meant
Michael simply had to make sure that we didn't finish the
race and he has won the championship, but, as I said at the
time, I knew Michael would do that under the circumstances. He did it to Damon Hill in 1994 and we had no
doubt that he would do it again. So it did put us under a lot
more pressure than perhaps we should have been.
Qualifying went well. We qualified on pole position, by
having done the same time as Michael, but having done it
before him, and the same time as Heinz. But, going into
the race, you just had to do everything you could to be
ready for that race and I suppose we were fairly well
embroiled in all that. I'm not aware of anything being
arranged, or anything being organised, between McLaren
and Williams beforehand, and I don't know how you would
[do anything] because McLaren weren't actually a power
threat in the race anyway. I think they qualified fifth and
seventh anyway and I think Damon was fourth on the grid,
Michael was second and Heinz was third. There was no
indication at that time that they would be an important
factor anyway. I think the thing is, as you say, that Ron and
Frank have a reasonably good respect for each other and I
think they had a common enemy in Ferrari.

I think there was to a certain extent, more rivalry
between Ferrari and McLaren and Ferrari and Williams
than there was between McLaren and Williams at that
stage. I think they had their opinions about Michael
Schumacher's tactics and Michael Schumacher's sort of
results on his way to the championship in 1995. And then,
going to Ferrari, all the same people went with him and I
think they carried that cloud of suspicion with them.
People were sceptical. We were sceptical. I think McLaren
were, too. So there was a joint scepticism about Ferrari's

tactics. But I wasn't aware of any arrangement and I don't see in hindsight what arrangement you would have worked before the race because they weren't going to be a factor. As for the race, there was obviously nobody around the two leaders. Frentzen had a problem with his rear tyres, which dropped him back at an early stage and that effectively left two cars out on their own. I mean, we were effectively a pit-stop ahead of everybody else. And Michael and Jacques had their own battle up to lap 48 or whatever it was. From that point, we were obviously protecting a damaged car, although we didn't know how damaged. Obviously we didn't want to drive any faster than we had to and I think, as far I understand it, Patrick spoke to Ron at that time to say 'if you (and they were catching us, fast enough to catch us before the finish) . . . if you catch us, we won't offer any defence because we can't afford to get into a battle and we can't afford to drive any faster than we have to'. Patrick then said to me, you know, 'There is no point defending ourselves if we are under attack. We are quite happy for McLaren to win this race. All we have got to do is finish in the points.' I had told Jacques that before-hand and said 'Look, if Michael drops out all you have to do is finish. Don't try any heroics on the last lap,' and I think he knew he had to finish in the points and had been briefed as such.

I think, if you look at the transcript from the radio, it says stuff about David's being very helpful or whatever. I don't think there was anything in that, other than the fact that they had agreed not to cause us any trouble. They hadn't hounded us down to get the win. It wasn't like they charged down on us as fast as possible. They actually kept their distance just in case we had a problem and that sort of thing. David, I think, was leading Mika at the time and JV was quite happy for David to win the race and, again, we spoke on the radio and I don't think you got it on the transcript. I think most of the transcript from JV people can't understand. It always says, 'Villeneuve replies, but we can't understand him.' But I can understand him and I think he said during the race, 'Is it David?' And I said 'Yes, it is Coulthard.' And, he said, 'That's no problem then'. I think that what happened then was that Ron gave them team orders to let Mika past David. So, actually, by the time it got to the last lap, or the last few laps, Mika was ahead of David – and JV was not as happy to let Mika win the race. So, we had a battle between myself and Jacques.

I had to remind him that all he had to do was finish and we didn't really want to piss him off. We just wanted to finish our race and if necessary get out of their way and let Mika Hakkinen win the race, but when he knew it was Mika he was a little bit more determined. 'Okay,' he said. 'I've only got another two laps to go so I can probably hold him off for two laps even if the car was a bit damaged.' So, I did, repeatedly, remind him, 'Look, you know'. At the end of the day, he is a driver and says 'Okay, the car feels good, I could just go a bit quicker,' but as an engineer, you know that 20 kilogrammes more force in one corner and whatever was broken, that we didn't know about at the time, might just collapse. We didn't know what the damage was and you just want to drive it as slowly as you can and get to the finish. If you try and outbrake Hakkinen into the last corner your front wheel might fall off. So I did repeat it to him and I think Patrick, from a technical point of view, just reminded him. I can't remember what his exact words were, but he reminded him that we are quite happy for a McLaren to win this race.

We didn't really care about the race win and, to be quite honest, there was never any thought in anybody at Williams's mind that anyone, whether they listened to the radio or not, would figure there was any collusion because, if you look back on it, what was the collusion? Is someone saying that McLaren actually helped us to win the championship? If they did, where? We cannot see where they helped us win the championship. If it is as simple as Patrick and Frank had an opportunity there to win a championship, and all Jacques had to do was finish in the top-six and they'd won a championship, and it was an opportunity to give Ron a race win, which might give them some bargaining power later on . . . I don't know what that situation is and I'm sure Frank and Patrick had their own agenda. Even so it doesn't affect anything. Having done enough to win the championship, we had the right to drive as slowly as we wanted for the last ten laps and if that gave Frank and Patrick more bargaining power later in the year or whatever, or if they were negotiating with one of Frank's drivers or Ron's drivers, or who knows, that is motor racing and that is business.

But it didn't affect the outcome or result of the race and it didn't detract from the importance of that race in the terms of the championship and everything. People don't really bother with the fact that Hakkinen won the race or that he ended up with four points more than he should have done in that championship or Jacques ended up with four points less than he should have done. It had no bearing on anything, unless you look at it from a horse-racing point of view that somebody put good money on Villeneuve winning the race and he didn't by virtue of the fact he let Hakkinen race. But we are not under those rules.

At the mention of horse-racing and gambling, I (the author) said: 'It is a very separate issue. It is the issue that blew up at the very first race of the following season, when the McLaren drivers swapped positions.'

At that stage [Clear continued], I don't think there was anybody in the sport who thought it wasn't part of the sport. Not necessarily to use your team-mate, but to use other teams. If you have got a good relationship with other teams — you know you make your own friends in this business. Drivers know that if you want to do well and you piss everybody off there comes a time when they are not going to get out of your way. They know who you are and you make your own luck. There was no feeling afterwards at Williams that that was a bit naughty or we shouldn't have done that. Nobody even gave it a second thought and when we saw all the transcripts and all the 'Jerezgate' stuff and we all figured that it was basically a smokescreen, put up by Ferrari, to block the fact that Michael had done what he had done in 1994 and deliberately driven into somebody to try to win the championship. That was the big issue and that was the big lack of sportsmanship that should have been questioned. It was questioned and should have been questioned. But suddenly it was turned on Frank and Patrick and Williams and Jock and Jacques and Ron Dennis! But everything that happened after lap 48 is really not significant unless you take the view that somebody put good money on Villeneuve to win the race.

How did it all affect you in the media storm after the race and before the hearing?

I would say that it didn't affect me at all. At Williams, it might sound disgraceful, but we just got on with doing next year's car and didn't pay any attention to it. I don't know who else you have talked to but I would be amazed if any of the key players in that incident would have thought anything of it. It was a big media hype. I don't think Michael ever thought it was of any interest and I don't get the impression that Michael or Jean Todt or whatever read all about. . . I must admit it did anger me because I looked at it purely from the point of view that I can't believe my integrity and Jacques' integrity and Patrick's integrity is being brought into question. Michael did what he did in front of 320 million viewers worldwide. That's what I thought about it.'

Clear admitted, too, that he knew teams listened to Williams's radio communications. He said:

We knew it used to happen and we knew Ferrari used to listen to us and Benetton were listening to us when Michael was at Benetton. Frank always flatly refused to do the same. I know during all the time when I was at Williams we never recorded or listened to other people's radio transmissions I know that Frank did not agree with it in principle and would not have it done. We never listened into it, but we knew very well that other people were listening to us.

It is obviously not sporting. If you defined motor racing during those couple of hours on a Sunday afternoon as a sport, it is not a sporting thing to do, is it?

I think I'd agree with you there. Absolutely.

Nowadays, there is not only that happening, but there is this business with photographers taking pictures of uncovered parts of the cars. The two are related to some degree because teams are spending a lot of money on pictures.

To be quite honest, I don't think we did a very good job of spying, ourselves. We could have brought a man to the circuit with a camera wearing civvies. We used to bring a design office person to the circuit every week and he wouldn't be recognised. We used to send him up and down the pit-lane and we used to get these pictures back of a Ferrari from 400 feet. Basically these guys only go to one race a year and they think its great and they photograph the car and they photograph the girls on the grid and we say 'You know that Ferrari looks like we see it every day. What we wanted really wanted was a photograph of . . . ' and they were like 'I didn't realise that.' At Williams we were fairly naïve in that respect. If there were teams employing photographers to do that very job then we were a long way behind and as I say the photographs that we did have were never particularly good. But I think we relied a lot more on the fact Patrick and myself and James Robinson and Gavin Fisher and people like that were at the circuit often enough to get a look at these things and we did tend to go up and down the pit-lane as much as possible. Something that Patrick is very good at is knowing what he is looking at. If he just had a glimpse at something on the grid he would come back and have a sketch of it and say that's what it looks like.

I don't know to what extent he has got a photographic memory, but he has got a very good eye for detail. That's worth 100 photographs, because he knows what he is looking at. He can stand over a car and ignore 95 per cent of it and just look at one bit. 'Oh, that's new, I haven't seen that before.' We send a draftsman down the pit-lane and he photographs the wing on a Ferrari and we say, 'We've seen that for the last six races, exactly the same.' I think it worked quite well that way. I think, having said that, that what teams are doing now, if they are employing photographers, or whatever, and all that sort of thing, it must be massively inefficient. You are just photographing things that you have seen day-in and day-out. These things with everybody having screens across the front of their garage now, what is that all about? It is pathetic, absolutely pathetic. I don't know why people do it and I wish somebody could sit me down and tell me why they do it. I would like to argue with anybody who thinks that there is anything you can learn, when those screens aren't put up, that you can't learn when those screens are there. We see the cars enough. We see them on the grid. They take the wheels and tyres off on the grid. Everybody does that. You look at photographs and things like this and you can see everything. It just spoils it for the public. The public sit in those grandstands. I think this is the first year were it has been so bad when everybody has had these screens across the garages . . . Bringing that sort of tactic into the public eye opens up the whole gamut of photographing things, espionage, spying, you know. But the other thing I've met, in the past, is . . . Well, I've worked with engineers who have been paid to come to my team by another team and who leave after two months and go back to the team they came from.

An engineer leaves a team, comes to your team, works for you and then goes back to the previous team. That's in the last five years?

About 10 years. I don't know of it much, but I know of it. That sort of thing is just . . .

Did it happen when you were at Williams?

No, I don't think it happened at Williams.

Has it happened here? At BAR?

No it hasn't happened here. I'm not prepared to say where it has happened.

That's for me to guess and you not to say?

But you know, those sort of things do happen. I think bringing them into the public eye makes them far more important now. I think as soon as the bloke handed his notice in and said, 'I don't like it here I'm going back to where I came from,' then everybody goes 'We know what your score is, you won't get a job here again – your card's marked.' But anyway it happens and bringing it into the public eye makes it an issue. It is like do you know they are doing that. It is like listening to radio. Yeah, we know they are listening to our radio, but we are not going to scramble it because as long as we don't tell you what fuel load we are running we could tell you loads of things that are meaningless.

Haven't the FIA said that you have to work on radio frequencies that are non-scrambled any more?

I think so. Everybody who has been an engineer and who has worked on radio during a Grand Prix knows that you don't talk about fuel loads, or what tyres you are on, or what type of tyre you are on. You just talk in code.

So, those examples you gave me of people moving teams. That is the exactly the sort of contrived thing that somebody would do to make up for the fact that they haven't got a worthwhile performance factor in that area themselves. They can't do the job. So they nick it off somebody else?

Yes.

And that it is ruled by money?

Yes.

Lots of teams who haven't necessarily been that successful have made a lot of money.

Yes.

People haven't won a thing, but they walk out with bags of money every night, and all the rest of it, and there are probably some people, you could say, who have been with Williams or McLaren . . . I'm not saying they are badly off, but they might have made a great deal more money?

Absolutely.

Do you know, and you don't have to name any of them, any time when there have been bribes offered?

Honestly, no.

That wouldn't surprise me.

What do you mean by a bribe?

Not a bribe to somebody who throws a result, but for some information. How did you do that or what are you up to? That kind of thing.

No.

It is probably the next thing.

Yeah.

It is certainly one of the things that people are going to have to be on the guard against.

Perhaps that is one of the good things about the way Formula One operates, technically, that there are actually very few people in a team who know why their car is fast, or not. There were only probably five people in the team [Williams], who knew all the figures of the car and I'm not saying I knew exactly why the car was quick, but I knew all the parameters of that car and I knew all the information if it was given to Ferrari would have told them where we were lacking. But, with only five people, and those five people being pretty senior people, your opportunity to bribe people is not going to be there because the Gavin Fishers, the Jock Clears and the Patrick Heads are not the guys you can bribe. The kind of guy you can bribe is a newer guy who feels he is not getting on as fast as he should . . . I think that Williams are a very, very honest team. I had a massive amount of respect for Patrick and Frank, just for that alone. There were certain things that I didn't agree with at Williams, but that it normal. To a large extent, when I come to a team like this [BAR] which has a lot of money and I am still working with one of the best drivers in the world, but still having to deal with all the other things that we have to deal with at BAR, it makes you appreciate Williams more and more. Most of that is the sheer integrity of Patrick and Frank, both in the true sense of the word and also in technical integrity. Patrick doesn't want to be bothered by all of the bullshit in Formula One. He just wants to make racing cars, that go fast, and that is what it is all about. All of his racing cars going fast speak for themselves. He could have had all the press conferences he likes over the last five years but nothing would have said as much as Ralf Schumacher's win in Canada. Everyone knows he is serious when you have a result like that. That is what it is all about and that is what makes Williams so special.

That is what is putting them back where they are now. They are four years away from their last championship and less than two years away from the bottom of their trough and that wasn't a big trough. Suddenly they are third last year and are back up again this year and that is because of the way they run their team. It is fantastic. That is what was galling about that whole incident in Jerez from where I was sitting. I was biased because I was at Williams, but I knew enough about Ferrari, and enough about McLaren, to think that I cannot believe people are pointing the finger at Williams, because if anybody in this sport handles themselves correctly it is Frank and Patrick. That's why we were particularly bitter about it being a smokescreen. Okay, create a smokescreen of some sort, but don't start questioning that sort of integrity. Then you really are clutching at straws, especially after having driven into somebody in the last race of the season.

Did Michael come and apologise to you afterwards?

No. He has never apologised for it and he has never conceded that it was anything but a mistake. If it was an error of judgement, he didn't have to apologise because, effectively, it gave Jacques the championship. If you look at it that way, he screwed up and gave Jacques the championship. To apologise would be to imply that he did something that he shouldn't really have done ... And he has still not admitted that he did something he shouldn't have done.

In Colnbrook, Max Mosley did his best to wipe clean the slate and buff up the image of Formula One after the Jerezgate hearing. He said that the McLaren tape revealed vehement arguments between Coulthard and the team when the Scot was ordered to allow Hakkinen to pass him and go on to victory. He said that there were many things to remember, many factors to consider.

> It is well known that everyone in Formula One tapes everyone else's radio conversations. Some of the other teams have been decoding McLaren's transmissions for some time, unknown, I think, to McLaren. All of this really needs to be put in the open. Next season, that will be part of the arrangement.

When it came to the question of how the transcripts were put in the public domain, by being given to *The Times*, Mosley's answers were very interesting. 'Once the whole issue was in the public domain, it clearly needed to be looked at quickly,' he said. Since Mosley was reported to have had dinner with Ecclestone and Todt, in London, in the week before the hearing and 24 hours before it was announced that it would take place at Colnbrook, and not in Paris, it is probable that Todt, or another Ferrari person, passed the transcripts to Ecclestone and Mosley that evening. Mosley, or Ecclestone, in theory at least, could then have ensured they were delivered to *The Times*. This action, unproven, would have heaped pressure on McLaren and Williams, the two rebel teams locked in dispute with them and the FIA over the terms of the 1997 Concorde Agreement. (The last thing they needed, at that time, was a scandal suggesting they had worked in collusion, as the FIA had claimed, concerning the result of the 1997 European Grand Prix.) Indeed, a deal, in which all sides were embarrassed, but not punished, in the glare of publicity that would follow the hearing was probably worked out at that time. Schumacher evaded the worst excesses possible. He was not sanctioned heavily, but received a light punishment (he said he would have done the safety campaign work voluntarily). The FIA statement, following the hearing, said:

> West McLaren Mercedes and Williams Grand Prix Engineering were able to show that there was no arrangement to fix the results of the 1997 European Grand Prix. For the future, in order to avoid possible misunderstandings and ambiguities, the World Motor Sport Council recommended that all radio transmissions between drivers

and their pits should be freely accessible by journalists and the public.

As to the 'road rage' ramming incident, by Schumacher on Villeneuve, on lap 48, the FIA and its president were clear in their views. In the statement, the FIA said:

The World Council found that Michael Schumacher's manoeuvre was an instinctive reaction and although deliberate not made with malice or premeditation. It was a serious error. The World Council decided to exclude Michael Schumacher from the results of the 1997 FIA Formula One World Championship for drivers. The final results of the FIA Formula One World Championship have been modified accordingly. The results of the Constructors' Championship remain unchanged. Michael Schumacher retains his points and victories recorded during the 1997 season. In lieu of any further penalty or fine, Michael Schumacher agreed to participate in the FIA European Road Safety campaign for a total of seven days in 1998.

And that, it seemed, was that. 'You have to remember,' Mosley explained, in his most sincere voice, mixing gravitas with a touch of theatre,

that both he and Villeneuve were under enormous pressure. They had the weight of their countries and their teams on their shoulders. There was one point between them and they had people shouting in their ears. It was an extraordinary set of circumstances. The drivers were hyped up, dealing with a tremendous amount of adrenalin, excitement and pressure. There is a great tendency to do something unwise in the heat of the moment. I do believe, quite sincerely, that there was no arrangement of the kind that we feared there might have been. Far from damaging Formula One, I think it actually benefits it, because it has become clear that it is being run as it should be run. Everyone concerned with Formula One is absolutely determined that no race will ever be fixed.

There was no doubt Villeneuve had slowed down dramatically on the last lap to allow the McLarens to pass him and finish first and second. He had told reporters in the immediate aftermath of the contest that

> He [Hakkinen] had stayed out of the battle in the first part of the race, when he was quicker than me and when he caught me, in the final laps, it was a question of either pushing like a maniac, risking going off with my car handling strangely, or seeing if he made a move, and then letting him through. David was also very close, so I didn't fight him either.

Yet it was apparent from the transcripts, too, that Clear told Villeneuve: 'Be aware that Hakkinen is now in position two. He probably wants to win. Very helpful.' Clear also said: 'DC is controlling Irvine.' And, as the leading trio began the final lap, Clear said: 'Hakkinen is immediately behind. Hakkinen has been very helpful. Don't let me down, Jacques. We discussed this.' The result stood. The trial ended. The sport moved on. The committee room episode was stored in the files and the club closed ranks. No more subterfuge, eh? No more collusion? No more courtroom dramas? What would Formula One be without them?

Part III: 1999
Two years later, in Sepang, Malaysia . . . It was dark, the night had fallen, but the temperature inside the Ferrari office in the paddock, even with the air-conditioning working, was in the high thirties. High humidity, too. Ross Brawn, the Ferrari technical director, was waving a red piece of bodywork and explaining its legality. It was the night of 17 October 1999. The items on display were bargeboards and they had been deemed questionable, perhaps irregular or illegal, in the aftermath of the Japanese Grand Prix that afternoon. Heavy sweat stains were visible everywhere. Strain was etched across many brows. It was late in the evening, the result was under protest and Ferrari were appealing. Michael Schumacher, recovered from a broken leg suffered at Silverstone in July, had returned vibrant and brilliant and fast. He had seized pole position and then gifted the race victory to his team-mate Eddie Irvine. Schumacher finished second to keep alive Ferrari's hopes of securing the drivers championship, with Irvine, for the first time in 20 years. McLaren argued that the Ferraris were illegal cars because of

the bargeboards, but the Italian team wanted to contest the case, in court, arguing that their way of doing things and their way of measuring them, and then of interpreting the measurements, was inside the law. The chaos brought more Formula One uproar, deep in the night, in the heat, and many people delayed their rush to Kuala Lumpur International Airport while the arguments raged.

Five days later, Paris, 22 October . . . The European autumn was on its way, windy, cool and damp. Ferrari's lawyers, a formidable team, glowed in their sharp suits. Outside the offices, the beautiful offices, of the FIA, in the Place de la Concorde, an ugly jumble of television trucks, cars, buses and people in plastic coats, hoods, long winter overcoats and strange headwear, stood on the pavements. They were waiting for a verdict from the FIA's International Court of Appeal. Thankfully, for the media army, tired from journeying to Asia and back, bored by waiting in the street, irritated by the propaganda war, the food was good in the restaurants within walking distance in this quarter of the French capital. The case was a *cause célèbre* in Formula One. Ferrari, with a team of men headed by Henri Peter, a smooth Swiss lawyer whose English was as precise as any British barristers, had chosen the Benetton–Briatore route to success on appeal in Paris. That meant a heavyweight team, imaginative casework, creative arguments. Even Irvine himself flew in to Paris. If his win stood, he could go back to Japan with a chance of fighting for the title. Thanks to his appearance, Ferrari's sleek lawyers, the ambiguity of the Formula One regulations and the need, perhaps, to offer the world another last-race televised showdown, their appeal was upheld. Ferrari won. McLaren, stunned and staggered by the decision, lost.

Inside the beautiful and grand old building, Ferrari had laid on a working media office for reporters complete with briefings from their own staff. A whisper here and a word there. But, said the traditionalists, the rulebook had been reinterpreted, if not rewritten. No, said Ferrari. No, said Max Mosley. In a court of law, as this was, it is the precise letter of the law that counts and in this case, the measurements of the barge-boards, there was enough ambiguity to allow for Ferrari's arguments to stand. In essence, law was used to beat the meaning of sport. But then, after all these years, that was nothing new to the Piranha Club . . . Surely, not. Ferrari had always been a team to find a way of reaching the best solution of all. And, in the end, it was

McLaren's year. Mika Hakkinen won in Japan. He won the title for a second year. Irvine was beaten. Ferrari lost it all again. But the noise and the celebrations and the talking and the controversy continued to echo on and on into the winter. The show continued. The sport is dead. Long live the sport.

9 New Boys and Hot Kitchens

Keith Wiggins is a nice guy. He has a laid-back kind of character, on the surface, but a steely determination underneath. He is into motor racing and in the mid-1990s he decided it was time to take his Pacific Racing team, a successful outfit in Formula 3000, based in Thetford in Norfolk, into Formula One. He did not worry too much about the recession of the time, or the fact that many other teams had aimed high and gone under.

> Recession or no recession, we're going to do it [he said]. I cannot help the timing. We have built up through every formula and we have won in each one. There is nowhere else to go. The motivation is to win. It's bloody hard to find money. But it is never going to be easy, so you have to do it sooner or later. I have found that people can relate to F1, whereas in F3000 it has always been difficult. At least you are in a market that everyone knows. The other thing is that the more you get into building an F1 team, the more you want to do it.

Wiggins team contested five races in 1994 and 17 in 1995 before folding with reported debts of £6 million. The Simtek team, run by Max Mosley's one-time protégé Nick Wirth, entered at the same time and gave up at the same time. Simtek ran in all 16 events in 1994, when they suffered the tragic experience of losing their driver Roland Ratzenberger, who was killed in qualifying at the San Marino Grand Prix at Imola, and then five in 1995. Simtek went down with debts of around £6 million. A year later, Lola entered the championship; a famous motor racing name, supposedly backed by a clever deal with Mastercard. The team failed to take part in the season-opening Australian Grand Prix and folded with debts of £6 million. The parent company, one of the sport's greatest car manufacturers, had to go into administration. All three had believed they could cope with the heat in the kitchen and show the club that the best of the new boys, if they were well prepared, could survive. 'I knew from the start of the whole thing, from the start of the season, that we were in the shit and we never got out of it,' said Wiggins. Lola never even went that far.

Since the irrepressible Eddie Jordan began strutting his stuff in dazzling green in 1991, a good bakers' dozen teams have been and gone in Formula One, their founders or principals fired by ambition and then eaten alive as they floundered in the scorching and unforgiving bear pit at the heart of top-level motor racing. The victims, the perished teams' chastened men, often passed through the Piranha Club at such speed, or in such a panic-stricken state of mind, that they had little opportunity to guess the value of the surroundings, count the paintings, taste the wine or understand the in-jokes. One glance through Jacques Deschenaux's Grand Prix Guide stirs a few memories. It is a sombre experience, like walking through a churchyard and reading the headstones:

AGS (1986–91, 48 races); Alfa Romeo (1950–85, 112), ATS (1977–84, 99), Brabham (1962–92, 394), BRM (1951–77, 197), Cooper (1950–69, 129), Dallara (1988–92, 78), Eagle (1966–69, 26), Ensign (1973–82, 99), Fittipaldi (1975–82, 104), Forti (1995–96, 23), Gordini (1950–56, 40), Hesketh (1974–78, 52), Honda (1964–68, 35), Lancia (1954–55, 4), Larrousse (1992–94, 48), Ligier (1976–96, 326), Lola (1962–97, 139), Lotus (1958–94, 491), March (1970–92, 230), Maserati (1950–60, 69), Matra (1967–72, 60), Mercedes (1954–55, 12), Onyx (1989–90, 17), Osella (1980–90, 132), Pacific (1994–95, 22), Parnelli (1974–76, 16), Penske (1974–76, 30), Porsche (1958–64, 31), Renault (1977–85, 123), Rial (1988–89, 20), Shadow (1973–80, 104), Simtek (1994–95, 21), Stewart (1997–99, 49), Surtees (1970–78, 118), Talbot (1950–51, 13), Tecno (1972–73, 11), Theodore (1978–83, 34), Tyrrell (1970–98, 418), Vanwall (1954–60, 28), Wolf (1977–79, 47), Zakspeed (1985–89, 54).

Some were famous names in the business. Brabham, Cooper, BRM, Ligier, Lotus, March and Tyrrell wrote their own chapters in the history of the sport before they perished or sold their assets or sold their names. Ligier became Prost; Tyrrell is British American Racing. Others were teams inspired and led by champion drivers, men like Stewart and Surtees, Brabham or Prost. Some had more than one go at making it work, like Lola. Some manufacturers, like Renault, came and went and came back again. Some like Mercedes came and went, but returned only as engine suppliers. For them all, the experience was a daunting, sometimes humbling and certainly an expensive affair. When Eddie Jordan came into the paddock, in his vivid Irish green, for the first time in 1991, his only protection was a budget for £6 million and a smile as wide as the Liffey. He finished the year with debts of more than £4 million and rising. In 1999, in his BAR team's maiden season in their own eye-catching livery in Formula One, after purchasing Tyrrell, Craig Pollock spent a reported sum of more than £120 million. His team finished 11th out of 11 and failed to score a point. But, like Jordan, he battled on. He was, at least, prepared for the strain.

Frenchmen say Alain Prost has aged ten years in the last three, but he is still in the club. Even the poorest teams now have budgets to drool over. For 2001, Prost and Minardi had built up war chests of more than £30 million each to spend a year scuffling around in the slipstream of the cars that revel in all the best television coverage. For them all, the risk is huge, the spending prolific. It may be a club for the quick and the dead, but it is also a place for the rich and the not-so-rich. The poor do not survive, unless they have deep pockets, understand thrift and have the kind of mixture of meticulous attention to detail and unwavering scruples that can guide any man through a maelstrom of ambition, power and speed. It takes something special for anyone to survive all this, emerge intact and make a profit in double-quick time, with their reputation intact. But someone did.

'It was by far the most difficult thing that I have ever undertaken,' said John Young Stewart, better known to the world as Jackie Stewart.

> It was the most complicated, the most confusing to understand, of the house rules, if you like, it was so plain difficult ... It was very difficult to have what I would call a strict business plan in place because there were so many unknowns. Not knowing what money would be coming in,

potentially, from all of the activities that, quite clearly, nearly everybody else was taking some benefit from . . . It certainly wasn't a level playing field.

Born on 11 June 1939 at Milton in Dunbartonshire, Scotland, Stewart's life has been a fairy tale of achievements and honours on the one hand and a succession of challenges and problems on the other. He is a dyslexic, a man obsessed by order, driven by a need to achieve, gripped by a sense of duty, fearful of failure and yet wondrous with people from all walks of life, elegant in motion, blessed with the eye of a marksman and the nerve of a three-times Formula One drivers' world champion. Growing up, tending the family garage, he made a point of serving petrol quickly and efficiently, keeping the forecourt clean and always working with a smile. He learned early on in life how to sell himself and he carried that lesson everywhere. He also developed good manners, believed in courtesies and benefited from all of his endeavours through a business career, developed with care after retiring from racing aged only 34. He had wonderful contracts, prestigious clients, a healthy bank balance and a life of uncomplicated bliss all laid out.

Then in 1997, at the age of 58, he decided to make a Formula One comeback, not as a driver of course, but as a team owner. And, to add emotional intensity, in a partnership with his racing-mad son Paul. Together, father and son, they looked like ripe pickings for the business; two more big dreamers heading for a brief career in the fast lane and then another entry in the statistical graveyards of the sport. But Stewart, senior, had a shrewd idea of what was going on, even if he found some of the obstacles were exceptional, to say the least.

Because Paul and I had been involved in running Paul Stewart Racing from little Formula Ford days to Formula Opel, Formula Vauxhall, Formula Three, Formula 3000 and because what we created had turned out to be the most successful racing team in the world, of its kind, multi-faceted and so on, we had an idea of what to do. Some of the drivers who came through that had gone on to great things – from David Coulthard to Dario Franchitti and Gil de Ferran to Castro Neves and Alan McNish to Juan Pablo Montoya. A whole lot of them have been very successful. Two of our drivers were first and second in the Indy 500 this year . . .

Talking, in the Jaguar Racing team's mobile motor home at the Canadian Grand Prix at Montreal in June 2001, Stewart was relaxed and studious, enjoying casting his mind back over achievements and successes associated with his hard work and care.

All of those things were relatively easy to do. For Formula One, our biggest responsibility was to secure an engine because as a new racing team, especially a start-up team, in Formula One it was vital. All of the start-up racing teams in the history of the sport had struggled to get any economic security and balance. The one thing that I felt was going to assure that for us was the securing of a factory engine. Now, for a brand new team that had never turned a wheel before, that was a very unusual thing to expect. It was a big issue and I spent an immense amount of time with Ford senior management going over the fact and at the time Sauber who had a supply of Ford factory engines were having a very unsuccessful period and Ford were extremely unhappy.

In fact, at the Canadian race in 1996, it was maybe at an all-time low and, going back on the Ford corporate jet from this race to Detroit, I was with the Ford senior management. There was four of us sitting together and they asked if I would help them make a decision about what they were going to do. I told them they should get out of Formula One because they weren't fully committed to it. 'You're either in, or you're out, and the way you're doing it, at the moment, is not giving you the chance to get the success that you expect, or want, by that association and affiliation to the sport's leading formula.' They said, 'No. We can't get out because the market will think it's wrong and in the rest of the world, lots of countries really want it.' I said, 'In that case you've got to do it differently than you're doing it just now.'

I wasn't going against Sauber. It was Ford. They were disappointed by Sauber in the way it was going. And then the question came back: would I get personally involved? And I said I would because I was under contract to them. And then they said, 'Would you be prepared to put a package together where you could be practically involved that would allow us to do this a different way?' I said 'yes'.

281

Paul and I and Rob Armstrong, our commercial director at Paul Stewart Racing, put a business plan together of our own and got it 'in principle' that Ford would supply to us the engines free of charge and supply to us also an amount of money that would assist us in our start up year, which was 1996, in order to be prepared for 1997. Now that in itself was a big step forward, but then we had to be sure that we had the right financial foundations and that was the biggest challenge of all on the basis that most of these other new teams were failing financially!

They would say, 'Well, we don't have all the money now, but by June we will have all the money,' and they were racing for the first half of the season hoping to get the second half of the season right. I would not go into that. So that was where we then started a very strong marketing initiative and we decided we were going to go for only blue chip companies and non-tobacco. That was against the whole trend of the paddock and for a new team to do that was almost bizarre because the cigarette money was the easiest money to get, if you had a good package.

But, because Jackie Stewart had won three world championships and is recognisable around the world, I knew I could be marketed and used by all the companies we went to see. It was one of the big magnets of the whole thing. So, we decided there had to be a telecommunications company and an IT company and I decided there had to be a financial services company. We needed fuel and oil. We needed tyres. The others we would look at, as we could see them fitting in to what I called 'blue chip, high prestige' companies. So, we got Hewlett Packard because I went straight to Lou Platt, who was the chairman of HP at the time, and I got on very well with him. They had been with us right from the beginning with a man called Alex Sozonoff, who I had met flying from Geneva to somewhere because he was based in Geneva. He was the Hewlett Packard man for Europe and we had built up a relationship because they came in on Paul Stewart Racing right at the beginning with a lot of equipment.

Then, for telecommunications, I went to Bert Roberts who was MCI World Con chairman and I did a deal on the telephone with him. We made two telephone calls and we agreed a three-year contract on the telephone.

Amazingly, Stewart admitted, he had never met Roberts.

But he knew my name and, again, that was where the benefit lay. This is where a Jackie Stewart, or an Alain Prost, or a Niki Lauda has a great advantage over most people, no matter who they are. You make the phone call and you get the answer. They, the most senior management people, almost always take your call and, as long as you're making sense to them, then they're interested to meet and if you go in and present logically, correctly and professionally then you've got a big advantage, but still because of your name. So we got that deal done and then I went to four different financial services institutions.

I went to the Bank of Scotland, who were with us in Formula Three, who were definitely interested, but they thought it would be too big for them and difficult for them to justify. And at that time I was asking for five million pounds. I went to the Royal Bank of Scotland with the same thing. I went to Standard Charter with the same thing and I went to HSBC. The two Scottish banks dropped out first and they didn't have the global reach. Standard Charter took quite a long time to drop out. They were seriously considering it, because of the Asia-Pacific region thing and so forth. HSBC, to begin with, were not what I would call enthusiastic. But as the vision was recognised, they changed their thinking. They were creating a new brand that nobody knew the name of then. It was Midland at that time in the UK and nobody knew what HSBC stood for. They'd moved back from Hong Kong. It was a British company, but nobody knew it, and they were linking up with their global operation.

It was a great corporate statement and it was youthful, dynamic, with big accounts. Ford Motor Company was one of their largest investors. So, in the end, I presented to the 22-person board in one of the best decision-making processes I have ever experienced in business. The chairman of the board then was Sir William Purves and the CEO was John Bond, now the chairman and knighted. They had me in at ten o'clock in the morning, I had a fourteen and a half minute presentation, they asked questions for a total of 45 minutes, including my fourteen and a half, and when I was asked to leave the chairman said: 'I will call you at three o'clock.' Yes, the same day! He called me on the dot at three o'clock and said that the board had agreed to go ahead with it, subject to contract. Amazing. . .

The most successful people are the best decision-makers, the less successful people paddle around it and by the time they make their decision the fire is already out and the enthusiasm is no longer there. So, anyway, we got the money together. We got the Texaco deal, which was very flaky for a while, right up, I think, to something like three days before the launch when we got a call, a real disruptive call, to say that they may not be going on after everything had been committed by one of their senior corporate officers. They wanted to walk away from it, but that was rectified at the last minute. We had enough money to ensure that we had absolutely no difficulty. None of them wanted one-year deals. We had absolutely no difficulty in knowing that we were going down the road economically sound. I wouldn't have done it without that.

Stewart also approached ING Barings, the Dutch bank whose image had suffered so badly after the 'Rogue Trader' affair; and, in a novel move he dealt personally with the prime minister of Malaysia with whom a twenty minutes appointment turned into a ninety minutes meeting and a firm sponsorship deal. Scrupulous attention to the housekeeping of the new business was a Stewart theme, once the sponsorship was put in place. He knew what it might cost to run the new enterprise, but admitted that trying to keep an engineering and design department in budget, when they wanted only to compete, to improve and to gain results, was 'a nightmare'. He continued:

We had a first-class financial director, who is still with us, with Jaguar Racing, Nigel Newton. We had Rob Armstrong, Paul [Stewart] and I all basically running the company and we were very tight on money. We really lived very frugally. We paid our bills before the end of every month. Nobody was ever not paid, or left waiting for money. So, therefore, we always got service because a lot of the teams didn't do that, even the rich teams. We got a tremendous amount of goodwill and there was a goodwill factor coming again from 'the Jackie and Paul show'. It was a family business – 'isn't it nice that that's happening?' So, we put ourselves into a situation where we had an enormous amount of goodwill travelling in our direction and I think, probably, that was the greatest currency we had.

The perception was, maybe, about how I did business and people knew that nobody was ever not going to get paid. That helped us. And the staff we got were amazing. Paul did all that, all the recruitment. I couldn't have done it without Paul. I wouldn't have done it, in the first place, without him. I had no need to go back into motor sport. Another thing that's important to say, too, is that I couldn't have done it when I retired from racing. I wasn't ready. I didn't know enough about business. I had not been through the corporate hierarchy or knew how to behave, to politic, to strategise, to present. I had to build credibility, believability and confidence that if Jackie Stewart was going to do something, he was going to do it well. All of those things are why these big multi-nationals bought in.

Stewart added that it was never in his or son Paul's original thoughts that the team could be sold. They were building something to last.

We were thinking long term. We were not thinking of turnover, or of somebody purchasing that company. You've got to have a financial structure and foundation that is strong and one that is not vulnerable. So that was our major focus. After that, you can sign designers, you can find fabricators, you can find engineers and mechanics, you can get PR people, you can get marketing people. It sounds so simple, but very few people do it and then they get over-confident and over-leverage themselves and then the crunch comes.

When the business was purchased, by Ford, I think I'm right in saying there was money in the bank. We had no overdraft at all. We never did have an overdraft. It was perhaps unique in our industry and our business world. The company was purchased, by Ford, at a very good rate. But, again, it was because the company was so clean. The due diligence that Ford did was very exhaustive in our case because here was a small business and they thought 'maybe we'll find something'. It was a very clean one because we had been so aggressive in our diligence ourselves not to be caught out like so many other teams had been.

For me, one of Bernie's greatest strengths, in his power position and his dominance of the teams, and the individuals, is that he has had to help so many of them out in times of trouble. There were more 'rain-cheques' out there, that he could call in at any time, than anyone would ever want. I wasn't concerned about that. I was concerned about my financial vulnerability, after having achieved all I had as a driver and having collected a large amount of money that would have kept me for the rest of my life without any difficulty. I was concerned that it could all be destroyed by a venture that some people were already saying I must have been mad to take on!

Driven, fastidious and workaholic, perhaps; but not mad. Stewart had planned his plan, calculated the risk, studied the odds and worked out, so far as possible, what he would be up against once inside the club. His homework was worth every second. He knew how he wanted it to be and he was ready to deal with it.

I am always very clear on my inabilities, or my abilities, or my downside risk. If you think of it in real terms, it was a risk management exercise. I had been in the risk management business at a time when motor racing really was dangerous. And the safety nets that I had in my professional life, whether it was taking a doctor round with me in a private plane, or having a doctor retained in every country that I raced in (and that Paul raced in later) so they would come at a moment's notice. My risk management was very important to it all. We spent as much time in the safety net business as we did in the building of the high technology effort. So, it was a really big and careful job that was done at the end of the day.

Interestingly, too, given the struggle that Alain Prost faced when he decided to buy Ligier and become a team owner in the winter of 1996–97, Stewart recognised that he had needed the many years of hard real world business experience, following his racing career, to prepare him for the job of launching his own family team. Not only that, he said, but he had two other advantages: his son, with him, and the fact he started without the baggage of a former team's reputation or name. But of these, he said, it was his age, experience and wisdom which counted most.

> The benefit of having not done it at the age of 34, or 36, or 38 even, four years after I retired when I still hadn't built up my reputation in the business world, is important. If I have a reputation in the business world today it is because I'm clean, because I deliver, because I do what I say I'm going to do, and I don't let people down. It's always dangerous to say that because somebody will say to you 'If he's going to talk about it like that, he's hiding something', but in our case, if we hadn't had that, it would not have occurred.

The key sponsor was HSBC and the key moment, the most daunting and suspenseful of the Stewart pre-launch period, came on the day he made his presentation and then retired to the offices of IMG in Chiswick to wait. Sir William Purves had said three o'clock in the afternoon and he meant it.

> I took the call on my own in an office. I knew it was very important, but to be honest with you, I wasn't totally sure they would make the decision to go ahead at that time. So, it wasn't a question of 'is it yes, or is it no?' It was a question of 'It's a very important call, but will they say come back in and we'll go through it again with a fine toothcomb?'

Since then, HSBC have remained loyal to Stewart, to Ford and to Jaguar Racing. 'Not only did they come in, but they have since doubled the money and then they've added to it since – and that was five years ago. So, they've increased their involvement.' Understandably, Stewart is proud of his achievements and his particular achievement in launching Stewart Grand Prix, building it into a profitable, stable going concern and then selling out to Ford for a figure understood to be adjacent to £100 million in July 1999, just three years after that first plane trip with the Ford executives when the original idea germinated. Ford had originally agreed to support the Stewart team with a £100 million five-year package including supplying engines and technical expertise. But they had grown impatient at the rate of progress towards any sustained and major success and had wanted to ensure their own and the team's financial stability.

At the Hungarian Grand Prix, in 1998, the Ford chairman Jacques Nasser was taken aback by the passion of the massed Ferrari following, a red hum of humanity in the main stand, and turned to Stewart. 'Why aren't they all white flags with a blue oval?' he asked. 'Look at all that passion. Why can't we get that?' Within seconds, both men knew what Nasser had felt and realised; Ford was not a team with passionate devotion. It did not have the image, the history or the traditions. It was not Ferrari. But Jaguar could be something like it. A brand name with an illustrious image and a pedigree in motor racing. This led to the takeover.

> I was 60 years of age and I was wondering what we should do [Stewart explained]. All my life I have been reasonably competitive and reasonably successful. I didn't drive racing cars to be a Formula One driver, to compete. I drove them to win races and to win championships. If we were not going to do that, as a team, there was no point in just being in the field. Not for me. We needed more money. We needed a wind tunnel. A wind tunnel costs £50 million. We needed all sorts of other facilities, equipment and people. We sold it well.

It was a move that ensured Stewart remained a rich man indeed and gave him the time, when it was truly needed, to give proper emotional and family support to Paul in 2000 when he was diagnosed with cancer and began prompt treatment under the supervision of the Mayo Clinic. The Stewart wealth of connections and money were put in perspective then and it was a happy day for the paddock when Paul reappeared, in Barcelona, in 2001.

For Jackie Stewart, however, it was not the end of his life in Formula One. To fulfil his contractual obligations, he remained a part of the Jaguar team, filling an ambassadorial role into which he poured as much personal attention, energy and preparation as he had done previously. His attention to detail and expectation of the highest standards has always shone through, as he admitted.

Yes, absolutely. It's one of the, for me, single most important elements of achieving success, whether it be doing a speech, or whether it be doing an appearance in a paddock club, or whether it be signing autographs or whether it be a meeting. This week, I've got about four or five very heavy meetings lined up. I will go into them with the same degree of commitment and single-mindedness because I say that I'm the president of the menial task division. I'm not very clever by comparison to others, certainly not academically or scholastically. So, I've had to rely on things that I am good at, which is what most people don't want to do. It is me that closes the door, it would be me who picked the paper off the floor or pulled the weed at the shooting school because if I do it then everybody has to do it.

But, more than anything else, I can't bear not doing it. Therefore, if I know I'm going to lose my focus, if something's bothering me that I haven't dealt with, why don't I deal with it now. In my life, for me the little things are so important, I do them right away. That way it's amazing how all the little things come into big things whether its pennies into pounds or millions of pounds. It doesn't matter.

Perhaps, because I'm dyslexic, because I can't read or write very well, I assume you're as dumb as I am. So, I want to be absolutely certain you've got it. It's amazing how that works because someone's perception of you is 'Oh, my God, if he's this pedantic about it, he's going to get it done' and that's how I am with these guys.

It was a different story in, and around, the paddock for Stewart the team owner. The club treated him as just another new boy. No favours. Wait your turn. See if you can survive first before you start asking for anything. It was not easy. At the Monaco Grand Prix in 1997, the Stewart team motor home was not allocated proper space in the paddock and had to be parked 'around the corner', beyond the yacht club, in a car park built into the rock face. 'I thought Jackie would prefer it if he was a bit nearer the royal palace,' quipped Bernie Ecclestone when the subject was raised. In the race, however, Rubens Barrichello produced a Boy's Own performance that left the team principal in tears of joy. He finished second. At the end of that year, rumours began circulating that the Stewart team was struggling to find money for 1998. Stewart's relationship with the club was strained and the FIA, in an unexpected move, spoke in public of the need for the team to show they were funded sufficiently to last the full year.

> The FIA turned round and said they were not accepting our entry without financial proof. It was a game. It was nonsense. Absolute nonsense. It was annoying because it was so poorly handled. It was totally unnecessary and it was like somebody firing a warning shot. It was just part of that little power game . . .

For the new boy, it was another school-yard experience and he knew it.

> Yes, it was tough. It was 'I'm the new boy on the block' time and we knew it [recalled Stewart]. Going into team principal meetings, and seeing the bizarre behaviour of those, and the overall influence that Bernie exercises on all of them, with Max in tandem, it was quite extraordinary. And it's an amazing closed club. I can't imagine another business this size in the world that is run like that. So, that was kind of a shock and as you are the new boy you know it means 'Don't think you're going to get any privileges' and then you suddenly do well in Monaco and that was almost a bad thing, if you like, to that effect. There we were, second, with ten or 15 laps to go, and Schumacher goes straight on at the first corner. If it hadn't been Michael Schumacher driving, the car would probably have stalled and we'd have won the race. That had its own effect because a lot of people in the paddock said, 'This is just what we don't need.' Then, trying to find out when we'd get any travel money. Or when we'd get any television money. Or any other income from our racing or any information on the breakdown of the financial distribution. At that time, the European Commission was very focused on this whole business and the threat of someone going and potentially spilling the beans was

there. Well, we had no beans to spill, because we didn't know anything, but we certainly weren't running out on a level playing field, as we would do in any other business I know. It was a very confusing time. There's no doubt about that.

More than anything, of course, Stewart proved he is a survivor. As a driver, he was a survivor of a time in racing when death was commonplace. He survived the business world without a formal scholastic education, as he has admitted, and he survived the Piranha Club.

In my opinion, Formula One needs the large corporations to come in to stabilise its behaviour and its practices. The infrastructure is not transparent and it surprised me that it is so fragile.

He knows he has been a lucky man. Others, like Craig Pollock, new on the block in 1999, after he had put together the big British American Tobacco and Reynard takeover of Tyrrell, and Bobby Rahal, Jaguar's chief operating officer, are still rising through the ranks. They are younger, fresher, from a different generation. Yet they share the Stewart vision of a modernised Formula One, a business unchained from the old ways of the Piranha Club and have other things in common with him. Pollock, to begin with, is a Scot and has spent much of his life in Switzerland. He is also, like them all, a self-made man. Rahal, an American, has spent his life in motor racing and has an old-fashioned feel for the sport that he has married to a modern way of doing business and conducting his life. He met the problems that bedevil the Piranha Club head-on in 2001 when he began activating his plans to improve Jaguar and found that, despite agreeing a contract with Adrian Newey to join him from McLaren, he had instead found a quick route to a High Court hearing. Both men, however, are fresh to the job, 20-odd years younger than Stewart and graduates.

Craig Pollock was born in Falkirk on 20 February 1956. His father was a grocer. He experienced a tough childhood that taught him his values and gave him inner steel that is visible within his piercing blue eyes. He was always determined to succeed. He loved sport, played high-level rugby at school, did some marshalling at Ingliston circuit, near his home, visited

Knockhill circuit, too, worked just hard enough and graduated from Jordanhill College, Glasgow, with a degree in sport and biology, before embarking on a teaching career.

He started teaching skiing and working as a physical education teacher at Keith Grammar School, in Scotland (so he could go skiing in Aviemore) before moving, after marrying his Swiss wife Barbara, to take a similar post at the exclusive Beau Soleil, College Alpin International, high up in the Alpes Vaudoises in French-speaking Switzerland, at Villars-sur-Ollon, a pretty village near Lac Leman. There he became director of sport and met Jacques Villeneuve, enrolled as a boarding pupil, following the death of his father Gilles Villeneuve, in 1983. He proved to be a daredevil star of the slopes. The two found a rapport, which became a close friendship that has lasted through many years. Villeneuve had learned to ski with the Canadian skier Steve Podborski and had a fearlessness that was inherited. When he grew up, moved on and started his racing career, Pollock went into business. He imported sports goods to Switzerland and Germany, then worked with a Japanese company, the Interhoba Group, owned by a close friend of the Honda family, rising to become managing director of a subsidiary involved in the sale of television rights in motor sport in Asia.

When he met Villeneuve again, in Japan, in 1992, it led to another career move as the young Canadian persuaded him to become his personal and business manager for his excursion into Formula Atlantic, in North America, where he was backed by Players. From there, the pair moved to Indycars, won the series, won the Indianapolis 500 and then, in 1996, came to Formula One. Villeneuve signed for the Williams team to partner Damon Hill, won the championship in 1997 and, soon after, followed Pollock to British American Racing (BAR), the team he had set up with support from British American Tobacco and Adrian Reynard, buying the declining Tyrrell team, for around £25 million, as its entry to the club before making a championship debut in 1999. A disappointing, pointless first season was followed by an alliance with Honda in 2000, a move that stabilised the new team after a rocky period inside and outside the boardroom. For Pollock, like Stewart, all of this was a lesson in survival.

British American Tobacco committed a reported £250 million to the BAR project in a five-year deal and it was Pollock's job, his challenge, as the managing director, to put the team together and make it happen. Persuading Villeneuve to join him was one of his first acts, but he had many drivers to select from once it became known, around the paddock, that a rich team was in town. 'I had so many guys, big-name drivers, approaching me for a drive, I almost lost count,' he said. 'Ten, at least. Some of their bosses would certainly be surprised if I revealed who they were.' When Pollock moved to recruit Michael Schumacher, from Ferrari, it sent out a message and it persuaded the Italians to improve their star's massive salary to £20 million annually. Like Stewart, he worked long hours to achieve his ambitions, driven on by his work ethic and his personal desire not to be outmanoeuvred as he had been in Indycar racing where he worked with great enthusiasm and success, but without any kind of equity holding to show for it at the end.

> I made up my mind that if I was running my own Formula One team, and I started to think about it in 1994, I wouldn't do it the same way as I had done the Indycar deal. This time, I wanted to be the boss and to make sure of that. I wanted to be in charge.

Like Stewart, he used relationships he had nurtured to help him build his team.

> When you are looking for such a high level of investment and funding there is no way you can do it by cold calling. You have to do it through relationships, trusts mutually developed, built up over the years. I have been fortunate that since 1985 I have been involved in sales, promotions and television rights and I have a huge network of powerful and influential friends and contacts in major businesses all over the world. Sometimes, you can pull on the contacts to open doors that would be closed to other people on the same mission ... But you have to be bold, you can't afford to blink or shy off or be timid. When you are asking somebody for £20 million, you have to look them straight in the eye and then justify. Luckily, I have every confidence in my capacity as a businessman and if something I have to offer is logical then I have no second thoughts about calling somebody up with my proposals. If I didn't have belief in my ideas then there is no way I

would even dare to make an approach to a company like British American Tobacco.

To succeed, also, and to fend off the counter-approaches from Benetton, McLaren and Williams (as is customary in the club, when one team smells a ripe sponsor, they all move in for the kill), Pollock knew he needed a fresh angle on promoting the sponsor.

> Our idea is that we will be different from every other team and in many ways. We will promote and openness and encourage a strong desire to be close to our audience. We won't be a team that is the private preserve, or toy, of a rich owner. Our fans will have a claim.

In short, he wanted to make BAR the Formula One 'team of the future'.

But it was a tough time for Pollock. He had to surrender his own private time, his family life and his relaxations and pas-times to the venture of making the BAR team happen. For a long period, he was commuting the Atlantic to talk to his friend Tom Moser, the head of global sponsorships at British American Tobacco. Then he was working in England, away from his home in Switzerland, setting up the team. 'I went weeks, some-times nearly two months, without seeing my wife, Barbara, and my son Scott and that was really tough on all of us,' he admit-ted. 'But, thank God, they understood.' Pollock shuttled between his home, near Villars, to a flat in the West End of London, or his apartment in Monte Carlo, working hour after hour on deals, meetings, proposals and team structures.

> I was getting to my desk at 5.30 am and staying until late at night – every night. The phones were on the go, non-stop. Even if it was wearying and time-consuming, I just rev-elled in it. We had 1,300 applications for just ten advertised jobs in the team.

If the setting up period was daunting and relentless, Pollock found entry to the club was traumatic. 'It has been one of the most important experiences of my life,' he said. 'I made mistakes and I got some things wrong, particularly inside the team. But it has all been part of the learning curve.' One result of his learning as he worked was an internal political struggle for control with Reynard, the founder technical director, who attempted to raise funds through a venture capital company, Cambridge Capital Partners, to launch a takeover bid. Like finding his way around the business, he survived that, too. He learned how to cope with the inner workings of the club, too. And, he realised, as well, that big budgets are not everything. A team needs to have the right people, the right funding and the right blend. In essence, it must remain a team. Too many inexperienced recruits were signed, but that period has been overcome.

> You can have two hundred or three hundred million dollars, but it doesn't mean that you will have a team that can win. It is how you use the budget that counts and you are only as good as the people you are hiring.

He recognised he had endured a difficult period to survive.

> I've had a baptism of fire and an accelerated learning process. If I hadn't gone through that, I wouldn't be here today and the team would not have survived [he told Formula One magazine in June 2001]. The bottom line is that the people who were after me have seen their plans backfire because it has made the rest of the team stronger.

As to the way in which the senior team owners had allegedly made life difficult for him in his first years as a new boy, Pollock was philosophical. He understood these things now.

> It was not a case of one individual being nasty to me. The top teams are not going to respect you just because you want respect. They will respect you for what you do. Not what you say. The nastiness has turned around into a good working relationship with the top team owners. If I want to go out, for a meal, with Flavio Briatore or Eddie Jordan, then I do. And Ron Dennis? Well, we do talk constructively. We have conversations now that we couldn't possibly have had in the first year because I was inexperienced and I didn't understand the inner workings of the paddock . . .

Pollock, the best-looking team owner, had survived. Briatore had been there before him, sneered at as a t-shirt salesman, made to feel unwelcome. He, too, had gone through the initiation process, the bullying in the playground. Together, at different times, each had walked in and done it and survived with a steely character and a twist of luck. They knew, like Stewart, what it took.

I am lucky, very lucky [said Stewart], that since 1969, when I won my first championship, I have built up a lot of important relationships. I have been lucky because this sport is so intoxicating to so many people in high places. I created relationships not by design, but simply because I was prepared to be open with them. I was prepared to be courteous to them and I was prepared to show them around and explain the sport. If I meet somebody who's highly successful, I'm really impressed because they've done something that's far and beyond anything that I've ever done. Most of the friends I have in this world are considerably more successful than me and I've always had the feeling that there's always something to learn. I had lunch with Henry Kissinger and Mick Jagger last Saturday ... Very impressive, different directions, and you know what? The same thing always happens with very successful achievers. They want to ask more questions of you than you of them and I went there to ask them questions ...

10   2001 – a Political Odyssey

Money, money, money – Part II

Paul Stoddart was born on 26 May 1955 in Coburg, Melbourne, Australia. A Victorian, by birth and nature, he came into Formula One with the same business attitudes he had carried through his successful life until, in January 2001, he took over the struggling Minardi team. Even then, he felt no pain, sensed no uncertainty and discerned no reason for changing his direct, open and straightforward attitude to deals and to people. Often unshaven and apparently without much affection for severe tailoring, Stoddart was a doer, not a talker. He liked achieving and in his life he had achieved much by applying his entrepreneurial skills to his love of anything that moved by land, sea or air. He was passionate about motor sports and had dreamt for many years of finding an opportunity to move into Formula One.

Like many members of the Piranha Club, Stoddart started out as a car dealer and part-time racer – think only of Eddie Jordan, Enzo Ferrari, Frank Williams or Bernie Ecclestone as four others who adopted similar routes to the Grand Prix world – and used his skills in trading and thinking on his feet to help fund his hobby. Then, the two began to merge, as they always do with men whose destiny it is to own a team in the Formula One World Championship. In Stoddart's case, however, it was by moving sideways into aviation that he found his fast track to the top. It happened when the Royal Australian Air Force approached him and asked him if he would be interested in purchasing their fleet of BA1-11 aircraft and reselling them. Stoddart did his homework and decided it was a deal worth risking.

Optimism, as often, had overcome judgement. The planes were difficult, if not impossible, to sell. So, like any good innovative risk-taking businessman, he decided to set up his own airline. At the time, he was barely into his twenties. He flew wealthy gamblers from the mainland of Australia to Tasmania where, because gambling was legal, while it remained illegal elsewhere Down Under at the time, many of them wanted to enjoy a bet. In some respects, the cynics might say, he has changed little since then . . . But much water has flowed under the Stoddart bridge since then.

Realising that he could make a good living from trading aircraft and their spare parts around the world, Stoddart moved rapidly. His business expanded with his quick thinking and his ambitions and he moved to England. Soon, he became an air business mogul, with a fleet of aircraft that included Boeing 747s and 737s and nearly 50 other planes. Most of them were leased out to other airlines as he focused his business on the charter market used by European businesses. He called his business European Aviation. His business thrived, running flat out and 24 hours a day to please the market and Stoddart became rich. In 1996, he was rich enough to return to his love of motor sport and begin to collect 'vintage' racing cars. In 2001, he was placed equal 51st, with Jackie Stewart, on the *Sunday Times* Rich List of British personalities.

By 2001, his European Aviation group employed 650 people, operated 35 jet aircraft and also ran one of the biggest spare parts businesses in the land. It funded his expansion in other areas and allowed his motor racing enthusiasm to become another business. European Formula Racing was created, growing from a company that acquired old cars from Tyrrell, from which he bought ten, to add to a collection that included a Brabham driven by Damon Hill and both a Minardi and a Benetton. By 1987, as a sponsor of the Tyrrell team, he was flying their staff to all the European races and learning the intricacies of Formula One. He became close friends with many people in the paddock and gathered an understanding of the business (as Craig Pollock had through his television sales work in Asia and his associations with Jacques Villeneuve in the mid-1990s).

When Tyrrell decided the time had come to sell their long-established Formula One racing operation, he was in a good position to buy, but was beaten to the deal by his friend Pollock who moved swiftly on behalf of British American Tobacco. When the Tyrrell team was sold, he bought much of their equipment and moved it to Ledbury in Gloucestershire, where he had a technical centre. Thwarted in his bid to buy Tyrrell, he bought the Edenbridge Formula 3000 operation instead and began to sponsor the Jordan team, flying the Dubliner and his men to the Grands Prix, before moving on to Arrows where his F3000 outfit, built out of the remains of Tyrrell and Edenbridge, was to become the Arrows junior team with fellow-Australian Mark Webber as a driver.

All of this, carefully planned and executed, was the work of a man with a mission and it was, therefore, no great surprise when he finally reached Formula One, as a team owner, by taking over Minardi in January 2001. He purchased a controlling, majority stake in the team from former owner Gabriele Rumi, who had himself previously bought into the ailing Italian outfit, a team sustained by enthusiasm, but bereft of results. Swiftly, he injected belief, money and organisation. Instead of despondency, there was determination. 'Money is obviously a necessary evil in Formula One,' said Stoddart, soon afterwards, when he announced that the little-known Spaniard Fernando Alonso was to be his first driver – and faced a barrage of questions about signing a 'pay-driver'.

> Like anyone, we've got to open our arms and to take as much as we can get of it. But, having said that, it would be quite wrong if I just made money the only motivator because it most certainly isn't. We haven't come this far to waste it all by putting a couple of drivers in the car that really can't drive. So you won't see that from us. We're hoping to have a young charger and then somebody with more experience alongside him.

They were bold words from a bold newcomer to the Piranha Club. He was full of life and full of belief and enthusiasm. He believed he could operate in Formula One as he had done before. Be genuine; tell the truth; judge people as you find them ... And he was prepared to fund the team heavily with his own money in the first year, while he put it on its feet and found the sponsors to fund a progressive package of improvements to turn the European Minardi team into winners.

> I have no fears about funding for this year. We are 75 per cent complete on a budget for the year, but we're still looking for a title sponsor. I believe we are the best value for

money in Formula One at this late stage and we have seven parties interested. We are realistic. We are not going to write cheques with our mouths. We have a five-year plan that is set in stone. In year one, we want to summarise, stabilise and rebuild. And in the next we will get an engine partner and climb up the field. In years three and four, we will be in the midfield and hopefully get a works engine deal. And in year five, we want to be regularly qualifying and finishing in the top ten.

It sounded bold and adventurous, even if, with a racing team based at Faenza, in central Italy, where the traditions of Minardi and its history remained, and a factory and administrative headquarters in England, it was clearly going to be a logistical challenge. Like Eddie Jordan, ten years before him, however, this man was not going to be beaten by anyone lacking his optimism, enthusiasm and energy. Stoddart was totally dedicated to succeeding. Like Pollock, he was prepared to work night and day. He could travel from Ledbury, where he also housed a Formula One two-seater venture, engine development and overhaul facilities and his other racing interests, to Faenza, he said, faster than most people could travel around the M25 to Heathrow airport. Yet, the cynics asked, how can he make it pay to bring a perennial failure like Minardi back to life?

The Italian team, run like a family by its founder Gian Carlo Minardi, had always struggled since entering Formula One in 1985. He had fought valiantly, enjoyed support from Ferrari, investment from Rumi and Flavio Briatore (who departed at the end of 1997) and various levels of sponsorship. In 2000, while the Prost team enjoyed a budget of around $130 million, Minardi had to manage on $60 million, but still beat their French rivals in the championship. The best deal that year came from Telefonica, the Spanish telecommunications group, which had talked of making a major investment in the team and in the Formula One business. Instead, in the end, they withdrew, leaving Minardi to flounder through lengthy and abortive talks with the Pan-American Sports Network to no avail.

Stoddart's arrival was compared to that of a white knight riding to the rescue, but it was a role he bashfully shied away from when drawn into discussion. Instead, he said, he was involved to turn Minardi into a force, to do something that clearly gave him a chance to realise his lifelong ambitions and, first, to ensure that the cars and the team were on the grid and in the game when the teams lined up in Albert Park, for the season-opening Australian Grand Prix, in his native Melbourne. Since he had no known engine deal, no drivers and sponsors to speak of, when he took over, it was a massive challenge, but one that was to be met with all his customary realism, humour and intelligence.

To all the romantics who had followed the rise and fall of Minardi with heartfelt sympathy, it was a wonderful story. But the bigger question that lurked behind the façade of this almost-pantomime act of apparent folly was: why did Minardi not find a buyer among the big manufacturers, particularly as they were said to be queuing up to find the means to take control of the sport? After all, it was barely a year since Renault purchased Benetton following the earlier deals that had seen Ford buy Stewart and BAR take over Tyrrell. Moreover, Mercedes-Benz, through Dailmer-Chrysler, and BMW were taking increasingly active interests in the business through their relationships with McLaren and Williams respectively. It looked like the age of the corporate manufacturer was upon Formula One. How, then, did Stoddart slip through their fingers and snap up Minardi so easily?

The answer, it seemed, was that the impending arrivals of Honda and Toyota had been resolved; that the former was only going to supply engines (to BAR and Jordan) while the latter was entering Formula One as the 12th, and final, permitted entrant to the championship, according to the existing Concorde Agreement. Toyota, having excelled and disgraced themselves in the Rally World Championship, therefore had no need to buy an existing franchise, and Minardi in turn were on sale at a time when the demand for Formula One teams was low. Stoddart's move was therefore as necessary as it was heroic to keep the grid and the television show at full capacity for the new season.

Suddenly, Stoddart was the name on everyone's lips. Even Ferrari were nudged aside by the massive media interest in the man from Melbourne who had rescued what was widely seen as just another lame duck European racing team. And, like the Old Man of Maranello, Stoddart knew how to play the game. Almost instinctively, he would let the right rumours persist and kill the bad ones swiftly. When, for example, Nigel Mansell's name was linked with the second seat at Minardi, the denial came gently and with an attachment; the 1992 champion could be in line to do some driving in the European Racing promotional two-seater car, but was unlikely to line up alongside the 19-year-old rookie Alonso on the grid in Melbourne. Mansell, after all, was 47, two years older than Stoddart himself.

Almost miraculously, by the standards of modern Formula One, Minardi succeeded in reaching Melbourne and taking part in the Australian Grand Prix. To a fanfare of congratulations and welcomes, Stoddart flew home as a hero and a saviour. Even without a car that was tested and proven, the paddock and his homeland were prepared to sing this man's praises. Just reviving Minardi was enough to do that, to bring out the best in everyone around him. He was wished well by every other team owner. On arrival in Australia, the fairy tale continued when the first European Minardi car, named the PS01, was unveiled at a fabulous launch held on the steps of Victoria's Parliament House. The house stopped its work for the occasion, in true Australian style, for the man who had brought a Formula One team back from the brink of extinction.

And that was not all for this new pioneer, cutting a swathe of refreshing and welcome candour through the oceans of techno-speak and corporate babbling in the sport. His cars and his drivers performed better than expected, both Alonso and Tarso Marques proving that the newly unveiled car had potential. This was exactly what Stoddart had dreamed of, a homecoming that was completed with two cars finishing well. The stage was set and the mugging of the team manager in Sao Paulo four weeks later, when the circus was in Brazil, could do nothing to halt the momentum. Setbacks were taken in their stride, an example set by Stoddart who said also that he relished his challenge and had enjoyed his forays into the early meetings of the club. 'I have found everyone to be incredibly helpful and I have been impressed with the whole set-up, the way Bernie operates and the way all the other teams go about their business,' he said in Albert Park. He was happy.

Having survived Melbourne, Kuala-Lumpur, Sao Paulo and Imola, the revitalised Minardi outfit made it to Barcelona complete with two fashionable new two-tier motor homes, one of which was originally built to order for the Sultan of Brunei. 'These new motor homes are just one more step on the road to turning the team into a strong midfield competitor within the next three years, both on and off the track,' said Stoddart, who also supplied a luxury private jet plane for the needs of his team members travelling from Italy. It was painted in the team livery and declared as 'stylish and relaxing' by the Italians. All was going well. In Stoddart's new world, the move to the Piranha Club had been as enjoyable as a bracing dip in Port Phillip Bay.

It all changed on Monday, 7 May 2001. It was a Bank Holiday in England, a day for vacations and rest. Stoddart, like most of the restless men who have at one time or another populated the membership of the Piranha Club, was keen to visit his factory, to check up on progress and to keep his desk clear. He walked through the main area of his offices and past a fax machine, a general one used by the staff. If he had not gone in on what was a holiday for his work force, he would not have been alone and therefore the first man to find the brief letter that lay in it, sent to him impersonally by Gustav Brunner. A native of Graz, in Austria, the 50-year-old engineer had been working for Stoddart as Minardi's Technical Director, a role in which he had earned many plaudits for his designs and the team's relative success.

The message, however, was brief and pointed. Stoddart picked it up and was stunned. It was the most gut-wrenching blow he could have received and it came as a total shock. Like Eddie Jordan, a decade or so earlier, he was being informed that a man he believed to be employed by his team, and under contract, had walked out. And he was being told by fax, a handwritten scrawled message, sent impersonally as if the previous four months meant nothing.

On Monday [he recounted, later that week, sitting under cover at the side of his motor home in the paddock at Spielberg, venue for the Austrian Grand Prix], I walked in to a fax. . . and I just happened to pick it up. Normally, I wouldn't. But it was addressed to me. It said, 'Paul, sorry. I do not have good news for you. I have signed with Toyota and I start with them tomorrow. The 2002 car, as you know, is designed. Sorry. Gustav.' It was handwritten. I've known him for years. And I've known him well, intensely so, this year. And I thought, and so did most of this pit lane, that he was a man of reasonable integrity and honesty. But I think we were wrong . . .

Stoddart was furious. This was not only a blow to his team, their progress and their ambitions, but also a personal blow. It was the kind of action that he had not experienced previously in his business life and had never anticipated. Yet, it was the kind of move that was never considered a surprise in the more Machiavellian world of Formula One. Indeed, only three weeks later, on Friday, 1 June, another extraordinary 'designer transfer' was to be announced, then denied, in a blaze of claims and counter-claims that set the Jaguar and McLaren teams at one another's technical throats over the signature of Adrian Newey. Stoddart's first thoughts about Toyota, their directors and management were unprintable.

The announcement from Toyota's headquarters in Cologne, Germany, came soon afterwards on the same day. After two stints at Ferrari, and other spells with teams as diverse as ATS, RAM, Rial, Leyton House and Zakspeed, Brunner was known as a very competent designer and engineer with plenty of experience. Until this episode, he had also been well-liked; but by leaving Stoddart, who felt hurt personally, in such fashion, he was selling his popularity for what most observers sensed to be a very lucrative offer from a Japanese company which had been banned from the Rally World Championship not many years previously when found cheating.

Stoddart was dismayed. Twenty-four hours later, he was fighting. In a statement, the European Minardi team announced it was set to take legal action against both Toyota and Brunner.

> We are obviously disappointed at this news [said Stoddart, in his official comments]. Gustav has been a trusted and highly regarded member of staff and for him to act in this way is totally incomprehensible to us. We are surprised and saddened that a company of Toyota's standing would seek to employ Mr Brunner, who has an irrevocable contract with Minardi until January 1, 2003. As such, European Minardi will be pursuing all of its options in law against both Mr Brunner and Toyota.

Deputy technical director Gabriele Tredozi took temporary day-to-day charge of the team's drawing office and technical staff at Faenza.

As the accusations flew from Faenza and Ledbury towards Cologne, the teams were gathering for the Austrian race and the paddock at Spielberg, tucked in the foothills of the Styrian Alps, near to the better-known village of Zeltweg, which was more synonymous with the breathtaking old Oesterreichring circuit, the awesome predecessor to the modern A1-Ring (named after a telecommunications company). There in the busy crowds jostling up and down the asphalt between the motor homes was an unexpected visitor: Toyota's media relations officer Andrea Ficarelli. His task, it transpired, was to defend his company's reputation at a difficult time.

'We employed Gustav Brunner after he told us that he had resigned from Minardi and he could join Toyota,' he explained. 'We have obviously no reason not to believe this version.' Ficarelli was unable to confirm paddock gossip suggesting that Brunner had been seduced away from Minardi, the team with the smallest budget, to join the world's third-largest car manufacturer, Toyota, by an offer of a three-year contract worth 12 million dollars. If this was true, of course, it was an offer that was equivalent to a sizeable part of the Minardi annual budget.

Understandably, given his position, Ficarelli also made it clear that Toyota did not believe it had played any part in any wrongdoing.

> Toyota is not involved at all because, if there is a problem between Minardi and Mr Brunner, it is a problem that doesn't legally involve Toyota [he added]. Our lawyer has said to Minardi that he is available to help, if we can help in any way, providing they send us the evidence that there is a valid contract between Minardi and Mr Brunner. We saw a copy of the contract that Mr Brunner provided to us and we have to say that Mr Brunner was absolutely free to leave the company based on the information that we have. If Minardi have any more evidence, we are happy to see this.

For Stoddart, it was like a red rag to a bull. He was livid, but controlled his anger. Visitors to his motor home were to be treated respectfully, but given the full story.

> We started proceedings first thing on Tuesday. We intend to pursue it to the fullest extent possible. We have been

wronged quite badly. As far as I am concerned, I want retribution for two things that were very wrong. One, what
was done; and, two, most importantly, the way it was done
. . . It is a bit like David and Goliath, isn't it? But the bigger
they are, the harder they fall.

And, he added, for good measure, that Brunner would not be
welcome back. 'He had 150 friends,' he said. 'Now, he's got 150
enemies.'

On that note, it was not difficult to understand the mood that
Stoddart was in as he spat out his words and opinions with an
almost blood thirsty relish for a courtroom fight. It was a good
time to ask him, the newest of the new boys, to register his
views on the 'club' and the business, just as he digested the
experience of being a victim. Had his view of Formula One
changed since January?

Yes, it has actually [he replied with typical honesty]. I
think when I came into it, it was such a mad rush to get
everything to Melbourne that we didn't have time to think
about any other aspect of the business. But I've learned, in
a very short space of time, that this is a demanding business. Very much more so than I had thought. It is demanding both in time and in motion. It is physical and mental.
You need to put the physical side into it, but the mental
part is incredibly more stressful and demanding than I
ever dreamed possible. And, as such, I've gone from enjoying a race weekend to not even knowing if we're going to
win or anything because you arrive on a Thursday and go
home on a Sunday and those four days are just washed
away in your life. You probably have 100 meetings of some
description and I don't think people appreciate just how
demanding it really is – and that's the biggest thing I've
learnt.

Asked about money, finding it, paying the bills, losing it and
dreaming of winning some, he was equally candid.

For me, it is still money going out. We were running on a
$50 million budget. That's aside from the cost of buying the
team. We've invested about $80 million. The team cost 50
and it took another 30 to fund the losses. So, our investment

will be in the vicinity of $70 or $80 million by the end of this year depending entirely upon what sponsorship we bring in. Or don't. So, I'm probably facing another 10 on top of what I expected, which is annoying, but I won't say totally unmanageable because we were sensible enough to know that for this year we might not attract any type of sponsor.

And I believe we've done a bit more than stand still. In this, there are two things: the business side and the motor sport side. On the business side, we've bought one-twelfth of F1. We've come into it, at a time, I think which is absolutely right for us, when the Concorde Agreement is undoubtedly going to be re-negotiated before its expiry. And in addition to that, we've come in at a time when another well-known company has invested the thick end of two billion dollars into it and they're not about to lose that option to get their return. So the timing was rather fortunate actually and if you put your business head on, forget about the notion of sport, or anything else, and ask: was our $50 million, in this, a good investment? The answer, I think, is, undoubtedly, yes . . . Would I like to do it again, next year? Most certainly not. This will be a properly funded team next year because we'll have the time to do it. As I talk now, we're negotiating with a couple of title sponsors and we've got an option with engines for next year.

We've surpassed all expectations, both of other people's and our own. We're ahead of our programme. We've taken a kicking this weekend, but nevertheless 'When the going gets tough, the tough get going.' We'll rise well and truly above that and I'm quite happy with our on-track performance, particularly that of Fernando, obviously. We're pretty reasonably relaxed really.

As he talked, there was hardly time for another question or a prompt. He wanted to unload himself of his feelings and his frustrations. The new kid on the block had suffered his first bloody nose at the hands of an arrogant newcomer who was not even in the neighbourhood yet.

Hopefully, we've been around long enough to know that knock-backs come from time to time. This one was totally unexpected and unjustified, but we'll rise above it. Many of the meetings this week have been along these lines – about putting things in place, not going out and just taking another named technical director. I don't believe that's the way to go, the way I believe you have to go forward is to have faith in the people that you believe in and that's what we're doing. We're trying to strengthen them and give them the chance to prove themselves and that is the route we're going down. We've got an ability now to go through a period of stability and, if that is the case, we're not going to suffer for some two years.

If I was in it for the short term, the only way I could recoup my losses would be to sell on, but because I'm in it for the long term then the way to go is to float the company, eventually, because I think the flotation of an F1 company is going to be an attractive proposition. So, I would not be at all uneasy about a flotation, the timing of which would need to be when the Concorde Agreement is re-negotiated, be that in 12 months' time, or five years' time. Because, only then, are you going to have stability in the sport – you're going to have longevity in the sport and you're going to be able to get a proper return out of the sport.

The flotation of an individual team is the team's prerogative. You might find, in the public forum, floating an F1 team today . . . There is a certain degree of secrecy and confidentiality around the Concorde Agreement. That would mean perhaps, under the proper auditing procedure, that you would be in breach of certain conditions if you did go down this route. Maybe you would, maybe you wouldn't. But, most certainly, what you could do is form a holding company and float that. And we could do that today. But I don't think today would be the right time to do it. All these options are open, but at the moment I don't see the need. Nor do I have the desire to get out of the team; quite the contrary. So, I think time will tell. I'm going to focus all my attention on what happens to the Concorde Agreement over the short term.

As anyone, with a reasonable working of Formula One and the Piranha Club, knows, any decision to make a major change in the way it works requires the support of all the members. It had, therefore, always been assumed this would be a stumbling block, as so often in the past, to any truly progressive evolution of the set-up, regardless of the deal by which the Kirch Group, run by the septuagenarian Leo Kirch, a German pay-per-view television mogul, acquired a majority stake in the Ecclestone family trust's Formula One holdings empire, SLEC, during April 2001.

Stoddart, however, with the advantage of being a newcomer with a fresh outlook, said he saw it quite differently. He saw a new future for the business. He saw a future in which the teams would each benefit from the growth of interest in the whole business, the 'show', only by securing that future through the prolongation of the Concorde Agreement, the binding contract between the teams, the sport's ruling body, the Fédération Internationale de l'Automobile (FIA) and the commercial rights holder. By May 2001, of course, the rights holder was effectively the trust set up by Bernie Ecclestone, known as SLEC, into which Kirch had invested, as Stoddart put it, the 'thick end of two billion dollars'. It was, Stoddart argued, in the interests of all parties involved to secure the long-term future value of the business, and of all those businesses involved, by extending the Concorde Agreement beyond 2007.

> It does take a unanimous decision to change anything [he confirmed]. And many things occur, particularly in a sporting nature; maybe one team, or person, for whatever reason best known to themselves, doesn't want to change something and the status quo remains. However, if you're talking about renegotiating the Concorde Agreement and you have a new shareholder who's invested a wickedly large amount of money into the commercial rights of F1, then that person can give their own investment an enhanced value. It's in their interest to negotiate a longer deal because, as has been reported in the press, the manufacturers are talking of going off and forming their own series. Well, there's nothing to stop them. They can, if they want to. That would clearly rip F1, as we know it today, apart and it would not be good for the shareholder. It would not be good for Bernie's remaining shareholding either and I don't believe it would be good for the teams. So the net result of that is that if you don't want to see that happen there has to be a bit of give. Now without breaching confidentiality, it's been well reported that of the TV

and commercial revenue in F1, it is split currently between the teams and Bernie's company SLEC, and it is then further split between the teams in a disproportionate way. If somebody, anybody, can suggest a formula which is deemed to be fairer than the existing one, that is probably going to be one of the few times when all of the teams will agree because, if it's in everybody's interest, then it's something that you can probably put forward. It doesn't matter who puts it forward, whether it be Bernie, whether it be Kirch, or whether it be one of the team owners.

If it's put forward and it's seen to be a 'win–win' situation for everyone, in so much as Kirch may end up with a smaller percentage, but with a longer, guaranteed period; a period by which they could then go and enhance the value of their investment by whatever means they want, then that's a good thing. Because, clearly, a five-year, or six-year agreement is nowhere near as good as a 25-year agreement, just to use any figures, for example. If, along the way, the teams were actually to earn more revenue than they earn today, and distribute it in a fairer way than they do today, that would, most likely, hypothetically, get the support of all the teams. So, I think then, and only then, would you actually see change – and it would take a situation like that to arise to do it.

Like all the rest of the club, even the free-speaking Stoddart was reluctant to say much more. The very future of the club itself was, by mid-season, the subject of considerable conjecture and much debate. It seemed, as 2001 unfolded, that Kirch was reluctant to talk to the manufacturers, or the teams, to ward off the threat of a breakaway series in Formula One. The manufacturers, led by Fiat, Ford, Renault and Mercedes-Benz, made their intentions clear with a series of provocative statements during the season.

All of this left Kirch in a strange position. He paid a reported two billion dollars for apparent control of a company that had a long-term, indeed extraordinarily long-term, deal to exploit the commercial rights of the sport, including all television rights (in a long-term deal that was extended by 100 years, to 2101 in May 2001), but found, on unwrapping this new purchase, that inside was not a solid item, but a product with only six years of real value remaining before, if the doom-mongers were to be believed, it shattered into pieces, at the end of the Concorde Agreement. To most observers, it seemed logical (and curious that this logic was apparently ignored) to move swiftly to sell shares in SLEC to the manufacturers, and thus persuade them not to form a breakaway series, or to persuade the teams to agree to a new long-term Concorde Agreement, in which they received a much-enhanced package of benefits, compared to previous agreements. This latter would, obviously, enhance the value of Kirch's holding and give it some long-term security. It would, also, permit Kirch to consider, as Ecclestone had done, flotation of his company. 'It would have incredibly more street value with a 25-year deal, than with a six-year deal,' said Stoddart.

The teams, however, were not going to fall over one another in a rush to sign a revised long-term Concorde Agreement unless the terms were right. They had, after all, to consider the benefits of the alternative route, which was likely to be a pro-posed new series, funded by the manufacturers. In effect, they were in a strong bargaining position, if they believed their unique expertise and experience was a product of lasting value. For the team owners, it was a delicate matter; and one, of course, that required the most concentrated effort to resolve. The threat of the breakaway series might not, after all, allow them to control any commercial rights and might, indeed, con-demn them to their roles as the highly paid performers, not the owners or rights-holders, in a travelling circus.

A deal with the manufacturers, on the one side, and with the new owners of SLEC and the commercial rights, on the other, appeared to be in their best interests, but only if it was all part of a new long term Concorde Agreement which gave everyone a fair share of the massive commercial and television income. And, to do this, continued revision of the complex, and secret, revenue streams, making the whole business transparent, and keeping everything in line with the requirements of such prying bodies as the European Commission, or the new anti-tobacco legislation, was required; in effect, the dismantling of the existing system and, with it, the dismantling of the club. Goodbye Darwin, hello democracy. But how many cheers for that?

In a modern age of advancing egalitarianism, the old survival system methods of operation were no longer appropriate. In the old system, due for revision, the income derived from the television and commercial revenues was distributed among the teams through two tiers of payments. One was a division of a section of that income between all of the participating teams on an equal basis. The second was a performance-related payment that guaranteed enormous rewards to the winners and the world champions and virtually nothing to any struggling team that finished outside the top ten. In the simplest sense, points earned prize-money; but this was of benefit more to the big, rich and successful teams than the strugglers at the back of the grid and many team owners felt that the time had come for a proper, equal split of the income derived from the business as a whole. Furthermore, an orthodox level of administrative transparency was needed. The days of payments, made and received, without explanation, without invoices or receipts, were numbered.

Stoddart, a scrapper and, it seemed, a born survivor, had to make do with what he could gather in from all sources as he worked to build up European Minardi in 2001. Understandably, he had his own views on the system, but through respect for the club rules kept them to himself. But, in one comment, he revealed his sympathies lay with the teams fighting for survival:

> It seems to me that the teams at the back end of the grid need the money more than the teams at the front. So, if I was going to have a disproportionate split, I'd have the ones at the back earning more. But, that's not going to happen. The only way forward with this is to have an equal split.

Talking in Spielberg, Stoddart could not hide his anger and frustration at the way in which Brunner had behaved. But also he could not hide, like everyone in Formula One, his huge admiration for the achievements and abilities of Bernie Ecclestone.

> Bernie will be running Formula One for the next five years. I, personally, worry about the day he wakes up and can't be bothered any more. He enjoys it. And the day he doesn't enjoy it is going to be a sorry, sad day for F1. It is another reason, sooner rather than later, to renegotiate the whole structure of how this runs. If it's done properly, I think the basis of renegotiating this structure will be the

first step to 'life after Bernie'. If there is a fair structure, that has no preferential treatment for anybody, and you have 12 teams competing for an equal share of the money, equal share of all the revenue, equal share of facilities, equal share of benefits, then you have the whole thing on a level footing. Perhaps, then, the management won't need to be as intense in its negotiations as it is today, when you have somebody feeling this is unfair. So that, by itself, provokes discussion and negotiation; and it's perhaps time, now, in Bernie's twilight years of F1, that we see it all put on a sound and fair and equal footing.

I'm not sure that the current position is unanimous. It's quite interesting, but, of course, in any government it wouldn't work. In any boardroom, it wouldn't work, because you can't have a deadlock that can't be broken. However, that's not for me to say. I think Bernie's the kind of guy that would like to see it all on a level footing. I can't speak for him, but if I'd built up anything like what he's built up, I'd want to pass on down the success story, which it is . . . And I can't second-guess Bernie's thoughts, but it wouldn't surprise me one little bit to see Bernie leave F1 in good shape and what we've been discussing would be a hell of a way to do it; because any other possible solution gives a reason for somebody to be unhappy. I think it's time now. F1 is such a major business, such a global business, that it has to be put on a level, it has to be fair to everybody, and I'm not sure that anybody would vote that down if it was put forward because so long as it was structured in a way that you could see that it was genuinely fair for everybody, then who's really going to complain? It's very hard to complain if it's fair.

This week, with Gustav, hit me quite personally. Apart from the fact the guy's a ****, it's knocked a bit of my confidence in people. This is a small team, it's done amazing things in such a short space of time and some ******** comes along and does this, and it reminds you of how vicious F1 can be. And when it's done so blatantly wrongly, against both law and morality, you do have to stand back and wonder why you bother getting up and getting involved with a shower of shit when this could happen. But it's one person and I'm not going to let one person destroy the morale of the team, which is probably one of the best

313

morales in this pit lane. So down to a person, we'll go out to prove a point and go on without him. But my one regret is exactly that.

As to the legal action, Stoddart said:

We've had one response from Toyota and none from Gustav, as we speak, so we're going to apply some pretty heavy shots. It's very hard. It was blatant. It's indefensible and that is what we will sue on. From the moral point of view, I wouldn't want him back. I'm bloody sure nobody in the team would accept him back. So that's not really an option. So I think our options lie in proper retribution in the law, to the damage that's been done to us, by both him and Toyota. And it's very hard for Toyota to walk away from this. I know there's been intense interest from the media, some saying there was no contract. Well, how the hell do they know? They [Toyota] refused the opportunity to see it when I offered it to them. I don't believe for one second that a company like that would be so negligent just to take somebody's word. 'Oh, I don't have a contract.' Especially, for this reported figure of 12 million dollars for three years. If that is true, then I don't think they gave a shit whether he had a contract or not and that's what has to be decided in the courts.

I've never had the feelings I've had this week about how low people can go. In fairness, yes, I have had a wide berth of businesses over the years and I've had people steal from me, I've had people do the wrong thing by me before. But I've never really had a person, at such a senior level, with such knowledge of the company, do anything like this. He's supposed to be the brains of the company. To just walk out, so blatantly disregard your contract, the people you work with, to effectively do a runner, from one country to another ... I certainly can't remember anything that's happened to me that would remotely resemble that. Yes, it does leave a bad taste and it does make you think that F1 is more ruthless than any business I've been involved in before. And I think that's probably fair to say. We've got to improve it, take something positive out of it. I suggest it's high time that people like Brunner, and the four or five other people at each team, who can really hurt a team badly, ought to be made to honour their contracts. We've had something called the Contracts Recognition Board (CRB), in respect of the drivers, for several years and, to my knowledge, I don't think it's ever been tested. (The CRB was created after Schumacher joined Benetton in 1991.) It's certainly had few, if any, reasons to be tested. The fact is that teams respect it and drivers respect it. I'm not the first person this has happened to, but I ought to be the last.

And if, out of this, F1 could be a lot better and accept that there are a handful of people in each company, that are key to that company's existence and that company's way forward, that they are as important as the driver, and, therefore, their contracts should be respected, as those of drivers are, it would be a good thing. If I have to be the catalyst for this to happen then so be it because it will make F1 a better sport.

Stoddart's request to create a CRB for team personnel was discussed at a meeting of team owners in Austria, briefly. They agreed to put it on an agenda for a future meeting. He was content with this. He was also content to let the club continue its progress towards reform. He respected Ecclestone and Max Mosley. He had faith in their ability.

We don't have meetings without one of them. Max is always the chairman. Max chairs the meetings. I think he does a bloody good job. He's an incredibly astute guy. He does a good job at controlling a bunch of people who don't see eye to eye on very much and, naturally, all have their own agendas. Max manages not only to keep it civil, but manages to move it forward. So, full credit to the guy. F1 is a global business. A lot of people read the papers and see Max gets crap for this and that. Everybody makes mistakes, but F1 would be a lot worse off without him. They've both done a good job for F1. They both have my vote every time. You have to sort it out and leave it in a clean fair state. If you do that I think a person could succeed Bernie. Maybe, that person could be Max. Maybe, it could be Ron Dennis. Maybe, it will be somebody we've ever heard of … I think a civil-minded, calm, intelligent individual could handle it provided F1 is handed over to that person on an equal footing. While it's not equal, it is going to be incredibly hard. I would not envy whoever has the job because they're going to have a lot of sorting out to do . . .

Two people have impressed me unbelievably. Two individuals who shall remain anonymous, but they're from very good teams. One by his sincerity, the other by the fact that, listening to him in meetings, I think 'F1's better off with you sitting there, because you make sense every time you open your mouth.' There are the quiet ones, those who have little to say, and those, sadly, who, when they do say something, you can see where it's going and it's usually not in the right direction, but they're in the minority. In general, people act in these meetings as they do in the pit lane, with one or two notable exceptions, and one guy stands out as a natural leader. No doubt about that. If you held a secret ballot, and people were serious, he would get the majority vote. If Bernie's successor was going to be a team owner, and it probably won't be, which of them is the best qualified to do the job? If they were honest about it, he'd probably get the vote.

But it will probably never be one of the team owners. It would be impossible for them to agree on anyone. People have got long memories. For instance, Toyota could bring in some ex-president, somebody who's beyond repute, but he'd never get my vote because of what they've just done to me. At the end of the day, you would have a situation where, although it may be the right way to go, you'd never get everybody to agree to doing it. Max would get my vote, but he probably wouldn't get other people's. So unless you actually have somebody who is completely dispassionate, and doesn't come along with a lot of baggage, and hasn't alienated any of the team owners along the way, you're not going to get the backing you need to govern this group. And on the other side of it, unless you have sorted it out on an equal footing, then that person's not going to be able to do their job, because they're going to spend more time sorting out bullshit than they are working with fact.

Formula One, at least the racing, is pretty much like I thought it would be. In fact, as a team, I think we are slightly ahead of our targets. Unfortunately, there is much more to Formula One than just the races. And the two things that have struck me are the amount of time that it consumes and the Gustav Brunner situation. That showed me the darker side of Formula One. I mean, the kind of dirty business like that, which I would rather not be involved in. Now, we are all big boys, so I hope something positive flows out of this situation. That is why I am pushing hard to get the Contract Recognition Board extended to include all the top guys in the teams; in every team. They are the guys that can make a difference. But this stuff, it has definitely shown me the dark side of Formula One and that's what I hope we can change.

Times have changed. Stoddart is one of the new breed. A man born in the 1950s, a team owner with his own experiences and visions. A man who thinks in a 'big business' way like Craig Pollock and Eddie Jordan. The old days are gone. Those days of Rob Walker, or Colin Chapman, or Ken Tyrrell, who was recovering from cancer in 2001, or even Max Mosley's March, have passed. Lotus borrowed money from Landhurst Leasing and went under. March, who in 1992 sold space on a race-by-race basis to local sponsors to be able to feed their mechanics on the road, went the same way. In Budapest, they discovered it was cheaper to rent stretched limos by the hour instead of hiring minibuses for the weekend.

So the whole team swept in and out of the circuit in three limos complete with cocktail bars and televisions. A case of needs must . . . [said a team mechanic at the time]. We were desperate. The money had run out. In Montreal, a local restaurant, hearing about our plight, fed us in return for space on the car. It gave us a few laughs.

It was out of such times that the Piranha Club emerged. Now, in the corporate age, such anecdotes no longer suit the business. The old stories of scrapes and feuds and wild fun belong in the past. They are part of the Formula One folklore and history. But strange things still happen. For example, on 1 June 2001, at 8.30 am in London, Jaguar Racing announced that Adrian Newey was to join them as Chief Technical Officer from August 2002. In a statement, Newey said: 'This has not been an easy decision for me to make . . . I have enjoyed hugely my four years to date at McLaren.' The same day, at 16.00, McLaren announced, 'Adrian Newey to stay at McLaren'. In his statement, Newey said:

Whilst I am delighted to confirm my intention to remain at McLaren International, and recognise that there are many exciting opportunities ahead, I regret any speculation which has been caused by my conversations with my good friend Bobby Rahal . . .

The saga continued, in similar vein, to the brink of a full High Court hearing before it was settled. But it proved, as ever, that the competition between the teams in Formula One remains as fierce in every way as it ever had been and that speed, clever designs, fast and brave driving and massive budgets will continue to dominate the sport.

According to *Eurobusiness*, one of the leading magazines that reported on Formula One's business affairs, the budgets for 2001 were as follows:

1. Ferrari (284.35 million dollars); 2. McLaren (274.55); 3. BAR (194.45); 4. Williams (192.95); 5. Benetton (180.85); 6. Jaguar (177.425); 7. Jordan (172.9); 8. Sauber (82.65); 9. Arrows (73.65); 10. Prost (47.5); 11. Toyota (47).

In 2001, Toyota, unloved by the club or the paddock, will join and boost the number of teams to 12 and number of cars on the grid to 24. By any measure, such figures prove that Formula One is a huge business. In February 2001, *Time* magazine was intrigued sufficiently by Formula One to run a report on the business. In it, Kate Noble reported 'for an industry that employs 40,000 people, generates 7.5 billion dollars in annual revenue and attracts television audiences of 500 million plus for each race, Formula One is surprisingly small . . . ' It went on to trace the share dealings which saw Bernie Ecclestone sell 50 per cent of SLEC to the German broadcaster EM.TV, in 2000; the crash in values of EM.TV's share prices; EM.TV majority owner Thomas Haffa's difficulties in finding the funds to complete his purchase; and then the Kirch Group's move, led by Leo Kirch, to buy a major holding in EM.TV to save the deal and also purchase a further 25 per cent of SLEC, as offered previously to EM.TV, as an option. The same article wrote of the consortium of European car manufacturers (Fiat, Daimler Chrysler, Renault, Ford and BMW) showing an interest in taking a stake in Formula One, or launching their own series. It also mentioned the settlement of the long-running competition investigation into Formula One by the European Commission, a move that had been interpreted widely as one that confirmed the sport was being given an official seal of approval in Europe.

Like most media observers, *Time* magazine was on the sidelines of the sport as it struggled through a period of apparent metamorphosis in public; a transition from Piranha Club to global corporate and sanitised sport-business. The struggle within the club and the sport about the next Concorde Agreement continued with the teams pointing out, in particular, that they receive too small a share of the television revenues compared to other sports and the manufacturers pressing for a voice at the table. (According to one source, while the Formula One teams receive 47 per cent of the television income, football clubs involved in the UEFA Champions League receive 75 per cent of the television income and clubs involved in the English Premier League receive 90 per cent.) The disputes and disagreements were all interlocked and the arguments and talks continued regularly as a backcloth to the 2001 FIA Formula One World Championship.

Despite the manufacturers' early claims to be earnest about creating a breakaway series, it was clear by the time of the British Grand Prix at Silverstone in July that this was unlikely. Indeed, a meeting of the team owners held at the circuit on the Saturday afternoon of that weekend welcomed in one of the manufacturers' key representatives to join them; Jurgen Hubbert, the senior figure at Mercedes-Benz. It was understood that Hubbert wanted the club to know that he was keen, on behalf of the car manufacturers' consortium, that their preferred option would be to negotiate and deal with the teams and play a part in the future of the Concorde Agreement. Hubbert, it was believed, told the meeting that he felt everyone should work together and that the teams and the manufacturers should negotiate together with Bernie Ecclestone and Leo Kirch to create a blueprint for the future.

It may, or may not, have signalled a sea change, but it certainly indicated that events were moving on. The same weekend saw a beautiful, small and red Ferrari on the Silverstone circuit with Michael Schumacher at the wheel. It was the car that Froilan Gonzalez of Argentina had driven to victory, to the great delight of Enzo Ferrari, on the same Northamptonshire circuit, in 1951. The car was a visual delicacy for the motor racing gourmet. It was owned by Bernie Ecclestone, just one from his wonderful collection. The car's motion around the redeveloped former wartime airfield thrilled the spectators and marked a half-century of scarlet continuity; it also, remarkably, confirmed Ecclestone's equally long participation in top-level motor racing. He had taken the sport a long way from those carefree, but dangerous days, and dragged it into a modern commercial and corporate era, well prepared for the twenty-first century. It was a long way, too, from the earliest days of F1CA and FOCA, a time when, as Ecclestone recalled, he sometimes allowed his temper to show.

I never wanted any titles, but I became president of FOCA, not because of the title, but for no other reason than that when you go and do deals in funny countries, they listen to you if you are a president! The first real meeting we had was with the Argentines in the Post House at Heathrow. That is when [Peter] Mackintosh [the FOCA secretary] did some sort of deal with them and it all went wrong. They sent the army over, the generals and everything else. I can remember the big Grundig tape recorder they had with them and I got so aggravated that I unplugged the tape recorder and ripped the tape off and threw it across the room! They were spouting so much rubbish and telling a lot of lies, trying to compromise poor Mackintosh . . .

Asked about his reflections on the progress made since he was climbing in and out of similar, if less powerful cars, to that pretty Ferrari in the late 1940s and early 1950s, he was typically modest and self-effacing. The paddock around him was awash with investments, technology, highly-paid engineers, drivers and staff and a colourful series of celebrities, sports stars, entertainers and politicians wandered by, enjoying the vibrant scenery. But he was not impressed.

'I don't look at things like that to be honest. I just do my job. Lot's of people have been 50 years in their jobs. This is what I do. I don't look back and I don't stop and think about it. I have been lucky enough to have super support, along the way, from people like Enzo Ferrrai, Colin Chapman and Teddy Mayer. These days, it is not so necessary, but in the early days, when you are building something, you really need it. They were very supportive. They helped me start the business. Other people today are reaping in the benefits of that.

Those who have known him for a long time are full of admiration and respect. Frank Williams recalled him buying Brabham and running the early meetings of the 1970s. He remembered one incident, in particular, at the Watkins Glen Motor Inn. 'He was there negotiating with the organiser from Mexico and the man, literally, excused himself to go to the lavatory . . . and never came back. He went out of the back window!' That, as Williams conceded with a smile, stuck in his mind. Of Ecclestone, the achiever, he said:

> In the big picture, we all know, and respect, that Bernie saw Formula One for what it could be. Over 30 years, he has moulded it into the activity that he thought would give it an important place in the world and a strong commercial base for the teams as well as creating a side of the business for himself. He has achieved his objectives very successfully. I think he has the admiration of all the teams for that. He really is a formidable individual in every sense of the world and he has created a worldwide sport pretty much single-handedly.

And, of Ecclestone, the man, he said he had

> a gifted business brain . . . He is intellectually very clever and level-headed. Clearly, he is very determined. He can also be very persuasive, when putting his deals together in the order in which he wanted them to stack up.

Could anyone else have done what Bernie did?

> Probably, but he wasn't in this part of the universe at the right time . . . I've always known it is impossible to second-guess Bernard. Like many very clever businessmen, you don't know what he is thinking.

And so to the future? A new set-up? A new structure? A new man at the top?

Formula One is an extremely dynamic activity [said Williams]. It never stands still. Certainly, over the last few years, it has accelerated. As Bernie has got more and more global television, the manufacturers are taking more and more interest and demonstrating their commitment and other major sponsors will come in. That's my theory. It's a major sport. A big event. That's what I repeat to Bernie. So, until the world unplugs itself, commercially, or oil is switched off all around the world, it will still, generally speaking, be popular. That's what I believe and that is why our company is prepared to invest.

As to a new leader to succeed Bernie, Williams was confident the right man would emerge.

My favourite comment is that in China there are at least 50 genuine world champions riding around on bikes, men we will never find. They'll never get to drive a car, but they have the right balance, the right mental approach, the toughness of mind, all the natural stuff. We want those people everywhere, you know? And you could replace the president of the United States in 24 hours. Right?

Index